New Frontiers of Democratic Participation at Work

Edited by
MICHAEL GOLD
Royal Holloway University of London

Routledge
Taylor & Francis Group

LONDON AND NEW YORK

First published 2003 by Ashgate Publishing

Reissued 2018 by Routledge
2 Park Square, Milton Park, Abingdon, Oxon OX14 4RN
711 Third Avenue, New York, NY 10017, USA

Routledge is an imprint of the Taylor & Francis Group, an informa business

A Library of Congress record exists under LC control number: 2002036106

ISBN 13: 978-1-138-71004-7 (hbk)
ISBN 13: 978-1-138-71001-6 (pbk)
ISBN 13: 978-1-315-19819-4 (ebk)

Contents

List of Figures and Tables

List of Abbreviations

ANACT	Agence Nationale pour l'Amélioration des Conditions de Travail (National Institute for the Improvement of Working Conditions) (F)
ANAES	Agence Nationale d'Accréditation et d'Evaluation en Santé (National Health Evaluation and Accreditation Agency) (F)
ARAN	Agenzia per la Rappresentanza Negoziale delle Pubbliche Amministrazioni (Agency for Representation in Public Service Bargaining) (I)
ARH	Agence Régionale de l'Hospitalisation (Regional Hospital Agency) (F)
ASL	Aziende Sanitarie Locali (Local Health Trusts) (I)
AWVN	General Employers' Association (NL)
BCI	Banca Commerciale Italiana (I)
BSE	Bovine spongiform encephalopathy ('mad cow disease')
CBI	Confederation of British Industry
CEEP	Centre Europeén de l'Entreprise Publique (European Centre of Enterprises with Public Participation)
CEO	Chief executive officer
CES	Conseil Economique et Social (Economic and Social Council) (F)
CES	Consejo Económico y Social (Economic and Social Council) (E)
CFDT	Confédération Française Démocratique du Travail (French Democratic Confederation of Labour)
CFE-CGC	Confédération Française de l'Encadrement - Confédération Générale des Cadres (French General Confederation of Managers)
CGIL	Confederazione Generale Italiana del Lavoro (Italian General Confederation of Labour)
CGT	Confédération Générale du Travail (General Confederation of Labour) (F)
CGT-FO	Confédération Générale du Travail-Force Ouvrière (General Confederation of Labour-Workers' Strength) (F)
CHSCT	Comité d'hygiène, sécurité et des conditions de travail (Workplace health and safety committee) (F)

CISL	Confederazione Italiana Sindacati Lavoratori (Italian Confederation of Workers)
CITUB	Confederation of Free Trade Unions in Bulgaria
CMTU	Confederation of Malta Trade Unions
CNEL	Consiglio Nazionale dell'Economia e del Lavoro (National Council for Economic and Labour Affairs) (I)
CNPF	Conseil National du Patronat Français (National Council of French Employers) (now MEDEF)
CNRS	Centre National de la Recherche Scientifique (National Centre for Scientific Research) (F)
CSSI	Commission du Service de Soins Infirmiers (Nursing Care Service Commission) (F)
DARES	Direction de l'Animation de la Recherche, des Etudes et des Statistiques (Directorate of Research, Studies and Statistics) (F)
DG	Directorate-General (of the European Commission)
EBO	Employee buy-out
EC	European Communities
ECB	European Central Bank
ECS	European Company Statute
EES	European Employment Strategy
EESC	Economic and Social Committee of the European Communities
EFFAT	European Federation of Trade Unions in Food, Agriculture and Tourism Sectors and Allied Branches
EIRO	*European Industrial Relations Observatory*
EIRR	*European Industrial Relations Review*
EMF	European Metalworkers' Federation
EMU	European Monetary Union
EPOC	Employee Participation in Organisational Change (research group)
ESC	Economic and social council
ESOP	Employee share-ownership plan
ETUC	European Trade Union Confederation
ETUI	European Trade Union Institute
EU	European Union
Eurocadres	Council of European Professional and Managerial Staff
EWC	European works council
EWCB	*European Works Councils Bulletin*

FEHP	Fédération des Etablissements de l'Hospitalisation Privée (Federation of Private Hospital Establishments) (F)
FERPA	European Federation of Retired and Elderly Persons
FHP	Fédération de l'Hospitalisation Privée (Private Hospital Federation) (F)
FNV	Federatie Nederlandse Vakbeweging (Dutch Trade Union Confederation)
FO	Force Ouvrière (Workers' Strength) (F)
GEM	Guze Ellul Mercer Foundation (Malta)
GWU	General Workers' Union (Malta)
HRM	Human resource management
ICT	Information and communications technology
IILS	International Institute for Labour Studies
ILO	International Labour Organization
INSEE	Institut National de la Statistique et des Etudes Economiques (National Institute of Statistics and Economic Studies) (F)
IRES	Institut de Recherches Economiques et Sociales (Institute for Economic and Social Research) (F)
ISTAT	Istituto Nazionale di Statistica (National Statistical Office) (I)
IT	Information technology
ITUC	Interregional trade union council
IUF	International Union of Food, Agricultural, Hotel, Restaurant, Catering, Tobacco and Allied Workers' Associations
LEST	Laboratoire d'Economie et de Sociologie du Travail (Institute of Labour Economics and Industrial Sociology) (F)
LO	Landsorganisasjonen i Norge (Norwegian Federation of Trade Unions)
LO	Landsorganisationen i Sverige (Swedish Federation of Trade Unions)
LTD	Loontechnische Dienst (Pay Research Service) (NL)
MCED	Malta Council for Economic Development (Malta)
MEBO	Management-employee buy-out
MEDEF	Mouvement des Entreprises de France (Movement of French Enterprises; formerly CNPF)
MLM	Maltese Labour Movement
MLP	Maltese Labour Party
MUBE	Malta Union of Bank Employees
MUT	Malta Union of Teachers

NAF	Norsk Arbeidsgiverforening (Norwegian Employers' Confederation; merged 1989 to form NHO)
NAP	National action plan for employment
NESC	National Economic and Social Council (Irl)
NGO	Non-governmental organization
NHO	Næringslivets Hovedorganisasjon (Confederation of Norwegian Business and Industry)
OKE	Economic and Social Council of Greece
OMC	Open method of coordination
RSU	Rappresentanza Sindacale Unitaria (Unified union representation) (I)
RWH	Reduction of working hours
SAP	Systems, Applications and Products in Data Processing
SE	Societas Europea (European Company)
SER	Sociaal-Economische Raad (Social and Economic Council) (NL)
SME	Small and middle-sized enterprise
SNB	Special negotiating body
SROS	Schéma Régional d'Organisation Sanitaire (Regional Health Organization Plan) (F)
SUD	Syndicats Solidaires, Unitaires et Démocratiques ('Democratic unified unions') (F)
TUE	Trade union education
UEAPME	Union Européenne des Artisans et des Petites et Moyennes Entreprises (European Union of Artisans and Small and Medium-sized Enterprises)
UĦM	Unjon Ħaddiema Magħqudin (Union of United Workers) (Malta)
UHP	Union de l'Hospitalisation Privée (Private Hospital Union) (F)
UIL	Unione Italiana del Lavoro (Italian Union of Labour)
UK	United Kingdom
UNICE	Union des Industries de la Communauté Europeénne (Union of Industrial and Employers' Confederations of Europe) (EU)
USA	United States of America
USL	Unità Sanitaria Locale (Local Health Authority) (I)
WPDC	Workers' Participation Development Centre (Malta)
WRI	Work Research Institute (Norway)

Notes on Contributors

Thérèse Beaupain has an MA in sociology from Columbia University (New York) and a PhD in social sciences from the Free University of Brussels, where she is now a lecturer in industrial relations. Her principal research interest has been the social dialogue process in Belgium, and she has acted as an expert for the ILO in this area. She has recently extended her field of interest to social dialogue within the European Union, with particular reference to European works councils.

Christofer Edling was recently appointed Torgny Segerstedt research fellow at the Swedish Centre for Advanced Studies in the Social Sciences. He received his PhD from Stockholm University, where he has been teaching since the mid-1990s. His research interests include the integration of sociological theory and method with the analysis of formal organizations.

Janine Goetschy is a senior research fellow at CNRS (National Centre for Scientific Research), attached to the group 'Travail et mobilité' at the University of Nanterre in France. She also lectures at the Free University of Brussels (Institut d'Etudes Européennes). She holds an MSc in industrial relations from the University of Bath (UK) and a PhD in political science from the Institute of Political Science in Paris. Her principal research interests focus on industrial relations and labour law regulation at EU level.

Michael Gold is senior lecturer in European business and employee relations at Royal Holloway University of London. He studied at the Universities of Oxford and Edinburgh, where he obtained his PhD. He worked for almost ten years at Incomes Data Services and at Industrial Relations Services, where he edited the *European Industrial Relations Review*. He has also worked at the University of Westminster and for the European Foundation for the Improvement of Living and Working Conditions in Dublin as a consultant.

Gérard Kester was an associate of the Institute of Social Studies in The Hague until 1997, and worked as a researcher or visiting professor at many other institutions as well. He has a PhD in social studies from Erasmus University in the Netherlands. He was founder of the Labour Studies Programme at the Institute of Social Studies, and founder and director (1981–97) of the African

Workers' Participation Development Programme (APADEP). His research projects have covered many areas of labour relations across the globe. He retired in 1998, but acts as technical advisor to FNV, the Dutch Trade Union Confederation.

Peter Leisink is associate professor of labour studies at the Utrecht School of Governance. He studied at the Universities of Utrecht and Wageningen, where he was awarded his PhD. He then lectured in the sociology of work and organization at Utrecht University, which was followed by a fellowship at the Industrial Relations Research Unit at Warwick University in 1993. He won a grant to establish a European research network on the effects of information and communication technology on work and organization. His publications also focus on organizational participation, industrial relations and globalization.

Helmut Martens has been a scientific researcher at the Regional Institute for Social Research in Dortmund since 1973 and a member of its research committee since 1984. He studied for his PhD in German literary and political sciences at the Technische Universität Hannover. His main research interests include codetermination and trade unions, transformation with respect to industrial relations in the new Federal regions of Eastern Germany, entrepreneurial networks and regional cooperation associations, the future of work and institutional theory.

Jacques Monat is a consultant who in recent years has worked for a variety of economic and social councils and the ETUI, amongst many other organizations. He obtained his Doctor of Law degree at Lyons University where he was appointed senior lecturer at its Labour Institute. He later went to Harvard University to study industrial relations. He then joined the ILO, where he was head of section of its Labour Law and Labour Relations Branch, and subsequently head of the participation programme of its International Institute for Labour Studies.

Philippe Mossé is a health economist at CNRS (National Centre for Scientific Research) in France. After his PhD, he spent a year at the University of California at Berkeley (USA). He is a member of LEST, in Aix en Provence. His main research areas are hospital management and the international comparison of health-care system reform. He is currently the scientific director of a DGXII research programme on direct participation in French and Italian hospitals, and directs a research programme on hospital restructuring for the French Ministry of Health.

Henri Pinaud works at the Laboratoire Georges Friedmann in Paris as a researcher in industrial relations. He was educated at the Sorbonne in Paris, where he obtained his PhD in sociology. He worked as a management consultant, and then joined CNRS (National Centre for Scientific Research) in 1983. He acted as the ETUC expert advising the European Foundation for the Improvement of Living and Working Conditions from 1984-95. He is currently coordinating a trade union research programme on direct worker participation in the reduction of working time in France, Germany and Italy.

Anna M. Ponzellini is a sociologist and senior researcher at the Pietro Seveso Regional Foundation in Milan, Italy. She also works at the Department of Social Studies, University of Brescia. She has been involved in many research projects on industrial relations, working time issues, equal opportunities and work/life balance. She has served as an expert for CNEL (Italian National Council for Economic and Labour Affairs) on a new law on working time and, in 1999, co-authored a handbook on the design of innovative working hours.

Thoralf Ulrik Qvale is research director at the Work Research Institute, Oslo, Norway, and head of the Institute's section on Enterprise Development and Innovation. He also holds a chair as professor of technology management at the Norwegian University of Science and Technology in Trondheim. His research interests cover industrial democracy and participation, industrial relations, action research, socio-technical design of workplaces, health and safety and the working environment.

Saviour Rizzo is research assistant and coordinator of educational courses at the Workers' Participation Development Centre at the University of Malta, where he obtained his BA and MEd degrees. He has written a manual on cooperatives (1984), co-edited a book on cooperative ways of working (1994) and edited a book on workers' participation at Malta Drydocks (1996). He has also published papers dealing with workers' education and the teaching of social studies.

Åke Sandberg is an associate professor and senior researcher at the National Swedish Institute for Working Life (Arbetslivsinstitutet) in Stockholm. He has an MBA from Gothenburg School of Economics and a PhD in sociology from Uppsala University. He has worked at the Royal Institute of Technology, Stockholm, Malmö University Centre and the Stockholm School of Economics. His research centres on new forms of management and employment, industrial networks and user-oriented design, with a recent focus on interactive media and multi-media industries, web journalism and call centres.

Joseph Vancell lectures at the Junior College of the University of Malta, where he obtained his BA and MEd degrees. He also works regularly at its Workers' Participation Development Centre. His current research interests centre on workers' education and development, and alternative teaching techniques. He was responsible for the Malta National Literacy Campaign at the Department for Education from 1992–96. He is also an established artist and producer of theatrical events.

Daniel Vaughan-Whitehead works at the European Commission, where he is responsible for social dialogue issues in the Eastward EU enlargement process. He holds a PhD from the European University Institute in Florence, and worked for the ILO between 1991–99. Over that period he was senior adviser to its Central and Eastern European Team in Budapest for more than six years. Currently Vice-President of the International Association for the Economics of Participation, he has been particularly active in promoting forms of workers' participation such as employee ownership in transition economies.

Edward Zammit is professor of industrial sociology and industrial relations in the Faculty of Economics, Management and Accountancy at the University of Malta. After taking degrees in philosophy and sociology, he completed his doctorate at the University of Oxford. He is also director of the Workers' Participation Development Centre at the University of Malta. His research covers various aspects of labour relations and workers' participation, with particular reference to Malta.

Foreword

The chapters in this book originated in papers presented at a seminar of the Scenario 21 network in December 2000 at the European Trade Union Institute in Brussels. We are a loosely-knit group of academics and researchers from across Europe who share an interest in promoting the ideals of industrial democracy and participation. We published a book in 1996 entitled *Trade Unions and Democratic Participation in Europe: a Scenario for the 21st Century*.[1] It argued that democratic participation must be based on the spread of codetermination and the increased active involvement of the unions in all forms of participation, including organizational and financial participation.

Our new book now revisits this territory, and analyses the 'new frontiers' of democratic participation at work that have been emerging over the last seven years or so. It examines EU and national dimensions, sectoral and company case studies and a variety of thematic aspects, such as the role of participation in social transformation. The purpose of the book is to illuminate the opportunities and challenges that lie ahead for unions and employee representatives alike as Europe evolves. We believe that the issues presented here should serve as a touchstone for further debate among everyone concerned with the future of work and its democratic organization.

During the preparation of this book, we were shocked to hear of the murder of Marco Biagi, the Italian labour lawyer, on 19 March 2002. We should like to dedicate these pages to his memory, as someone deeply committed to exploring and researching the frontiers of democratic participation at work.

Michael Gold
Editor
September 2002

Note

1   Kester, G. and Pinaud, H. (eds) (1996), *Trade Unions and Democratic Participation in Europe: a Scenario for the 21st Century*, Avebury, Aldershot.

Acknowledgements

This book would not have been possible without the administrative and financial support that the European Trade Union Institute has given the Scenario 21 network over the years. We should like to record our grateful thanks to its Director, Reiner Hoffmann, and to all its staff. However, the views expressed by contributors are their own and do not necessarily reflect those of other members of the network or of the ETUI.

Chapter 1

Introduction: New Frontiers of Democratic Participation at Work

Gérard Kester, Edward Zammit and Michael Gold

The book *Trade Unions and Democratic Participation: a Scenario for the 21st Century* was published in 1996. This study took a broad and a long view: it traced the evolution of democratic participation in some 10 European countries back to the post-World War II era, evaluated the state of the art at the end of the twentieth century, and considered the main options for the next century. The overall conclusion of the study was that democratic worker participation should be further strengthened and that this was possible only with renewed and persistent trade union support. Furthermore, the support by trade unions for democratic participation provides an opportunity and lever at the same time for their own renewal. Four major propositions were formulated (Kester and Pinaud, 1996c).

1   Different forms of participation (including traditional collective bargaining, codetermination and organizational and financial participation) are neither mutually exclusive nor incompatible with each other. On the contrary, their effect can be cumulative and mutually reinforcing. Implemented separately, they lose their meaning and effectiveness; implemented in synergy, they assume a dynamic force.

2   Rapid and major shifts in the labour market, in the nature of employment contracts, technology, forms of work organization, globalization, culture and ideology and so on, demand an innovative approach to democratic participation. They increase the need to link problems of the shop-floor and the enterprise to both local/regional and sector (meso-)levels as well as to national and international (macro-)level labour issues, and to regulate these with possibly new forms of democratic participation.

3   A sustained spread of democratic participation is possible only under appropriate conditions, including a framework to provide facilities for research, information, education, training, publications, media, consultancy

and legal advice, as well as an institutionalized framework for cooperation between trade unions and university research.

4   An innovative approach to democratic participation at the workplace level and beyond poses a particular challenge to the trade union movement to provide the necessary support. In recent years, trade unions have lost the initiative over the development of certain important forms of participation. A comprehensive hold over labour issues and all forms of workers' participation may be achieved only by trade unions. These have to promote a democratic culture of solidarity in which workers fight for their own rights and the rights of others, building solid democratic institutions in the economy.

These four main propositions (formulated as hypotheses) constitute the dimensions of what was termed 'Scenario 21'. Admittedly, they were rather abstract and needed to be elaborated along more specific parameters. To this end, multiple consultations were held between academic researchers and trade unionists in the Scenario 21 network, to examine key issues and frontier areas of future research conducive to the implementation of Scenario 21. New research projects were set up, including comparative research between several European countries, and researchers conducting projects relevant to the above mentioned hypotheses were invited to analyse their results in the perspective of one or more of the hypotheses of Scenario 21. In one country, Germany, a follow-up publication to the Scenario 21 book was published, putting emphasis on the relationship between representative worker participation and direct participation, in a trade union perspective (Kissler et al., 1997).

A main characteristic of participation is its dynamic nature. Like democracy in general (Sklar, 1987), participation is a lengthy, prolonged developmental process. It includes the digesting of experience gained and the drawing on new ideas, events, actions, policies and strategies that either directly or indirectly increase (but may also reduce) worker influence. This perspective of participation as a process has been brilliantly elaborated by Daniel Mothe in his book *Autogestion Goutte à Goutte* (Mothe, 1980). Rather than a quantum leap in the form of one grand revolution, he sees the participation process as a chain of little revolutions. Democratic participation is a dynamic process that has to be constantly proposed, learned and defended. Several other studies have emphasized that it is necessary to take the broader and the longer view, to understand the nature of participation as a learning process that leads to the gradual further democratization of labour relations. One worldwide comparative study devoted to this very perspective demonstrates that whatever the fate of worker participation, worker control or worker self-management at different moments of history, the subject matter appears to retain a fundamental attraction. This analysis of participation leads the author to define participation as a process, a movement that sets in motion a democratic way of thinking -- even when the actual forms of participation have functioned with great defects (Bayat, 1991).

Sketching the situation that prevails at the start of the twenty-first century with broad strokes, we may observe several main dimensions to the participation process. Human-centred direct worker participation is threatened by lean production (Sandberg, 1995), and its development is currently mainly in the hands of management (Pinaud, 1996). The internationalization of works councils in Europe was an important step forward, but the current agenda of the trade union movement does not include participation as a high priority (Kester and Pinaud, 1996b). The employers' camp has seized the main initiative for developing workplace participation. This has become linked sometimes with certain forms of human resource management, such as total quality management, and sometimes with shares in capital ownership and reward, possibly with government support (Vaughan-Whitehead, 1996).

It is more controversial to consider the track record of self-management on the one hand and of participatory forms on the other. The twentieth century experiences of Utopian work organizations without money (such as kibbutzim), without managers (several worker take-over experiences) or without markets have generally failed. The theory of self-management has contributed enormously to the setting-up of such enterprises on a more realistic yet principled basis. Yugoslavia made an impressive start with nationwide self-management in the 1960s, and then showed that a real alternative to the classical capitalist firm was possible (Vanek, 1972). However, the lack of a market economy disrupted earlier successes and increasing control by the Communist Party made the process less and less democratic. Regional conflicts emerged and ethnic cleansing dealt the final blow to a country that was once the proud reference point for democratic participation. The upshot is that, apart from an impressive number of cooperatives, especially Mondragón in Spain, a number of firms in North America and a few experiments elsewhere, pure self-management has never yet managed to reach a critical mass. A number of hope-raising cases have not made it. To quote a few: Algerian self-management remained an unborn baby (Clegg, 1971); attempts in Peru to create a social-property sector in the 1970s proved over-ambitious (Knight, 1975); in Mali, an attempt to turn a public firm into a self-managed one instead of privatizing it also failed (Kester and Sidibe, 1986); and the Malta Drydocks, with 3,000 workers, had to surrender its self-management system in 1996 after more than 20 years (Zammit, 2001).

Institutionalized forms of representative worker participation in Europe, on the other hand, have indeed reached a critical mass. They have developed into more democratic, meaningful and effective instruments of worker representation, and have also become self-perpetuating. History has its own logic, and today some forms of partnership rather than unilateral imposition are more likely to provide a feasible strategy. Here participation is developing as a win-win game for the various actors involved. The role of capital is not eliminated but put under greater democratic control. Privatization can be made more palatable if opportunities are taken to redefine the role of professional management and capital. At levels beyond the firm 'it is precisely the economic non-representation of billions of people that is the source of the greatest inhumanity and injustice in our world' (Vanek, 1987, p. 14). More democratized labour relations or the strengthening of democratic participation can be important steps in the direction of a more just and democratic society.

This introductory chapter gives an overview of the rest of the book and seeks to illustrate, with specific case study material, innovative developments in each of the four propositions formulated above.

Towards more Concerted Democratic Participation at the Workplace

Heller et al. (1998) have recently described and evaluated nearly half a century of experience and research on the democratization of work organizations, digesting the accumulated research outcomes of the well-known Industrial Democracy in Europe project and the Decisions in Organization project. They set out to learn the lessons of past empirical experience in all honesty: identifying the bottlenecks, disappointments, failed objectives, even shattered dreams, but also the positive achievements. They conclude that participation can work, but only under the appropriate conditions. As for the design of participation, they advise that an *interlocking multi-level decision making structure* should be matched by a similarly *interlocking multi-level participation structure*: they plead for a holistic, systematic approach to employee participation (Heller et al., 1998). Their study fully confirms the first proposition of Scenario 21. Heller et al. also assess the prospective developments during the first decades of the twenty-first century, when they expect increased possibilities for participation in ways that are independent of convictions and ideologies. Work organizations, they argue, will become coalitions among various interests and allow patterns where team networks play an increasingly important role.

Most of the chapters in this publication address similar frontier problem areas of democratic participation at the workplace. Edling and Sandberg write about new forms of management and work organization in Swedish workplaces, whilst Qvale analyses a new and comprehensive 'turnaround' organizational paradigm in the off-shore petrochemical industry in Norway. Leisink compares employee perceptions of democratic participation with existing practice and attempts at institutional innovation in the information and communications industry in the Netherlands, evaluating the implications for trade union policy. Pinaud and Ponzellini each address union and worker involvement in reducing working time. Mossé examines hospital reform and democratic participation in France and Italy. Zammit, Rizzo and Vancell show – with reference to Malta's General Workers' Union – how trade union education may contribute both to reinforcing trade union objectives and to promoting democratic participation. Goetschy adds to the discussion the important and highly relevant dimension of EU social policy, encompassing recent developments in employment policy at the European and national levels. Gold examines the significance of the now well-established European works councils and the ways in which their influence may be strengthened within transnational companies. Monat and Beaupain provide an overview of the role of economic and social councils in promoting forms of social dialogue, whilst Vaughan-Whitehead examines the Central and Eastern European experiences of privatization and/or financial participation as a lever for participation in decision making. Finally, Martens contributes a wide-ranging analysis of how the crisis of 'Fordist' institutions has affected participation at work in the 'new economy' in Germany.

These chapters provide rich new insights based on empirical studies. Qvale observes that, in view of the current development of more flexible, participative and integrated forms of work organization, the complex system for representative democracy is becoming less adequate. One of the problems to be tackled is the stubborn, institutionalized culture of work organization, which causes resistance to change among middle managers, workers and shop stewards. They fear loss of power, while the existing administrative systems and collective agreements appear unable to support new ways of working. The headquarters' fear of loss of control and corporate synergies are also living realities in bipartite or tripartite change ventures today. Qvale argues, with reference to mainstream theory, that the answer to organizational change cannot be found in a piecemeal, one-factor change procedure, but only by a 'turnaround', resulting in a new organizational paradigm. He presents a major study of the clash of two 'philosophies' of worker representation (participation versus adversarialism) in off-shore petrochemical firms in Norway, and the long and difficult process of accommodating them in a participatory framework in which both the directly elected worker representatives and trade union officers can jointly influence important policy decision making.

The study of hospital reform and democratic participation in France and Italy, reported by Mossé, is an undertaking directly stemming from earlier theoretical work of the Scenario 21 network. In both countries, hospitals are reformed by rationalization and sharper cost effectiveness whilst at the same time seeking to improve quality of service. Mossé's is a comparative study that takes one of the central hypotheses of Scenario 21 as a starting point: hospital reform will be effective to the extent that the different forms of direct and indirect participation become coherent. The absence of such coherence, the hypothesis adds, will destabilize hospital staff and thereby affect hospital reform in a negative fashion.

Both countries seek the same reforms but their trade union situation is quite different. French trade unions have a tradition of centralized bargaining which trickles down to the workplace level. The different stances on labour issues by the three main trade union confederations trickle down as well. Italy has a multi-union structure like France, as well as numerous autonomous trade unions. But Italian bargaining practice has a two-tier structure: one tier at national level and one within the enterprise. At the national level, trade union rivalry predominates as in France, but at the enterprise level, the situation is very different. In Italy, the various trade unions constitute a common platform at sector and workplace level where they nurture a culture of consensus. However, the preliminary findings of the study provide no evidence that this culture of consensus makes a significant difference, though the consolidated findings may allow firmer conclusions to be drawn.

The study by Edling and Sandberg deals with new forms of management and work and their relation to the trade union role in a participative framework. It presents some fundamental background information that is required for a realistic, down-to-earth discussion of democratic participation and the part played by the unions in contemporary work organizations. The study addresses the characteristics and extent of new management, flat organization, decentralized decision making, flexibility and cooperative labour relations in a Swedish context. There, unlike in America or Japan, they argue, a more 'competing union tradition of ideas exists, with values like quality of work, autonomy and democracy at the workplace'. On the basis of empirical data coupled with a broad survey of contemporary literature on the subject, they find that the elements characterized as the 'new' organizational forms and methods of management are to be found in varying degrees within Swedish working life. For instance, quality circles and development groups are found at more than half the workplaces. On the other hand, the authors find no correlation between new management and a flat organizational structure even though policy decisions may be decentralized. They also find that the establishments exhibiting an 'aggregate measure of new management' are fairly uncommon. New management is most common in large establishments within the private sector, with the engineering industry at the forefront. Furthermore, the larger the proportion of white-collar workers among the employees, the higher the extent of new management.

Unexpectedly, the authors reveal that union influence is perceived by management as being stronger and labour relations more cooperative in establishments with new management. Ironically, the authors speculate that had the union organization indeed been strong enough – such as in a situation of full employment – it would probably have resisted effectively the closure of plants with the latest work organization and production technology like the ones at Uddevalla and Kalmar. Thus the study by Edling and Sandberg further underlines some of the main arguments of Scenario 21, including the compatibility of collective bargaining and forms of democratic worker participation.

Leisink's chapter explores democratic participation in the information and communications industry in the Netherlands. The majority of these firms employ fewer than 50 employees and labour relations are subject either to 'cheerful anarchy' or to more regular individual and collective negotiations and consultations between employees and management in the bigger companies. Leisink insists on building up his arguments 'from below': what do the employees themselves want? Very interestingly, he notes in various studies that there is an *increasing* desire among significant categories of employee to have access to group decision making and company decision making, and in fact, in the majority of cases, direct participation by way of group delegation and group consultation is practised in the information and communications industry. This growing 'participation propensity' (Walker, 1974) appears to be nourished by concerns about individual interests rather than wider societal interests. Hence there is a preference for (and actual practice of) one-to-one negotiations with employers, informal or formal group consultations, and in terms of indirect participation, a preference for works councils and a (growing?) hesitation to be represented by trade unions in collective bargaining. Where works councils exist (in the Netherlands in companies with 50 or more employees – a legal provision which is not always implemented), they are often also used as bargaining instruments to negotiate employment conditions and remain the sole form of indirect democratic participation. In other words, the trade unions do not get involved. A further most interesting finding mentioned in Leisink's chapter is that a majority of employees (between 55 and 70 per cent in different studies) prefer trade unions and works councils *together* to represent the work force. This argument clearly bolsters Qvale's observations about the prospects for reconciling adversarial and participative labour relations. There is a symbiotic relationship between collective bargaining and works councils. The borderlines between them become either blurred or subject to greater tension, and this is to a great extent influenced by the trade union's stand on certain issues. Do the works councils represent group or sectional interests, or do they (also) fight for the wider questions of employee solidarity? Such questions put the trade union in a most delicate position. They may generate important policy debates within union structures, as Leisink reports, unless the unions stick rigidly to their traditionally militant roles, as seems to be the case in France (see chapter 10 by Pinaud).

European Works Councils and the European Employment Strategy

Two further chapters complement the exploration of the frontiers of workplace democratization. The most remarkable landmark in European industrial relations over the last decade of the twentieth century was the long awaited adoption of the directive on European works councils (EWCs) by the European Union in 1994 (Goetschy, 1996; Gold and Hall, 1994). By 2002, some 700 EWCs had been set up in the 1,874 companies covered by the directive, a density approaching 40 per cent (ETUI, 2002). The European Union has made significant funds available to monitor and support the establishment, functioning and development of EWCs, which have provided fruitful evidence for the Europeanization of social and employment practice across the continent.

In his chapter, Gold discusses EWCs in terms of their overall impact on the newly emerging European employment policy. He argues that part of the support that EWCs have been winning from certain employers comes from their realization that EWCs can play an important role in promoting the now fashionable, 'company-friendly' and 'supply-side' approaches to human resource management, employability and flexibility. This is in line with current EU policy for dealing with the still widespread unemployment problem, that is, by steering a middle course between the regulatory approach of the interventionists, who arguably focused too narrowly on the rights of workers, and the free market orientation of the neo-liberals. Nevertheless, there are indications that unions are managing to secure certain trade-offs through EWCs and thereby gaining genuine influence over a widening number of issues at the European-group level of transnational companies.

Furthermore, as Goetschy reveals in her chapter, the current European Employment Strategy stresses multi-governance – through social partnership and dialogue – as its identifying feature, and national policies are expected to be coordinated around the EU guidelines. These guidelines structure the form and content of the national action plans for employment that must be drawn up every year by member states for submission to the Commission. This process is creating a new bargaining arena for the social partners with a direct bearing on national industrial relations practices. In other words, new potential areas for worker participation are being opened in relation to influence on managerial prerogatives, working conditions, job content and better prospects for job security in both present and/or future jobs, amongst others. These two chapters, taken together, illustrate the ways in which unions, given resolve, may take advantage of shifts towards supply-side policies at all levels of the EU economy to shape their own agendas and work to their own priorities.

Financial Participation: a Lever for Other Forms of Democratic Participation?

The 1990s also prompted a 'new deal' for financial participation. The accelerated transition to a neo-liberal economy has shifted the emphasis towards profit-sharing and employee share-ownership schemes initiated and encouraged by both employers and government. In the 1980s the Conservative government in the UK widely introduced 'people's capitalism' schemes. Initial studies have shown that these schemes tended to reduce the influence of workers in decision making and began to erode collective bargaining, dividing different groups of workers in a 'thirst for gold' (Baddon et al., 1989). Blinder adds later that schemes of financial participation function better where these are combined with institutions of employee participation in decision making and that employee share-ownership plans (ESOPs) in particular are most likely to flourish in a participatory environment (Blinder, 1990). Similarly, Central and Eastern Europe became a surprising laboratory of economic democracy. The privatization trend that characterized this area was initially expected to follow classical capitalist paradigms. However, a much wider range of ownership and management schemes sprang up. Empirical evidence was produced showing that financial participation schemes can lead to positive effects on the motivation and productivity of workers, as well as on organizational performance and innovation (Vaughan-Whitehead, 1995). The fears expressed by many policy advisors at the beginning of the transition period regarding the negative implications of employee ownership proved to be largely exaggerated (Uvalic and Vaughan-Whitehead, 1997).

In this book, Vaughan-Whitehead gives a comprehensive overview of the role of the trade unions in the privatization process in the countries of Central and Eastern Europe. Focusing on employee ownership and works councils in these transition economies, Vaughan-Whitehead examines the unions' role in helping workers to become owners and their subsequent failure to ensure the survival of employee ownership. He attributes this failure to a number of factors, including the lack of shareholders' participation rights, and traces the most recent developments across the individual countries in question, concluding that the unions need to formulate greater coherence in their policies in support of employee ownership.

Towards more Inclusive Democratic Participation

Labour markets and labour relations are currently in rapid transition in Europe. The boundaries between 'inside' and 'outside' the workplace are becoming vaguer as there is a shift away from secure and long-term employment contracts to short-term contracts, and away from full-time to part-time employment and to higher labour turnover. The proportion of temporary or seasonal labour, home-workers, the unemployed, marginalized workers (such as women, young people and migrants), and the socially excluded rises. The problems of energy supplies, natural resources, the environment, migration, population increase and so on all have major consequences for the world of labour and production. In addition, those who do not have a full-time or tenured job, as well as the marginalized and the excluded, seek the opportunity to express themselves, to exert influence, to share in the fruits of the economy and to codetermine their future. A debate on this trade union challenge was launched through the Scenario 21 project.

We have just entered a new century in which industrial and labour relations are expected to change quite fundamentally. Even if we do not share the opinion of Forrester (1996) that thinking in terms of full employment has already become an anachronism, we cannot nevertheless help observing a steady trend from secure employment to employability, from fixed conditions to flexibility, from established work organizations to adaptability. This is the clear message of the Green Paper published by the European Commission, *Partnership for a New Organization of Work* (1997), the subsequent employment communications and guidelines, and now embodied in the European Economic Strategy, as Goetschy shows in her chapter. Rapidly expanding schemes of financial participation have introduced many workers to capital ownership. Though it is important not to exaggerate the trends (Bradley et al., 2000), many workers choose or have to accept part-time work or freelance or self-employment status. The development of democracy has implied that not only the conditions and the mode of production, but also the effects and results of production, are questioned by a broad spectrum of organizations in civil society.

Apart from the issues that can be dealt with democratically in the context of one workplace, there are many labour issues that cross the boundaries of workplaces or that exist in the labour market or in society without specific reference to an (organized) place of work. We may call them 'transversal' labour issues, and these cannot be regulated in traditional enterprise-based institutions of democratic participation.

Classical industrial relations theory continues to be primarily conceptualized within the interaction between three major actors: organized employers, government and the waged/salaried workers and their organizations (Dunlop, 1958). This theory is enshrined in the structure of the International Labour Organization, and is institutionalized deeply and widely in the industrialized countries. For a long time, and especially as long as Europe was characterized by full employment and more or less stable employment contracts, tripartism was a strong industrial relations instrument, and the welfare state its result. When that context changed in Europe (as evidenced by structural unemployment, a weakening of the welfare state, social exclusion and so on), the existing institutional frameworks continued but could not adequately serve as the most effective instruments to cope with new environment. There is a wide range of issues in which new labour participation strategies could be developed. These include the physical environment, the labour market, quality of life in general, (lifelong) education and training, and also internationalization and globalization. Can the traditional institutions of labour relations cope with the micro-, meso- and macro-level issues confronting the world of labour tomorrow? Tripartite industrial relations are extremely important but carry with them the threat of creating a coalition made up of those who have what they need and of marginalizing the dispossessed – of concentrating on the present at the cost of the future. Consensus between strong social partners of production may well encourage vested interests to take precedence while the traditional structures in which labour relations are handled gradually ossify (Kester and Pinaud, 1996a). Beyond the enterprise, more or less traditional tripartite consultation structures can yield important macro-social and economic results for workers (Visser and Hemerijck, 1997), but are in dire need of restructuring and re-orientation (Treu, 1992; Trebilcock, 1994).

Three chapters on transversal labour issues are included in this book: one by Pinaud on the reduction of working time in France, one by Ponzellini on the reduction of working time in Italy and one by Monat and Beaupain on the role of economic and social councils in social dialogue.

Linking Macro Issues to the Employee at Home and Work

Pinaud investigates the response of trade unions and institutions to direct and indirect forms of participation on such a 'transversal issue' as the reduction of working hours (RWH). Reduction of working hours touches three important, different dimensions: macro-economically, it is a device to curb unemployment; managerially, a device for flexibility; and sociologically, a device for improved quality of both working and home life. It is a particular challenge to democratic participation as it implies tripartite negotiation at national level, direct and indirect forms of participation at the workplace, as well as individual choices concerning the quality of life in general. In his chapter, Pinaud introduces us to the debate and experience of this issue in France. Shorter hours are not viewed 'from above' but 'from below'. Pinaud's assumption is that, as workers are directly affected by decisions on shorter hours both at work and at home, they must have a keen interest in gaining access to these decisions. But on the basis of his analysis of recent experience, he cannot but conclude that RWH has become part of the traditional ball game of government, management and professional trade unionists and remote from the workers themselves. We must ask why this opportunity for direct participation was missed when, in France, so much space had been created, by law, for direct expression by workers.

Trade unions have, and apparently very legitimately, put all their emphasis on the employment creation objective of RWH. But, as Pinaud rightly questions, why did the trade unions not take this golden opportunity to make use of existing direct participation structures to consult workers on draft RWH agreements? Why not include the issues that the workers themselves find important? Ironically, Pinaud continues, where workers did gain some influence, it was through non-union direct participation or non-union staff representation. Pinaud maintains that the failure to exploit the participation potential of the introduction of RWH was a setback for both trade unionism and industrial relations in France.

Pinaud's remarks raise the more general question of the spectrum of possibilities of trade union innovation in dealing with questions of solidarity when it comes to transversal issues. In this respect, reference may be made to the statement on goals and principles by the Dutch union confederation, FNV (1997). This may serve as an example (not a model) of a trade union attempt to broaden its concept of solidarity to include 'unprotected' and often non-unionized categories of workers such as migrants, women and the unemployed.

Ponzellini's chapter on the reduction of working time in Italy presents some stark contrasts with the French experience. Ponzellini notes the results of generalized reductions in working time over the 1980s and observes that the focus of bargaining has since shifted towards making working time more flexible. Still more recently, new forms of bargaining have evolved aimed at combining the needs of both employers and workers: employers gain by intensifying use of plant while workers gain by improving their work/life balance. The key point about this is that these new arrangements are driven from the bottom up – by the everyday requirements of workers, particularly women – rather than from the top down by the policies designed centrally by the unions (which nevertheless continue to campaign for generalized reductions in working time as well).

Amongst the unions, the term 'flexibility' began with negative connotations, as they perceived it as a set of means used by employers to undermine alleged rigidities and to intensify the pace of work. Indeed, companies have given priority to their own commercial and technical objectives over a long period, and of course many still do. However, attitudes began to change over the 1990s. Ponzellini examines how differing organizational needs for flexibility – such as optimization of the use of capital, extension of opening hours in service sectors and pressures to adapt rapidly to fluctuations in demand for certain products – have led to different responses by companies according to their own special circumstances. Meanwhile, particularly with the growth of female employment, the principal issue facing increasing numbers of workers is not 'how much' work to do, but 'when' to do it. Indeed, it has become increasingly clear not only that male and female workers have different requirements in this respect, but also that their needs evolve over time as they enter successive phases of life. The coincidence of these developments – company needs for flexibility and worker needs for improved work/life balance – has led to increasing 'destandardization' of working hours in company-level agreements in Italy over the last 10 years or so.

Ponzellini carefully analyzes the content of four such agreements across a variety of sectors in both manufacturing and services. She acknowledges that her cases remain limited in scope and still largely symbolic, but at the same time she highlights some crucial points, notably that improved work/life balance can be achieved at zero cost to companies and that, therefore, the company is the best level to achieve such results. Overall, her chapter concludes that the notion of 'standard working hours' will continue to bend under mounting pressures. The challenge for the unions is that these pressures will continue to erode their representational status amongst workforces. On the other hand, they may enhance the importance of company-level bargaining and hence the unions' ability to provide individualized responses to workers' needs.

Tripartism Visited and Revisited

Tripartite mechanisms, as argued by Monat and Beaupain, have been important factors in the democratic process, bringing the traditional social partners together in a context of democratic participation. But democracy is an ongoing process. Its development increasingly includes citizens in decision-making processes at all levels. This demands a spirit of openness rather than a dogged dependency on existing structures. As Touraine has stated, the long movement of descent of democracy to civil society, triggered by trade union action and industrial democracy, will continue. From political democracy to social democracy to cultural democracy: everyday activities are increasingly linked to dialogue and political decision making (Touraine, 1994; Dahrendorf, 1996). Touraine places much emphasis on human rights, citizenship and civil society, and on the importance of participative democracy for development. In a radical criticism of the socialist tradition, Keane strongly pleads for the democratization of civil society, which allows all citizens to participate in the democratic process. His examination of the theoretical and institutional roots of the deepening crisis of European socialism is an important contribution to understanding the participative void in what he sees as leftist dogmatic democracy (Keane, 1988). However, an 'institutional' answer to multi-partite and multi-faceted labour relations is implicit in a number of mechanisms of social dialogue that already exist. Trebilcock provides a survey of such mechanisms, and from her statistics it can be deduced that of a total of 56 tripartite structures in the industrialized countries she surveyed, 23 are 'tripartite plus'. That is – apart from government, employers and trade unions – they include experts and members of other social organizations, such as consumers' associations, environmentalists, farmers and craftworkers, amongst others (Trebilcock, 1994). Yet her study puts full emphasis on the functioning and achievements of tripartism, which is not surprising as tripartism continues to be the locus of power.

In their chapter, Monat and Beaupain present an up-to-date survey of economic and social councils across Europe. They observe that the majority of such councils have a consultative nature, though in certain countries intersectoral agreements may be concluded. They run through the origins and legal bases of the councils and their composition and operations, and pay particular attention to developments in Central and Eastern Europe and at EU level, focusing on the role of the Economic and Social Committee and the social dialogue process. The authors examine a number of the challenges faced by economic and social councils, such as managing the trade-offs between consensus and efficiency and their relationship with political democracy and civil society. However, they conclude that the work of these councils underpins all four of the propositions outlined on the first page of this introduction.

Towards Greater Investment in the Development of Participation

Participation is a dynamic ongoing process of policy and strategy formulation, of designing and redesigning structures and procedures, based on evaluation of experience, and taking into account opinions and expectations of workers, their leaders, management and employers. This observation implies that the gradual approach requires coordination, organization and support.

In Europe there has been historically definite support from governments, particularly where they have legislated for participation structures. The interesting feature is not only that the institutions of participation have been given a legal basis, but also that their development has been supported. In a number of European countries, the law provides funds from the company budget for education, advice, logistical and administrative support, time-off and training. These facilities were created as a result, not least, of trade union struggle and tough trade union/management and trade union/government negotiations. University institutions – often in cooperation with the trade union movement – have also been eager to assume a monitoring role (see chapters 17 to 24 in Kester and Pinaud, 1996a). However, over the past 10 years or so, this support appears to have been sharply decreasing (Zammit, 1996). Furthermore, whether in Europe or elsewhere, most studies do not consider the support for the functioning and development of democratic participation to be adequate. Such studies include the longitudinal European surveys of Heller et al. (1998), an analysis of the situation in Africa (Adu-Amankwah and Kester, 1999) and a recent cross-continental study of works councils (Markey and Monat, 1997).

It is true that for mainstream democratic participation (direct and indirect representation, especially through works councils), supporting structures have been created, as mentioned earlier, with respect to education, training and expert advice, paid for out of company budgets. In a small country like the Netherlands alone, an estimated €200 million per year must be provided by law for the education and training of elected works council members. However, it would appear to be time to evaluate more effectively whether the current levels of support are really sufficient for the development of democratic participation. In particular, we must assess the level of support necessary to provide adequate responses to the new frontiers of democratic participation.

The chapter by Zammit, Rizzo and Vancell discusses the issue of trade union education for workers' participation. On the basis of a case study analysing the experience of the General Workers' Union in Malta, they illustrate how trade union education can serve both the functional and reproductive ends of the union while simultaneously promoting transformative goals according to the opportunities which present themselves historically from time to time. Nevertheless, the extent of educational support required for an effective participation culture to develop is far beyond what any union can offer. It requires nothing less than the full support of the state as well as the collaboration of the voluntary and private sectors.

Revisiting Scenario 21

In the above pages references have been made to the wide diversity of chapters in this book, all dealing with new developments in democratic participation at work. However, it is not easy to interpret the accumulated research data obtained across different countries and sectors of the economy. Our earlier publication

(Kester and Pinaud, 1996a) set out the assumptions concerning Scenario 21, so we focus here on analysing the extent to which the data now available confirm, qualify or reject the propositions launched over five years ago.

Guiding Principles

Revisiting the 'guiding principles' for a strategy on democratic participation (Kester, 1996), we observe that most of them remain relevant. It is interesting to note that in several chapters of this book – for example, those by Mossé and Pinaud – reference is made to democratic participation as a felt need of workers. Leisink even observes an increasing propensity to participation. Furthermore, he notes that the right to participation is being exercised independently of trade union membership: workers may want to participate through trade unions or they may want to participate directly, without any trade union intervention, in conformity with the principle of the freedom of association. Such developments confirm that participation is not the exclusive domain of 'leftist' political forces but is an 'ideology in its own right'. In the earlier Scenario 21 publication, fears were expressed by the authors that the momentum to develop democratic participation, which had long been sustained by trade unions, was slipping away. This was said to be the combined result of the farewell to traditional socialism and the embrace of neo-liberalism even by social democratic forces. Yet, as the chapters reported here show, there are many new initiatives and innovative formats of democratic participation that are taking shape.

One guiding principle mentioned in the earlier Scenario 21 publication deserves further scrutiny, namely that the origin of the right to democratic participation can be found in labour and not in capital ownership. Several chapters in the present volume suggest important modifications in this respect. Participation was long seen as an integral component of the *workers' struggle*, often with the strong support of trade unions and governments to the left of the political spectrum. Management and employers had been diligent in the process. They tolerated democratic participation in general but dressed it up with their own values: greater cooperation, better communications and flows of information, improved management/worker relations, social harmony, reduction of industrial conflict and so on. All these serve management's interest as they may increase efficiency and productivity. In the tug-of-war over the direction and significance of the development of participation, all groups in power tend to promote their own objectives (Poole, 1986).

However, as the contributions of Qvale and particularly Goetschy and Gold show, another inroad into the participation game – if not another philosophy

– is that of social *partnership*. Edling and Sandberg put the emphasis of their analysis of new forms of management and work organization in Swedish workplaces on *cooperation*, with union influence still going strong and a new ideological perspective from the management side. Participation can be open to a positive sum game. The old in-fighting between trade unions and management/employers over objectives, scope and direction of participation can be substituted by a new kind of process. The realization of shared objectives now becomes a central issue along with the development of a shared culture, legitimate for all involved, so that different roles can be played in cultural congruence. The study by Leisink also points in this direction, and would appear to suggest that the workers themselves become increasingly supportive of such a new way of thinking. Ironically, in a number of countries, employers may be closer to the partnership model than trade unions because of the supposed convergence between democracy and efficiency (Gautrat, 1999). The right to democratic participation may then be found in partnership. Democratic participation, it would appear, is no longer primarily a *battleground* between capital and labour, implying a zero sum, or win-lose game, but a *common challenge*, a win-win game that forces all parties to reconsider the rules of the game and the roles of the actors. However, Martens, in his chapter, also reminds us quite rightly of the complexities of the social transformations we are living through and points out the scale of the challenge involved in establishing such new models of participation.

Scenario 21

The 'bread and butter' and 'consolidation' scenarios, and the scenario 'for growth of democratic participation' (or Scenario 21), were elaborated in the Kester and Pinaud volume (1996a) with special reference to possible trade union roles and strategies. In the chapters reviewed in this introduction, there are no real cases of the 'bread and butter' scenario in which trade unions concentrate exclusively on bargaining over pay and terms and conditions, and leave the initiative and practice of any form of participation to management and workers. However, a number of cases reported here (both Pinaud's and Ponzellini's studies of the reduction of working hours and Mossé's study of hospital reform) come close to the 'consolidation' scenario. This is essentially the combination or rather – we might say – the cohabitation of collective bargaining and codetermination at company level, but without an active trade union role in *strengthening* codetermination or managerial and financial participation.

Qvale reports on a case that comes close to Scenario 21: the development and spread of codetermination and increased trade union involvement in all forms of participation including organizational and financial participation. The cases reported by Leisink as well as Edling and Sandberg would appear to fit in between the consolidation scenario and Scenario 21, though more inclined towards the latter. Quite obviously, this 'classification' of the different contributions is a rough guide and, as already observed in the earlier publication, the three scenarios may in reality overlap (Kester and Pinaud, 1996c). Yet, for the sake of our argument here it would appear useful to elaborate on the consequences of the above mentioned cases in the perspective of the assumptions underpinning these scenarios.

A first assumed consequence of the consolidation scenario is a division in the representation of workers' interests, in the context of unions on the one hand and in the context of management – such as forms of direct participation – on the other. The study by Pinaud confirms this most clearly: the introduction and implementation of shorter working hours, he says, was conducted through traditional industrial relations processes despite the rich potential for direct participation. The further assumption was that the duality of representation would 'undoubtedly be exploited by employers' (Kester and Pinaud, 1996c, p. 51). This does not appear to be the case in the story of shorter hours, where management did not see it as an opportunity to introduce participative management unilaterally. A most significant finding in the study by Leisink is that the majority of employees in the information and communications industry want a combination of bargaining and works councils to represent their interests. This is of particular importance because a further assumption of the consolidation scenario was that the lack of trade union involvement in participation would lead to increased corporatism, and that there would be a shift away from collective forms of representation towards individually based forms. Without trade union involvement, works councils may easily become breeding-grounds for collective egoism. Leisink indeed mentions that works councils are little inclined to raise wider issues of solidarity (such as gender or ethnic issues). He also reports that the absence of trade union representation in the small and medium-sized enterprise sector he studied means that individually based forms of representation are on the increase. Pinaud makes the same observation but attributes it to trade union indifference.

In view of these very tentative observations, which are subject to further testing, it is important to refer again to the need to revise the guiding principle on the origin of the right to democratic participation. The assumption that duality of representation would undoubtedly be exploited by employers has to be critically modified under the 'social partnership ideology'. In the chapters by Goetschy, Gold, Martens, Pinaud and particularly Leisink, it emerges that initiatives may also come from the workers' side. On the other hand, the mere absence or indifference of a trade union may produce new forms of representation, both for the purposes of bargaining and codetermination/ comanagement, which may be exploited by management *and/or* by workers. The consequences of this assumed non-trade union context may lead to some likely consequences including: individualization of labour relations, progressive fragmentation and a dual labour relations system in which the better-offs obtain a positive deal for themselves and leave the trade unions to deal with negative aspects and to represent the worse-offs. This may eventually lead to further reductions in trade union membership and loss of trade union power and influence. This scenario would appear to present a challenge for trade unions, that is, to prevent this vicious circle from turning into a self-fulfilling prophecy. This challenge has been picked up by trade unions in the Netherlands and Italy, as Leisink and Ponzellini respectively suggest, but much less so in France, where Pinaud's study laments the lost opportunities for trade unions.

Many of the consequences assumed for the consolidation scenario are absent in the case described by Qvale. Here the trade unions play an active part in coordinating the different forms of participation, by adopting a multi-track strategy as a constructive social partner. In particular, as it was assumed (Kester and Pinaud, 1996c) that trade union support for involvement in all forms of participation would make it possible for them to balance individual, group and collective interests, then such a strategy will clearly strengthen the trade unions.

Trade Unions

Many of the chapters in this book reflect the transformations to which trade unions and labour markets across the industrialized world have been subject in recent years. Leisink, for example, investigates the articulation of individualized interests through one-to-one negotiations between workers and employers, and in the new economy, on which he writes, he observes employee preferences for representation through works councils rather than trade unions. Similarly, Qvale points out that complex forms of representative democracy at work lose their appeal under pressure from more adaptable forms of work organization. Edling and Sandberg focus on the extent of 'new' methods of management, including decentralized decision making, flexibility and cooperative labour relations, and their impact on the functioning of the unions. Pinaud and Ponzellini examine the role – explicit or otherwise – of the work/life balance in recent reductions in working time.

Some observers take these developments – individualization, new forms of work organization and management and work/life balance, amongst others, set against a backdrop of generally declining union membership – as indicators of a transition from a 'Fordist' to 'post-Fordist' society. Martens, in his chapter on social transformation, self-organization at work and participation in Germany, tackles these issues head on. He argues that the system of industrial relations in Germany, and notably the unions, works councils and codetermination, are the 'children of Fordism' and are still to face up to what he calls 'the worst of the adaptation crisis'. He makes his case by considering 10 arguments. Reflecting other chapters in the book, these include the evidence of workers' perceptions of the future of their own work, the evolution of managerial models of participation and the emergence of the 'labour entrepreneur', the worker who operates in a greater atmosphere of autonomy and internalizes the entrepreneurial requirements of his or her employer in the light of market demands.

Martens acknowledges the legacy of codetermination in consolidating social consensus in Germany following the horrors of the Second World War. Nevertheless, he stresses that education in trade union activity must relate to workers' own experiences of change if it is to provide a basis for understanding social realities. According to a recent survey of its members carried out by IG Metall, the German metalworking union, these experiences and expectations have now evolved so far that the unions must prioritize the development of new, viable models of activity. This task becomes particularly acute as Martens envisages workers as 'citizens', whom the unions must recruit individually to survive by offering specific advantages over non-membership (Leisink makes very similar points in his own chapter). Yet Martens is not unduly pessimistic. He concludes that only 'dogmatic neo-liberals' could believe that the world of work will be based in the future only on the market. He emphasizes the significance of continuities, and declares that 'a stable future for society requires stable institutional change in many of the key institutions of the old labour society'.

There is here a paradox of trade union representativeness and legitimacy. Trade unions are under-represented or not represented at all in many small and medium-sized enterprises and in the new economy. For a long time, trade unions have been conditioned to deal with the representation of interests of workers in large-scale organizations and on broader sectoral and national levels.

They have acquired professional expertise and developed their infrastructure for that purpose. As Pinaud observes in his contribution to this book, the trade unions in France put the emphasis on 'quantitative' demands, which attract massive worker support, at the expense of 'qualitative' or individual demands. This gives rise, Pinaud continues, to the classic but stubbornly oligarchical tendency: a small nucleus of professionals and activists take decisions on behalf of 'the workers' who are consulted only to rubber-stamp trade union decisions. Indeed Pinaud's study, like Leisink's, confirms that the workers recognize the need for trade unions to tackle collective questions through solidarity. However, they also feel that their qualitative/individual needs are not being adequately represented by trade unions, so they turn to other channels of representation or participation. Yet when electing their own representatives, they appear to be simply re-inventing the trade union wheel.

We may venture to suggest that a cultural gap has come to exist between traditional trade unionism and the ambitions, expectations and perspectives of workers in new sectors and elsewhere. In particular, the individualism and materialism among young workers clearly does not conform to the established pattern of solidarity in trade unionism. Admittedly, this is a complex issue, as the positions of both workers and trade unions are backed by good arguments. When the workers come to terms with management – through direct participation or works councils – the trade unions suspect that employers' real intentions are to fulfil their own narrowly corporate demands. When trade unions negotiate the terms of employment in the wider context of socio-economic issues and solidarity, workers fear that their own immediate interests may be traded off against issues about which they are not adequately informed by the unions.

Under Scenario 21, it might be possible to reduce this cultural gap considerably, as the issue would appear to be one of misunderstanding rather than of disagreement. We can, after all, observe misunderstandings or lack of understanding – rather than disagreements based on principle – between employers and unions over which procedures to use to handle contrasting issues, such as those where mutual interests are concerned rather than conflicting interests, individual rather than collective aspirations, and qualitative rather than quantitative demands. Indeed, democratic participation is not a major item on the agenda of most trade unions, and neither is it on the agenda of political parties. The fourth proposition on Scenario 21, summarized at the start of this chapter, maintained that an innovative approach to democratic participation at the workplace level and beyond would be more successful if the union movement were willing to take up the challenge and provide the necessary support. By actively involving themselves in the entire spectrum of direct and indirect participation, the trade unions may regain legitimacy for their triple role. This consists in defending both their members' material interests (business unionism) and their individual and qualitative interests (participative unionism) as well as the interests of workers in general (inclusive unionism). Unions need to explain all three roles to demonstrate their complementarity and to mobilize the widest possible support for them, primarily among workers, but also among management and the general public. Trade unions hold a strategic position as they are present at all levels, from the workplace right up to international arenas. They can therefore 'broker' grass-roots experiences and expectations at all levels of decision making by taking into account broader issues of social and economic justice and solidarity. In this way, the unions may be able to break down misunderstandings over the scope and purpose of different forms of participation.

This may well be the most important mission for the trade union movement in the twenty-first century. If it fails, there is the risk of further social disintegration and the erosion of democracy. If it succeeds, a new reflective partnership could develop with potential benefits for all. For this to happen, a 'turnaround' change is necessary, so aptly described by Qvale in chapter 8. We conclude that, judging from his study, the prospects may not be unrealistic.

References

Adu-Amankwah, K. and Kester, G. (eds) (1999), *How to Make Democratic Participation a Success? An African Trade Union Challenge*, Textua, Rotterdam.

Albert, M. (1991), *Capitalisme contre Capitalisme*, Seuil, Paris.

Anstey, M. (1997), *Labour Relations in Transition*, Port Elisabeth, Anstey (self-publisher).

Baddon, L., Hunter, L., Hyman, J., Leopold, J. and Ramsay, H. (1989), *People's Capitalism? A Critical Analysis of Profit-Sharing and Employee Share Ownership*, Routledge, London/New York.

Bayat, A. (1991), *Work, Politics and Power: An International Perspective on Workers' Control and Self-management*, Zed Books, London, and Monthly Review Press, New York.

Blinder, A.S. (ed.) (1990), *Paying for Productivity: a Look at the Evidence*, The Brookings Institution, Washington.

Bradley, H., Erickson, M., Stephenson, C. and Williams, S. (2000), *Myths at Work*, Polity, Cambridge.

Clegg, I. (1971), *Workers' Self-management in Algeria*, Allen Lane, London.

Commission of the European Communities (1997), *Partnership for a New Organization of Work*, Green Paper, April, Commission of the EC, Brussels.

Dahrendorf, R. (1996), 'Economic Opportunity, Civil Society and Political Liberty', *Development and Change*, Vol. 27, No. 2, pp. 229–49.

Dunlop, J. (1958), *Industrial Relations Systems*, Holt, New York.
ETUI (2002), *European Works Councils – Multinationals Database 2002* (CD-ROM), edited by Kerckhofs, P. and Pas, I., European Trade Union Institute, Brussels.
FNV (1997), 'FNV Statement on Aims and Ideals; Ratified on 30 May 1997', Federatie Nederlandse Vakbeweging, Amsterdam.
Forrester, V. (1996), *L'Horreur Economique*, Fayard, Paris.
Gautrat, J. (1999), 'Le statut de l'expression', in Le Tron, M., Pinaud, H. and Chouraqui, A. (eds), *Syndicalisme et démocratie dans l'entreprise*, L'Harmattan, Paris, pp. 187–206.
Goetschy, J. (1996), 'Participation and Building Social Europe', in Kester, G. and Pinaud, H. (eds), *Trade Unions and Democratic Participation in Europe: A Scenario for the 21st Century*, Avebury Press, Aldershot, pp. 27–33.
Gold, M. and Hall, M. (1994), 'Statutory European Works Councils: the Final Countdown?', *Industrial Relations Journal*, Vol. 25, No. 3, September, pp. 177–86.
Heller, F., Pusic, E., Strauss, G. and Wilpert, B. (1998), *Organizational Participation: Myth and Reality*, Oxford University Press, Oxford/New York.
Keane, J. (1988), *Democracy and Civil Society*, Verso, London/New York.
Kester, G. (1996), 'Guiding Principles for a Strategy for Democratic Participation', in Kester, G. and Pinaud, H. (eds), *Trade Unions and Democratic Participation in Europe: A Scenario for the 21st Century*, Avebury Press, Aldershot, pp. 35–48.
Kester, G. and Pinaud, H. (eds) (1996a), *Trade Unions and Democratic Participation in Europe: A Scenario for the 21st Century: A Scenario for the 21st Century*, Avebury Press, Aldershot.
Kester, G. and Pinaud, H. (1996b), 'Democratic Participation: A Challenge for Democracy', in Kester, G. and Pinaud, H. (eds), *Trade Unions and Democratic Participation in Europe: A Scenario for the 21st Century*, Avebury Press, Aldershot, pp. 1–9.
Kester, G. and Pinaud, H. (1996c), 'The Decline, Consolidation or Growth of Participation?', in Kester, G. and Pinaud, H. (eds), *Trade Unions and Democratic Participation in Europe: A Scenario for the 21st Century*, Avebury Press, Aldershot, pp. 49-63.
Kester, G. and Sidibe, O. (1986), 'Petite Fleur de l'Esprit Autogestionnaire au Sahel: l'apprentissage de la participation responsable à l'entreprise Malienne du bois', ENA, Bamako.
Kissler, L., Greiffenstein, R. and West, K. (eds) (1997), *Erneuerung der Mitbestimmung durch demokratische Partizipation: das Szenario 21 und seine Bedeutung für die Mitbestimmung in Deutschland*, Schuren Verlag, Marburg.
Knight, P.T. (1975), 'New Forms of Economic Organization in Peru: Towards Workers' Self-Management', in Lowenthal, A.F. (ed.), *The Peruvian Experiment. Continuity and Change under Military Rule*, Princeton University Press, Princeton, New Jersey, pp. 350–401.
Leisink, P., van Leemput, J. and Vilrokx, J. (eds) (1996), *The Challenge to Trade Unions in Europe: Innovation or Adaptation?*, Edward Elgar, Cheltenham.
Markey, R. and Monat, J. (eds) (1997), *Innovation and Employee Participation through Works Councils*, Avebury, Aldershot.
Mothe, D. (1980), *L'Autogestion Goutte à Goutte*, Le Centurion, Paris.
Pinaud, H. (1996), 'The Role of Social Actors during Recent Developments in Worker Participation in Ten Countries of Western Europe', in Kester, G. and Pinaud, H. (eds), *Trade Unions and Democratic Participation in Europe: A Scenario for the 21st Century*, Avebury Press, Aldershot, pp. 11–25.
Poole, M. (1986), *Towards a New Industrial Democracy: Workers' Participation in Industry*, Routledge and Kegan Paul, London/New York.

Regini, M. (ed.) (1992), *The Future of Labour Movements*, Sage, London.

Sandberg, Å. (ed.) (1995), *Enriching Production: Perspectives on Volvo's Uddevalla Plant as an Alternative to Lean Production*, Avebury, Aldershot/Brookfield.

Sklar, R. (1987), 'Developmental Democracy', *Comparative Studies in Society and History*, Vol. 29, No. 4, pp. 696–8.

Touraine, A. (1994), *Qu'est-ce que la démocratie?*, Fayard, Paris.

Trebilcock, A. (ed.) (1994), *Towards Social Dialogue. Tripartite Co-operation in National Economic and Social Policy Making*, International Labour Organization, Geneva.

Treu, T. (ed.) (1992), *Participation in Public Policy-making: The Role of Trade Unions and Employers' Associations*, Walter de Gruyter, Berlin/New York.

Uvalic, M. and Vaughan-Whitehead, D. (eds) (1997), *Privatization Surprises in Transition Economies: Employee-Ownership in Central and Eastern Europe*, Edward Elgar, Cheltenham.

Vanek, J. (1972), *The Economics of Workers' Management: A Yugoslav Case Study*, Allen and Unwin, London.

Vanek, J. (1987), 'Towards a Just, Efficient and Fully Democratic Society', in Jones, D. and Svejnar, J. (eds), *Advances in the Economic Analysis of Participatory and Labor-managed Firms*, vol. II, JAI Press, Greenwich, London.

Van Ruysseveldt, J. and Visser, J. (eds) (1996), *Industrial Relations in Europe: Traditions and Transitions*, Sage, London.

Vaughan-Whitehead, D. (ed.) (1995), *Workers' Financial Participation: East-West Experiences*, International Labour Organization, Geneva.

Vaughan-Whitehead, D. (1996), 'Financial Participation: A New Challenge for Trade Unions', in Kester, G. and Pinaud, H. (eds), *Trade Unions and Democratic Participation in Europe: A Scenario for the 21st Century*, Avebury Press, Aldershot, pp. 161–82.

Visser, J. and Hemerijck, A. (1997), *'A Dutch Miracle': Job Growth, Welfare Reform and Corporatism in the Netherlands*, Amsterdam University Press, Amsterdam.

Walker, K. (1974), 'Workers' Participation in Management: Problems and Prospects', *Bulletin of the International Institute of Labour Studies*, Vol. XII, International Labour Organization, Geneva.

Zammit, E. (1996), 'Introduction to Trade Union-University Co-operation on Democratic Participation', in Kester, G. and Pinaud, H. (eds), *Trade Unions and Democratic Participation in Europe: A Scenario for the 21st Century*, Avebury Press, Aldershot, pp. 199–208.

Zammit, E. (2001), 'Efficiency versus Democracy in the Workplace? A Postscript on Self-management at Malta Drydocks', in Markey, R., Gollan, P., Hodgkinson, A., Chouraqui, A. and Veersma, U. (eds), *Models of Employee Participation in a Changing Global Environment*, Ashgate, Aldershot, pp. 161–75.

PART I
EU AND NATIONAL
DIMENSIONS

Chapter 2

EU Social Policy and Developments in Worker Involvement

Janine Goetschy

Arrangements for worker involvement at EU level hold several records in the history of EU social policy. They count among the first issues to be placed on the EU social agenda, they have been the longest to remain on that agenda, and they have proved to be amongst the most controversial. Over the years, they have been the object of highly adversarial discussions that have taken a series of twists and turns resulting from the significant institutional diversity of member states with respect to worker involvement. However, even though the various EU legislative proposals governing this area have undergone major changes of content and development over the years, the only one to be adopted until very recently was the European works councils (EWC) directive, in 1994 (see chapter 3). The changes in the content of other, successive, proposals and their ultimate fate have been closely linked to the evolution of EU social policy as well as to national developments and debates on industrial democracy and to the increasing speed of EU economic integration. With the development of the internal market, the advent of European Monetary Union (EMU), growing company size and ever-advancing strategies on corporate restructuring and relocation, company change – to be accepted by employees – has required more and more appropriate systems for worker information/consultation and even participation.

This chapter will examine precisely why and how, after 30 years of debate, the regulation and directive implementing the European Company Statute were eventually adopted in October 2001, following the compromise texts adopted by the Council in December 2000. It will also examine the reasons for the rapid progress on the directive establishing a general framework for informing and consulting employees at national level, which led to its adoption in February 2002.

Meanwhile, apart from the various substantive legal instruments (the 1994 EWC directive, the European Company Statute and the directive on national information/consultation), worker and union involvement has also been developing at the EU level in more indirect forms, especially during the 1990s, through several other means. These include the EU social dialogue and Euro-collective bargaining since the Maastricht Treaty (1992); parts of the European Employment Strategy formalized by the Amsterdam Treaty (1997); and, more recently, broader forms of macro-economic social dialogue, such as the broad economic guidelines (1992), the Cologne process (1999) and the Lisbon coordination approach (2000). An increasing diversification of forms of union involvement has thus been taking place at EU level, accompanied by the developing wave of national social pacts in numerous European countries throughout the 1990s. This chapter will also investigate the reasons behind such a diversification of means of union involvement, the complementary or competing interlinkages between them and their functioning and likely consequences.

Diversification of Forms of Union Involvement at EU Level

Over the 1990s, participatory frameworks designed at the EU level witnessed increasing diversification, as follows.

• Progress on the collective bargaining side, with the advent of Euro-agreements following the Maastricht Social Agreement annexed to the Maastricht Treaty (1992), which granted the EU social partners a collective bargaining role.
• Progress on EU legislative measures in the field of worker involvement.
• The introduction of the European Employment Strategy (EES), which represented a new method ('the open method of coordination') for coordinating national employment policies with implications for social partnership at EU, national, regional and enterprise levels.
• Encouragement to exchange good practice between social partnership experiments across different member states.

The motives for such a diversification of means for union participation at the EU level were based on the quest for greater legitimacy and efficiency for EU social policy and the EU economic integration process as a whole. The search for legitimacy was of a twofold nature (Scharpf, 1999). To enhance legitimacy 'by input', it was expected that there should be greater involvement from the EU social partners (ETUC, UNICE, and CEEP) in EU rule-making procedures at EU level (directly through Euro-agreements or through formal consultation in the legislative process). More generally, greater involvement was also expected from the many and various political and social actors engaged in the construction of social Europe (for example, the introduction of a codecision role for the European Parliament in the Amsterdam Treaty was a move in that direction). To enhance legitimacy 'by output', the quantity and quality of decisions taken at EU level in the social field had also to be improved. Furthermore, setbacks experienced later on at the EU level in the 1990s with respect both to the legislative and contractual routes for decision making justified the adoption of the 'open method of coordination' for policy issues which were either not yet within the EU's competence on social affairs (as prescribed by the Treaty) or were so but subject to unanimous voting and highly contentious. The open method of coordination appeared then as the only way forward for issues corresponding to urgent national social priorities (such as employment and social protection) but for which the classic EU methods (the legislative and contractual routes) were lacking or insufficiently efficient to advance at EU level.

Indeed, neither the enlarged sphere of EU social competence nor the chance for the social partners to negotiate Euro-agreements led to great activity either on the part of the Commission (in its capacity to propose directives) or on the part of the EU social partners (in their capacity to negotiate). Only three Euro-agreements have been reached so far (parental leave, 1995; part-time work, 1997; and short-term contracts, 1998). A few other attempts at negotiation failed in the meantime (for example, on temporary work) (Keller and Sörries, 1999; Keller and Bansbach, 2000).

Increasing the legitimacy and efficiency of the EU on social and employment matters became even more vital towards the mid-1990s if the whole EMU project, which by then had entered its final phase, were not to be placed at risk. The Renault Vilvoorde case, pessimistic public opinion about EMU's implications for employment, the future of public services and corporate relocations had been generating serious tension for some time. They cried out for the EU to tackle the most urgent social and employment issues within the framework of a diversified set of normative and institutional means for union involvement.

The diversification of normative means in themselves as well as the specific features of the management by objectives of the European Employment Strategy (EES) has entailed a proliferation of discussion/transaction/ negotiation forums at EU, national, regional, sectoral and enterprise levels. In turn, these forums integrate a multiplicity of social and political actors – such as EU institutions, member states, EU-level and national-level social partners and associations – which allows us to speak clearly about a multi-level process of governance. These forums or frameworks for action, however, vary greatly among themselves at the lower levels: their capacity to empower actors, their proactive nature and the legal status of measures they adopt differ widely. Yet what characterizes the creation of social Europe in the 1990s was precisely the intention:

a) to adopt EU measures allowing the intervention of successive levels below to adapt them to local institutional diversity and circumstances, and thereby satisfy the 'subsidiarity principle';

b) to make sure that measures were properly implemented by involving to a greater degree a wider range of actors (indeed, effective implementation may be achieved by other means, such as management by objectives, benchmarking, evaluation processes and the use of harmonized statistics, other than just through the use of legally binding measures); and

c) to promote proactive thinking (for example, through methods of worker involvement at company level; governance by recurring methods, such as the annual employment guidelines; the use of broad economic guidelines; and the Lisbon approach with 10-year targets on employment rates, growth and so on).

Risks of Competition between EU Regulatory Methods

Three major criticisms are often addressed towards the diversification of regulatory methods including Euro-agreements, directives, EU employment guidelines, exchange of good practice and, more recently, the open method of coordination. These criticisms focus on the complexity and work overload for actors and institutions that such multi-level governance entails; the relative lack of coordination between those various regulatory tools; and the risk of regulatory competition.

The first criticism is difficult to overcome, though an improvement can be expected with the development over time of learning processes rendering political and social actors more able to cope with complex issues and procedures. Lack of coordination can be reduced partly through procedural interlinkages between the law and the contractual method on the one hand and the open method of coordination and legal and contractual aspects on the other. Hence, in this respect, the complex links that have been developing between the law and the implementation of the existing Euro-agreements are interesting to note. Indeed, these existing Euro-agreements have been closely associated with the threat of intervention by the European Commission with a legislative measure in case of failure to agree during negotiations. Furthermore, the Euro-agreements have been turned into directives, which could in turn be implemented either through national legislation or through national collective bargaining. Generally speaking, to satisfy national diversity, more and more EU directives in the employment and social field are now intended to allow for a greater national margin of manoeuvre, and are thought of in terms of functional equivalents rather than identical measures. Some directives (such as those covering European works councils, the European Company Statute and national level information/consultation) even open up the content for negotiation first and envisage reference provisions only if negotiations were to fail. In this way, they set rules allowing for a great variety of national solutions.

If we now turn to the EES, which is, according to the Treaty, first and foremost a matter for the member states and EU institutions, then that too reveals interesting developments with respect to better articulation with the social partners.

The European Employment Strategy and its Link with Social Partnership

Though formalized within the Amsterdam Treaty (1997), the idea for a European employment strategy had already been initiated in the Delors White Paper, *Growth, Competitiveness and Employment* (1993), and operationalized on a pragmatic basis by the Essen procedure following the European Council in December 1994. Following Amsterdam, it had been implemented before the Treaty had formally come into force on the basis of the employment guidelines of the special Luxembourg summit (November 1997). Since then the EES has reached what might be called its own 'cruising speed'.

However, with the Lisbon European Council (March 2000), the EES was given a new impetus. During this summit, the member states agreed an ambitious new strategic goal for the EU over the next 10 years: 'to become the most competitive and dynamic knowledge economy in the world, capable of durable economic growth, of higher employment levels and jobs of a better quality and of improved social cohesion'. It set three major objectives relating to employment policy to be met by 2010: the goal of full employment; the raising of employment rates with quantified targets (70 per cent on average and 60 per cent for women); and an annual growth rate of 3 per cent over the same period. It is the first time that a European Council had issued conclusions of such a concrete nature with 60 actions covering 10 different fields. It took, however, nine months of hard debate and negotiation between the member states before reaching agreement on a strategy in which 'political orientations' should take the lead over economic matters (to be decided at an annual spring summit of European heads of state and government) and in which more virtuous circles were expected from closer articulation between various policy fields (macro-economic goals, structural economic reforms, labour market reforms, social cohesion and the modernization of social protection). The underlying assumption was that EU economic integration and reforms are not ends in themselves, but must support employment and social cohesion. Similarly, social cohesion and high employment levels underpin conditions for economic growth.

Since the Lisbon European Council, the EES has also been referred to as the 'open method of coordination'. This is because it represents a new regulatory method for creating a social Europe which is supposed to be complementary to the already existing instruments at EU level, namely legislation, European collective agreements and social dialogue, structural funds, support programmes, the integration processes of various policy fields, analysis and research. Indeed, since the 1980s and especially over the 1990s, a majority of member states have had to face high levels of unemployment and decreasing employment rates. However, employment levels and performances are highly diverse across the EU member states.

The EES process as designed by the Treaty is the following. Each year common European employment guidelines are drawn up and adopted by the Council (Social Affairs and Ecofin) by qualified majority vote. They then have to be formulated into national employment policies on which each member state must report to the Commission and the Council in their annual 'national action plans'. An annual evaluation then takes place on the basis of which the Council may address recommendations to member states. Such recommendations to individual states deemed not to have followed the guidelines have no obligatory effect, but could be politically powerful. The Employment Committee participates in the EES as an advisory body. Governments are expected to associate trade union and employer organizations at various levels both when formulating and implementing their national action plans for employment (NAPs). Three elements characterize the Employment Title in the Treaty:

- it is based on the previous experience of the Essen procedure;
- the approach to employment is inspired by the existing convergence process in the macro-economic field; and

- though employment is an issue of common concern for both the national and EU levels, it is the national level that remains primarily responsible for employment policies and achievements.

Since the Luxembourg summit in autumn 1997, the annual European employment guidelines have been set out under four pillars:

a) improving employability (aimed at improving the access of the unemployed to the labour market through two explicit objectives, namely developing a 'preventive approach' to avoid long-term unemployment and implementing 'activation policies');

b) developing entrepreneurship (making it easier to start and run a new business, and to recruit people for it by reducing administrative constraints and rendering taxation more employment friendly);

c) encouraging adaptability both for employees and businesses (entailing the modernization of work organization and other forms of adaptability in enterprises); and

d) strengthening equal opportunity policies (involving a gender main-streaming approach across all four pillars, tackling the gender gap, reconciling work and family life and facilitating reintegration into the labour market).

Around 20 such EU guidelines are established each year with only a few of them corresponding to quantified targets. Up until now there has been considerable continuity with respect to the EU annual guidelines: they have been more or less identical every year.

The EES procedure places social dialogue and collective bargaining between the two sides of industry at the heart of the strategy in several ways. Trade union and employer organizations are expected to participate in the EES at various levels when drawing up and implementing their national action plans (NAPs). They are supposed to be closely involved in the implementation of some of the employment guidelines, especially those related to the so-called 'third pillar' on 'adaptability'. The aim is to create compromises between job creation or preservation and the need for flexibility in work organization, working time or employment contracts at differing levels, such as the company, the region, the sector or intersectoral level. These compromises are broadly associated with a 'supply-side' approach to active labour market policy. In this context, a new equilibrium has to be found urgently between flexibility and job security for which collective bargaining is a crucial tool. More recently, education and life-long learning have also become essential priorities of the EES which the social partners are expected to cover.

How have the social partners at national level been involved in producing the NAPs? At both the drawing up and implementation phases the social partners have been insufficiently involved in the process, which has centred all too often on government. On the whole, the consultation process over the NAPs has not really generated new initiatives from the social partners or new national strategies towards unemployment. Though consultations over the NAPs generally take place only at central level, it is usually not the senior representatives of the employers or unions who are involved. This contrasts with the experience in negotiating social pacts at national levels; in such cases, top representatives of the union and employers' organizations are invariably the protagonists (Foden, 1999).

What changes are observable in the 2001 guidelines with respect to the links between the EES and social partnership? The social partners have been strenuously urged to strengthen their own contribution to the guidelines (a request also repeated at the Feira Council in June 2000). More specifically, the social partners are expected to create 'a process within the process' whereby they are responsible for developing and reporting on actions within their own sphere. They have been given exclusive responsibility for the implementation of two guidelines in the adaptability pillar. These are guideline 13 on the modernization of work organization and guideline 15 on the contribution of education and life-long learning to adaptability; on both issues they are supposed to negotiate agreements. Furthermore, with respect to work modernization, they are expected to produce an annual report detailing the achievements of these negotiations and how far they have been implemented, with their impact on employment and the labour market. Such a reporting process had also been planned later on for education and life-long learning by the Social Agenda, adopted at Nice in December 2000. This stipulated that the social partners should report to the Council of Social Affairs by the end of 2001 on agreements at all levels reached in this field. Moreover, the social partners are also invited, but this time in cooperation with the member states, to strengthen their contribution to active policies to combat emerging employment bottlenecks (guideline G.6), to combat undeclared work (G.9), to take part in local action for employment (G.11), to tackle gender gaps (G.17) and to reconcile work and family life (G.18).

The role of the social partners in the EES can be multi-faceted. The European social partners, together with their national counterparts, may themselves define which of the existing guidelines should be subject to benchmarks, the criteria for such benchmarks and whatever further action (such as negotiation) should be taken. They would then assume a role in improving the implementation of the guidelines within their overall framework.

Some objectives of the employment guidelines, and hence their implementation, could also be taken care of by the EU social dialogue itself (sectoral or intersectoral). This could lead to joint opinions or agreements. Such initiatives, driven by the Essen employment process and later on by the EES, have already resulted in agreements in various sectors (civil aviation, telecommunications, commerce, agriculture and tanning) as well as in the three intersectoral or cross-industry agreements on parental leave, part time work and fixed term employment contracts. This covers implementation and dissemination of the guidelines outside their general framework. The sectoral agreement on teleworking in telecommunications concluded in February 2001 gives a few hints about the ways in which the EES and the social dialogue may be linked.

The social partners could also, within the framework of the EU sectoral or intersectoral social dialogue, propose and elaborate new guidelines of their own which could then be adopted by the Council. This would entail a role of initiative on their part.

Furthermore, the European social partners may also, on the basis of national 'institutional' good practice, monitor the participation of their national counterparts in the drawing up and implementation of national action plans. They could encourage at national level a more coherent approach between the four pillars of the EES and promote greater integration amongst the different policy fields (such as macro-economic policy and reforms to taxation, the labour market and social protection) in order to improve national employment performance. This should lead to a better and closer articulation between the NAPs and the dynamics of national social pacts, in those countries where they exist. The lack of interlinkages between the two is one of the weak points of the EES.

Finally, appropriate procedural methods are required for an effective link up to take place between the EES and collective bargaining at European and national levels. The annual report on adaptability required under the 2001 guidelines[1] is a first step in this direction, as is the report on life-long learning required at the end of 2001 by the Social Agenda. In addition to these requirements to report by given deadlines, the content of the EES guidelines could be linked more closely to measures already existing in the EU *acquis communautaire*, such as the information/consultation of workers, the three European framework agreements and the numerous opinions issued in the context of the intersectoral social dialogue (Bercusson, 2000). Meanwhile, greater access to the different sources of EU funding would also help to define and promote more effectively the role of the social partners in the EES (the reform of the structural funds in the framework of Agenda 2000 is already a step in this direction).

Links between the EES and National Social Pacts

Though the employment guidelines do refer to national bargaining regarding employability, adaptability, education and training and equal opportunities, it has to be acknowledged that in practice the links between the internal dynamics of national social pacts and the sometimes rather formalistic preparation of the NAPs have appeared rather weak (Léonard, 2001). Without going into a detailed comparison between countries, this shortcoming is frequently revealed by the fact that the consultation of the social partners over the NAPs does not generally involve the highest levels of the trade union or employer hierarchy, whereas the negotiation of national social pacts does indeed involve participation by top-level employer and union representatives. Moreover, it has frequently seemed to be the case that, whereas the national social pacts of the 1990s (Italy, Portugal, Spain, Ireland, Netherlands, Finland and Denmark) gave rise to innovative and imaginative initiatives, the implementation of the employment guidelines has led to no such strong impetus.

To establish links between the NAPs as presented in the EES framework and the national social pacts is no straightforward matter because they are based upon, and yet create a tension between, two rather contradictory rationales (Rhodes, 2002). Whereas the EES aims to achieve better European convergence of national employment policies, the national social pacts are generally speaking competitive in nature, seeking to exploit national advantages in order to improve the competitive position of the national economy in the overall European or global arena. Several authors have deplored the downward spiral characteristic of such pacts (Streeck, 1999), whereas the aim of the EES is, precisely, to stem this downward spiral by defining convergent goals among member states on employability, entrepreneurship, adaptability of businesses and individuals, and equal opportunity between the sexes. The general idea of the EES is indeed to promote high employment rates and a reduction of unemployment, but not at any price and at a rate that is fairly comparable among the countries where progress is most needed (Germany, France, Italy, Spain, Finland and Greece). 'Not at any price' means that unemployment has to be reduced and the employment rate raised but only on certain conditions.

These include the preservation of quality jobs (with respect to the period of contract, working conditions, level of skills, pay levels and so on), the protection of social welfare and the avoidance of tax competition between countries. This twofold tension – European coordination in the EES and the NAPs alongside national competition in the social pacts – is not necessarily harmful in itself. However, the national social pacts are supposed, as the bottom line, not to export 'external negativities' to the other member states, whereas the EES seeks precisely to remedy some of these 'external negativities'. Indeed, let us recall that the EU employment guidelines are not confined to the labour market in the strictest sense, but that they substantially encroach upon aspects of social protection, education, social, tax, pay and regional exclusion, and seek to achieve convergence of certain aspects of these policies. In addition, beyond the EES which covers above all, it is true, structural reforms of the labour market, the other forms of European macro-economic convergence that are being developed may also contribute to curbing this downward spiral which is suspiciously present in the national social pacts of a competitive type.

Social pacts concluded in individual member states during the 1990s have shown that, at national level, institutional aspects of exercising power within companies have been temporarily shelved in favour of efforts to find fundamentally new compromises on employment (and its distribution in society), social protection and solidarity amongst citizens and between generations. The national social pacts of the 1970s had proved to be essentially redistributive in aiming at pay restraint in return for changes in social protection, taxation and increased powers for mechanisms for employee representation. Pacts in the 1990s, by contrast, tackled social issues with employment and social protection policies as the cornerstones, while information, consultation and representation bodies have not generally seen their institutional powers widened over recent years by national reforms. Moreover, employers often increasingly tended to see such bodies as a burdensome cost: this is why France, for example, in recent years has rationalized the operation of works councils and worker representatives in an effort to reduce their cost to companies, especially small and medium-sized enterprises (SMEs). The main priority over the 1990s has been to use already existing structures for worker involvement and collective bargaining to deal with substantive issues such as flexibility, work organization, working time, employment and so on. Several other chapters in this book describe and assess the exact role and importance of these structures over that decade in monitoring company organizational and strategic change, at a time of increasing competition and globalization. The fact that at national level very little widening of their formal institutional powers took place over the last 15 years goes some way to explaining why issues of workers' information and consultation – added to the great institutional diversity between member states – have for so long failed to make progress at EU level.

New Impetus for Directives on Worker Involvement

The 1990s witnessed intensifying competition, enterprise relocations, plant closures and corporate globalization through mergers and acquisitions (around 300 per year). In this context, the need for appropriate institutions and procedures for information and consultation over corporate change was becoming more and more acute. The international economic context as well as national political scenes had been changing a great deal since the 1970s. The 1970s had been a period of worker militancy and power on the labour side and hence the heyday of both new forms of work organization and national debates on industrial democracy (Brannen, 1983). By contrast, during the period two decades later information and consultation issues turned from an offensive to a more defensive character, and were in a way much more management oriented.

For more than 30 years, worker information, consultation and participation issues have been on the EU agenda. Proposals for directives on those issues had been subject to serious disputes and recurrent failures until the first breakthrough took place with the European works councils directive in 1994 (outlined in chapter 3). In December 2000, the Nice European Council concluding the French Presidency reached political agreement on the European Company Statute (ECS). This was a major proposal for a directive on worker involvement on which all 15 member states agreed; a unanimous position was necessary as the Treaty requires unanimity for directives entailing elements of codetermination. Indeed, the ECS was at last formally adopted by the Council on 8 October 2001.

This agreement also accelerated the unblocking of yet another proposed directive, the directive on informing and consulting workers at national level. During the Council of Social Affairs Ministers on 20 December 2000, it appeared that this directive was likely to be accepted as soon as the necessary majority required for its adoption could be achieved under the Swedish Presidency. In this case a qualified majority vote was sufficient as it touched only on questions of information and consultation. A formal debate was not possible, however, on 20 December as the UK invoked the procedural rules requesting a certain period of delay and warning before an issue can be put on the agenda. However, the directive was eventually formally adopted under the Spanish Presidency, on 18 February 2002, and came into force on its publication in the Official Journal on 23 March 2002 (EIRR, 2002b).

Apart from these two recent political successes, the EU Social Policy Agenda for the next five years was also adopted by the member states at the Nice summit. This clearly retained worker involvement as one of its six priorities under the heading 'anticipating and capitalizing on change in the working environment by creating a new balance between flexibility and security'. On the legislative side, the Social Policy Agenda reckoned that by 2002, apart from the adoption of the directives on the ECS and information/consultation at national level, a review and revision of the current European works council directive would also have taken place. Thereafter, by 2003, reviews of directives on collective dismissals, business transfers and employer insolvency were planned, as well as by 2004 an 'exchange of views' on individual dismissals.

On the social dialogue side, social partners are urged to hold talks and possibly negotiations on work organization, new forms of work, employability measures, adaptability and data protection issues. The aims of such a dialogue are various: to encourage enterprise modernization and improve labour relations; and to develop a trade-off between greater security for workers in exchange for greater flexibility on their part. Most of these questions are closely linked to the EES (see above). On the part of enterprises, greater adaptability is expected too, along with greater social responsibility when they undertake changes to managerial and strategic policy. Moreover, the Social Policy Agenda stresses the importance of the macro-economic dialogue, that is, the Cologne process whereby certain European institutions (such as the European Commission, Council and European Central Bank) and the social partners mutually adjust in an anticipated manner their respective monetary, macro-economic, employment and pay policies. Finally, a European Observatory for Monitoring Change was to be set up within the European Foundation for the Improvement of Living and Working Conditions in Dublin. This formalizes the work previously performed by the high-level group on economic and social implications of industrial change, chaired by Pehr Gyllenhammar and established by the Commission in January 1998.

The European Company Statute

First proposed by the European Commission in 1970, the ECS failed to be approved at successive Councils of Ministers due to the great diversity of existing institutional structures and traditions regarding worker involvement in the various EU member states. Controversy centred especially around the fact that some member states with strong statutory requirements, such as Germany with its board-level representation, feared that the European company (*Societas Europea*, or SE) could be used as a means to avoid more stringent national prescriptions. On the other hand, countries with comparatively weak statutory systems of worker involvement or no statutory rights at all (such as Ireland, Spain and the UK) were concerned that the SE would be used as a means to import stronger regulations. In 1997, the high-level group chaired by Etienne Davignon managed to break the deadlock and relaunch the debate on the basis of the experience acquired with the European works councils directive. The new draft text proposed by the Luxembourg Presidency in 1997 provided for negotiations between management and a special negotiating committee of employee representatives over the type of provisions that should apply to the SE; statutory fall-back arrangements would apply only if negotiations broke down. Before the Nice summit (2000), Spain was the only country remaining opposed to the French draft text. Spanish approval was finally obtained in Nice in exchange for some potential EU financial help to its fishing fleet and because the final text was highly flexible. Indeed, the deal was reached in Nice by making the national implementation of certain fall-back provisions optional: in other words, the text does not require the transposition of the worker participation provisions (those on board representation) of the ECS into national legislation. Hence the Nice European Council agreement on the ECS stated the following:

> [T]he Nice agreement ... will leave member states the option of whether to transpose into their national law the reference provisions relating to participation applicable to European companies constituted by merger. In order for a European company to be registered in a member state which has not transposed those reference provisions, an agreement [between the social partners] must be concluded on the arrangements for worker involvement, including participation, or none of the companies involved must have been governed by participation rules prior to registration of the European company (European Council, 2000).

The formal adoption of the ECS directive took place in October 2001; from 2004 onwards a company will be able to register as a *Societas Europea* (EIRR, 2002a). The ECS comprises a regulation concerning the legal and fiscal aspects of the SE, and a separate directive on worker involvement. It is essentially the latter which had remained a contentious issue for so many years. Whereas the Internal Market Council decided on the regulation, the Social Affairs Council decided on the directive. Both texts had to be forwarded to the European Parliament for consultation as the wording had changed so much since 1990 when it had been last consulted on the issue.

What are the major elements of the ECS? An SE may be formed in different ways: by a merger of existing companies from different EU member states; by the formation of a joint holding company or a subsidiary by existing companies from different EU member states; or by the conversion of an existing national company. To each of those different contexts for setting up an SE, specific worker involvement provisions apply.

A negotiation process takes places between a special negotiating body (SNB) and management as to the features of worker involvement in the planned SE. A set of rules specifies how this (temporary) special negotiating body is to be composed and the various subjects the negotiations must cover. These include the coverage and duration of the agreement, composition of the worker involvement body, its competences and procedures, the frequency of meetings and its financial resources – this body then negotiates the exact nature of the (final) representative body. The inclusion of board-level participation in the agreement is optional except in the case of the 'conversion' of an existing national company. In such a case, the agreement may not provide for a lower level of worker involvement: where the national company already had board-level representation, such participation automatically becomes a compulsory part of the agreement. In the 'other types of SE' (merger, formation of a holding company or formation of a subsidiary), where board-level representation existed, a lower level of worker involvement may be agreed, but only by a two-thirds majority of the SNB. Furthermore, in order for an SE formed by merger to be registered in a member state which has not transposed the provisions of the ECS on board-level representation into national legislation, special rules apply.

Four outcomes are possible:

a) a decision not to start or terminate negotiations, whereupon only the national provisions on information/consultation in the various countries where the SE operates will apply; this applies in the case of a merger, holding company or common subsidiary, but not in case of a conversion of an existing national company which has board-level participation arrangements and which must remain;

b) a written agreement on the worker involvement arrangements to apply to the SE;

c) an agreement to apply the fall-back reference provisions; or

d) failure to reach agreement within the deadline (six months, which may be extended up to one year) in which case the reference provisions apply.

How can we evaluate the ECS? It seems obvious that this directive is highly complex and flexible, and respects national institutional diversity, a feature which led the way to its final adoption. Compared with the EWC directive, it shares points of comparison and contrast. The comparisons include: the preference for negotiated solutions with statutory provisions applying only in the case of failure to agree; the procedure involving the special negotiating body; the subject matter the agreement must cover; and the content of the statutory provisions. As to points of contrast, the ECS directive is more progressive with respect to content. For example, it provides in certain cases for board-level employee 'participation' and the statutory provisions for rights to information and consultation exceed those of the EWC directive.

We must now consider the advantages of an SE for business (Liaisons Sociales Europe, 2001). First, companies operating across several member states through various subsidiaries will be able to register as one single company on the basis of a single set of rules, with a single annual reporting system, a single tax declaration and a single legal framework for their employees. All those aspects had previously been governed by different national laws. This will bring important cost savings and reduce administrative complications. Second, the ECS will facilitate cross-border company mergers and thus accelerate restructuring, which will enable companies to make the best of the potential presented by the single internal market and be in a better situation to face up to globalization. They will be able to register in those countries where the tax system and legislative framework are most advantageous to them. Such a choice remains possible, as the SE is only an option for companies. Third, the ECS will allow much greater flexibility in the internal management of the various subsidiaries with respect to organizational or fiscal matters. Fourth, headquarters can thus be more easily relocated from one member state to another without the company having to dissolve itself. Fifth, it will provide companies with greater visibility, and financial markets will benefit from greater transparency and hopefully trust as to companies' activities. Among the sectors most interested in the ECS are included motor manufacturing, construction, oil, chemicals, banking and insurance.

And what might be the advantages from an employee perspective? On the one hand, the ECS sets up basic rights and guarantees on social aspects when companies choose to change their legal basis. The comparison of the ECS with the EWC directive shows that their rights are wider in the former. It can add the 'participation' dimension at EU level in situations where it was previously restricted to only certain national subsidiaries. Indeed the participation element figures in the statutory reference provisions. It allows for the intervention of worker representatives during the early phases of the restructuring process. On the other hand though, the ECS is a powerful tool for companies wishing to speed up restructuring and strategic change, which worker representatives are not so keen to see occurring as restructuring most often entails uncertainties, greater flexibility and reductions in employment. With or without the ECS, those mergers and that restructuring might however take place anyway, and the directive on worker involvement in the ECS at least gives them some legal guarantees.

F. Vasquez, Associate Head of Unit in the Directorate-General for Employment at the European Commission, has remarked:

> The major difficulty with the forthcoming negotiations over the European Company (and the major difference with the EWC directive) will consist in the fact that these two sets of negotiation will inevitably overlap and take place at the same time in most cases. One set will focus on the type of worker involvement regime to be introduced into the European Company and the other will focus on the social and employment consequences of the restructuring operation which the choice of the European Company often implies (Liaisons Sociales Europe, 2001).

These two sets of negotiation are, therefore, very likely to be interrelated. This implies that the setting up of a European Company might often be linked to much broader and more crucial negotiations on important substantive matters; such interrelationships might indeed seriously affect the way in which the European Company Statute is implemented.

Conclusions

Over the 1990s, a strategy of diversification of regulatory methods has clearly been developing at EU level: two new instruments, euro-collective bargaining and the open method of coordination (through the EES), have been added to the classic legislative instrument. Moreover, taken separately, each of these three methods has granted a more important role to social partners both at the EU and national levels: the content of EU directives is now subject to their formal consultation *ex ante* and they can also have a greater say in their implementation *ex post*. Social partners may design and conclude agreements autonomously and they have also been requested to take part more actively in the EES. Furthermore, the social partners were invited to participate in the so-called Cologne process (1999) consisting in a dialogue between the European Central Bank, the Council and the Commission on monetary, macro-economic, employment and pay policies. Such developments, which were meant to give a larger say to the social partners in the shaping of EU social and employment reforms, have led to what has been variously termed 'multi-level governance' (Marks et al., 1996) and 'deliberative governance' (Teague, 2001). Two explicit reasons motivated those important EU regulatory changes. On the one hand, it was expected that improved legitimacy of EU decision making would result – that is, improved legitimacy by input (the involvement of a greater number of actors is supposed to make it more democratic) and improved legitimacy by output (better decisions *per se* and more efficient implementation). On the other hand, it was intended to take better account of the diversity of national labour relations and labour institutions, and hence the implementation of 'active subsidiarity'.

However, apart from the risk of the fragmentation of EU rule-making, and even internal competition amongst its elements, we should also stress the inherent complexity of such developments. Amongst these, the following could be particularly highlighted for leading to a very complex situation.

- The increasing interconnection of policy fields and the better understanding of their mutual links (with the Lisbon approach, employment policies, structural reform of labour markets and other economic institutions, policies on macro-economics, innovation and social exclusion, training and education, and modernization of social protection all expected to foster virtuous circles).[2]
- The multiplicity of actors involved in the various EU coordination policies (monetary authorities, EU institutions, governments, local authorities and social partners, amongst many others).
- The multiplicity of discussion/negotiation forums and coordination procedures (such as the broad economic guidelines and the Luxembourg, Cologne, Cardiff and Lisbon processes).

* The varying significance of the role of the social partners in these developments, barely nascent in some, but highly critical in others, depending on the process at stake.

Furthermore, it is far from clear at the moment which guidance levels and which actors will become the most important and determinant. What seems to be emerging, however, is that the various EU coordination processes and EU macro-economic policies (especially the EES, the monetary policy of the European Central Bank (ECB), the broad economic guidelines, the growth and stability pact, the Lisbon approach, and to a lesser degree for the time being the Cologne coordination process) are increasingly shaping the margin of manoeuvre of negotiators at lower levels. The fact that priorities set by the EU (defined in EU coordination processes and EU policies) are often reflected in national social pacts, does not prevent the latter from being 'competitive' national pacts. The EES, for example, defines more and more the normative frameworks within which employment issues must be viewed, through its employment-friendly tax policies, its 'flexsecurity' and worker mobility concepts and so on. The EES also sets quantitative targets which governments and social partners at lower levels have to satisfy, and curtails the scope for other bargaining issues so that ever greater efforts (with respect to matters like flexibility, duration of contracts, working conditions, working time and company restructuring) have to be made by unions and employees in the name of preserving or creating employment. With employment as the major priority, this might lead to situations where the employer increasingly legitimizes organizational change for the sake of saving jobs. In these ways, EU coordination processes and especially the EES tend to influence more and more the 'epistemic frame of reference' that shapes the nature of the discussions held amongst management and worker representatives even though they take place at decentralized company level.

As a substantive issue, mechanisms for EU worker involvement witnessed rapid progress at the Nice European Council which broke the deadlock on the European Company Statute, an instrument first proposed by the Commission 30 years ago. This step forward also accelerated political consensus around the directive on national information/consultation. The unfreezing of these proposals was linked to several factors. Advances had been made since 1997 under the auspices of the High-Level Davignon group, which tried to learn from the more successful EWC directive in 1994 and from the experience of its implementation since then. The major elements in its success included the adoption of a negotiation process prior to the eventual implementation of the reference provisions of the directive on the one hand, and the taking into account to a very large extent of national institutional diversity on the other. Furthermore, the repeated demands for worker flexibility, mobility and training alongside the sometimes expressed expectation that workers should be involved in company restructuring – points stressed by all official EU-level documents, the EES and the Lisbon approach – had to be followed up sooner or later by more concrete EU legal measures on worker involvement. Moreover, large companies were pressing for less costly and faster restructuring. In the context of European economic integration and globalization, such pressures would be eased by the adoption of the regulation concerning the legal and fiscal aspects of the European Company Statute, the latter itself being dependent on the adoption of the directive on worker involvement. Finally, the Nice Treaty reforms were seen as very poor with respect to social and employment issues by many observers, who were very disappointed that, for example, social protection remained subject to unanimous voting. Some positive social results had, therefore, to be provided in other ways by the Nice Council and the French Presidency, which proved advantageous to the European Company Statute.

Notes

1   What have been the more general changes observable in the 2001 employment guidelines? Though the content of the four pillars has remained basically quite similar to the content of guidelines 2000, a horizontal section of five general prescriptions has been introduced to capture the objectives of the Lisbon summit: a) the overall aim of full employment is emphasized, prompting member states to monitor their national employment rates and female employment rate in order to achieve 70 per cent and 60 per cent respectively by 2010 (by encouraging higher employment rates among women and older workers through policies in support of active ageing); b) education and lifelong learning are stressed as new Lisbon priorities, and are of special relevance for the pillar on employability and adaptability; c) social partners are expected to play a more prominent role in the EES, especially in the adaptability pillar with a new reporting procedure and are clearly invited to define their own contribution at EU level; d) member states are invited to pay attention to all four pillars and take care of the coherence between them when transforming the guidelines into national policies; and e) the quality of jobs (that is, jobs with good working conditions, health and safety, remuneration, training facilities, gender equality, balance between flexibility and job security, and quality of industrial relations) has clearly become a priority alongside the aim of increasing the employment rate, an issue which lies at the heart of social partner activity.

2   The Lisbon approach (2000) aimed at integrating economic and social policy fields (including the reform of the macro-economic structure and labour markets, and enhancing policies to combat social exclusion and modernize social protection). Through its annual spring European summit, it attempts to provide the major medium-term economic and

social orientations for EU integration and to give convergent objectives to the variety of integrationist processes mentioned above and to place special emphasis on the adoption of broad economic policy guidelines in line with the employment guidelines.

References

Bercusson, B. (2000), 'The European Employment Strategy and the EC Institutional Structure of Social and Labour Law', SALTSA-Arbetslivsinstitutet seminar, 9–10 October, Brussels.

Biagi, M. (2000), 'The Impact of the European Employment Strategy on the Role of Labour Law and Industrial Relations', *The International Journal of Comparative Labour Law and Industrial Relations,* Vol. 16, No. 2, pp. 155–73.

Brannen, P. (1983), *Authority and Participation in Industry*, Batsford Academic, London.

Commission of the European Communities (2000), *Joint Employment Report 2000*, Commission and Council, Brussels.

Commission of the European Communities (2001), *Council Decision of 19 January on Guidelines for Member States' Employment Policies for the Year 2001* (COM 2001 1/63/ EC), Brussels.

Cram, L. (1997), *Policy-making in the European Union. Conceptual Lenses and the Integration Process*, Routledge, London.

Ebbinghaus, B. and Visser, J. (2000), *Trade Unions in Western Europe since 1945*, Macmillan, Basingstoke.

EIRR (2001), 'European Company Statute close to Adoption', *European Industrial Relations Review*, February, No. 325, pp. 14–16.

EIRR (2002a), 'European Company Statute Adopted', *European Industrial Relations Review*, January, No. 336, pp. 21–5.

EIRR (2002b), 'New Working Time and Consultation Directives in Force', *European Industrial Relations Review*, May, No. 340, pp. 13–17.

European Council (2000), *Conclusions of the French Presidency*, Nice.

Falkner, G. (1998), *EU Social Policy in the 1990s: Towards a Corporatist Policy Community*, Routledge, London.

Foden, D. (1999), 'The Role of Social Partners in the European Employment Strategy', *Transfer*, Vol. 5, No. 4, pp. 215–45.

Goetschy, J. and Pochet, P. (1997), 'The Treaty of Amsterdam: A New Approach to Economic and Social Affairs?', *Transfer*, Vol. 3, No. 3, pp. 607–22.

Goetschy, J. (1999), 'The European Employment Strategy: Genesis and Development', *European Journal of Industrial Relations,* Vol. 5, No. 2, pp. 117–37.

Goetschy, J. (2000), 'The European Employment Strategy: Strengths and Weaknesses', *European Community Studies Association Review,* Vol. 13, No. 3.

Goetschy, J. (2002), 'The European Employment Strategy, Multi-level Governance and Policy Co-ordination: Past, Present and Future', in Zeitlin, J. and Trubek, D. (eds), *Governing Work and Welfare in a New Economy: European and American Experiments*, Blackwell, Oxford.

Gold, M., Cressey, P. and Gill, C. (2000), 'Employment, Employment, Employment: Is Europe Working?', *Industrial Relations Journal*, Vol. 31, No. 4, pp. 275–91.

Hyman, R. (1999), 'European Industrial Relations: From Regulation to Deregulation to Re-regulation?' IREC, 1999 conference, Aix en Provence, May.

Keller, B. and Bansbach, M. (2000), 'Social Dialogue: an Interim Report on Recent Results and Prospects', *Industrial Relations Journal*, Vol. 31, No. 4, pp. 291–308.

Keller, B. and Sörries, B. (1999), 'Sectoral Social Dialogue: New Opportunities or More Impasses?', *Industrial Relations Journal*, Vol. 30, No. 4, pp. 330–45.

Kenner, J. (1999), 'The EC Employment Title and the Third Way: Making Soft Law Work?', *The International Journal of Comparative Labour Law and Industrial Relations*, Vol. 15, No. 1, pp. 33–60.

Léonard, E. (2001), 'Industrial Relations and the Regulation of Employment in Europe', *European Journal of Industrial Relations*, Vol. 7, No. 1, pp. 27–47.

Liaisons Sociales Europe (2001), 'La société européenne au service des entreprises et des salariés', 28 February, No. 27, pp. 2–3.

Lönnroth, J. (2000), 'The European Employment Strategy: a Model for Open Co-ordination and the Role of the Social Partners', SALTSA-Arbetslivsinstitutet seminar, 9–10 October, Brussels.

Majone, G. (1996), *Regulating Europe*, Routledge, London.

Marginson, P. (2000), 'The Eurocompany and Euro Industrial Relations', *European Journal of Industrial Relations*, Vol. 6, No. 1, pp. 9–35.

Marks, G., Scharpf, F.W., Schmitter, P.C. and Streeck, W. (eds) (1996), *Governance in the European Union*, Sage, London.

Rhodes, M. (2002), 'The Political Economy of Social Pacts', in Zeitlin, J. and Trubek, D. (eds), *Governing Work and Welfare in a New Economy: European and American Experiments*, Blackwell, Oxford.

Scharpf, F. (1999), *Governing in Europe. Effective and Democratic?*, Oxford University Press, Oxford.

Schmid, G. (1995), 'Is Full Employment Still Possible? Transitional Labour Markets as a New Strategy of Labour Market Policy', *Economic and Industrial Democracy*, Vol. 16, pp. 429–56.

Streeck, W. (1999), 'Competitive Solidarity: Rethinking the European Social Model', 11th annual meeting on SASE, 8–11 June, Madison, Wisconsin.

Teague, P. (2001), 'Deliberative Governance and EU Social Policy', *European Journal of Industrial Relations*, Vol. 7, No. 1, pp. 7–26.

Traxler, F., Blaschke, S. and Kittel, B. (2000), *National Labor Relations in Internationalized Markets*, Oxford University Press, Oxford.

Chapter 3

European Works Councils: Who Benefits?

Michael Gold

Social and employment policy in the European Union has been subject to extensive change over the last 10 years or so, in both form and content. The emphasis dominant throughout most of the 1970s and 1980s on the extension of workers' rights through binding EU legislation gave way, in the 1990s, to a greater diversification of aims and means in the search for improved relevance, legitimacy and efficiency. The poor performance of the EU in employment creation, when compared with the USA, was highlighted in the Commission's White Paper, *Growth, Competitiveness and Employment*, in 1993 and led to the conclusions of the Essen Council the following year. These mark a key moment in redefining the aims of EU social policy. The Essen Council recommended: the promotion of investment in vocational training; increasing the employment intensity of growth; the reduction of non-wage labour costs; a shift towards active labour market policy; and special measures to target groups particularly hard-hit by unemployment.

At the same time, the EU began to develop more inclusive means of involving the social partners in the formulation of employment policy. These means included the more intensive use of social dialogue following the Maastricht Treaty and the integration of the social partners into the various stages of drawing up employment policy. These developments came to a head in the employment title of the Amsterdam Treaty (1997) which requires the member states to draw up national action plans for employment (NAPs) on an annual basis, a process in which the social partners are supposed to be fully involved. The NAPs are submitted to the Commission and published as a means of diffusing best practice.

These steps consolidated the concept of the European Employment Strategy (EES), which was subsequently refined at the Lisbon Council in 2000. There, member states agreed on exacting new aims, including full employment, the raising of employment rates and sustainable growth within the creation of a dynamic European knowledge economy. The means required to achieve the aims of the EES include a broad range of regulatory methods that support and complement existing legislative methods, such as social dialogue, EU-level collective bargaining and policy diffusion. The term 'open method of coordination' (OMC) refers to this more diffuse and complex network of decision making that embraces both wider areas of competence, such as employment and social protection, and a wider range of actors, notably employers and unions at all levels (for a discussion of these processes, see chapter 2 in this book by Goetschy).

These developments, from Essen onwards, have been characterized by some commentators as the new supply-side employment policy agenda, with its origins in European monetary integration and the discrediting of 'tax and spend' economic policies.[1] The EES reflects the apparently growing consensus amongst economists and experts on the best ways to combat unemployment within the mixed EU economies (Dyson, 1994). It steers a middle course between the regulatory approach of the interventionists, who focused rather narrowly on the rights of workers, and the free market orientation of the neo-liberals, by reflecting a supply-side orientation based on appropriate forms of intervention. Teague is broadly correct when he points out that 'a double-edged process of change is underway' (1999, p. 58). He argues that 'the often pragmatic search for labour market reform by governments to rein in excessive regulation without entirely abandoning social protection principles has unintentionally created a "modernizing" employment policy agenda' (1999, p. 59).

Indeed, running parallel with these 'modernizing' tendencies in *external* labour markets to promote employment, the evolution of European works councils (EWCs) can be understood as part of the creation of supply-side approaches to *internal* labour markets within the multi-national companies covered by the EWC directive. Employers, unions and employee representatives also form part of the 'epistemic community' – the community of ideas, views and norms (Haas, 1992) – that has embraced supply-side approaches over the 1990s. The formal power of employee representatives within companies operating in Europe has been extended in recent years only in relation to EWCs. The principal reason for this extension, it is argued here, is that certain employers have understood the key role that EWCs can play in promoting internal labour market policies based on 'company-friendly' supply-side approaches.

Within the context of the themes explored in this book, the challenge presented to employee representatives and trade unions by this opportunity is significant. One of the propositions outlined in chapter 1 is that intensifying degrees of competition and globalization demand 'innovative approaches to democratic participation'. This proposition highlights the need to link problems of the shop-floor and enterprise to national and international developments and to regulate them, where necessary, through new forms of participation. European works councils, as institutionalized, legally-enforceable bodies, now provide exactly this kind of innovative approach linking such levels of representation and thereby help to plug the 'representation gap' at European level in multinational companies. The consolidation of EWCs will, in turn, require employee representatives to create appropriate mechanisms to sustain their activity and influence by means of research, training and the provision of expert advice, without which they risk degenerating into little more than talking shops controlled or manipulated by employers. Overall, then, EWCs very much present a 'new frontier' of democracy at work, both in terms of their potential for securing new levels of representation at EU-level and in terms of engendering the support infrastructures required to make them genuinely effective.

The remainder of this chapter examines the ways in which EWCs are operating in practice and reviews some of the theories advanced so far to explain their operation and prospects. It also analyses management attitudes towards EWCs and the strategies that employee representatives and unions might adopt to maximize their potential for influence.

European Works Councils

Attempts made by the Commission to introduce some form of worker participation at EU-level into companies, from board level downwards, has presented a confused and confusing story over the last 30 years. It covers the draft Fifth directive, the European Company Statute, the draft Vredeling directive and the European works councils directive as the best known protagonists, with a supporting cast of many more measures covering areas like health and safety and redundancies (Cressey, 1993; Knutsen, 1997). However, few would disagree with the view that the European works councils directive has proved to be the most important initiative on worker consultation in the EU so far (Cressey, 1997).

The directive was eventually adopted by the Council in September 1994, following much controversy and bitter opposition from organized employers' interests (Gold and Hall, 1994). Member states were given two years to implement the terms of the directive (by September 1996) and then companies were given a further three years to establish European works councils, where required (by September 1999). The directive applies to all transnational companies with at least 1,000 employees in the European Union, of whom at least 150 are based in a second member state, wherever the headquarters might be located. The directive was adopted under the opt-out provisions of the Maastricht Treaty, which originally excluded its application to the UK. However, the Labour government signed up to the social chapter shortly after its election in 1997, and passed the regulations necessary to integrate UK companies into its provisions from January 2000.

The directive also required the Commission to review its operation within five years of its adoption (that is, by September 1999). The Commission adopted its report in April 2000, but focused only on the transposition of its terms in member states covered in 1994 (at that stage, only 12). The Commission stated that it was still too early to give a full assessment of the directive, as it would be necessary to take into account the terms of the European Company Statute (since adopted in October 2001) and the directive establishing a general framework for informing and consulting employees at national level in the EU (since adopted in February 2002). However, the report did highlight a number of problems, including the low level of transnational information and consultation in certain agreements, the absence of provisions governing restructuring and the need to ensure timeliness of information (EWCB, 2000a).

By 2002, the total number of EWCs had reached some 700, with 1,874 companies identified as falling within the scope of the directive, a density of 37 per cent (ETUI, 2002). By the end of 1999, there were already 507 attested EWCs, 386 of which had been set up under Article 13 of the directive and a further 121 which had been set up under Article 6 (Carley and Marginson, 2000). Article 13 had granted exemptions from the directive to those multinationals that negotiated voluntary agreements establishing EWCs, an option available until September 1996, whilst Article 6 requires such negotiations between the central management of eligible companies and a special negotiating body comprising employee representatives. So far, there is only one example of an Article 7 EWC, set up in accordance with the subsidiary requirements of the directive (Lecher et al., 2002, p. 51).

There is now a voluminous and growing literature analysing the development of EWCs, which falls broadly into several overlapping categories. First, there are guides to the directive itself, which adopt a generally legal orientation and explain what it says and how it should be implemented, along with analyses of its background, the kinds of companies covered and so on (Hall et al., 1995; Colaianni, 1996; Blanpain, 1999).

Second, there are analyses of EWC agreements themselves – their constitutions, functions, membership, facilities and rights, amongst other formal characteristics. This material is associated with work carried out under the auspices of the European Foundation for the Improvement of Living and Working Conditions in Dublin (Bonneton et al., 1996; Marginson et al., 1998; Carley and Marginson, 2000), or else relies heavily upon it. For example, by drawing on European Foundation sources, Rivest (1996) demonstrated that there was a sectoral influence on the early formation of EWCs through trade union activity, particularly in food and construction. More recently, Gilman and Marginson (2002), also drawing on these updated sources, have explored the factors influencing the 'constrained choices' made by management and employee representatives in negotiating EWC agreements. They conclude that a 'learning effect' has spread innovatory features of EWCs across to new agreements, over and above the effects deriving from the legislative framework of the EWC directive itself and from sectoral influences and the national industrial relations systems in individual member states.

Third, there is growing interest in the theoretical implications of EWCs for the evolution of industrial relations at European level. Debates have centred on a variety of overlapping themes, including the corporatist tendencies implicit in the establishment of EWCs (Knutsen, 1997; Streeck, 1997a; Streeck, 1997b), their contribution to the 'Europeanization' of industrial relations (Marginson, 2000; Lecher et al., 2002) and the prospects for the development of European-level collective bargaining (Marginson and Sisson, 1998), amongst others.

Finally, there has been an accumulation of case study material based on questionnaire and interview surveys of EWCs. Some of these have focused on individual companies (Cressey, 1998; Lecher et al., 2002; Weston and Martínez Lucio, 1997; Whittall, 2000; Wills, 2000), whilst others have focused on sectors like chemicals and metalworking (Lecher et al., 1999), food, banking and insurance (Lecher et al., 2001) or the motor industry (Hancké, 2000). The *European Works Councils Bulletin* has also published an impressive array of case studies, recent examples focusing on Sharp (EWCB, 2000b), Volkswagen (EWCB, 2002a) and Electrolux (EWCB, 2002b). Analysis of this case study material has provided a wealth of insights into the 'interior life' or social dynamics of EWCs, particularly their relationships with management, trade unions, members and national systems of employee representation. It centres on the practice of EWCs rather than their formal constitutions. There is now therefore a gathering corpus of material – albeit partial and sometimes inconsistent – on the role they play within their host company's internal labour market. Investigation has centred, for example, on the degree to which they help or hinder management in promoting commitment, flexible working practices, equal opportunities, training and other human resource policies and the degree to which they manage to remain independent in protecting workers' interests. Just as there has been a shift towards 'supply-side' approaches to external labour markets at macro-economic level, there is increasing evidence that EWCs generally support a shift towards similar approaches to internal labour markets at micro-economic level in line with 'soft' approaches to human resource management.

The context for this shift lies in the increasingly competitive global market faced by multinational companies. The pressures exerted on companies by globalization have induced companies to adopt whole batteries of measures including not least the introduction of decentralized business units, new technological processes and innovatory management techniques. The latter embrace cultural change programmes, total quality management, flexible working practices and benchmarking measures designed to strengthen processes of strategic control (Goold, 1991). Associated with these techniques is indeed the rise of 'soft' forms of human resource management (HRM) designed – according to Guest (1987) – to secure four principal goals: commitment (workers' identification with the interests of the organization); flexibility (their willingness to adapt to change); quality (work to the highest standards); and integration (the matching of human resource policy and practice with the requirements of business strategy). Though the efficacy of these techniques in securing better performance is often ambiguous or open to dispute, the discourse of commitment and flexibility in HRM has become the new orthodoxy. Few textbooks fail to mention somewhere that 'people are a company's most important asset' (for a review of this literature, see Redman and Wilkinson, 2001). The apparent triumph of HRM has, of course, also been underpinned by changes in the employment structure, the rise of the service sector, generally declining union memberships across Europe and a crisis of representation at work. These elements have all, in one way or another, led to a shift in the balance of power within companies towards management, the material base on which human resource management discourse has flourished.

Then, into this turbulent environment, there arrived the EWC directive, a kind of ugly duckling regarded with suspicion or shunned to begin with by the management of virtually all the multinational companies affected. Despite this, almost 10 years after taking effect, there is mounting evidence that the ugly duckling has lost its down and is even turning into a swan, at least in the eyes of certain managements. The purpose of this chapter is to plot the changing attitudes towards the directive, to observe how it has been very often adapted to serve management interests and how European works councillors and the unions have managed to use EWCs to their own advantage.

Management Attitudes

From the very beginning, managements with experience of the prototype, voluntary EWCs have been aware of their advantages. Even in the early 1990s, management pointed out that EWCs helped them to explain corporate strategy, facilitate company restructuring, foster international contacts and exchange views and create a sense of belonging to an international company (Gold and Hall, 1992, p. 48). Since then, virtually every empirical study of EWCs has reinforced these findings. Lamers, for example, uses the term 'added value' to refer to the benefits of EWCs. The Dutch managers covered in her survey mentioned several aspects of the potential added value of EWCs, which they saw as 'supplementing the internationalization process within groups' and providing 'a European-level platform to discuss strategies and transnational matters with an international employee representation' (1998, p. 183). Managers attending a conference organized jointly by CEEP, ETUC and UNICE in Brussels in April 1999 emphasized similar positive effects. These included creating greater understanding of the company's policies, facilitating cross-border restructuring and enabling cooperation between management and employee representatives on new policy initiatives (EWCB, 1999b).

The impact of a EWC in securing an attitude shift amongst employee representatives was reported by managers involved in the NatWest Staff Council. They were impressed that 'members of the Council were increasingly using the language of "us" to refer to the bank and its employees rather than "us and them", differentiating between employees and management' (EWCB 1999c, p. 16). Indeed, Wills notes a change in attitude amongst those employers who have introduced EWCs. Those who have not yet done so report concerns over the potentially injurious effects of EWCs, such as increased bureaucracy, expense and duplication. However, those who have already introduced a EWC are appreciably more favourable. They see the main advantages of EWCs in involving employees in the business, exchanging information, getting management views over to employees and hearing the voice of employees. On this basis, Wills concludes that 'the perception of EWCs appears to be worse than the reality' (1998a, p. 26).

Models of European Works Councils

The question then arises: what is, in fact, the 'reality' of EWCs? What impact are they having on the internal dynamics of multinational companies? Or on human resource strategies?

The literature so far has developed four sets of models of EWCs (Marginson et al., 1998; Lecher and Rüb, 1999; Lecher et al., 1999 and 2001; Schulten, 1996). The research, carried out by Marginson et al. (1998) into 386 voluntary (Article 13) agreements, makes a simple distinction between 'active' EWCs on the one hand and 'formal' or 'symbolic' EWCs on the other. The former encourage representatives to share views and ideas outside the formal structures of EWC meetings through provision of employee-side meetings only, access to independent experts, coordinating committees or executives and rights to negotiate agendas. The latter, by contrast, do not. However, this distinction does not adequately reflect the evolving practice of EWCs – as opposed to the agreements on which they are based – and further research has refined this duality through the empirical investigation into the actual functioning of EWCs.

Lecher and Rüb (1999), for example, have detected three likely lines of development amongst EWCs. First, the EWC may be perceived by its members as merely an extension of their own national systems of industrial relations (national orientation). Or, second, the EWC acts as the hub of a radial communication structure allowing group management to consult on the basis of its own priorities (national parent company dominance). Or, third, all members use the EWC to create a genuine 'combine' that 'works on collectively agreed issues and projects – that is, not merely as an extension of the national, but as an authentically European actor' (EWC collective) (1999, p. 20). An example of an EWC collective may be found at Bull where the EWC successfully intervened to stop the transfer of production from France to the UK by applying the principle 'whoever wins the order makes the goods' (1999, p. 16).

However, Lecher et al. (2001) later on identify four categories of EWCs following their extensive research into further case studies. These are: the symbolic EWC; the service EWC; the project-oriented EWC; and the participative EWC. These categories are based on four sets of relationships or fields of interaction: the EWC's relationship with management; with the national framework of employee representation; with the trade unions; and with its own workforce, or members. For each set of relationships, the authors set out a gradation of influence – from non-existent or weak to strong – which marks out the EWC on a scale. They assign it a category according to its overall ranking across all four sets of relationships, whilst fully acknowledging the difficulties that may be involved in this process. Their conceptions of these categories are broadly as follows.

- The *symbolic* EWC is one which, though 'formally established, does not truly operate' (Lecher et al., 2001, p. 54). Its functions are generally restricted to annual meetings with group management and it is unable or unwilling to achieve any kind of internal cohesion.
- The *service* EWC, by contrast, acts as a forum for 'the mutual exchange of information and provision of support between employee representatives' (Lecher et al., 2001, p. 54). It functions as a hub for communication channels and may provide a further range of services, such as conveying national-level problems to group management or even mediating in national disputes.
- The role of the *project-oriented* EWC, however, extends further than this, as it 'defines sets of tasks for itself (projects), which it can implement independently of management' (Lecher et al., 2001, p. 56). It strives to create autonomy for itself and develops its own strategy on a systematic basis.
- Finally, the *participative* EWC attempts to widen its sphere of activity beyond information and consultation and 'move on towards formalized consultative procedures, negotiations and the conclusion of agreements ...' (Lecher et al., 2001, p. 57). It perceives itself as an instrument for representing the common interests of employees at the European level through involvement in the relevant corporate decision-making processes.

In the course of a thorough analysis, the authors conclude that of their 15 case studies, six EWCs were symbolic, four were service-oriented, two were project-oriented and the remaining three were participative, though of course these allocations are not meant to be seen as static. EWCs may well develop over time, and indeed regress, or else present various hybrid forms.

It is clearly in the interests of both employee representatives and trade unions to work towards creating genuinely project-oriented or participative EWCs. Unless they succeed, there will always remain the suspicion that EWCs will predominantly serve the interests of employers. Indeed, the positive attitudes registered by employers noted above with respect to their EWCs are undoubtedly based on the extent to which they are able to control their agendas and activities. The more independent the EWC the less likely the chance that it will merely reflect management interests.

To what extent, however, are employee representatives and unions able to create participative EWCs? In an attempt to answer this question, Schulten develops his own model of EWCs that contrasts the level of labour/management cooperation with the degree of labour/labour cooperation, which includes networking, that exists between different segments of employee interests represented on the EWC (Schulten, 1996). He argues that there is evidence that employee representatives' ability to network and sustain a EWC between meetings may well provide the key to explaining the evolution of participative EWCs. Schulten refers, in this context, to 'autonomous European co-operation networks' (1996, p. 317) by which he means the quality of the relationships between national and local employee representatives within the company. He derives a model to explain the possible evolutionary dynamic of EWCs, based on their capacity to mobilize and promote such networks.

Degree of labour/labour cooperation network	Level of management/labour cooperation	
	Low	High
High	Quadrant 2 No recognition of EWC	Quadrant 3 EWC collective
Low	Quadrant 1 Atomized	Quadrant 4 Formal EWC only

Figure 3.1   Model of EWC practice

Source: Adapted from Schulten (1996, p. 318).

Quadrant 1, where there is both low management/labour cooperation and low levels of networking, depicts those companies where employees remain atomized at European level. They may have organized some initial meetings but there are no regular contacts and no EWC.

Quadrant 2, with low levels of management/labour cooperation but high levels of networking, illustrates the case of a company where employee representatives have developed systems of informal cooperation networking but where management is resisting recognition of a EWC.

Quadrant 3 covers 'EWC collectives' which combines both high levels of management/labour cooperation with high levels of networking. In such cases, not only has management recognized the EWC but the employee representatives also maintain regular contact through meetings to exchange views and information and build up independence from management information systems.

Quadrant 4 represents the existence of a formal EWC with high levels of management/labour cooperation but low levels of networking. Such EWCs operate at the bare minimum level and probably meet just once a year, with no contact amongst their members in between times.

The contrasts between the models drawn up by Lecher et al. on the one hand and Schulten on the other are instructive. Lecher et al. focus purely on the nature of the EWC as an institution, whereas Schulten looks more widely at the problem of recognition and the networking of employees outside the framework of an EWC. His quadrant 1 is a reminder of the woeful position of employees who are faced by hostile management and, for whatever reason, have not managed to build up their own international links. Quadrant 2 underlines the significant point that cooperation networks amongst employees may well exist even though management does not recognize a EWC (Digital was an early example of such a case).

However, as he points out, quadrants 1 and 2 should gradually disappear as the EWC directive comes to be fully implemented. Indeed, it is hardly coincidental that Lecher et al., publishing their own findings between three and five years after Schulten, focus rather on the operation and functioning of established EWCs. The problems of recognition that exercised Schulten had receded as a problem by 1999, once the directive had come into force.

Nevertheless, this leaves an important gap between quadrants 3 and 4 in Schulten's model, and it is on these two quadrants that Lecher et al. implicitly focus. Broadly, quadrant 3 covers three of Lecher et al.'s categories – service-oriented, project-oriented and participative – whilst quadrant 4 covers their symbolic category. In other words, by unpacking categories within these two quadrants, Lecher et al. bear witness to the considerable leap forward – in terms of both quantity and quality and efficiency – of EWCs in the second half of the 1990s. Not only had their numbers increased dramatically but so had their 'interior life', the dynamics of their scope and influence.

Employee representatives and unions are likely to face strong pressures to remain in quadrant 4, with a formal or symbolic EWC only. Indeed, there are numerous factors that might underpin such pressures. For example, company structure had been hypothesized from the outset as a potential barrier to the formation of viable EWCs. Marginson and Sisson (1994) argued that companies operating in diversified product markets or with divisionalized structures would find it particularly difficult to establish a group-level EWC that would adequately reflect the interests of all its employees. Indeed, the response by certain employers sympathetic to EWCs has been to set up divisional-level EWCs. The EWC at Thomson Consumer Electronics operates separately from that of Thomson CSF, whilst BP established a EWC for each of its three divisions (BP Oil Europe, BP Chemicals and BP Exploration). By contrast, some commentators have pointed out that employers could damage the chances of success of EWCs by restricting their scope to all European-group level operations, however little they may have in common.

Of course, unions and employee representatives confront further major obstacles in building up the networks required to move into quadrant 3. Lecher et al. list a variety of factors impeding EWC initiatives. These include lack of interest on the part of employee representatives, lack of trade union capacity, low level of employer willingness, absence of key preconditions in the field of employee representation (such as decentralized employee representation at national levels or insufficient legal protection) and procedural factors (such as the deterrent effect of complex systems (2002, p. 170)). Lack of time, resources and appropriate skills (such as languages) may also act as obvious constraints on the effectiveness of EWCs. Or indeed members may perceive the EWC as simply an extension of their own domestic industrial relations system (the national orientation noted above) or they may be unable to prevent – or even connive in – group management's interests in using it to set its own narrow priorities (national parent company dominance). In other cases, employees may simply confront hostile management attitudes. At PepsiCo, for example, employee representatives attending the inaugural meeting of their EWC in 1996 were allegedly 'forcibly barred' from speaking to trade union officials. They were also shadowed by a PepsiCo human resources manager and had their airline tickets withheld until they had signed a deal excluding trade union involvement (Overell, 1997).

European Works Councils as 'Symbolic' Bodies

It is argued here that the favourable attitudes of employers – in those cases where employers are indeed favourable – reflect an experience of EWCs that is so far based predominantly in quadrant 4, that is of the EWC as a symbolic or formal entity. Employers' 'reality' (Wills, 1998a, p. 26) is, then, one in which they have retained the fundamental control over the direction and structure of EWCs, thus allowing them to deploy them in line with their own agendas. These agendas are set increasingly in the context of rigorous international competition requiring – from the industrial relations point of view – the introduction of new technologies, production techniques and management practices that have become the core activity of human resource analysts.

We have already noted above that six of the 15 case studies observed by Lecher et al. (2001) fell into the symbolic category, and there is further evidence that this is how management would prefer to keep EWCs. Wills (1999), for example, conducted a survey of 17 Article 13 agreements in UK companies, 65 per cent of which had been initiated by management. Amongst the disadvantages, 71 per cent complained of the financial expense involved, 71 per cent that they raised the expectations of employees and 50 per cent that they fostered transnational trade unionism. Yet despite this, their views of the advantages of EWCs were significant. When asked about the impact of EWCs on employee relations, some 71 per cent stated that they fostered identification with the corporate mission, 64 per cent that they widened an understanding of management, 50 per cent that they improved communications between staff at different levels and 38 per cent that they promoted partnership. Indeed, Wills observed that management accounts of restructuring and redundancies led to a sense of vulnerability amongst employee representatives and a reduced will to resist, whilst the use of comparative performance indicators often pitted workers in different locations against one another. Her in-depth study of one UK-based EWC over a three-year cycle similarly led her to conclude that EWCs were 'an arm of management-led communications systems designed to facilitate one-way information flow at the workplace' (2000, p. 101).

Rather similar results emerged from a survey of 10 UK-based companies, designed to assess their costs and benefits, carried out under the auspices of the UK Department of Trade and Industry (Weber et al., 2000). Six companies in the sample feared that the EWC would have an immediate impact on raising employees' expectations with respect to restructuring and employment and working conditions, though four did not believe that there would be any such effect. Similarly, six of the 10 companies reported concerns that the EWC increased bureaucracy and placed burdens on management time. Yet, significantly there was 'no perception that the outcome of management decisions was essentially changed by the consultation process' (Weber et al., 2000, p. 19). Indeed, in terms of benefits, five of the 10 companies stated that there was an immediate positive impact on the ability both to exchange information with employee representatives and to involve the employees more closely in the business. Three companies believed that there was an immediate impact on their ability to improve employees' understanding of the business, though two stated that the impact would take from two to five years to become apparent. Their focus was exclusively on such 'soft' areas of HRM (improving commitment, communications and so on) and not at all on 'hard' areas (such as productivity and business strategy).

Indeed, most interestingly – or chillingly, depending on the perspective – companies unwittingly reflected the terminology of the academic analysts noted above in referring to the symbolic value of the EWCs: 'In terms of benefits of EWCs ... [eight] companies perceived such forums primarily to have *symbolic* value in terms of demonstrating a positive commitment to employees' (Weber et al., 2000, p. 20 [emphasis added]).

The Potential of EWCs

Nevertheless, even the most pessimistic commentators acknowledge that EWCs may have 'considerable potential' (Ramsay, 1997a, p. 320) or that workers need to 'realize the power they have to make the EWCs work for them' (Wills, 1998c, p. 125). Indeed, just as governments and employers have had to compromise over the modernizing employment agenda with respect to external labour markets, so too multinational companies have had on occasion to compromise with respect to restructuring their internal labour markets. And just as social pacts across a variety of countries have allowed complex trade-offs between the social partners at national level (Casey and Gold, 2000), so too there is evidence that unions have played a key role in securing advantages for their members at company level through EWCs. The 'double-edged process of change' noted by Teague operates at all levels, not just the national.

Danone, for example, which has 'arguably the most advanced of all transnational information and consultation arrangements' (EWCB, 1997, p. 4), negotiated in 1997 new provisions at group level to be implemented at local levels in cases of changes affecting jobs or working conditions. These provisions covered training, consultation, redeployment and union rights and would assist workers particularly in those countries where they were weakest (notably the UK and Eastern Europe). They were agreed by management and the International Union of Food, Agricultural, Hotel, Restaurant, Catering, Tobacco and Allied Workers' Associations (IUF).

In June 2001, the EWC at Club Méditerranée concluded a joint declaration on subcontracting, which protects the working conditions of subcontracted workers wherever they operate, a move particularly welcomed by the European Trade Union Confederation. This initiative had been taken by the European Federation of Trade Unions in Food, Agriculture and Tourism (EFFAT), which is represented on the EWC and coordinates the trade union representatives who make up the employee side (EWCB, 2001a).

And management, EWC employee representatives and an official from the European Metalworkers' Federation (EMF) at General Motors Europe reached a third framework agreement on group-level restructuring in October 2001. This allows for cost savings and reductions in capacity, with adjustments in employment levels undertaken through early retirement and 'separation programmes', without site closures or enforced redundancies (EWCB, 2001b). Air France, Suez Lyonnaise des Eaux and Vivendi are further examples of multinational companies that have signed codes of corporate conduct, with most cases involving international trade union organizations (EWCB, 2001a).

The role of the trade unions, then, particularly at EU level through the European industry federations, has proved vital in providing the leadership and innovatory flair required to establish EWCs in the first place and then enhance their influence within companies. However, one of the key variables in these examples of success has been the ability of EWC members to mobilize and organize between meetings. One of the problems is that the EWC directive itself emerged not from a bottom-up process of mass popular demand but from top-down pressure from the union hierarchies (Turner, 1996). Nevertheless, examples of success reveal the potential for unions to lead EWCs into a more engaged and activist phase (quadrant 3 in Schulten's formulation, or project-orientation/participative categories in that of Lecher et al.). Sometimes, this includes the involvement of the EWC in helping to mobilize mass protests, as at Unilever in February 1999 (EWCB, 1999a, p. 4) and Michelin in September 1999, in both cases over job losses and failure to consult (EWCB, 1999d, p. 4). In both instances, the unions had organized the action, supported by the respective EWCs.

In particular, other researchers have analysed the role of networking in promoting the effectiveness of EWCs. Networking may be constrained by a wide variety of factors, including organizational structure, divisional activities and management communication systems, as well as national industrial relations systems and concerns of unions over loss of control. Nevertheless, it contributes markedly to information flows amongst EWC members and hence to their influence on the EWC (Weston and Martínez Lucio, 1997). It is therefore not surprising that when EWC members are asked what they would do to improve the operation of their EWC, most favour more regular meetings and better communications (Wills, 1998b, p. 25). The role of an executive committee, elected by the EWC to carry forward its tasks between full meetings, has also been found to contribute greatly to the promotion of networking.

Some researchers have now gone further in identifying categories of networking. Lecher et al. distinguish good practice networks, project networks and action networks (2001, p. 109). The principal function of good practice networks is to consolidate the functioning of the EWC within the company by transferring ideas and knowledge, whilst project networks emerge with the growing awareness of problems and issues in common that require solutions. Action networks, by contrast, become an integral part of the operation of the EWC by helping to coordinate policies and positions on issues relevant to the entire workforce, for example, through lobbying, agreeing on areas for possible negotiation or even promoting consultation in the appropriate sectoral forums. The dynamics of building up transnational networks have been monitored in a three-year project at Kværner, the engineering and construction group. The process involved ensuring access to personal computers, appropriate training, language training and awareness, and dealing with lack of confidence. The aim, apparently successfully achieved, was to create 'liberating structures' through the creation of 'an atmosphere of collective supportiveness' (Tully, 2000, p. 17).

Overall, then, EWCs may simply provide a forum for the communication of management policy and strategy. In such cases, it is likely to act as a formal arrangement only and it is not surprising that management reports 'soft' rather than 'hard' advantages, as reported by Weber et al. (2000) and Wills (1999). That is, management sees the advantages of EWCs as a forum to exchange information, getting management views over to employees and promoting a European-level corporate culture. It tends to see fewer advantages in developing business strategy, managing change or enhancing productivity. This is very much in line with the supply-side approaches to human resource management noted earlier. However, there is clearly potential for increasing the influence of EWCs, a point returned to in the conclusions.

Conclusions

There have been several types of change in employment practices at European level over recent years, which have been reflected both in this chapter and in chapter 2 by Goetschy. One change is that employers are increasingly appreciating the advantages of EWCs as a means of improving communications and projecting the company at European level. The second, mirrored at national level, is that employment promotion and social protection are now dominating the EU agenda. The third is the development of the way in which the EU tackles social issues: legislative and contractual regulation has been joined by a process of coordination of national policy around EU guidelines as laid down in the European Employment Strategy. This coordination seems to have become the norm and has spread from the coordination of employment policy and macro-economic and pay policies to structural policy on the goods, services and capital markets and, in the foreseeable future, social protection and information society policy as well.

The identifying feature of this coordination is that it forms part of a multi-governance process. The employment guidelines lay down certain performance indicators and commitments in principle from member states, to which they must respond each year by submitting national action plans for employment to the Commission. At lower levels of the process, new discussion and bargaining forums have been created for the social partners, local and national authorities, and other organizations. These provide the focus for potential agreements, and the more detailed working out of implementation and monitoring. Such multi-governance, as orchestrated by the EU, will foster new interactions and developments within social and industrial relations practice at all levels, such as national social pacts or in the content of collective bargaining.

Furthermore, it is clear that the EU guidelines – employability, entrepreneurship, adaptability and equal opportunities – are in keeping with national trends. Against a backdrop of intensifying competition resulting from globalization and European integration, 1990s employment policies aim to give substantial advantages to both companies and to individuals. They give advantages to companies in terms of lower costs through pay restraint and labour market flexibility, and to individuals through education and training, skills and better rights at work, at the pre-supply level rather than at the redistributive or demand level. The fact that the discussions at the Lisbon summit in 2000 focused on the knowledge society, education and training clearly confirmed this trend.

So far, these coordination procedures, which have such an impact on workers, are still largely the preserve of the member states, the EU institutions and national or EU-level trade union and employers' organizations. However, the general thrust of the guidelines is to support or adjust trends already in place for the last 10 years or so within the member states. While these trends allow for national diversity, they also go some way towards 'Europeanizing' national, pluralist understandings of the notion of flexibility, which underlie structural employment reforms. This 'Europeanization' produces a process of legitimation and acceptance of pluralist norms and practices of flexibility and the changes in behaviour expected of employees.

Such trends provide the essential context for analysing processes at lower levels of industrial relations activity as well, particularly the evolution of the practice of EWCs. Managers involved argue that their orientation towards commitment, communications, training and flexible working should improve their companies' profitability and thereby strengthen the chances of both finding employment and keeping it. Such an orientation should also improve everyday working conditions more generally along with pay, as flexibility affects weekly, annual and even lifetime working hours and working methods.

EWCs should clearly not be rejected altogether as agencies for articulating and advancing worker interests as some commentators imply. Rather, it has been argued here that EWCs provide the institutional setting for advances that may be made by employee representatives and unions at European level, provided that they are able to overcome the barriers to their effectiveness and operate efficiently outside the formal constraints of timetabled meetings. In this way EWCs will prove best able to mobilize the 'modernizing agenda' to their own advantage. Indeed, as EWC constitutions have come up for renegotiation, there have been many examples of improvements. These include widening national coverage to embrace Central and Eastern Europe and sometimes the whole world, setting up executive committees to carry tasks forward between meetings and improving the scope for information, consultation and negotiation, amongst much else. What is most striking at the moment is the sheer diversity of practice amongst the EWCs studied so far (a tiny proportion, in fact, of the 700 already in existence), ranging from barely functioning symbols to influential and genuinely participative bodies. Indeed, each case study presents a different story or narrative. The background of the company in question, the nature and style of its management, the constraints imposed by the sector, the strength and leadership of the unions and employee representatives, the overall balance of forces and the personalities involved all contribute to the backdrop against which the 'action' unfolds. When successful, however, it is clear that EWCs combine internal cohesion with strategic vision (Hyman, 2000). To achieve this combination, the role of the unions at all levels – national, sectoral and EU – will prove essential.

Note

1   Supply-side economic policies are associated with the attempt to dismantle alleged rigidities in the operation of the 'free market'. Such policies include cutting tax rates, the substitution of monetarism for wage and price controls as a curb on inflation, the abolition of credit and exchange controls, the opening up of financial markets, the deregulation of transport networks and the intensification of competition in the public sector through the introduction of internal markets, privatization and contracting out. In the employment sphere, supply-side policies centre on introducing greater flexibility into the labour market either through negotiations with the unions or through reducing their influence by one means or another (Minford, 1991).

References

Blanpain, R. (1999), *European Works Councils in Multinational Enterprises: Background, Working and Experience*, Working Paper No. 83 (Multinational Enterprises Programme), ILO, Geneva.

Bonneton, P., Carley, M., Hall, M. and Krieger, H. (1996), *Review of Current Agreements on Information and Consultation in European Multinationals*, EF/96/10/EN, European Foundation for the Improvement of Living and Working Conditions, Dublin.

Carley, M. and Marginson, P. (2000), *Negotiating EWCs under the Directive: A Comparative Analysis of Article 6 and Article 13 Agreements*, European Foundation for the Improvement of Living and Working Conditions, Dublin.

Casey, B. and Gold, M. (2000), *Social Partnership and Economic Performance. The Case of Europe*, Edward Elgar, Cheltenham.

Colaianni, T. (1996), *European Works Councils: A Legal and Practical Guide*, Sweet and Maxwell, London.

Cressey, P. (1993), 'Employee Participation', in Gold, M. (ed.), *The Social Dimension. Employment Policy in the European Community*, Macmillan, Basingstoke, pp. 85–104.

Cressey, P. (1997), 'Transnational Works Councils and Macro European Developments', in Markey, R. and Monat, J. (eds), *Innovation and Employee Participation through Works Councils. International Case Studies*, Avebury, Aldershot, pp. 29–48.

Cressey, P. (1998), 'European works councils in practice', *Human Resource Management Journal*, Vol. 8, No. 1, pp. 67–79.

Dyson, K. (1994), *Elusive Union. The Process of Economic and Monetary Union in Europe*, Longman, London and New York.

ETUI (2002), *European Works Councils – Multinationals Database 2002* (CD-ROM) edited by Kerckhofs, P. and Pas, I., European Trade Union Institute, Brussels.

EWCB (1997), 'Danone Joint Text Tackles Redundancies and Closures', No. 10, July/August, p. 4.

EWCB (1999a), 'European Action Day Organised at Unilever', No. 20, March/April, p. 4.

EWCB (1999b), 'Social Partners Review Developments of EWCs', No. 21, May/June, pp. 6–8.

EWCB (1999c), 'The NatWest Staff Council Reviewed', No. 23, September/October, pp. 14–17.

EWCB (1999d), 'Michelin Agrees EWC ... and Announces Job Losses', No. 24, November/December, p. 4.

EWCB (2000a), 'Commission Assesses Implementation of EWC's Directive', No.28, July/August, pp. 4–6.

EWCB (2000b), 'Four Years in the Life of the Sharp EWC', No. 30, November/December, pp. 11–15.

EWCB (2001a), 'Air France EWC Signs Social and Ethical Charter', No. 35, September/October, pp. 7–9.

EWCB (2001b), 'GM EWC Reaches Agreement on Opel Restructuring', No. 36, November/December, pp. 8–10.

EWCB (2002a), 'The Volkswagen EWC and National Employee Representation Structures', No. 37, January/February, pp. 12–15.

EWCB (2002b), 'The Evolution of the Electrolux Works Council', No. 39, May/June, pp. 13–16.

Gilman, M. and Marginson, P. (2002), 'Negotiating European Works Councils: Contours of Constrained Choice', *Industrial Relations Journal*, Vol. 33, No. 1, March, pp. 36–51.

Gold, M. and Hall, M. (1992), *Report on European-level Information and Consultation in Multinational Companies – an Evaluation of Practice*, European Foundation for the Improvement of Living and Working Conditions, Dublin.

Gold, M. and Hall, M. (1994), 'Statutory European Works Councils: The Final Countdown?' *Industrial Relations Journal*, Vol. 25, No. 3, September, pp. 177–86.

Goold, M. (1991), 'Strategic Control in the Decentralized Firm', *Sloan Management Review*, Vol. 32, No. 2, Winter, pp. 69–81.

Guest, D. (1987), 'Human Resource Management and Industrial Relations', *Journal of Management Studies*, Vol. 24, No. 5, September, pp. 503–21.

Haas, P.M. (1992), 'Introduction: Epistemic Communities and International Policy Coordination', *International Organization*, Vol. 46, No.1, pp. 1–35.

Hall, M., Carley, M., Gold, M., Marginson, P. and Sisson, K. (1995), *European Works Councils: Planning for the Directive*, Eclipse Group, London and Industrial Relations Research Unit, University of Warwick.

Hancké, B. (2000), 'European Works Councils and Industrial Restructuring in the European Motor Industry', *European Journal of Industrial Relations*, Vol. 6, No. 1, pp. 35–59.

Hyman, R. (2000), 'Editorial', *European Journal of Industrial Relations*, Vol. 6, No. 1, pp. 5–7.

Knutsen, P. (1997), 'Corporatist Tendencies in the Euro-polity: The European Union Directive of 22 September 1994, on European Works Councils', *Economic and Industrial Democracy*, Vol. 18, No. 2, May, pp. 289–323.

Lamers, J. (1998), *The Added Value of European Works Councils*, AWVN, Harlem.

Lecher, W. and Rüb, S. (1999), 'The Constitution of European Works Councils: From Information Forum to Social Actor?' *European Journal of Industrial Relations*, Vol. 5, No. 1, pp. 7–25.

Lecher, W., Nagel, B. and Platzer, H.-W. (1999), *The Establishment of European Works Councils. From Information Committee to Social Actor*, Ashgate, Aldershot.

Lecher, W., Platzer, H.-W., Rüb, S. and Weiner, K.-P. (2001), *European Works Councils. Developments, Types and Networking*, Ashgate, Aldershot.

Lecher, W., Platzer, H.-W., Rüb, S. and Weiner, K.-P. (2002), *European Works Councils: Negotiated Europeanization*, Ashgate, Aldershot.

Majone, G. (1993), 'The European Community between Social Policy and Social Regulation', *Journal of Common Market Studies*, Vol. 31, No. 2, pp. 153–70.

Marginson, P. (2000), 'The Eurocompany and Euro Industrial Relations', *European Journal of Industrial Relations*, Vol. 6, No. 1, pp. 9–34.

Marginson, P. and Sisson, K. (1994), 'The Structure of Transnational Capital in Europe: The Emerging Euro-company and its Implications for Industrial Relations' in Ferner, A. and Hyman, R. (eds), *Industrial Relations in the New Europe*, Blackwell, Oxford, pp. 15–51.

Marginson, P. and Sisson, K. (1998), 'European Collective Bargaining: A Virtual Prospect?', *Journal of Common Market Studies*, Vol. 36, No. 4, pp. 505–28.

Marginson, P., Gilman, M., Jacobi, O. and Krieger, H. (1998), *Negotiating European Works Councils: An Analysis of Agreements under Article 13*, European Foundation for the Improvement of Living and Working Conditions, Dublin.

Minford, P. (1991), *The Supply Side Revolution in Britain*, Elgar/Institute of Economic Affairs, Aldershot.

Overell, S. (1997), 'Union Court Threat if PepsiCo Will not Talk', *People Management*, 12 June, p. 13.

Ramsay, H. (1997a), 'Fool's Gold? European Works Councils and Workplace Democracy', *Industrial Relations Journal*, Vol. 28, No. 4, December, pp. 314–22.

Ramsay, H. (1997b), 'Solidarity at Last? International Trade Unionism approaching the Millenium', *Economic and Industrial Democracy*, Vol. 18, No. 4, November, pp. 503–37.

Redman, T. and Wilkinson, A. (2001), 'In Search of Human Resource Management', in Redman, T. and Wilkinson, A. (eds), *Contemporary Human Resource Management*, Financial Times/ Prentice Hall, London.

Rivest, C. (1996), 'Voluntary European Works Councils', *European Journal of Industrial Relations*, Vol. 2, No. 2, July, pp. 235–53.

Schulten, T. (1996), 'European Works Councils: Prospects for a New System of European Industrial Relations', *European Journal of Industrial Relations*, Vol. 2, No. 3, November, pp. 303–24.

Streeck, W. (1997a), *Citizenship under Regime Competition: The Case of the 'European Works Councils'*, Jean Monnet Chair paper No. 42, April, European University Institute, Florence.

Streeck, W. (1997b), 'Neither European nor Works Councils: A Reply to Paul Knutsen', *Economic and Industrial Democracy*, Vol. 18, pp. 325–7.

Teague, P. (1999), 'Reshaping Employment Regimes in Europe: Policy Shifts alongside Boundary Change', *Journal of Public Policy*, Vol. 19, No. 1, pp. 33–62.

Transfer (1999), whole issue, Vol. 5, No. 3, Autumn, European Trade Union Institute.

Tully, B. (2000), 'Developing an EWC Network at Kværner', *European Works Councils Bulletin*, No. 30, November/December, pp. 15–17.

Turner, L. (1996), 'The Europeanization of Labour: Structure before Action', *European Journal of Industrial Relations*, Vol. 2, No. 3, November, pp. 325–44.

Weber, T., Foster, P. and Egriboz, K.L. (2000), *Costs and Benefits of the European Works Councils Directive*, Employment Relations Research Series No. 9, Department of Trade and Industry, London.

Weston, S. and Martínez Lucio, M. (1997), 'Trade Unions, Management and European Works Councils: Opening Pandora's Box?', *International Journal of Human Resource Management*, Vol. 8, No. 6, December, pp. 764–79.

Whittall, M. (2000), 'The BMW European Works Council: A Cause of European Industrial Relations Optimism?', *European Journal of Industrial Relations*, Vol. 6, No. 1, pp. 61–83.

Wills, J. (1998a), 'Making the Best of it? Managerial Attitudes towards, and Experiences of, European Works Councils in UK-owned Multi-national Firms', working paper No. 3, January, University of Southampton, Department of Geography.

Wills, J. (1998b), 'The Experience and Implications of European Works Councils in the UK', working paper No. 4, January, University of Southampton, Department of Geography.

Wills, J. (1998c), 'Taking on the Cosmocorps? Experiments in Transnational Labor Organization', *Economic Geography*, Vol. 74, No. 2, pp. 111–30.

Wills, J. (1999), 'European Works Councils in British firms', *Human Resource Management Journal*, Vol. 9, No. 4, pp. 19–38.

Wills, J. (2000), 'Great Expectations: Three Years in the Life of a European Works Council', *European Journal of Industrial Relations*, Vol. 6, No. 1, pp. 85–107.

Chapter 4

The Role of Economic and Social Councils in Social Dialogue[1]

Jacques Monat and Thérèse Beaupain

Introduction

Mention has been made, in our previous volume on possible scenarios for democratic participation in the twenty-first century (Kester and Pinaud, 1996), of the importance and interactions of the various levels of participation. These include the macro-level (both national and international), meso-level (regional, sectoral and local) and micro-level (company/group of companies, plant or establishment and shop floor). It should also be recalled that Jaroslav Vanek always insisted on the need for supporting structures for the development of democratic participation (Vanek, 1971). Institutions of the type analysed in this chapter – economic and social councils – are, for example, a source of research and expertise that are very useful, *inter alia*, for training, as well as an important source of information and publications. Such functions form an aspect of our third proposition on democratic participation – on the conditions required to promote its extension – discussed in the introduction to this book.

However, this new volume attempts not only to check the scenarios, hypotheses and proposals of the previous one but also to analyse innovative aspects of developments which have occurred in the meantime. It may seem inappropriate at first glance to deal with economic and social councils and similar institutions (hereafter ESCs), which were sometimes set up in the 1920s if not earlier. However, we have to consider that most forms and institutions of employee participation, whether direct (involving the employees themselves) or indirect (through representatives), are far from being new. Works councils for instance date back to the last quarter of the nineteenth century and modern collective bargaining to the beginning of the twentieth century. Safety delegates, who appeared first in mining, and board representation (a subject of debate in Germany as early as 1848) date back at least to the 1920s. Semi-autonomous groups originate in the Bata factory at Zlyn, then in Czechoslovakia, between the two world wars, tripartite management of social security schemes can be found at the end of the 1940s and quality circles and other expression groups were largely influenced by the old Scanlon Plan (Lesieur, 1958). Furthermore, self-management and cooperatives had already been created in the nineteenth century.

What is probably more interesting, in the absence of entirely new forms of participation, is to examine how existing institutions are adapting to new circumstances or issues and put to maximum use. Not even financial participation – or profit sharing in particular – is a new phenomenon. Employee share ownership appears, however, to have expanded mostly in recent years but to have had a significant impact on participation in decision making only in exceptional cases, such as certain employee share-ownership plans (ESOPs), take-overs or buy-outs and in Central and Eastern Europe (see chapter 12 by Vaughan-Whitehead). What is perhaps the most innovative is the role for contractual and/or legislative regulation played by the European social dialogue – both intersectoral and sectoral – which will be analysed below. In this context, ESCs are by definition a major instrument of 'partnership' and remain a definite fixture today both in business and labour relations as well.

This chapter, while supplemented by analysis of social dialogue, focuses on economic and social councils or similar institutions in Europe. These were already the subject of a report by the European Trade Union Institute (ETUI) in 1990, but are now less associated with national economic planning and rather more with economic and social policy in general. In spite of criticisms here and there on their cost and efficiency, few of them have been suppressed, though in general they have undergone reforms. Some, like the Belgian National Labour Council, are directly involved in collective bargaining, while most of the others provide opportunities for informal contacts amongst the social partners. These have a non-negligible, even if difficult to measure, influence on collective bargaining at macro- and meso-levels, as well as often to a certain extent on the enterprise level, including the new type of pact for employment and competitiveness (European Foundation, 2000). It is also common for ESCs to deal with health and safety or environmental issues, and more generally with the quality of working and living conditions, along with education and training, including lifelong education and further training, pensions and other forms of social protection, financial participation and so on.

This chapter investigates in depth the contribution, either direct or indirect, of ESCs to participation within enterprises, collective bargaining at various levels and industrial relations in general. It goes without saying that they contribute to varying degrees, depending in particular on the level of participation, less for instance on direct participation at shop-floor level or information and consultation in enterprises, except in the case of studies and reports or debates related to a given form of participation. Moreover, it has been considered appropriate to place the whole subject in the wider perspective of social dialogue, in particular due to the globalization and Europeanization of industrial relations. This includes the development of a Social Europe and the European social dialogue in the framework of the institutions of the European Union (EU), including the Economic and Social Committee of the European Communities, according to its full official title (hereafter abbreviated to EESC).

Therefore we shall deal here with a collective concept of democracy (polls or votes being an individual form of political democracy), namely, the influence of organized civil society or 'intermediate bodies' on political, economic and social decisions or policies. Other forms of influence, of course, also exist, including lobbying, strikes, boycotts, rallies or demonstrations and possibly opinion surveys (or street interviews in the media). However, the forms examined in the present chapter tend in general to reach some degree of consensus on the basis of preliminary studies, debates and/or consultations. A brief comparison will later be made with political democracy, based on political parties and the mandate given through votes to representatives in parliament or other public bodies. A possible complementarity will appear. Finally, it is also possible to take the view that the links between social dialogue and civil dialogue evoked above and examined below constitute a 'new frontier' for democratic participation and trade union action beyond the usual tripartism and traditional industrial relations.

Some Definitions

In a report submitted to the International Labour Conference, the International Labour Organization indicated that the expression 'social dialogue' is often used interchangeably with the term 'tripartite concertation', while it admitted too that 'other groups besides employers and workers are sometimes also involved in tripartite cooperation. For example, some self-employed workers such as farmers, craftsmen or small shopkeepers or groups such as co-operatives ...' (ILO, 1996, p. 6). Furthermore, later on in this chapter, we shall notice a trend to complement social dialogue by civil dialogue. This takes place, for example, by including an increasing diversity of non-governmental organizations (such as associations representing consumers, the family and environmental interests) within its remit, or at least by consulting them regularly or when appropriate when they are not represented in ESCs.

In a recent opinion, the EESC defined 'civil society' as a global concept covering all forms of social action by individuals or groups outside and independent from public authorities and 'organized civil society' as all structures where the members deal with general interest through a democratic process based on debate and consensus, being at the same time mediators between public authorities and citizens (Economic and Social Committee, 1999, paras 5.1, 7.1 and 8.1). And a report submitted in December 1999 to a meeting on social dialogue of the International Labour Office stated the following:

> What is meant by 'social dialogue'? In its most diffuse and general usage, it seems little more than another term for industrial relations, involving collective bargaining and other means of pursuing agreement between employers and representatives of workers. In a second meaning, it is distinguished from collective bargaining, indicating a process of exchanging information and viewpoints, which may ultimately facilitate successful negotiation but is not itself a negotiating process. In a third sense, it indicates a particular institutional configuration designed to encourage consensual or positive-sum interaction. Fourthly, it may denote a normative orientation towards 'social partnership' and the avoidance of conflict (Hyman, 2000, p. 1).

We may also wonder whether 'social dialogue' does not tend nowadays to be used as synonymous with 'participation' and sometimes even to replace it. This certainly corresponds to a fashion, but since labels may be important, this one may seem more 'neutral' between social actors, more flexible and not necessarily conducive to formal bargaining, with its risk of labour disputes, or to co-management or codetermination. It implies instead some degree of co-responsibility and appropriate balance of power. A major objective remains a fair distribution of effort on the one hand and results on the other, as well as quality of work and life.

In the following pages we shall first briefly examine the various types and powers of ESCs in Western Europe, their historical origins and legal basis, composition, organization and functioning. We shall emphasize their possible role and limitations concerning the development of democratic participation in enterprises and in industrial relations in general. A special part will be devoted to the trend towards having such institutions in Central and Eastern Europe as well as in some countries of Southern Europe with a view to EU enlargement. A further section will deal with the Economic and Social Committee of the EU, followed by one devoted to 'European social dialogue'. Our concluding remarks will consider various criticisms of ESCs and assess the factors that may facilitate or hinder their operation. We shall end by looking at the prospects for the future of democratic participation in comparison with our 1996 hypotheses, scenarios or proposals and the new frontier between social dialogue and civil dialogue.

Various Types and Powers of Tripartite Bodies

In addition to traditional ESCs or similar institutions, there are numerous specialized bodies (covering for instance vocational training, employment policy, working conditions, prevention of occupational hazards and protection of the disabled) where social partners are consulted, sometimes by ministries or related organs. There are an estimated 300 such bodies in France (Caire, in Trebilcock, 1994) and the Netherlands. Some of these bodies manage functions like social security on a bipartite or tripartite basis (as in France and Italy), or various schemes for vocational training.

Typology of Economic and Social Committees

Within the scope of the present study centring on Western Europe, a major distinction may be made between National Economic Councils, National Labour Councils – of which Belgium has both – and National Economic and Social Councils, as in France, Greece, Ireland, Italy, Luxembourg, Portugal and Spain. The Netherlands has an important Labour Foundation, a bipartite body where possibilities for agreement, in particular but not exclusively on wages and other conditions of work, are explored and opinions issued. In both practical and geographical terms it is very close to the Social and Economic Council (SER). In Belgium, the Central Economic Council and the National Labour Council are similarly located in the same building. Finland has only an Economic Council. In France it was decided after World War II to have in addition a National Labour Council, but this was never set up. Historically the 'social partnership' system of Austria (ILO, 1986; Traxler, in Trebilcock, 1994) appeared to be a special case in many respects, with various bodies such as its Parity Commission for Wages and Prices and its subcommittees. However, at present in fact only two are active: the Subcommittee on Wages and the Consultative Committee for Economic and Social Issues, to a large extent similar to an ESC. The latter discusses practically all questions of economic policy of major significance. Its secretariat is provided jointly by the Economic Chamber and the Chamber of Labour, representing respectively employers and workers. Whatever the country and its structures for social dialogue, the importance of informal contacts, up to top levels of public authorities and social partners, remains vital.

There is a further distinction between national and regional Economic and Social Councils or similar bodies, as in the case of France. Belgium has such bodies for the major federal components of the country (Flemish or French-speaking parts, and Brussels), as do Italy and Spain. There is even a cantonal ESC in Geneva and a municipal version in France, at Issy-les-Moulineaux near Paris.

Powers

The powers of the ESCs are in general of a consultative nature, except in some countries, in particular Belgium, where since 1968 national interoccupational collective agreements, which may be given binding legal force by a special decree, are also formally concluded in the National Labour Council. Among the 77 collective agreements concluded in the Belgian National Labour Council and often revised several times, a number has led to general progress in conditions of work and powers of representative bodies within the enterprise. Now they are largely 'framework agreements' or agreements implementing EU directives. In countries like Portugal (where the ESC was preceded by a 'social concertation' body), macro-level agreements have been concluded on economic and social policy, covering to a large extent some kind of incomes policy (Nascimento Rodrigues, n.d.; Fajertag and Pochet, 1997; EIRObserver, 1999). However in practice many ESCs pave the way for various types of agreement or their activity is supplemented by more or less informal agreements reached in a related body, as is the case in the Dutch Labour Foundation vis-à-vis the SER.

Consultation in general is initiated by government as a whole or by a minister, or, more seldom, by parliament, while in most countries ESCs may also take the initiative of issuing an opinion (right of initiative), a proposal or a recommendation. In France, where criticism has been levelled at the relative frequency of appointments as members of the ESC of politicians who had lost their seats in elections, it has been pointed out that connections with high-level decision makers may facilitate requests for consultation and/or the follow-up of opinions issued. Sometimes consultation is mandatory, for instance concerning social security or labour legislation. In the Netherlands, various Acts provided for a mandatory consultation of the SER over measures relating to a wide range of economic and social issues, but in 1995 the Dutch

Parliament revoked its prerogative to be consulted on economic and social policy before government introduces a new bill. In several countries, including France, Luxembourg and Spain, such a body must present a report each year on the economic and social situation of the country, and in Belgium on the state of competitiveness. This may be used for the purposes of collective bargaining, being considered as largely impartial. Opinions issued are usually based on a preliminary study and debate and published with the corresponding report. In any case the preparation of reports, studies and surveys on a broad range of subjects is one of the most important activities of such bodies. In the recent past this range has tended to be even larger.

Moreover, the Dutch SER has some degree of regulatory power, participating in the implementation of certain types of legislation. In 1970 it issued a code of conduct governing mergers, and it monitors its application. In Italy, under the Constitution, the National Council for Economic and Labour Affairs (CNEL) may submit bills to parliament, but more informal arrangements are used and the annual budget law is subject to separate consultations of the social partners. It has also been given the task of setting up a data bank on collective agreements. ESCs may also play a statutory or informal role in the settlement of major labour disputes.

Origins and Legal Basis

France has at present one of the oldest ESCs, established in 1925, when it was called the National Economic Council. Corresponding more or less to an interest in partnership or to the pressures for an incomes policy, there was an initial wave of setting up such bodies after World War II, a period of reconstruction and searching for consensus. The present French Council was set up in 1946, with its previous title; the Belgian Central Economic Council in 1948; the Dutch SER in 1950, with the Dutch Labour Foundation established as early as 1945; the Belgian National Labour Council in 1952, succeeding an informal structure set up at the end of 1944 after a social pact; and the Austrian Parity Commission in 1953. Several of them were largely the result of clandestine contacts during the war between employers' circles and trade unionists resisting Nazi occupation and wishing to maintain some kind of partnership after the war, especially in Belgium and the Netherlands. A second wave occurred around the 1960s: Italy 1957, Finland 1966, Luxembourg 1966 and Ireland 1973.[2] The third wave took place in the 1990s: Portugal and Spain in 1991 and a new Economic and Social Committee (OKE) in Greece in 1995 (a previous one having been set up in 1978 but dismantled in 1982). In Portugal and Spain it was one of the final steps in the return to democracy.

Since 1960 there has been a Recommendation (No. 113) of the International Labour Organization concerning consultation at national and industry levels on economic and social matters, supplemented by very useful 'observations' of the International Labour Conference.

In some cases the national Constitution provides for such a body (as in France, Portugal, Spain and Italy),[3] or a special act was required or – as in Ireland – a decree. In Portugal, as indicated earlier, it was preceded in 1984 by a Council for Social Concertation, which became one of its permanent committees.

Composition

The size of ESCs varies greatly from one country to another, especially if economic and social issues are dealt with by two separate bodies, as in Belgium. The largest ESC in Western Europe is that of France, which has 231 members, but is seen as a third Constitutional Assembly. The Italian CNEL has 111 members since its reinforcement in terms of membership and powers in the recent past.

The dilemma is to have a sufficiently widely representative body to cover a maximum number of interest groups or components of civil society, while at the same time not being too large to maintain efficiency and speedy response if required. We shall examine later, when dealing with organization, techniques such as the use of subcommittees, which help to overcome this dilemma. Still, such bodies, as well as political assemblies, 'have yet to reflect the increasing importance of women in society' (Duruflé, 1995, p. 380).

A large membership clearly enables a greater diversity of organizations to be represented. In France, for instance, in recent years five trade union confederations (excluding agriculture but including middle management and executives) plus the National Federation of Autonomous Trade Unions, have had representatives on the national ESC. It also includes a wide variety of others, such as the federation of teachers, the confederation of professionals, four organizations for private enterprise, nine agricultural organizations, credit and mutual institutions, five artisans' organizations and many others. There were also nine representatives of economic and social activities overseas. In Italy, out of a total of 111 members, the CNEL now has 18 representatives of self-employed workers. There is a comparable breadth of representation on

Portugal's High Council of Science and Technology, which also embraces the universities, family associations and women's associations. Greece, Portugal and Spain have representatives of consumers. Since 1998 the community and voluntary sector, including a representative from the national organization of the unemployed and one from the national youth council, has had representation on the Irish National Economic and Social Council (NESC). A few countries, like Greece, Ireland and Portugal, have representatives of regional and/or local authorities.

While some institutions are bipartite, such as the Belgian National Labour Council or the Dutch Labour Foundation, others are tripartite and, as we have seen in the case of France and various other countries, more than tripartite. However, if 'tripartite' is taken to mean the same number of employers', employees' and other representatives, the last category does not necessarily cover government representatives. While some countries have, like Ireland, Luxembourg and Portugal, representatives of ministries or of the government, most institutions have so-called independent experts in the third category, either appointed by government (often having been proposed by economic or social organizations) or co-opted by other members. While on the Dutch SER they constitute one third (experts in economics, law, finance and social matters), along with the employers' and workers' representatives, the proportion varies in other countries. In France, in addition to the 231 members mentioned above, there are 72 'section members' appointed for two years, who assume the role of experts in their section but do not attend plenary sessions, while 40 members are appointed for their special competence in economic, social, scientific or cultural fields. Everywhere the presence of independent experts may result in less heated discussion with a more scientific or technical approach. However, on the Belgian National Labour Council the trend is towards resorting to experts accompanying a member, in general from his/her organization. This is also possible in committees. In Italy, in addition to the 12 experts who are members, the CNEL may commission outside research.

In some cases the members are chosen by the most representative organizations, in particular those of employers and workers, while in others they are appointed by the government, in general after appropriate consultations or among candidates proposed by their organization.

Organization and Functions

In France, the chairperson of the Economic and Social Council is elected by the members themselves for a period of two and a half years, while the term of office of the members themselves is five years. While in most countries the appointment or election is for the same period as that of the members (usually four years but only three in Ireland and two on the Dutch SER), on the Belgian Labour Council there is no time limit. In the bipartite Dutch Labour Foundation, the chair alternates between an employer and a worker representative. In Finland the prime minister chairs the Economic Council.

For the functioning of ESCs, the role of the secretary general as well as that of the bureau officers, where they exist, is important. The 12 members of the Bureau of the Dutch SER, for example, are representatives of the major interests in the country. They meet twice a year with delegates from the government. In addition there is a variable number of support staff.[4] However, in Austria the Secretariat of the Parity Commission was traditionally provided by the Federal Chancellery, and high-level experts considered it an honour to cooperate on a voluntary basis. In France a statistical unit is seconded by the National Institute of Statistics and Economic Studies (INSEE).

As already mentioned, in practice, studies, opinions and debates are largely prepared within subcommittees. They may be of a permanent or temporary nature, even set up on an ad hoc basis, or simply working groups or working parties. They usually deal with the economic situation, finance, education and training, social affairs and other related areas. In general they meet in private session, while plenary meetings of ESCs are, with few exceptions, public in countries like France, Italy, the Netherlands and Portugal. Government members or senior civil servants may be invited to attend plenary sessions, possibly also those of subcommittees. Everywhere publicity of activities, opinions and reports issued is constantly increasing through such means as mass media and multi-media, including the Internet. In France, opinions and reports are traditionally published in a special series of the Official Gazette. In various countries the result of votes as well as dissenting opinions are also published.

The Italian CNEL has several 'observatories' (for example on fiscal reform and crime). Its studies are often supplemented by related seminars, such as on employment, social policy, research or transportation policy. In France and Portugal meetings are also organized by the national ESC.

In general the budget is covered by the government but there are exceptions. The Dutch SER, for example, is mostly financed by a supplementary levy added to contributions to Chambers of Commerce and Industry, while in Greece the 1994 Act launching the new ESC (OKE) provides that 'financing from other resources is possible, if this is accepted by the General Assembly'.

Remuneration of members varies greatly from one country to another. In a number of cases, most of an ESC's budget is devoted to the remuneration of members and support staff, sometimes not leaving much for field studies and/or consultation of outside experts. In a few countries, such as Ireland, members receive just travel allowances.

Exchanges of information and experience are regularly organized on an international basis, and in July 1999 the International Association of Economic and Social Councils was set up, with its secretariat in Paris. It covers about 50 countries.

Central and Eastern Europe and Enlargement of the EU

The transition towards a market economy and a democratic society was obviously influenced by the experience of Western Europe. Shortly before the political change, Hungary set up an Interests Reconciliation Council somewhat similar to the Portuguese equivalent at that time. It quickly became a major body for tripartite social dialogue and negotiations, macro-level policies, including incomes and wages, and legislation, as well as the settlement of various labour disputes (such as a taxi and lorry drivers' blockade in the 1990s). However, it encountered increasing difficulties with the growth of multi-national companies, banks and insurance companies and non-governmental organizations (NGOs), in addition to various political or social tensions. In 1999 new reformed structures were introduced. First, there was an Economic Council for consultations on economic policy with a wider representation of economic actors beyond national trade union confederations and employers' associations (chambers of commerce, the financial sector and multi-national companies, amongst others). Second, a National Labour Council was established, less powerful than the Economic Council but retaining functions pertaining to labour issues, such as minimum pay, annual growth of earnings in the business sector and pre-legislative consultations. Finally, various other new councils were also set up, including a social council, a council of the elderly, a council of the handicapped and a council for the representation of women, involving a great number of NGOs.

Soon after the political change, a Council was set up in the then Czechoslovak Republic, which was replaced by two similar bodies after the split between the Czech Republic and Slovakia. Now in the latter country the institution corresponds to a Council for Economic and Social Consultation. In Bulgaria a National Commission for Coordination of Interests was established as a result of a tripartite general agreement of 1990 and a Standing Tripartite Committee in 1991. Initially the social partners were involved in order to try to ensure the implementation of socially difficult economic reforms. More recently Economic and Social Councils were established in Croatia, Romania and Slovenia. In the Russian Federation a national tripartite commission with up to 250 members was established by presidential decree in the mid-1990s. In most other countries of Central and Eastern Europe, governments have decided, since the second half of the 1990s, to introduce some form of national tripartite council for consultations and negotiations over a broad range of industrial relations, social and economic issues, including the repercussions of privatization and restructuring, such as redundancy and unemployment. This is the case for instance in Estonia. In Poland a tripartite commission on socio-economic issues, though merely consultative, had been established by 1994. In the same country several tripartite committees at ministerial and departmental level had existed since 1991. As in other countries, active tripartite discussions occur on an informal basis in addition to ad hoc tripartite meetings, notably on labour legislation. Slovakia has tripartite bodies at industry level. Initially the representatives of large state enterprises had a special influence in such bodies in this region, but this is tending to decrease.

Enlargement of the EU towards Central and Eastern Europe requires tripartite structures for social dialogue to be more and more active in order to prevent the formal perpetuation of the dominance of the state (Vaughan-Whitehead, 2000). This will emphasize the importance of representative socio-economic organizations, including at regional and sectoral levels, enabling increased reliance on social pacts and collective agreements, which are more flexible than legislation alone. In such a context, the creation of trade union integration commissions should be noted. In 1996 the ETUC installed such integration commissions, with ETUC affiliates or observer members, into each candidate country. This may help to avoid the by-passing of trade unions. Twice a year, the coordinator of each of these commissions meets at the ETUC for debriefing.

Enlargement will also extend to Southern Europe and the Mediterranean Basin. Turkey already has an ESC, and the Greek part of Cyprus has a tripartite Labour Advisory Board. Malta meanwhile has a forum for a better economy and a tripartite council for its economic development (MCED) with 13 members and various working groups (Attard, 1995).

The Economic and Social Committee of the EU

The Economic and Social Committee (EESC) was set up by the 1957 Treaty of Rome, whilst the Single European Act (1986), the Treaty of Maastricht (1992) and the Treaty of Amsterdam (1997) have all reinforced its role. Its 222 members are nominated by national governments and appointed on a personal basis by the Council of the European Union for a renewable four-year term of office. They belong to one of three groups: employers, workers or various interests (ranging from farming to commerce, transport, the professions, cooperatives, mutual associations, small and medium-sized enterprises and environmental and consumer protection).

The task of the members is to issue opinions on matters referred to the EESC by the Commission and the Council, as well as the European Parliament pursuant to the Treaty of Amsterdam. Consultation of the EESC by the Commission or the Council is mandatory in many cases and optional in others, but it may also adopt opinions on its own initiative. The above-mentioned Act and Treaties extended the range of issues that have to be referred to this Committee: regional, environmental and employment policy, broad guidelines for economic policy and combating social exclusion, amongst others. It now produces an average of 180 opinions per year (15 per cent on its own initiative), totalling some 3,500 opinions between 1957 and the beginning of 2001. All opinions are forwarded to the EU decision-making bodies and then published in the Official Journal of the European Communities. The European Commission regularly reports on the follow up. In recent years the activities of the EESC have been reinforced by various meetings such as symposia and other events aiming at bringing the EU closer to the people and to civil society.

Every two years the EESC elects a bureau made up of 21 members, a president and two vice-presidents. The committee has six sections, which resemble parliamentary committees. They cover: economic and monetary union and social cohesion; single market, production and consumption; transport, energy, infrastructure and the information society; employment, social affairs and citizenship; agriculture, rural development and the environment; and external relations. Section opinions are drafted by tripartite study groups ranging from three to 15 members, including a rapporteur assisted by an expert. *Ad hoc* subcommittees for specific issues may also be set up, but since 1994 it has had a permanent Single Market Observatory or monitoring unit of 21 members, to draw attention to malfunctions and recommend remedies (twice a year it holds a Single Market Forum to review developments). Opinions are adopted at the plenary sessions on the basis of section opinions by a simple majority. Meetings are held some 10 times per year.

Links exist with regional and national ESCs, especially exchanges of information and joint discussions. The EESC participates in the international meetings of ESCs. It also has links with interest groups and similar bodies of non-member countries and groups of countries, in particular the Mediterranean, the Asian Caribbean and Pacific group, Central and Eastern Europe, Latin America (such as the Mercosur consultative forum) and the European Economic Area. It regularly distributes a number of publications, including its main opinions in brochure format, a monthly newsletter and an annual report, though there remain criticisms that the EESC has not made itself sufficiently well known (Lemercier, 1997). The EESC has a Secretary General who reports to the President, and a staff of 130 who work exclusively for it. In addition, since January 1995, it has shared with the European Committee of the Regions[5] a common core of departments whose staff, numbering 523, are mostly members of the EESC's secretariat.

The EESC is also facing the problem, already mentioned, of the increasing complexity of civil society, and in particular how to represent NGOs in an appropriate manner. An interesting point is that representatives of cooperatives and other representatives of its third group (various interests) may on occasion have affinities with the workers' group, especially when adopting opinions in the social field or on agricultural matters. Nevertheless, this group is sometimes criticized for including organizations that in fact represent employers and could be transferred to its employers' group, thereby opening new possibilities for NGOs and other organizations following a new balancing act between the groups. However, such a balance is not easy to reach and fears have also been expressed that more NGOs might reinforce the weight of the workers' group. These problems, in addition to possible cost reductions, are under examination and the EESC Secretary-General has set up working groups for that purpose, as well as for improving the setting of priorities and communications. Further to the Nice Summit in 2000, the Nice Treaty once ratified provides for a maximum of 350 members of the EESC in the case of EU enlargement, a number not higher than the membership of the Committee of the Regions, and envisages their distribution amongst all member states. An appointment by the Council on a qualified majority would suffice.

Contrary to what may happen in a number of national ESCs, it is not uncommon for the EESC to deal with highly topical and controversial issues, such as bovine spongiform encephalopathy (BSE or 'mad cow disease') and genetic modification in agriculture. In such cases, the EESC may request any of its sections to draw up an information report.

On the whole the EESC is not a forum for negotiation on European social dialogue, but it may clarify respective areas of possible consensus and divergence. It also helps EU enlargement, not only by promoting through its own experience autonomy and representativity of the social partners, but also through various activities such as meetings organized in different countries.

European Social Dialogue

The Treaty of Rome which established the EESC, and the summits of June 1974 and June 1984, provided for the participation of social partners in economic and social policy. The next major step forward for EU-level participation was the European social dialogue, launched in 1985 with a process of informal and voluntary dialogue at Val Duchesse by the then President of the Commission, Jacques Delors. One working party dealt with economic and social problems and another with new technologies, organization of work and adaptability of workers. Several joint opinions and statements, covering areas like macro-economic issues, the labour market and training resulted (Gold, 1998). A further stage of development began with the Social Protocol and Agreement, basically negotiated and agreed by the social partners themselves in October 1991. It was first annexed to the Maastricht Treaty in 1992 and later on, after the end of the opt out of the United Kingdom, integrated into the Amsterdam Treaty in 1997. It gave the social partners at the intersectoral level, ETUC, UNICE and CEEP,[6] the opportunity to conclude binding framework agreements voluntarily, which define only broad principles and objectives at EU level. Detailed implementation is then left up to the social partners in the member states, in accordance with national laws and practices, as a substitute for legislation that may be proposed by the Commission. The Maastricht Treaty also gave a role to the social partners in all social policy initiatives: they have to be consulted twice, generally 'on the possible direction of Community action' as well as, more specifically, 'on the content of the envisaged proposal'.

By 1990, CEEP and ETUC had already concluded an agreement on training measures in energy distribution and rail transport, and a European framework agreement covering training and safety and health in the public sector. In more recent years, the European social partners have negotiated three framework agreements on:

- parental leave, signed in 1995 by ETUC, UNICE and CEEP, the content of which was incorporated into a Council Directive of 3 June 1996;
- part-time work, concluded by the same European social partners, which gave rise to a Council Directive of 15 December 1997; and
- fixed-term contracts, which was ratified in Warsaw by the organizations concerned in March 1999, and became Council Directive of 28 June 1999.

In agriculture, a European framework agreement on the improvement of paid employment was reached in 1997, to be implemented through agreements at national level. In 1998, working time in agriculture was also dealt with by European-level agreements.

However negotiations, though important, are only part of the social dialogue process. It serves as a forum in which the social partners, at both pan-European and sectoral levels, can examine together current changes in the EU (such as enlargement and restructuring) and discuss how to deal with them through the EU institutions. In addition to the EESC, the European social partners also play an active role on numerous advisory and consultative committees (on health and safety, equal rights and so on) and in the European Social Fund. They have a regular interface with the Social Affairs and Labour Council, the governor of the European Central Bank and the 'troïka' of heads of government prior to each six-monthly summit meeting, which corresponds to a 'macro-economic dialogue'. Since 1992 there has also been a new Social Dialogue Committee, which set up thematic working groups, including one on vocational education and training, while the Standing Committee on Employment, established by the European Council in 1970, was restructured in 1999.

At the sectoral level, the new regulation of the Social Protocol annexed to the Treaty of Maastricht is also supposed to be applicable. The Commission itself has stressed the importance of this particular level in its Communication, *Adapting and Promoting Social Dialogue at Community Level*, adopted in May 1998, which mapped out the way ahead for social dialogue with respect to information, consultation and negotiation. Moreover, the Commission decided in 1998 to establish a new framework for sectoral dialogue at the European level. New sectoral dialogue committees – replacing all previous sectoral dialogue structures – have been set up (26 by the beginning of 2001) and now constitute the key forum for sectoral dialogue (consultation, joint action and negotiations). These new sectoral dialogue committees started preparing studies, joint opinions, statements, agreements and joint actions (for example on training), and in some sectors (initially clothing, footwear and commerce), codes of conduct. Agreements concluded in such committees are comparable to collective agreements, but must be put into effect at national level. Agreements in air and maritime transport have been implemented through the directive process. Various sectors, until the recent past, had only informal working parties, while non-structured discussion groups exist in some ten sectors, including chemicals, printing/media and business services. The telecommunications sector adopted new guidelines for the organization of telework in February 2001. These guidelines provide a framework for the implementation of teleworking in this sector. They follow on from a joint political statement made by the social partners in this sector as a contribution to the March 2000 Lisbon European Council. The conclusions of this Council focus on a 10-year strategy for the European economy including a framework for specific employment and training targets.

All this is in line with the principle of subsidiarity, promoting action and agreements at the lowest level possible, to solve problems closest to those who may be affected through their representatives. The importance of this principle will further increase with EU enlargement, due to the widely differing traditions and cultures of new members.

Conclusions: Prospects and New Frontiers between Social and Civil Dialogue

As already pointed out by the European Trade Union Institute, 'there is no ideal model of economic and social committee. It varies in accordance with the past and the traditions of each country, as with its economic and social structures' (ETUI, 1990, p. 65). Such diversity may be especially appropriate with EU enlargement.

It has also to be admitted that on the whole, possibly at different periods, countries without ESCs such as Germany or Sweden may have had good economic and social results, while corporatist or neo-corporatist structures may have delivered good results in others (see for instance, Treu, 1992). Literature on the evaluation of ESCs as such is not very abundant (Trebilcock, 1994; Freyssinet, 1996; Visser and Hemerijck, 1997), the latter being not entirely negative towards the Dutch SER but more positive towards the bipartite Labour Foundation. An ILO report concluded in an overall assessment: 'tripartite co-operation – which was never without its problems – is now subject to both favourable and unfavourable influences ... these difficulties have not prevented it from being practised to a large extent or from adjusting to its new environment' (ILO, 1996, p. 27). The Dutch SER was one of the most severely criticized, but probably as a result of special circumstances (*inter alia* the expansion of the social protection system with very widespread resort to invalidity pensions and delays in issuing sensitive opinions), though it was retained, with modifications. Some countries, like Italy and Portugal, were generally able to conclude important social pacts, while others, such as Belgium, tried but did not succeed (Fajertag and Pochet, 1997).

One of the reasons for the criticism voiced from time to time was an excessive search for consensus. For example, within the EESC it was occasionally impossible to agree on a given subject, or votes on a joint opinion were largely divided. Meanwhile, in France, the Teulade Report on pensions, published by the Economic and Social Council in July 1999, was considered by many as too optimistic. A recent evaluation of European social dialogue, at both intersectoral and sectoral levels, underlines that at the first of these levels '[t]he existing judgements point in opposing directions' but that:

> the social partners' right to be consulted on proposals in the social field and to opt for agreement-based rather than legislative measures now makes them central players in the European social arena ... On the other hand, the increase of opportunities for the social partners has not led to overwhelming results (Keller and Bansbach, 2000, pp. 292–4).

The same authors, while recognizing the progress made by the European sectoral dialogue, do not support the optimistic assessment by some outside commentators (p. 300). In this respect, it will be interesting to observe the extent to which the social partners take up the challenge of the Commission's Communication, adopted in June 2002, designed to raise the profile and effectiveness of the social dialogue and improve its coherence between national and EU levels. It proposes a 'tripartite social summit for growth and employment' to be held annually on the eve of the spring European Council, bringing together the Presidency of the Council, the President of the Commission and EU-level social partners to discuss the social and economic situation. The Communication also calls on the social partners to expand their joint work programmes with the aim of concluding agreements that can be incorporated into Community legislation.

One of the difficulties facing the institutions dealt with in the present chapter is to have a large enough membership to be representative of civil society, or social interests in general, but not so large as to impair efficiency. In various countries, such as Italy or Sweden, trade unions try to go beyond their traditional membership, for example, by organizing people like the self-employed, the unemployed or pensioners. However, representativeness may then suffer from a multiplicity of rival aspiring social partners, or, notably at the sectoral level, from an absence of representative organizations on one side or the other. Efforts are being made, such as the cooperation agreement concluded at the end of 1998 between UNICE and the European Union of Artisans and Small and Medium-sized Enterprises (UEAPME), to extend the role of the latter in the various instances of European social dialogue, at least in the form of prior consultation by UNICE and observer status. In addition, as indicated earlier, there is a trend towards wider membership, in particular with NGOs. Already in the most recent ESCs, such as the Portuguese and Spanish cases, a broader range of associations have been represented (such as those for consumers, the family and environmental protection). In Ireland, there has been since 1987 an economic policy programme that has been renewed every three years by the social partners. Furthermore, since 1997, in addition to the traditional tripartite representatives, representatives of women, the unemployed, the homeless, the disabled and members of the cooperative movement, amongst others, have also been assimilated. When appropriate, the EESC consults NGOs not represented on it, organizes symposia and so on. In September 1995, a Platform of European Social NGOs was set up, uniting some 25 European NGOs claiming together to represent thousands of institutions and networks in the voluntary sector across Europe. Later, together with the ETUC, it issued a joint position paper and other joint declarations on issues of common concern. The Platform has pointed out that the aim of NGOs is not to compete with the social partners but to cooperate with them.

Practically everywhere, whatever the size of the institution, preparatory work is largely carried out within sections, subcommittees or other smaller units. The assistance of outside or inside experts is also of considerable importance. Moreover, there is an increasing tendency to reinforce links and cooperation with other bodies at lower levels, especially regional ones, even if the latter are themselves sometimes criticized (Dupont, 2000).

Efficiency is also measured by the length of response. While sensitive issues can sometimes be 'cooled off' by delaying the publication of a joint opinion, there has recently been a trend in several countries to react rapidly, if necessary, sometimes in order to take a stand before other institutions, such as parliament. The Dutch reform of the SER in 1992, for instance, fixed a deadline of two months for consultation concerning important economic or social measures, while previously in some extreme cases it could take several years to reach a minimum of consensus. It also happened that the SER gave verbal opinions, which were neither published nor discussed publicly in plenary, for instance to provide arguments for a minister at an EU meeting. In France, since 1984, in cases of urgency, there has been a deadline of one month for issuing an opinion. Spanish legislation also allows the imposition of a deadline on the ESC of a maximum of ten days, while Greek legislation allows for one of 15 days in extremely urgent cases.

Another problem is to have top-level representatives for active follow-up and fruitful contacts with government and parliament as well as to enhance the image of the ESCs in public opinion. In countries where membership is declining, participation of trade unions at macro-level clearly offers an opportunity to regain a non-negligible influence. However, the question of absenteeism may have to be faced and various solutions try to diminish this. Examples include the linking of remuneration to attendance and the appointment of deputy members as in Belgium, Luxembourg and the Netherlands (in Portugal it is possible but not obligatory to have deputy members). In Luxembourg, the ESC may propose replacing a member in case of absence from more than five ESC meetings without substitution by the deputy member, or if no valid explanation has been submitted to the chairperson. Some degree of absenteeism may be attributable to representatives keeping in touch with their constituents or their usual activities. Obviously their organizations must themselves make an effort to increase their own internal democratic participation and avoid appearing too bureaucratic. It is doubtful that increasing the presence of professional or highly specialized representatives on national and supranational bodies would undermine workers' identification with trade unions, given the rapid changes in the composition of the workforce that is currently taking place. However, here again, an active policy of information and internal democracy is probably what matters most.

The follow up of the ESC's work is of prime importance. The French Economic and Social Council, for instance, finally obtained annual reports on the follow up to its opinions from the government. Appropriate contacts can also facilitate the same process. This is the case for example on the Dutch SER where it is not uncommon for representatives of ministries to attend SER meetings as observers. In general, experience has shown that government must give the impetus for an equitable sharing of sacrifices for the success of such institutions. The independence of each organization represented must be respected (conversely, commitments entered into must be actually implemented).

Criticism of ESCs may be increasing in an era less prone than previously to collective values and rather more inclined towards the free interplay of market forces designed to enhance competitiveness in a global economy. The long experience of social concertation and incomes policies of countries like Finland or Norway was nevertheless very useful for their competitiveness, as well as social pacts of the Portuguese ESC. Even now, the Belgian Central Economic Council is very active in maintaining competitiveness in the framework of an Act of 26 July 1996. Indeed, revitalizing ESCs seems not only possible but actually practical. The Italian CNEL, for instance, was subject recently to a far-reaching enlargement of both its membership and activities, and exchanges of ideas and experience are especially active between ESCs, not least through their new International Association.

Due to the interdependence of levels of participation there must be sufficient information and training of the social partners and other members of civil society to link the micro-level of enterprises with the macro-levels, both national and international. This link is particularly important at the European level, through European works councils and European social dialogue institutions and practices.

Last but not least, a basic question has often been raised regarding the possible complementarity, rather than competition, between ESCs and political institutions.[7] This is a major aspect of democratic participation. Increasingly a 'democratic deficit' is being felt. The complexity and technicality of most issues to be dealt with in the political arena gives a special importance to the knowledge and experience of the various social groups represented within ESCs. Obviously parliamentary work, as well as that of other political assemblies, is largely prepared within committees and by experts either from political parties or public authorities. But this complexity and technicality is probably one of the main reasons for falling levels of electoral turn-out across many industrialized countries, including Switzerland, which frequently calls on its citizens to vote in its system of direct democracy. On the other hand, the quality of studies, reports and debates within most ESCs is largely recognized. If major components of democracy are the freedom, pluralism and participation of the people concerned in the decision making that will affect them:

> they contribute to the attempts to achieve a working consensus on economic and social policy matters, a process which is of considerable importance in a democratic society insofar as it enables a broadening of political democracy to incorporate economic and social democracy as well (ETUI, 1990, p. 7).

Therefore it is clear from the present chapter that for trade unions and existing institutions the new frontier is between democratic participation and social dialogue on the one hand and civil society on the other. It is significant that in October 1999 the EESC held a first convention on organized civil society at European level and that in December 2000 an important conference took place in Warsaw entitled 'From social dialogue towards civil dialogue', in cooperation with the International Association of Economic and Social Councils and similar institutions, the ILO and the EESC.

If European social dialogue at both intersectoral and sectoral levels is in general not considered part of independent collective bargaining (Keller and Bansbach, 2000; Keller and Sörries, 1999), it is beyond any doubt, even if it could still expand, that it usefully supplements it. This confirms the possible complementarity of collective bargaining and other forms of participation, which is one of the main propositions contained in the introduction to this book. In addition to other aspects dealt with elsewhere in the present book, such as European works councils, European social dialogue demonstrates the increasing Europeanization of industrial relations. It is significant, for instance, that several national ESCs are constantly reinforcing their activities concerning Europe, for example in Belgium and France, where the ESCs have recently set up new structures to deal with European issues.

It has also been mentioned above that the range of issues dealt with by ESCs is constantly expanding. Further examples can be found in the recent creation in Spain of a committee concerning women at work and in the creation in the French ESC of a special 'delegation' for gender issues. At the request of the government, the French ESC published an opinion in April 2001 designed to improve the provisions of a draft bill on bullying at work. The opinion covered its extension to the civil service, its recognition as an occupational disease and proposed the same penal sanctions as for sexual harassment.

On the whole it appears that ESCs as well as the process of European social dialogue are in line with the four major propositions outlined in the introduction.

- The various forms of concertation and sometimes co-determination described here can reinforce and be in synergy with traditional collective bargaining. For example since the end of the 1980s the Belgian Central Economic Council has had a great influence on wages and employment policies at industry and enterprise levels.
- The institutions covered in this chapter have in a number of cases adopted innovative approaches, or at least have been able to adapt in order to link enterprise problems to meso-levels (local/regional or branch levels) as well as to macro-levels (national and international, especially European),

thereby significantly increasing democratic participation. For example, negotiations of the fourth Irish national agreement (1997–99) included an extension of partnership to the enterprise level and in 2000 the Italian ESC issued a publication on participation within enterprises and its prospects.

- ESCs are an important source of both information through various media and high-quality research which may be very useful for industrial relations in general and democratic participation in particular, including collective bargaining, education, training, consultancy and universities. Sometimes ESC research reports even make a contribution to public policy discussions in areas where to issue definitive conclusions would not be appropriate.
- Trade unions may find in such institutions major opportunities for influence and a place where workers may not only fight for their own rights but also for the rights of others, contributing at the same time to a culture of solidarity and the building of solid democratic institutions in the economy.

In our earlier volume (Kester and Pinaud, 1996), the 'growth scenario' referred to the advisability of an active trade union support for and coordination of the various forms and levels of participation, seeking to strengthen democratic participation at meso- and macro- (including international) levels. It was pointed out that in such a scenario existing forms of participation would be improved and expanded. Vaughan-Whitehead now sees a trend at the European level of codetermination towards 'shared social governance' (2000, p. 390). Involvement of trade unions in the various forms and levels of participation also makes it possible for them to balance individual, group and collective interests, giving them a new importance. What has been described and analysed in the present chapter may not have significance for all existing forms and levels of participation, and entirely new forms have seldom been initiated. Nevertheless, the contribution of ESCs and European social dialogue, and their prospects for the future, even though shortcomings remain and improvements are still possible, largely confirm the value and feasibility of our hypotheses and expectations.

Notes

1   This chapter greatly benefited from our attendance at an international meeting of ESCs and visits to several national and European institutions, their specialists and documentation

units, and in particular the ETUI, ETUC, DGV of the European Commission and the EESC. Since a comprehensive list of contacts would be too long, here we can only express our gratitude to all those who agreed to be interviewed or provide information. However, special thanks are due to Professor Marcel Bourlard, Director of the ILO Liaison Office in Brussels, and to the coordinator of this work, Mrs Jytte Bendixen of the ETUI.

2   A previous Council in Ireland, dating back to the 1960s, was dissolved in 1970.

3   The National Council for Economic and Labour Affairs (Consiglio Nazionale dell'Economia e del Lavoro, CNEL) was set up by an Act of Parliament in 1957, though it was also provided for in the Constitution of 1947. Similarly, in Spain, the Economic and Social Council (Consejo Económico y Social, CES) was set up by an Act of 1991, but had been envisaged in the Constitution of 1978.

4   Support staff may sometimes number around 100, or even more. There are some 150 full-time staff for the French ESC and Dutch SER, but far fewer in Greece, Ireland, Luxembourg and Portugal (about three-quarters being administrative and one quarter research staff, very often with civil service status, or special status as in Luxembourg or the Netherlands).

5   This body, composed of locally or regionally elected representatives of the member states, is the same size as the EESC. For more detail on the Committee of the Regions, see Office for Publications of the European Communities (1999), pp. 30–31.

6   ETUC: European Trade Union Confederation; UNICE: Union of Industrial and Employers' Confederations in Europe; CEEP: European Centre for Enterprises with Public Participation. The ETUC incorporates the Council of European Professional and Managerial Staff (Eurocadres) and the European Federation of Retired and Elderly Persons (FERPA). It coordinates the activities of 38 Interregional Trade Union Councils (ITUCs) organizing trade union cooperation in cross-border areas.

7   See, in particular, Conseil économique et social (1992). In a message to the meeting summarized in this publication, the then French prime minister pointed out that consultative assemblies are not competing with political institutions but are, on the contrary, their partners, contributing to the clarity and quality of democratic debate.

References

Attard, L. (1995), *Malta Council for Economic Development*. MBA Dissertation submitted to Brunel University, Uxbridge, mimeo.

Bodineau, P. (1994), *Les conseils économiques et sociaux*, Presses Universitaires de France, (*Que sais-je?* series), Paris.

Casale, G. (ed.), (1999), *Social Dialogue in Central and Eastern Europe*, International Labour Office, ILO-CEET, Budapest.

CNEL (1992), *The Economic and Social Councils in Europe: Roles and Perspectives*, Edizioni Scientifiche Italiane, Naples.

Commission of the European Communities (2000), *The Commission and Non-Governmental Organizations: Building a Stronger Partnership*, Discussion Paper COM (2000) 11 Final, Brussels.

Conseil central de l'économie (2000), Les comités de dialogue sectoriel européens, *Lettre mensuelle socio-économique*, 56, Brussels.

Conseil économique et social (1992), *Les assemblées consultatives concurrentes ou partenaires des instances politiques?*, CES, Paris.

Draus, F. (2001), *Social Dialogue in European Union Candidate Countries – Overview*, ETUC/UNICE/CEEP/UEAPME, Brussels.

Dupont, G. (2000), 'Les conseils économiques et sociaux régionaux n'ont pas trouvé leur place', *Le Monde*, 12 December, p. 16.

Duruflé, B. (1995), Resumé of questionnaire responses, in *Les conseils économiques et sociaux et institutions similaires (données comparatives)*, Conselho económico e social, Lisbon.

Economic and Social Committee (1999), Opinion 851/99, Brussels.

European Foundation for the Improvement of Living and Working Conditions (2000), *Communiqué*, No. 10, December, p. 1.

EIRObserver (1999), comparative supplement (insert), Issue No. 4, European Foundation for the Improvement of Living and Working Conditions, Dublin.

ETUI (1990), *The Role of Economic and Social Councils in Western Europe*, mimeo, European Trade Union Institute, Brussels.

Fajertag, G. and Pochet, P. (eds) (1997), *Social Pacts in Europe*, ETUI, Brussels.

Freyssinet, J. (1996), *Le Conseil économique et social*, La Documentation française, Paris.

Gold, M. (1998), 'Social Partnership at the EU Level: Initiatives, Problems and Implications for Member States', in Hine, D. and Kassim, H. (eds), *Beyond the Market. The EU and National Social Policy*, Routledge, London, pp. 107–33.

Heller, F., Pusic, E., Strauss, G. and Wilpert, B. (1998), *Organizational Participation: Myth and Reality*, Oxford University Press, Oxford/New York.

Hyman, R. (2000), *Social Dialogue in Western Europe: 'The State of the Art'*, Social Dialogue Papers, WP1, International Labour Office, Geneva.

ILO (1986), *The Trade Union Situation and Industrial Relations in Austria*, International Labour Office, Geneva.

ILO (1996), *Tripartite Consultation at the National Level on Economic and Social Policy*, Report VI, International Labour Conference, 83rd Session, International Labour Office, Geneva.

ILO (1997–98). *World Labour Report: Industrial Relations, Democracy and Social Stability*, International Labour Office, Geneva.

Keane, J. (1998), *Democracy and Civil Society*, Verso, London/New York.

Keller, B. and Bansbach, M. (2000), 'Social Dialogue: An Interim Report on Recent Results and Prospects', *Industrial Relations Journal*, Vol. 31(4), pp. 291–305.

Keller, B. and Sörries, B. (1999), 'The New European Social Dialogue: Old Wine in New Bottles', *Journal of European Social Policy*, Vol. 9, pp. 111–25.

Kester, G and Pinaud, H. (eds) (1996), *Trade Unions and Democratic Participation in Europe*, Avebury, Aldershot.

Kyloh, R. (ed.) (1995), *Tripartism on Trial: Tripartite Consultations and Negotiations in Central and Eastern Europe*, ILO-CEET, Geneva.

Lemercier, M. (1997), *Europe: quel partenariat social en réponse aux défis actuels? Ou quel comité économique et social pour demain?*, Institut d'études européennes, Louvain.

Lesieur, F. (ed.) (1958), *The Scanlon Plan: A Frontier in Labour-Management Co-operation*, MIT Press, Cambridge, MA.

Nascimento Rodrigues, H. (n.d.), 'Os Acordos de Concertação Social', in Barreto, A. (ed.), *A situação social em Portugal, 1960–1995*, ICS, University of Lisbon, Lisbon.

Office for Publications of the European Communities (1999), *Serving the European Union – A Citizen's Guide to the Institutions of the European Union*, Luxembourg.

Trebilcock, A. (ed.) (1994), *Towards Social Dialogue. Tripartite Co-operation in National Economic and Social Policy-making*, International Labour Office, Geneva.

Treu, T. (ed.) (1992), *Participation in Public Policy-making: The Role of Trade Unions and Employers' Associations*, Walter de Gruyter, Berlin and New York.

Vanek, J. (1971), *The Participatory Economy. An Evolutionary Hypothesis and a Strategy for Development*, Cornell University Press, Ithaca/New York.

Vaughan-Whitehead, D. (2000), 'Social Dialogue in EU Enlargement: Acquis and Responsibilities', *Transfer*, Vol. 6(3), pp. 387–98.

Visser, J. and Hemerijck, A. (1997), *A Dutch Miracle: Job Growth, Welfare Reform and Corporatism in the Netherlands*, Amsterdam University Press, Amsterdam.

PART II
SECTORAL AND COMPANY
CASE STUDIES

Chapter 5

Making Sense of Democratic Participation in the Dutch Information and Communications Industry

Peter Leisink

Introduction

In the Netherlands there is not much tradition of representative democratic participation in the information and communications technology (ICT) industry. A majority of firms employ fewer than 50 workers while a works council is mandatory only when the number of employees exceeds 50. Collective bargaining has not gained a firm foothold outside the former public telecom and broadcasting companies and the printing and publishing industry. Many workers in the ICT industry have their employment conditions determined on an individual basis, making them into special cases since four out of five workers in the Netherlands overall are covered by collective agreements. Obviously, trade unions are not happy with this situation and continually attempt to find ways to open a negotiating process, starting with individual employers but with a view to achieving sectoral agreements in the longer run. However, only a few employers have so far been interested in engaging in such negotiations.

An evaluation of the state of democratic participation in the information and communications industry tends to turn quickly into a matter of ideological positions. Employers claim that unions have no right to demand collective bargaining since only a few workers are unionized. They also hold the view that collective agreements are a straitjacket that does not fit the circumstances of the individual firm, and consequently some firms prefer to negotiate with the works council. There are also employers, however, who claim that the high-skilled workers whom they employ are well able to promote their own interests and negotiate their employment conditions on an individual basis. Furthermore, some employers claim that higher educational levels, individualization and the emergence of a knowledge society can very well be combined with individualization of employment relations, of which their firms are the innovators. On the other hand, trade unions claim that the regulation of employment conditions on an individual basis leads to arbitrary regulation dominated by the employer, since individual workers do not have the information, the negotiating skills or the power to enter into these negotiations as an equal partner. The idea of negotiations between the employer and the works council has been accepted by unions only in the exceptional circumstances that no sectoral agreement exists. Unions then hope that this will prepare the ground for themselves but are concerned about the outcome because they think that works councils do not hold the same values of worker solidarity as unions do. Unions reject as rhetoric the suggestion by employers that high-skilled workers view employment not as wage dependency but as a business partnership and that they prefer to arrange employment conditions on an individual basis. The comparatively favourable employment conditions which workers in the ICT industry enjoyed in the 1980s and 1990s were regarded by unions as a temporary exception: as soon as economic recession caused reorganization and policies to cut labour costs, workers would then discover the need for union organization and collective bargaining.

What about the workers in the ICT industry themselves? Both employers and unions claim to speak on behalf of the workers, but what are the views of the workers themselves? This chapter aims to give an idea of their views on democratic participation and workers' interests and to assess them in the context of their industries. Rather than taking the position that workers in the ICT industry should have a specific view, which would imply adopting unions' or employers' views as the normative reference point, this chapter argues that all these views actually exist as frames of meaning in interaction with which workers themselves come to make sense of democratic participation. The chapter first explains the theoretical perspective underlying this approach. It then describes the various frameworks which give meaning to democratic participation and workers' interests. Against this background, it goes on to analyze the views of ICT workers on democratic participation and workers' interests and finally discusses the implications of these views for trade union policies.

Theoretical Perspective

In an interesting article which is directly relevant to the issue of workers' interests, Bourdieu (1987) discusses the question of what constitutes a social class. He argues that objectivist theoretical approaches including the Marxist tradition, which claim that workers' interests can be deduced from an objective analysis of the position of labour in a capitalist economic system, suffer from what he calls the 'theoreticist illusion' (Bourdieu, 1987, p. 7). To be sure, Bourdieu does not argue that an objective analysis of the position of labour in a capitalist economic system is wrong and redundant as such. On the contrary, an objectivist analysis must be made as one moment in the analysis of class society. However, it is false to suppose that the class interests which are derived from this objectivist analysis will also be found when the workers' consciousness is examined. When workers appear to define their interests as subjectively different from what objective class analysis would lead one to suppose, Marxists tend to explain this by claiming that these workers have a false consciousness due to the media and other ideological apparatuses in a capitalist society, and claim that ultimately workers will develop a notion of class interests that corresponds to their objective position in society. This Marxist kind of explanation suffers from a theoreticist illusion, Bourdieu argues, because it presupposes that objective positions and relations in a class society will enforce themselves subjectively, thereby neglecting the occurrence of other social forces which also attempt to influence the definition of interests. Thus, the way in which people in a certain position come to *understand* their position and interests subjectively is the outcome of various social forces – in the specific form of trade unions, professional associations, political parties, women's and ethnic organizations and so on – which all attempt to impose their definition of interests. Therefore, Bourdieu concludes, in order to understand what makes a social class we must combine the objectivist and the subjectivist analysis.

An initial benefit of the type of analysis which Bourdieu proposes is that organizational views on democratic participation and workers' interests which were sketched in the introduction to this chapter can be understood as the result of social forces. Bourdieu must also be read as saying that an objective analysis of social positions must be made in order to understand and explain the particular views, values, working and living practices, in short the culture of particular categories of people. Making this kind of objective analysis and combining it with the analysis of the subjective views of people can help avoid the voluntarist tendency in constructivist authors such as Weick (1995) and De Moor (1995), who suggest that people define situations and construct social practices and organizations merely as they choose. This theoretical view neglects the social structures of signification and domination that enable and constrain the (sensemaking) activities of actors (Giddens, 1984). More concretely, people define situations but they do so while drawing on the historically created sets of meanings that exist in a community. In addition, their power to define cannot be detached from the economic, cultural and social resources which they can dispose of and which are differentially distributed over social positions, so that, for example, employer and employee generally do not have equal power to define the situation that will dominate in the workplace. This theoretical perspective, which includes both the competent and creative activity of agents and the social contexts of interaction, as well as the recursive relations between agency and structure, is known by labels such as structuration theory (Giddens, 1984) and genetic structuralism (Bourdieu, 1987).

Adopting this theoretical perspective in the research on how workers in ICT sectors of industry make sense of democratic participation and workers' interests requires that we not only investigate the definitions which they have developed subjectively, but also analyse their social situation. The latter amounts in principle to an elaborate investigation which is very demanding to carry out in practice. However, this chapter attempts to honour this requirement by paying attention to the various frameworks for making sense of democratic participation and workers' interests that are present in these sectors; to some extent it is also possible to take into account the variety of sectors and job categories. Thus we can appreciate some of the objective contexts and constraints in the ICT sectors of industry with which workers interact to make sense of democratic participation and workers' interests in a diversity of ways. A related kind of approach has been elaborated by Christensen and Westenholz (1998) in their study of employee representatives as company strategic actors. They show how three different cognitive frameworks (of collective bargaining, codetermination and co-management) offer diverse definitions and values which constitute employees as actors through their membership of a union and/or a firm. The way in which employees appropriate these frameworks infuses their methods of co-authoring and co-performing the participation 'drama'. Similarly, the various cognitive frameworks that exist in sectors of the ICT industry can also be seen as relevant contexts on which workers' definitions draw.

Participation Frameworks

It can be expected that some of the main forms of democratic participation (Pinaud, 1996) can be found in sectors or firms in the ICT industry. As forms of indirect participation collective bargaining and codetermination are relevant, and as a form of direct participation organizational participation is also a relevant framework. In the context of the Dutch industrial relations system, these respective cognitive frameworks conceive of democratic participation and workers' interests in different ways (Leisink, 1996).

Collective bargaining represents a framework of democratic participation and workers' interests which takes as its starting point the position of the worker in a capitalist economy in opening up forms of action aimed at solidarity between all workers ('equal wages for equal jobs'). Industrial unionism has been dominant since 1945. Workers in a particular sector of industry are organized in an industrial union, which usually has branches for specific sectors of industry. Collective bargaining cognitively orientates democratic participation and workers' interests not at a professional or workplace level, but at a sectoral level. Worker solidarity is even more encompassing than this, in the sense that unions harmonize their proposals for collective bargaining policy at the level of the national centre of their confederation. The main significance of the collective bargaining framework is in the normative orientation it provides for workers' interests. Most union federations in the Netherlands subscribe to the principle of inclusive unionism (Visser, 1987), which means that they claim to represent all workers, including those out of work because of unemployment or disability, and not just the membership's interests. Although the overall unionization rate in the Netherlands is only about 25 per cent, the unions' inclusive bargaining policies in conjunction with institutional features of the industrial relations system (such as the principle of declaring collective agreements generally binding) result in a strong institutional influence for this framework.

Codetermination represents another form of indirect participation, but its institutionalization through works councils carries a cognitive framework which is very different from collective bargaining. This framework makes sense of democratic participation as a form of industrial citizenship. Employees as members of a firm have a right to discuss matters of mutual interest with their management through their works council representatives. All employees have a right to elect their representatives and any employee can be elected as a representative, irrespective of trade union membership. Although in practice about two thirds of works council members are trade union members, this does not turn the works council into a trade union instrument. The mission of the works council is embedded in legislation which defines it as contributing to 'the proper functioning of the firm in all its goals' and to 'the consultation with the employees and the representation of the firm's employees'. In principle works councils can raise any issue which they regard as significant but they have special legal rights of approval/veto in the area of the company's social policies and rights of advice in the area of financial and strategic policies. Trade unions have attempted to orientate their members who serve on works councils towards wider, more inclusive definitions of workers' interests, but in general works councils conceive of workers' interests as involving the employment conditions of the workers employed by the firm and are little inclined to raise issues of wider social concern such as the promotion of labour participation of women and ethnic minorities (Klein and Evers, 1994; Van het Kaar and Looise, 1999).

While works councils are mandatory for firms employing 50 or more employees, direct participation is not a legal requirement. This means that organizational participation in its various forms, such as quality circles, is dependent on the cooperation if not the initiative of the management. Organizational participation offers forms of direct participation to individual employees or groups of employees on the operation of work methods and enhances employee autonomy through such arrangements as delegation or teamwork. The cooperation of management in initiating such forms of direct participation has been dependent on the positive effects they are believed to have on employee motivation and company performance. The motives of the great majority of managers in the Netherlands for introducing direct participation is their belief that direct participation has positive effects on both company performance (such as improvements in quality and reductions in costs) and quality of work, and the belief that employees have a right to participation (Huijgen and Benders, 1998; EPOC research group, 1997). In this framework, employees are constituted as actors in the firm to the extent that managers think that their workplace offers chances for improving company performance and quality of work through forms of direct participation. The representation of workers' interests in the area of quality of work is directly related to improvement of company performance.

A New Frontier

Obviously, these three cognitive frameworks – collective bargaining, codetermination and direct participation – offer very different representations of democratic participation and workers' interests. The social actors who have historically initiated these cognitive frameworks are also different: the trade unions, the state and the employers/management respectively. Over the years, all frameworks have come to include cognitive and normative elements held by other actors, but they compete with each other for dominance in the ideological field, that is, for imposing a particular view of democratic participation and workers' interests as the cognitively and morally 'right' one. This competition takes place for instance through public debates in the media and at conferences; another 'battlefield' is the winning of support among workers. Studying this process in newly emerging industries such as the ICT industry is of interest because these industries have no established traditions – or they exist only in subsectors of these newly developing industries – and so, on the one hand, workers are relatively less constrained in their sensemaking while, on the other hand, traditional frameworks must attempt to assert themselves to reproduce their continuity. Therefore, studying the way in which workers in the emerging ICT industry make sense of democratic participation and workers' interests is of more general interest because of what it can reveal about the cognitive and normative appeal of the various views on democratic participation and worker solidarity in a society which is changing through such processes as individualization, multiculturalism, informatization and globalization. Thus, the ICT industry offers a view of a new frontier of democratic participation.

Frameworks of Meaning in the ICT industry

The ICT industry is newly emerging, so a brief description of it is required if only because the kind of sectors and firms which are included under its heading differs between authors. Then an indication will be given of the frameworks of meaning with respect to democratic participation which exist in the industry.

The Information and Communications Industry

The term 'information and communications industry' is not a recognized term in the standard industrial classification system. This may explain why different definitions exist. A common element in most analyses is that information and communication technologies are regarded as the basis for the convergence of a set of previously separate industries. These include computers (hardware and software) and telecommunications. This is the definition of the ICT industry – in a narrow sense – used in a recent report, *Working in the ICT Sector: Under What Conditions?* (Computable, FNV Bondgenoten, 2000), which will be used in this chapter.

Another definition also includes media firms because they create, organize and produce the content for multimedia or new media such as the Internet, which are regarded as a distinctive feature of ICT convergence. Thus several authors (such as Hummel, 1998; Leisink, Teunen and Boumans, 2000; Michel, 1997; and Sandberg, 1998) include in their definition of the ICT industry firms from the media industries: printing and publishing, broadcasting and the audiovisual industry, photography, news and journalist agencies, public relations and advertizing agencies. This chapter will focus on the computer, telecommunications and media industries.

The Collective Bargaining Framework

In a survey of 2,430 firms from the ICT industry in this broad sense, involved in the production of multimedia, the majority of firms did not engage in collective bargaining with trade unions. Some 61 per cent of small firms employing fewer than five employees and 54 per cent of 'large' firms employing five or more employees arranged employment conditions on an individual basis with each employee. Of the large firms, 19 per cent regulated employment conditions in line with a sectoral collective agreement, 15 per cent regulated them through a company-level collective agreement and 13 per cent applied a combination of collective agreement plus individual arrangements (Leisink, Teunen and Boumans, 2000, pp. 109–10). Major differences exist between firms depending on their sector. In the graphics industry, for instance, collective bargaining is dominant with only 5 per cent of firms setting employment conditions on an individual basis, but in the IT sector, advertizing agencies and the audiovisual industry as many as 65 to 80 per cent of all firms set employment conditions on an individual basis only.

A survey of 1,689 workers in the IT and telecoms sector (Computable, FNV Bondgenoten, 2000) reveals somewhat different data, which may be partly related to the fact that employees rather than firms from the sector were interviewed, and the fact that 40 per cent of them were trade union members. Indeed, their union was the co-organizer of the survey and sent 5,000 of its members a questionnaire. Some 69 per cent of the workers in the IT and telecoms sectors have their employment relations regulated by a collective agreement and 23 per cent have their conditions set on an individual basis. When there is a collective agreement, it is only rarely the union that represents the workers. Only 19 per cent of the workers report a collective bargaining framework with the union as their representative, while 39 per cent report that their collective agreement was negotiated by the works council and a further 33 per cent work under a set of conditions that is unilaterally decided by the firm.

The lack of sectoral agreements in the IT sector is partly owing to the absence of representative organizations of employers (Van Liempt and Van Uffelen, 2000). There are several organizations representing parts of the sector but none of them has more than a few hundred members. One of the biggest employer organizations is V-ICT-Nederland, which organizes about 300 firms selling and distributing computer hardware and offering maintenance services. This employer organization has actually engaged in negotiations with the trade unions, and the collective agreement concluded in 1997 offers a framework which firms can adapt to their local situation. Their hope was that the framework character would be attractive to other firms, but so far attempts at extending the agreement to other parts of the IT sector have met with little success. In addition, some 20 company-level collective agreements exist, which cover some of the largest software houses, such as Roccade, the former state computer centre with about 4,000 employees. In the case of these 20 company collective agreements, works councils represent the employees together with the trade unions, and in some cases the works council has a stronger position than the trade unions in the negotiating process and in the implementation of the agreement. This reflects the lack of representativeness of the unions, which organize only between 5 and 10 per cent of all IT employees, but it is also a result of the employers' preference not to negotiate with unions because they are associated with traditional collectivist and antagonistic views which can result in straitjacket agreements and conflicts (Van Liempt and Van Uffelen, 2000; Bijlsma and Van het Kaar, 1999).

The Codetermination Framework

With respect to the incidence of works councils in the ICT industry, it is necessary first to point out that only between 1 and 2 per cent of all firms in the ICT industry (in the broad sense) actually employ 50 or more employees, which means that some 500 to 1,000 firms legally qualify to set one up. Data from a research project which has a different breakdown of industries would seem to suggest that between 64 and 90 per cent of large communications firms have a works council (Oeij and Stoppelenburg, 1998), but more detailed information about IT and telecom firms shows that only 150 firms have a works council out of the 480 that are legally required to have one (Seifert, 2000).

In addition to size thresholds, the majority of firms producing multimedia applications have not been active for more than five years and have started in an atmosphere which some describe as 'a group of friends' or 'cheerful anarchy'. There is little time for meetings and, when there is, they take place in a café. It is only with the growth of the firm that the need for more professional personnel management arises, and it is then that some not only organize group consultation on a more regular basis but also establish a works council.

Works councils in ICT firms are involved in regulating the basic employment conditions of their employees such as pay, working hours and job descriptions, and in this process they voice the issues that are typical of ICT employees, which range from training, development and career opportunities offered by the firm, to the pressure of work and opportunities for part-time work in the more established firms (Lenderink, 2000; Seifert, 2000). Their focus is on the individual firm and its workforce.

The Direct Participation Framework

In the Netherlands the incidence of direct participation appears higher than the European average: the latest research of firms with a works council showed that almost all firms (97 per cent) also practised some form of group consultation, 46 per cent had quality circles and 43 per cent had self-managed work teams (Van het Kaar and Looise, 1999). These data refer to firms employing 50 or more employees; other research reveals that 76 per cent of firms employing more than 10 employees practise some form of group consultation and that the scope of consultation has broadened from operational work issues to issues of personnel management (Van het Kaar and Looise, 2000). A 1993 survey by a public supervision body states that in about half of all firms with group consultation, this had also included employment conditions such as overtime payments and compensation for travelling expenses (LTD, 1993). This proportion has undoubtedly increased since.

Group consultation appears to be a common phenomenon in ICT firms if advertizing agencies, almost all of which have fewer than 50 employees, are anything to go by. A survey of employees in advertizing agencies (included as a subsector in the broad definition of the ICT industry) showed that two-thirds of all employees took part in group consultation (Van Wijk, 2000). Account, secretarial and support staff participation in group consultation is just below average, but so is that of highly skilled art directors and copywriters. On the other hand, managers and media, financial and personnel specialists' participation in group consultation is above average.

An extra reason for ICT firms to practise group delegation and group consultation has to do with knowledge sharing. Offering employees a job with scope for creativity, research and development appears to make ICT firms attractive in the tight labour market. However, for the firm to benefit from the professional expertise which the individual employee acquires, the exchange of knowledge must be organized. One way of doing this is through creating self-managed project teams with rotating membership and frequent group seminars. Such platforms can also play a role in the more mundane issues of personnel management. With the professionalization of personnel management in ICT firms, forms of direct participation are getting more systematic attention, but, in general, informal consultation appears to be the rule, particularly in small firms.

This section has attempted to sketch the incidence of three different forms of democratic participation in the ICT industry. An overall assessment cannot be made, however, since there is a strong degree of variability regarding segments of the industry, size and age of firms. In some segments, such as printing, publishing and public broadcasting, sectoral collective bargaining exists in combination with representative participation through works councils and direct participation at workplace level. Other segments, such as advertizing agencies, software houses and internet providers, have no tradition of sectoral collective bargaining at all; only some firms practise collective bargaining at firm level and offer an opportunity for representative participation through works councils while direct participation appears to be more prevalent.

These varied patterns of democratic participation are themselves a product of the (inter)action of employees, employers and other actors in the industry, and in that sense their views about democratic participation and workers' interests have gone into their making. These patterns also represent cognitive frameworks in the context of the workplace with which employees interact to develop and articulate their own views.

Employees' Views on Democratic Participation and Workers' Interests

This section will explore the views of employees in the ICT industry with respect to two topics. First, it will examine their views concerning the various forms of democratic participation: what do employees think about collective bargaining, trade unions, works councils and direct participation? Second, it will ask: what are the interests that employees in the ICT industry regard as important, and how do their views compare with inclusive union views on workers' interests?

Collective Bargaining and Representative Participation

Employees in IT and telecom firms prefer some kind of collective regulation of their employment conditions; only 11 per cent do not want any regulation because they prefer to arrange their employment contracts on an individual basis. However, contrary to the tradition of industrial unionism and its preference for collective agreements for an entire industry, 38 per cent of employees prefer a company agreement, 24 per cent prefer an agreement at the level of a subsector of the industry, and only 16 per cent prefer a collective agreement covering the entire ICT industry (Computable, FNV Bondgenoten, 2000). While collective bargaining as a form of democratic participation is thus clearly embedded in the views of IT employees, they do not generally share the view that trade unions (should) represent the workers in collective bargaining with the employer. Only 9 per cent of ICT employees subscribe to the idea of trade unions representing the workers in collective bargaining, while 28 per cent prefer the works council as their only representative. The majority (55 per cent), however, prefer trade unions and works councils together to represent workers in collective bargaining. Interestingly, it is also the view of trade union members that trade unions and works councils should represent workers together in collective bargaining. Only 7 per cent regard trade unions as their only representative in collective bargaining, while 73 per cent prefer trade unions and works councils in combination.

Comparing the subjective views of ICT employees on democratic participation with the present situation of collective bargaining and worker representation, we can observe that the employees' views generally reflect and support the objective situation. The research finds that 80 per cent of ICT employees have their employment conditions currently regulated in one way or other, while 78 per cent indeed prefer some kind of regulation. However, there are two important contrasts. First, while one-third of the ICT employees currently have their employment conditions regulated unilaterally by their firm, almost all employees prefer to be represented in collective bargaining by the works council and/or trade unions. Second, while 19 per cent of the ICT employees currently have their employment conditions regulated by an agreement concluded by the trade unions, only 6 per cent prefer the unions to be their only representative. The claim of trade unions, that they are the sole representative of the workers in collective bargaining and that works councils can play a role in the implementation of (parts of) the agreement, does not meet with much support among ICT employees. The majority of ICT employees (55 per cent) regard trade unions as the representative of the workers in collective bargaining only in combination with works councils, and 28 per cent prefer only the works council as their representative.

Van Wijk (2000) reports a survey of employees of advertizing agencies which represent the commercial side of the ICT industry. Advertizing agencies have never had a collective agreement and trade union membership is almost non-existent. Only 1 per cent of their employees are union members, and 9 per cent are members of a professional association. Earlier research concerning employees of advertizing agencies (Leisink and Spaninks, 1994) found that almost all employees (88 per cent) preferred to determine their employment conditions on an individual basis rather than through any kind of collective agreement. At present the situation has slightly changed, since 78 per cent now report that they prefer individual arrangements over collective agreements. Particularly production and studio employees show a more than average preference for collective agreements, but this is not a general characteristic of lower skilled employees because secretarial assistants, for instance, comply fully with the average preference for individual arrangements. Although the proportion of employees preferring a collective agreement regulating basic employment conditions for the sector has increased from 9 per cent in 1992 to 20 per cent in 1999, collective bargaining is obviously not directly associated with democratic participation by most employees in advertizing agencies.

Direct Participation

The survey of employees in advertizing agencies also examined their views about employee participation in decision making at agency level and about group consultation (Van Wijk, 2000). Since most advertizing agencies employ fewer than 50 employees there is no legal requirement for them to have a works council. However, there may be some form of informal council, or employees can be consulted about company decisions on an individual basis. While in 1992 only 21 per cent of all employees reported that they were consulted about company decisions, now 38 per cent indicate that they are consulted and 8 per cent that they participate as co-decision maker. Managers and professional staff are most involved, and so are secretarial assistants, while account, production and studio assistants are least involved. There is however no direct positive correlation between participation in decision making and employee evaluation of company decision making. Although account, production and studio staff are less satisfied than average about company decision making (between 25 per cent and 29 per cent versus an average of 23 per cent dissatisfaction), account managers (32 per cent) and art designers and copywriters (37 per cent) are even more dissatisfied despite the fact that they participate more than average in company decision making. While more employees participated in company decision making in 1999 compared with 1992, more still had the view that they should have an even greater say in company decision making (50 per cent in 1999, against 39 per cent in 1992). Indeed, two-thirds of all employees participate in group consultation, with account, production and studio staff as well as secretarial assistants, art designers and copywriters being least involved. Nevertheless, almost half of all employees felt that they should have a greater say in group decision making.

Thus, for employees in advertizing agencies, democratic participation does not mean collective bargaining but direct participation through group consultation and company decision making. The views of employees in advertizing agencies generally reflect and support the current situation of democratic participation. Interestingly, however, more employees than in 1992 now emphasize that they must have more say in group and company decision making, although the proportion of participants has actually risen. This means that direct participation in group decision making as well as participation in company decision making has acquired greater significance for employees.

Workers' Interests

It was explained above that industrial unionism was introduced in the Netherlands after World War II, because this was thought to be the best way to safeguard worker solidarity. At the time it meant the end of white-collar unions, at least those affiliated to the socialist, Catholic and Protestant confederations that existed in the Netherlands. Occupational categories were integrated into collective agreements covering industrial sectors so that the principle of solidarity could be implemented more effectively. On the grounds of the same principle, unions preferred sectoral agreements over company agreements in order to avoid fragmentation, and in accordance with this idea unions also opposed company agreements negotiated by works councils. Industrial unionism and sectoral collective agreements thereby formed the bedrock of the Dutch system. It is precisely this system, however, which is undermined by the views of ICT employees. A minority of IT and telecom employees and a great majority of advertizing employees do not prefer a collective agreement at all, and of those IT and telecom employees who do, the largest proportion prefers a company agreement. In addition, we may question whether those ICT employees who want unions together with the works council to represent them in collective bargaining do so because they support the unions' view on inclusive worker solidarity or because they pragmatically appreciate the unions' expertise in collective bargaining.

And when we examine ICT employees' preferences concerning pay, working hours and other employment conditions, another feature emerges which does not sit easily with traditional trade union views on workers' interests. Trade unions have until recently understood solidarity as 'equality' and have operationalized this through standard regulations. In the case of working hours, trade unions have felt that a collective reduction of working hours is both in the interest of workers and in the interest of the unemployed, and have therefore not wanted collective agreements to offer employees a choice (whereas part-time work was considered an individual choice to give up the rights to a full-time job on a voluntary basis). When IT and telecom employees were asked to comment on the importance they would attach to a number of topics if they were to have a collective agreement, 83 per cent chose the possibility of part-time work, 82 per cent indicated that they wanted the option between financial compensation for overtime work and compensation through extra time off, and 69 per cent would like to have the possibility of buying extra time off. By contrast, a collective reduction of working hours was preferred by only 42 per cent (Computable, FNV Bondgenoten, 2000). These preferences illustrate the diversity of opinions of ICT employees and their wish for individual autonomy instead of standardized collectivity.

Advertizing employees articulate a similar kind of diversity of preferences. Many of them work long hours, but while the majority would like to work shorter hours, opinions diverge as to the number of preferred hours, ranging from less than 30 hours to between 45 and 50 hours. This diversity of preferences is no doubt also the reason why 82 per cent of all employees have a positive attitude towards introducing greater flexibility into employment conditions (Van Wijk, 2000).

Implications for Trade Union Policies

Employees in the ICT industry make sense of their interests from the perspective of their own status in work and life, and this results in a diversity of meanings. For instance, young employees attach great importance to their company's policies on training and career development, female employees with young children attach great importance to part-time work and flexible working hours, male employees with young children attach great importance to childcare facilities, while employees without children at home attach great importance to sabbatical leave opportunities. This obvious diversity does not lead to a broad understanding of joint interests.

The diversity of the labour force is now probably greater than it was 50 years ago, but even then diversity existed and trade unions saw the reconciliation of different interests as part of their function. Notwithstanding the traditional image of solidarity, trade union programmes for collective bargaining have always reflected the dominant concerns of the hegemonic groups, Hyman argues (1996), and solidarity has always been a historical construct. A significant difference between then and now, however, is that few employees in the ICT industry join unions and, as a consequence, there is no platform for a 'multi-cultural' debate between the various categories of employees with different views on democratic participation and workers' interests. ICT employees want to arrange their employment conditions directly in line with their interests as they see them and, therefore, prefer their works council or themselves to negotiate with their employer. The tight ICT labour market and the fact that about two out of three employees in the ICT industry have had higher education (Computable, FNV Bondgenoten, 2000; Van Wijk, 2000), no doubt contribute to the employees' sense of being able to arrange employment conditions on an individual basis. Such direct and individual fixing of employment conditions at company level can, of course, have negative repercussions for employees with a weak position in the labour market. Interestingly, however, the lowest skilled employees in advertizing agencies do not differ much from the higher skilled employees with respect to their preference for arranging employment conditions on an individual basis.

This sketch of ICT employees' views of workers' interests and democratic participation is not unique to the ICT industry, and it contains various elements that have been known to the trade unions for a number of years. During the 1990s debates within the trade unions resulted in several initiatives to cope with the emerging 'new' employee and the employers' need for differentiation. Some of these initiatives will be reviewed briefly, and then we shall discuss the extent to which they meet the aspirations of ICT employees, as analysed here.

Union Initiatives to Accommodate Diversity

Differentiation and decentralization made an impact on trade union policies and industrial relations during the 1990s. Central coordination at the confederate level of wage demands and programmes for collective bargaining has become less detailed; general principles and directions are agreed but it is left to the unions themselves to elaborate the collective bargaining policies for their own sectors. In some sectors, agreements have been modernized and offer a framework concerning such issues as work schedules and duty rosters which may be negotiated at company level, where the works council or the trade union can represent the workers. However, in these agreements it is the unions that act as the workers' representative and it is the unions that decide the issues to be left to the company level and the style of workplace negotiations. Individual employees or groups of employees can only have as much choice as the unions want to leave them.

During the 1990s unions also discussed in a more specific sense the implications of trends towards individualization and multiculturalism. One policy document of the FNV (Federatie Nederlandse Vakbeweging, the biggest trade union confederation in the Netherlands), for instance, reads: 'Our society is becoming increasingly multi-coloured and some categories of workers demand a greater say. As a consequence, greater diversity of work schedules and career opportunities is needed, occasionally even at the level of the individual employee' (FNV, 1993, p. 15). While this document recognizes the need for diversity, it does not grant the individual employee the right or the opportunity to make his or her own choice. The latter topic has been covered by a later policy document entitled *Making Your Own Choice?* (FNV, 1999). In this document the FNV explains that it wants to promote the interests of every individual employee, the interests of all employees collectively and that it wants to realise a number of social goals. Differentiation of employment conditions is desirable only on certain conditions and within certain constraints because individual interests and collective interests do not always run parallel, argues the FNV. Equal treatment and certainty are the points of departure which require that in the areas of pay, working hours and social security, collective agreements concluded by the unions are actually required. Only sectors and firms that have a collective agreement and good social policies can, according to the FNV, qualify for agreements that offer a certain degree of individual choice of employment conditions. The degree of choice is restricted, however. For instance, the FNV accepts that workers may opt to work one hour extra per day in order to save for extra days off or sabbatical leave, or that workers may opt to pay a greater percentage of their salary into their pension scheme. The FNV does not, however, accept that workers may opt to sell holidays in exchange for higher income, the reason being that this would contravene its social goal of promoting full employment by reducing the number of working hours.

In addition, since 1997 the FNV has discussed plans to give works councils a greater role in the preparation and implementation of collective agreements, but not in their actual negotiation and conclusion. This is regarded as the unions' prerogative because unions are independent and professional negotiators whose goal it is to conclude an agreement based on solidarity. The principle of solidarity and requisite bargaining strength do not permit the delegation of employment conditions such as pay, working hours and social security to the works council for negotiation with the employer. However, works councils can play a role in giving advice to union negotiators and, once unions have concluded a collective agreement, works councils can consult the employer on the implementation of those issues which the unions have left for the workplace level to determine.

Union Initiatives Evaluated

While union initiatives may go a long way in meeting the wish for tailor-made arrangements in sectors where collective agreements exist, the question here is whether these ideas match up with the meaning that ICT employees attribute to democratic participation and workers' interests.

If the views of IT, telecom and advertising employees as reported by recent surveys are representative of ICT employees in general, the unions can have little hope that they will be able to recruit employees on the basis of their plans. Three significant differences come to the fore when employees' views and union plans are compared. First, those employees who see a need for collective agreements do not regard the unions as their sole representative. Unlike the unions which claim collective bargaining as their exclusive prerogative, the majority of IT and telecom employees want unions and works councils together to represent the workers in negotiations with the employer. A significant minority of employees regard the works council as their only representative. A majority of advertising employees want to negotiate employment conditions on an individual basis themselves. Second, unions prefer collective agreements at sectoral level and regard the regulation of basic employment conditions (pay, working hours and social security) as a package. However, IT and telecom employees prefer collective agreements at company or workplace level and have such diverse preferences with respect to these basic employment conditions that they cannot be covered by standard regulations, unless a substantial degree of choice is allowed that the unions do not find acceptable. An example is the diversity of advertising employees' preferences concerning working hours. Another example is that 61 per cent of IT and telecom employees want the chance to sell back holiday entitlements, which is exactly what the unions reject because it goes against the collective goal of full employment. Third, ICT employees accept variations in employment conditions which unions find unacceptable because of the sense they make of solidarity. Typical instances of solidaristic trade union policy of the 1980s and 1990s, such as the prevention of wide pay differentials or the collective reduction of working hours, are supported by only 42 per cent of IT and telecom employees (and this percentage may be even lower if the over-representation of union members in the survey response is corrected). The restrictions which unions – because of the principle of solidarity – place on the degree of choice which individual employees may exercise are much too tight to accommodate the diversity and range of options which ICT employees want to have.

It is interesting to observe that FNV Bondgenoten, the union which organizes employees in the IT sector, has concluded collective agreements which do not comply with the conditions set out in the FNV policy documents. The actual practice of workplace relations is different from the guidelines of formal policy. FNV Bondgenoten has accepted a negotiating role for works councils as well as a degree of flexibility and choice concerning basic employment conditions, which far exceed the official FNV policy but which have been accepted because without them no agreement would have been possible. This practical experience has also prompted FNV Bondgenoten to propose that it may decide autonomously the degree of flexibility and choice concerning employment conditions that may be offered by collective agreements which it concludes (*Volkskrant*, 11 August 2000). This proposal has fired a debate at the confederate level in which the public sector union, Abavakabo FNV, has opposed the private sector union, FNV Bondgenoten, on the grounds that collective provisions such as childcare can no longer be maintained if employees can choose whether or not they want to contribute towards them.

Challenges to Solidarity and Democratic Participation

This debate amongst the unions illustrates the need for further examination of the principle of solidarity (Leisink, 1997). On the one hand, solidarity was the basis of the friendly societies of the nineteenth century (Hyman, 1996), which used the financial strength of the collectivity of members to offer material support to individuals on whom the misfortune of illness, disability or unemployment had fallen. This meaning of solidarity is related to the mutual insurance of members with common work-related interests against involuntarily incurred misfortunes. It would be hard to claim that childcare comes under this heading. Childcare as well as a number of other collective goods, such as vocational training, have come to be organized collectively because they are hard, if not impossible, for the individual firm to provide for and because their provision as a collective obligation prevents free-rider behaviour. On the other hand, solidarity is called on as a normative principle to legitimize a line of action such as a reduction of pay differentials, which people holding other values will not subscribe to. It is interesting to note that even the modest degree of variation in employment conditions, which is created by the restricted choice which the FNV finds acceptable for individual employees to exercise, causes a complete split of opinion among the union membership: half the membership finds such variations acceptable and the other half does not (Van Rij, 1995).

These differences of opinion should be recognized and debated when unions want to engage with employees in the ICT industry. Adopting the morally superior stance of solidarity will not in itself bridge the actual gap between unions and ICT employees. If unions were to enter such a debate openly they would see many of their most cherished ideas challenged. ICT employees will tend to dismiss the trade union view on solidarity as out of touch with the reality of the ICT labour market, where shortages of labour offer little or no chance of a job to the unemployed; thus solidarity with the unemployed will not be appreciated as a sensible argument by ICT employees who wish to sell back their holidays. In addition, the unreflective paternalism of the union claim to represent the workers in collective bargaining is unlikely to convince ICT employees that unions support the goal of democratic participation. Trade unions are likely to approach ICT employees with their own slant on collective bargaining rights. This is a paradigm alien to the ICT industry which will be felt by ICT employees as remote from, if not contradictory to, their own views on direct participation and works councils. Only if trade unions are willing to engage in a dialogue with ICT employees, respecting their multi-cultural differences and willing to accept that the outcome will probably be different from the way in which solidarity and worker representation are understood in longstanding trade union strongholds like public transport and the construction industry, only then will there be a basis for developing a practice of context-sensitive collective bargaining along the direct participation track.

This latter point refers to the guiding principles for a strategy for democratic participation, as formulated by Kester (1996). Kester (1996, p. 44) regards the tendency to view collective bargaining and participation as contradictory as erroneous, and instead argues the case for a twin-track strategy for developing both bargaining and participation. However, he fails to consider that the practical implications of this principle vary widely between a situation where collective bargaining and trade union representation are established and a situation where they are practically non-existent, as in the ICT industry. In the former situation unions can make space for a direct participation track and can even attempt to make the participation and collective bargaining track mutually reinforcing. In the latter situation, however, the tension between the two tracks which is related to the different orientations underlying both, can seriously affect the viability of collective bargaining when, as in the case of the ICT industry, direct participation with its cognitive framework is dominant and employees feel no need for the trade union/collective bargaining framework with its traditional antagonistic and collectivist values.

Conclusions

Direct participation by way of group delegation and group consultation appears to be the most widely favoured and practised form of democratic participation in the ICT industry. ICT employees make sense of democratic participation primarily as direct participation. These forms of direct participation are not restricted to operational production matters only, but include such matters as work schedules which employees consider significant for their work and life. In addition, many ICT firms promote special interest groups and knowledge platforms which have an important function in the exchange and development of knowledge within the firm. Many employees like to participate in these out of professional interest and because they serve as a forum to discuss company policies with management. Because of the tight labour market in which the ICT industry finds itself, management often promotes this type of direct participation as a way of binding their employees into the organization by creating a learning environment and innovative culture. In this way the management can respond to the motivation of most ICT employees who favour working for a company which offers good opportunities for training and development (Computable, FNV Bondgenoten, 2000). Indirect participation through works councils represents a cognitive framework for workers' interests and democratic participation which is more in line with the views of ICT employees than representation by unions. However, this form of democratic participation is mandatory only for firms that employ 50 employees or more while only between 1 and 2 per cent of all ICT firms actually employ that number of employees.

Democratic participation through representation by trade unions in collective bargaining does not find much support amongst ICT employees.

Apart from some pockets of traditional unionism, such as the former public telecom company, public broadcasting and the printing and publishing industry, union membership is very low, ranging from almost no membership in advertising agencies to 5 to 10 per cent membership in IT firms. The relative absence of collective agreements concluded by trade unions is in line with this overall low rate of unionization. At least as important as an indicator of the slight future chances of democratic participation through trade unions is the considerable gap between ICT employees' views about democratic participation and workers' interests, and traditional union views. The real cultural gap between the two concerns the legitimacy of the union claim to represent the workers in collective bargaining and the meaning given to workers' interests. ICT employees vary between their wish to arrange employment conditions on an individual basis (as in advertising agencies) and their wish to regulate employment conditions at company level, but they certainly do not wish to have their employment conditions regulated by unions at the sectoral level. Underlying these attitudes is a concept of workers' interests which gives priority to individual and company circumstances and an emphasis to autonomy and flexibility at the workplace level rather than solidarity at sectoral level.

For a long time trade unions have wanted to believe that employees in the computer industry were no different from workers in general and would discover the need for union organization and collective bargaining when economic recession caused restructuring. This belief has not been confirmed (Leisink, 1997). While internet firms have recently been brought down to earth with a bump when 'old' economic laws prompted major reorganizations, ICT employees have not become increasingly interested in union assistance. Indeed, it can be argued that, in fact, other categories of worker are developing views of workers' interests that are more or less closely similar to the views of the ICT employees reported here. In many industries, employees want a work situation geared to their private life and its changing phases. This concerns primarily working time, and it is no coincidence that unions began about a decade ago to accept a role for works councils in implementing working time arrangements at company and shopfloor level and have recently accepted a limited degree of *à la carte* choice by individual employees. So far, however, these changes have been forced upon the unions by the threat of unilateral employer initiatives and/or by the threat of declining membership, particularly among high-skilled employees and in new sectors of the economy. Unions have not modernized their concept of employment and workers' interests, and this is the main reason for the cultural gap with the views of ICT employees and highly skilled and female employees. Rather than modernizing the concept of workers' interests in relation to the traditional value of solidarity and the new value of autonomy, most unions have invested in offering new services such as financial discounts. It appears that such new services have been appreciated by the existing membership but have hardly attracted new members, and indeed why would 'new' employees join the unions for these services if they can also be obtained elsewhere?

However, some small-scale innovations have taken place which may give a hint of a more fundamental modernization. The union in the arts and audiovisual sector has opened a service for the self-employed who can delegate their tax and administrative responsibilities to a union agency, which is a free service for those who join the union and but has to be paid for by those who do not. About 10 per cent of the union membership now appears to consist of the self-employed and the union believes that this positive tally is related to the fact that it is actively establishing itself as a combination of both union and professional association. In promoting this identity the union broadens the concept of employment to embrace not only the traditional wage dependency of workers but also professional interests, and this obviously appeals to the sense which the self-employed make of themselves. Another innovation may be found in the structure of the collective agreement in the graphics sector, which has been transformed into a multi-tiered framework agreement. At the sectoral level the agreement establishes only minimum levels of pay and social provisions (such as social security, training and labour market policies), the parameters of working hours and related minimum compensation. In addition, the sectoral agreement specifies procedural rules for collective bargaining at lower levels, namely the subsector and workplace level. At these levels, negotiations cover improvements in employment conditions, which may involve substantive changes of sectoral level rules on the conditions required for employees to give consent to be covered by the agreement in question. That is, it is the employees themselves who, directly or through their works council representatives, may be involved in negotiations at workplace level and who decide for themselves whether or not they want to be assisted by union officials. This concept of a multi-tiered framework agreement explicitly derives from a perspective that attempts to combine solidarity (at sectoral level) with autonomy (at workplace level), and has been welcomed as a sound arrangement by both employers and employees since its introduction in 1997. The structure of the graphics sector agreement resembles the type of company agreement which some IT firms have concluded with trade unions (Van Liempt and Van Uffelen, 2000). For instance, the IT firm Roccade was successful in managing the diversity of internal agreements that previously existed in the software houses, out of which it grew, through the introduction of a framework agreement. This offers the scope for choice and tailor-made arrangements at the unit, workplace and individual level, and was refined in collaboration with the works councils and the employees through intensive use of meetings, e-mails and other communication media (Van Liempt and Van Uffelen, 2000).

These examples show that a substantial modernization of collective bargaining frameworks and understandings of workers' interests is possible, and they confirm that a multi-track strategy of collective bargaining, co-determination and direct participation can take place in situations where they were perhaps least expected. As yet these remain rare cases, but they may prove to be attractive examples of democratic participation well worth following.

References

Bijlsma, A. and Van het Kaar, R. (1999), 'Ondernemingsraad en arbeidsvoorwaarden', in Van het Kaar, R. and Looise, J. (eds), *De volwassen OR*, OR-informatie/Samson, Alphen aan den Rijn, pp. 151–75.

Bourdieu, P. (1987), 'What Makes a Social Class? On the Theoretical and Practical Existence of Groups', *Berkeley Journal of Sociology*, Vol. XXXII, pp. 1–17.

Christensen, S. and Westenholz, A. (1998), *Employee Representatives in Governance of Companies Participating in a Dramatic Quest*, Copenhagen Business School, Copenhagen.

Computable, FNV Bondgenoten (2000), *Werken in de ICT sector: onder welke voorwaarden?*, FNV-Pers, Amsterdam.

De Moor, W. (1995), *Teamwerk en participatief management*, Bohn Stafleu Van Loghum, Houten/Diegem.

EPOC research group (1997), *New Forms of Work Organization. Can Europe Realise its Potential?*, Office for Official Publications of the European Communities, Luxembourg.

FNV (1993), *Veelkleurige vooruitzichten*, Federatie Nederlandse Vakbeweging, Amsterdam.

FNV (1999), *Zelf kiezen? FNV-beleidsnotitie over keuzemogelijkheden in de CAO*, Federatie Nederlandse Vakbeweging, Amsterdam.

Giddens, A. (1984), *The Constitution of Society*, Polity Press, Cambridge.

Huijgen, F. and Benders, J. (1998), 'Het vallende kwartje: directe participatie in Nederland en Europa', *Tijdschrift voor Arbeidsvraagstukken*, Vol. 14, No. 2, pp. 113–27.

Hummel, R. (1998), 'Which Multimedia Jobs?', *Medien Journal*, Vol. 22, No. 1, pp. 3–12.

Hyman, R. (1996), 'Changing Union Identities in Europe', in Leisink, P., Van Leemput, J. and Vilrokx, J. (eds), *The Challenges to Trade Unions in Europe*, Edward Elgar, Cheltenham, UK and Brookfield, US, pp. 53–73.

Kester, G. (1996), 'Guiding Principles for a Strategy for Democratic Participation', in Kester, G. and Pinaud, H. (eds), *Trade Unions and Democratic Participation in Europe*, Avebury, Aldershot, pp. 35–48.

Klein, H. and Evers, D.G. (1994), *Maatschappelijke betrokkenheid van ondernemingsraden*, Ministerie van Sociale Zaken en Werkgelegenheid, 's Gravenhage.

Leisink, P. (1996), 'Trade Unions and Worker Participation in the Netherlands', in Kester, G. and Pinaud, H. (eds), *Trade Unions and Democratic Participation in Europe*, Avebury, Aldershot, pp. 95–103.

Leisink, P. (1997), 'New Union Constituencies Call for Differentiated Agendas and Democratic Participation', *Transfer*, Vol. 3, No. 3, pp. 534–50.

Leisink, P. and Spaninks, L. (1994), 'Arbeidsverhoudingen zonder collectieve regulering; het voorbeeld van de reclamebranche', *Tijdschrift voor Arbeid en Bewustzijn*, Vol. 18, No. 1, pp. 34–40.

Leisink, P., Teunen, J. and Boumans, J. (2000), *Multimedia: de pioniersfase voorbij*, GOC, Veenendaal.

Lenderink, A. (2000), 'Installing HRM', *PW*, 15 January, pp. 16–21.

LTD (1993), *Werkoverleg in het Nederlandse bedrijfsleven in 1992*, Loontechnische Dienst, Ministerie van Sociale Zaken en Werkgelegenheid, The Hague.

Michel, L. (1997), 'Qualifikationsanforderungen in der Multimediawirtschaft', in von Haaren, K. and Hensche, D. (eds), *Arbeit im Multimedia-Zeitalter*, VSA, Hamburg, pp. 41–50.

Oeij, P. and Stoppelenburg, P. (1998), *Naleving van de Wet op de Ondernemingsraden, stand van zaken 1997*, SZW/VUGA, The Hague.

Pinaud, H. (1996), 'The Role of Social Actors during Recent Developments in Worker Participation in Ten Countries of Western Europe', in Kester, G. and Pinaud, H. (eds), *Trade Unions and Democratic Participation in Europe*, Avebury, Aldershot, pp. 11–25.

Sandberg, Å. (1998), *New Media in Sweden*, Arbetslivsinstitutet, Solna.

Seifert, F. (2000), 'ICT'er wil meer dan loon en leasebak', *OR-Informatie*, Vol. 26, No. 7, pp. 30–33.

Van het Kaar, R. and Looise, J. (1999), *De volwassen OR*, OR-Informatie/Samson, Alphen aan den Rijn.

Van Liempt, A. and Van Uffelen, A. (2000), 'Arbeidsverhoudingen in ontwikkeling: het ambivalente karakter van arbeidsvoorwaardenregelingen in de ICT sector', *Sociaal Maandblad Arbeid*, Vol. 55, No. 6, pp. 244–52.

Van Rij, C. (1995), *Flexibilisering van de arbeid. Een opiniepeiling onder het FNV-Ledenpanel*, Universiteit van Amsterdam, Amsterdam.

Van Wijk, E. (2000), *Nu nog beter!?!*, Utrecht University, Utrecht.

Visser, J. (1987), *In Search of Inclusive Unionism*, Amsterdam University, Amsterdam.

Weick, K. (1995), *Sensemaking in Organizations*, Sage, Thousand Oaks/London/New Delhi.

Chapter 6

French and Italian Hospitals: the Long Road towards Autonomy

Philippe Mossé

Governments across the industrialized world are in the process of implementing wide-ranging reforms to rationalize their health systems, all of whose operations – economic, occupational, technical and social – are, as a result, undergoing major changes.

Neither France nor Italy has escaped these changes, whose pace has become much faster since the beginning of the 1990s, and which are reflected particularly in the emergence of new players and institutions. Part one of this chapter investigates the nature of these reforms undergone by French and Italian hospitals over the last 10 or so years. These reforms have gone together with structural and shorter-term developments specific to their respective labour relations systems which are themselves changing – these are analysed in part two. There has been an interaction between these two areas, namely organizational reform and labour relations, especially at the micro-level, and the broad outline of a study of this interaction, funded by DGXII of the European Commission, is reviewed in part three.

French and Italian Hospitals in the 1990s: Fundamental Reforms

France: Regionalization and its Problems

In France, a new law in 1991 placed the emphasis on budgetary and policy planning and cooperation between the state and sickness insurance funds to help match health provision with needs. Under this law, the region was seen as the relevant level for organizing health care. New bodies external to hospitals – the health agencies and conferences – were set up to oversee and monitor the introduction of these reforms.

The purpose of the national health conference, for instance, is to lay down national guidelines in respect of health and economic objectives. Meanwhile, the National Health Evaluation and Accreditation Agency (Agence Nationale d'Accréditation et d'Evaluation en Santé, ANAES) has three tasks. It is responsible for producing and disseminating the reference standards for health practices drawn up by experts, for evaluating hospital and outpatient health care and for accreditation. In order to regulate the sector, the agencies and conferences are therefore involved in an ongoing process of creating tight sets of recommendations and incentives designed to have a substantial impact on the running of hospitals. Building on these reforms, a further initiative in 1996 introduced a new player, the Regional Hospital Agency (Agence Régionale de l'Hospitalisation, ARH). Each of the 26 French regions has one of these agencies, which has responsibilities for both budgetary (quantitative) and policy (qualitative) regulation to help promote the hospital system.

Contracting is the main method being used to implement these reforms. Since 1991, each hospital has had to negotiate an establishment plan defining its medical and social priorities for the following five years. Using this plan as a basis, the statutory orders of April 1996 introduced a new procedure for regulating agreements between each hospital and the ARH. This procedure takes the form of a contract specifying objectives and resources over the five-year period. To be valid, it has to comply with the guidelines of the Regional Health Organization Plan (Schéma Régional d'Organisation Sanitaire, SROS). Taking public health priorities as a starting point, this regional plan defines needs in terms of equipment for each individual hospital. This is a dynamic procedure that encourages staff to take part in formulating the terms of the contract, which has helped, in turn, to breathe new life into existing and new consultation structures (such as the service councils and so on). Overall, it has provided a framework for the process of rationalization, underpinned by a quest for quality at a lower cost. It attempts to tap different types of expertise and competence to be found at each point in the system.

At the same time, there has been a substantial drop in the number of short-stay beds in recent years. Maternity services, for example, are a particular case in point since restructuring, involving the concentration and gradual disappearance of establishments handling fewer than 300 births per year. The disappearance of a total of 40,000 in-patient beds in the public sector and 20,000 in the private sector between 1990 and 1997 is especially surprising when it is borne in mind that there had been a massive and constant increase over preceding decades (Mossé et al., 1999).

These changes have been possible, however, only because they have gone hand in hand with changes in the role and location of hospital service provision; there has been no decline in the demand for hospitals as such. Indeed, according to DARES (the Directorate of Research, Studies and Statistics), the number of admissions continued to rise between 1983 and 1999, while capacity fell. This apparent arithmetical paradox can be explained by the continuing and spectacular drop in the average length of stay. By reducing the length of stay, and thereby substantially increasing the concentration of care required, hospitals have created new needs for aftercare and peripheral services. In France, for example, there has been a major increase in days spent in long-stay establishments.

It should not be assumed from this diversification, however, that care services are no longer the prerogative of hospitals. Indeed, the proliferation of methods of patient care is offering hospitals a much wider range of choices. In the private sector this is being reflected, for instance, in a sudden and massive increase in outpatient rather than conventional surgery. Between 1983 and 1995, surgical bed occupancy rates fell from 82 per cent to 75 per cent in the private profit-making sector. Other practices, paving the way for similar reductions, have been introduced into the public sector. External consultations have also increased steadily, reaching a figure of 50 million per year in 1997.

These changes have accompanied radical changes in hospital employment. Although over a million people nowadays work in French hospitals (in contrast with 300,000 in 1970), this growth has not been linear. From the point of view of types of employment, there has been a much greater increase in the numbers of care workers than in the numbers of technical and logistical workers.

Italy: Autonomy and the National Health Service

There have been three major reforms of the Italian health system since the mid-1970s: in 1978, 1992 and 1999. The reform to unify health care in Italy really started with the creation of the national health service under the terms of the law of 23 December 1978.

According to the opening articles of this law, this institution is defined as:

> all the functions, structures, services and activities required to promote, maintain and recover the physical and mental health of the population as a whole, without discrimination based on individual or social conditions, according to methods that ensure equal treatment of citizens by the service.

For the first time, this law introduced the principles of equality and equity into the health system in Italy. The reform that created the national health service made Local Health Authorities (Unità Sanitarie Locali, USLs) responsible for supplying hospital services and local preventative services. The geographical areas covered by the USLs corresponded directly to their parent regions responsible for the funding quota from the national health fund. This fund itself is allocated on the basis of the number of inhabitants.

The national health service is institutionally organized at three levels: the central or state level; the regional level, with powers of legislation over medical insurance, provided that the principles laid down by the state are respected; and the local, decentralized level made up of communes and 'mountain communities' (groups of small communes) that provide health services through local health units and base districts. The regions may use their own funds to supplement state funds when health expenditure on their inhabitants is greater than the funding guaranteed by the national fund. They pay their own contributions into the regional fund chiefly on the basis of the number of inhabitants covered by each health unit.

However, by the beginning of the 1990s, it had become evident that the structure of the national health service needed to be redesigned to tackle the problems brought about by the institutional and financial crisis. Legislative decree 502/1992 introduced many innovative elements. It launched, in particular, a genuine reform of the health service using an institutional and economic approach through which its continuing public nature could be made compatible with the introduction of competitive elements able to ensure greater efficiency. The innovations introduced by this second reform should be seen in this light:

- regionalization of the system, including greater autonomy in decision making and relative economic and financial responsibility for regions;
- conversion of health facilities into 'enterprises'; hospitals were thus converted into *aziende* or 'hospital trusts' and the USL became the Local Health Trusts (Aziende Sanitarie Locali, ASLs);
- introduction of a system of health facility funding based on services provided and remunerated in accordance with tariffs decided at a higher level; and
- introduction of a system of approval/accreditation and greater competition between public and private centres in order to recognize the principle of the free choice of citizens as consumers.

This paved the way for competition between public and private health facilities. The private facilities that existed alongside the public system had, after the reform, to comply with the service standards and offer the guarantees required to obtain payment, by public health facilities, for services provided to patients at the same rates as for services provided by the public sector.

The USL/ASLs are responsible for supplying health care to the population. They have their own health-care facilities, but also enter into agreements with private hospitals and services. In 1978 there were over 650 USLs, a figure that has now fallen to 220 for Italy as a whole. Since 1997, 60 per cent of hospitals have been funded by the diagnostic related group (DRG) method. This method is used to describe medical activity on the basis of the case mix. It has been gradually introduced to replace the systems based on per diem or global budgeting that were the dominant methods used to allocate resources during the 1970s and 1980s.

The third reform, introduced in 1999, builds on and refines the general principles of the preceding reform. This third health reform law entitled *Standards for the Rationalization of the National Health Service* (legislative decree 229/99) has recently been enacted, but has now been followed by a fourth one launched in mid-2001. This succession of reforms has shaped the new Italian health-care system, and in substance:

- it confirms the importance of the national health service as 'a resource by which the system meets the constitutional task of health protection';
- it continues and completes the regionalization of the system and the conversion of national health service facilities into enterprises. In this respect, decree 502/92 is amended by decree 229/99, making it compulsory for hospitals to adopt a 'private law instrument';
- it enhances the role of communes in the area of social and health planning at both regional and local levels, without transferring other responsibilities for direct management of the national health service;
- it stresses the need to promote and evaluate the quality of health-care, in particular highlighting the requirement to train workers;
- it redefines the type of contract of employment for chief medical officers; and
- it includes scientific research into health among the objectives of the national health service.

Despite this rationalization, in contrast to France, there do not seem to have been the same trends in the structure of hospital employment brought about by the increasing number of care workers. The number of public or private hospitals regulated by agreement (1,465) is falling following the closure or redeployment of facilities with fewer than 120 beds. According to data from ISTAT (the Italian National Statistical Office), the number of beds (310,000) fell by 8.6 per cent between 1992 and 1996, coming close to the objective of an average of 5.5 beds per 1,000 inhabitants. In Italy, as in most developed countries, the average length of stay has fallen substantially. Over the same period, the bed occupancy rate increased from 71 per cent to 74 per cent, while the hospitalization rate per 1,000 inhabitants increased from 158 to 162 (levels which are amongst the lowest in the European Union). There is, however, a major divide between the Centre and North and the South of Italy, where fewer beds are available (4.8 per 1,000 inhabitants) and where the bed occupancy rate is also lower (70.2 per cent). Private hospitals are therefore a basic alternative to the public sector in Southern Italy and account for between 20 and 25 per cent of total hospitalization in some regions (in comparison with a national average of 11 per cent).

Same Problems, Different Contexts

Analysis of the changes that have taken place in the French and Italian health systems reveals a number of similarities between the two countries. Over the last 20 years, the reforms introduced into each system have all been geared towards rationalization to combine control of health expenditure with the maintenance and improvement of service quality. The main features of reform from an institutional point of view are the regionalization of systems, the increased autonomy and responsibility of health facilities and the establishment of new agencies responsible for evaluation.

Meanwhile, all members of hospital staff in both the French and Italian health systems have been requested to give their points of view about what should be done to improve the next phases of development. In this new context, industrial relations are no longer seen as a system within which groups of actors are in competition to increase their share of a given and predetermined resource. From now on, the main goal of industrial relations (in the style of Dunlop, 1958) is not to define the best way to share a given cake but rather – as far as hospital regulation is concerned – to establish the best procedures to agree common goals and resolve consequent disputes. When uncertainty dominates, defining the rules of the game, as well as its goals, is the new function of the industrial relations system. In the health-care field, it is a complex matter to achieve this aim because hospitals are not conventional firms. Indeed, they are located at the heart of the welfare state and social solidarity, and constitute a costly public service where efficiency has to be demonstrated. They also constitute the workplace where, on a daily basis, a huge number of professionals are active.

Given these features, the Scenario 21 propositions have to be slightly adapted to fit the dynamics of the hospital sector (see chapter 1 of this book).

Proposition 1 The efficiency of hospital organization depends on the relative weighting of the different types of participation. The hypothesis here is that hospital performance depends on the coherence between forms of participation such as collective bargaining, codetermination, direct 'organizational' participation and financial participation (Pinaud et al., 1999) on the one hand, and the various conceptions of the hospital and its mission on the other. A commitment by trade unions to direct participation depends on prior conditions and cannot be the result of a technocratic decision.

Proposition 2 When there is no agreement about the type of targeted efficiency sought, the stress placed on quality requirements confuses hospital staff. Indeed, traditional management tools are based on quantitative indicators (such as activity indices or the number of avoidable deaths). By contrast, quality assurance processes involve interaction and coordination. As health outcomes are not easy to define in an operational way, growing levels of professional specialization tend to jeopardize the employee involvement required to achieve them.

Proposition 3 Working time and its reduction and reorganization (revealing tensions between work and home life) reflect the diversity of tasks undertaken in hospitals, which are places of both socialization and service provision. This leads to a very wide range of individual working hours. Regulated in most cases at an informal and individual level, this range is perceived by some people as a guarantee of quality and commitment, while for others it is a fairly major source of dysfunction.

In all three cases – the role of the unions, quality assurance and the organization of working time – an efficient, operational approach would lay the foundations for an agreement on procedures, rather than try and implement generalized solutions that have already been to some extent tried and tested in other socio-economic contexts (Mossé, 1997). On one hand, the similar timescale for these reforms in France and Italy is as striking as the similarity of the resources and techniques utilized for the purpose. On the other, standing back for a moment from a technocratic and managerial point of view, they seem to have been grafted on to contexts with differing histories, approaches and structures.

We should undoubtedly draw the conclusion from our brief review of these developments in France and Italy that the reforms in question are not the result of the introduction on a massive scale of new management methods. Rather, they can be seen as the different, and societally defined, impact of a wave of rationalizations on specific national features of the health services that it was vainly seeking to remove.

Industrial Relations: Autonomy and Representation

France: Nationally Defined Rules

From the point of view of internal regulation, the health sector in France has two separate mechanisms for the public and private sectors. The private sector is itself divided into two: the commercial health sector (such as private profit-making clinics, dental and medical surgeries) and the non profit-making association or mutual sector. In the public health sector, as in the public service as a whole, regulations and agreements are negotiated before the government legislates, taking the statement of conclusions agreed by the partners as its starting point.

At national level, there is no formal bargaining policy for the public health sector. There is, nevertheless, considerable scope for bargaining between the established social partners. The state intervenes in this bargaining only as a 'referee'.

Since November 1988, when there was widespread industrial unrest, there has been intensive bargaining in two main areas of the public health sector. The first area concerns working conditions. A system for evaluating initiatives to improve working conditions has been set up. This new strategy is providing the trade unions with a new legitimacy, as they are being recognized as the key player in finding solutions to actual problems as they occur. The agreement signed on 14 March 2000 by the Minister for Health and the representative trade unions, with the exception of the CGT, confirms and consolidates this policy. The second area concerns job classifications. The main issue here is one of reformulating the classification grid and of differentiating classifications as a function of occupational specialisms, and then pay increases in turn as a function of these specialisms.

As it is under state supervision, the private non profit-making sector is subject to the same operating rules as public hospitals.

In the private commercial or for-profit health sector, the social partners, both employers' organizations and trade unions, are the main players. A private hospital owner used to sign up to one of two different collective agreements negotiated by either the Private Hospital Union (Union de l'Hospitalisation Privée, UHP) or the French Federation of Private Hospital Establishments (Fédération des Etablissements de l'Hospitalisation Privée, FEHP). To facilitate staff mobility between private hospitals that are more and more often involved in mergers, the two employers' unions themselves merged in July 2001 under the name of the Private Hospital Federation (Fédération de l'Hospitalisation Privée, FHP). As a result, there is now only one collective agreement for the whole commercial health sector.

Job classifications are revised according to various criteria: degree of autonomy at work, the evolving nature of the post, the specific nature of working methods used and so on. Revisions are linked to pay scales. There have been major demands at workplace or clinic level in this area. The result is that many established work practices are difficult to call into question when they are not matched by a counterpart in terms of pay. Pay increases are, in any case, often awarded to obtain some kind of industrial peace, leaving problems concerning issues like working hours unresolved.

In each establishment, bargaining generally takes place within formal bodies: establishment-level technical committees, works councils or employee delegates in the private sector. It is compulsory for all enterprises, whether public or private, to establish a workplace health and safety committee (comité d'hygiène, de sécurité et des conditions de travail, CHSCT). This is a classic mechanism of representational or indirect participation.

The 1991 reform paved the way for two new bodies providing a new framework for participation: the Nursing Care Service Commission (Commission du Service de Soins Infirmiers, CSSI) and the Service Council (Conseil de Service). The CSSI was set up so that the nursing profession could be recognized at the level of the establishment as a whole. In achieving this, nurses now tend to act as a new counter-balance between doctors and managers. However, while the CSSI is having a fairly major impact on the formulation of the establishment plan, its impact on the relative strength of the parties involved at local level still remains to be seen.

The service council is in most cases led by a nursing executive. It was set up to provide a body for multi-occupational participation. In practice, this body is difficult to operate as the specific interests of each occupational group represented (such as nurses) tend to impede discussions and proposals. However, as service council meetings are open to the staff of the whole unit, it can be seen as an instrument for direct participation. Maybe because direct participation can also be seen as a threat to the development of trade unionism (Pinaud et al., 1999), unionists are reluctant to involve themselves in the service council.

Our analysis therefore reveals the bargaining system in France to be, generally, a centralized one (Guégan, 1995). The national framework is rigorous and represents a constraint that leaves little scope for subsectoral initiatives. Employees are little more than consumers of the bargaining 'product' and are not proactive players. This outcome is not surprising in France where employees who are not trade union members benefit from the results of bargaining in the same way as employees who are indeed union members. In the health sector, this is reinforced by the highly bureaucratic nature of the operating rules. Furthermore, over and above these institutional aspects, one of the main features of the French union landscape is the competition or even conflict between unions. Separate strategies may therefore be implemented especially at the *federal* level (that is, the national level for a given economic sector) or even at the *confederal* level (which gathers together all economic sectors at the national level).

Italy: a National Agency as a Key Actor

In Italy, the national health service has over 685,000 employees, or 24 per cent of the public service. In this sector, employment relationships and industrial relations are governed by laws and regulations that apply across all sectors of the public service. The law that regulates employment relationships and industrial relations dates from 1973. Over the years, it has been amended on many occasions, in particular by the reform of 1993, followed by other legislative amendments, the most important of which were in 1997 and 1998. All national health service employees have a contract of employment defined by a collective agreement. For all categories of health employee, such as nurses, doctors, administrative and ancillary staff, these contracts reflect regulations formulated at two levels. The national level, the pillar of the structure, corresponds to the national collective agreement. At enterprise level, managers may also have supplementary contracts specific to certain public sector services.

In the case of *normative* rules, there is a four-year cycle of negotiations. These rules govern in particular the parameters used to set pay increases in the medium term. They may include the projected rate of inflation, guarantees to protect purchasing power, general economic and labour market trends, and even aspects of competitiveness and growth specific to the health sector. National *pay* rules, by contrast, follow a two-year cycle. The data used include in particular a comparison between the projected and actual rates of inflation over the previous two years, and here again the impact of monetary and fiscal policies are taken into account.

At enterprise level, bargaining takes place every four years. Bargaining covers topics separate from those discussed at national level. Local pay variations are possible. Pay increases may vary according to economic results, such as productivity, quality and competitiveness. These local variations are termed the participatory component of pay.

For employers at national level, the Agency for Public Service Bargaining Representation (Agenzia per la Rappresentanza Negoziale delle Pubbliche Amministrazioni, ARAN), which was established by law 29/1993, is the sole representative body. Its powers were strengthened by the reform of November 1997. This agency was set up to prevent direct interference by political parties in matters of collective bargaining. It follows guidelines drawn up by the employers' coordination committee (the sector committee attended by regional health administrators).

> The various administrations [such as the Ministry of Health, Ministry of Education and local government] are entitled to send specific guidelines to ARAN, before negotiations start, and must be continually kept up to date during the negotiation process. ARAN is also obliged to obtain their consent to the proposed agreement before final approval (the law refers to a favourable opinion having to be 'in place before government authorization'). For ... hospitals these powers are exercised by specialized sector committees created for the purpose. These reforms make ARAN less a technical and operational agency strictly dependent on central government and more similar to an agency in the service of the administrations it represents and by which it is also financed (Bordogna et al., 1999, p. 110).

From the point of view of employees, the players are the unions' representatives from the health sector and the confederations to which they are affiliated. The existence of unitary union representation bodies (rappresentanze sindacali unitarie, RSU) at the hospital level makes it possible to discuss and coordinate the positions that the unions should jointly adopt with respect to management. This pragmatic alliance does not abolish differences in strategy, but at the hospital level it may act as a kind of local think tank. Differences are discussed at national level and hammered out with a view to reaching a consensus, which is then expressed at local union level.

In terms of union presence, there is a general level of union density in the health sector of some 50 per cent, with much higher levels among medical and non-medical managers (between 65 and 70 per cent). Levels are traditionally very high and in practice involve close to half the public sector. There are also unions that are not affiliated to the three largest confederations (CGIL, CISL and UIL). These are the so-called 'autonomous unions', which are often organized on occupational or even corporatist lines and not according to the principle of the sector or subsector like those affiliated to the CGIL, CISL and UIL.

Occupational unions are significant among non-management staff (over 22 per cent of elected representatives on the works councils), and account for the vast majority of managers and even more so of doctors, for whom there are few trade unions affiliated to the largest confederations. Among employees such as nurses and technical staff, there are 101 trade unions of this type. There are a further 80 among doctors and 43 among non-medical managers. However, most of these 224 organizations account for less than 0.1 per cent of the total bargaining delegations in the three groups mentioned above. Furthermore, because of their diversity, they raise problems of recognition and balance within the overall labour relations system.

These problems have been recently regulated by new rules on representativeness. Law 396/97 makes representativeness subject in practice to a double criterion of membership and electoral results in the RSU. The threshold has been set at 5 per cent. The aim was to bring the number of representative organizations down to some five or six per occupational category. The first elections under this new system were held at the end of 1998, when there was a very high turnout (ranging from 75 to 80 per cent). At the level of national bargaining, there are now four 'first-level' or federal unions and five confederations representing employees; nine 'first-level' unions and nine confederations representing doctors; and seven 'first-level' unions and six confederations representing administrative management.

The first agreements concluded under national collective bargaining were planned to cover the period 1998–2001 across the following areas:

- pay increases linked to the rates of inflation projected by the government and parliament, supplemented at decentralized level by negotiation of the 'participatory' component of pay;
- development of participation and consultation over enterprise reorganization programmes and the application of the new job classification system;

- a new job classification system reducing the number of grades from eight to four with the possibility of pay advancement per grade; and
- flexibility and reductions in working hours accompanied by incentives for part-time working according to guidelines contained in the general agreement. This area includes the reduction of working time enabling staff working '3/8' hours systems or hours alternating over several weeks to reduce their hours from 36 to 35 per week.

Participation and Reform: the Odd Couple?

Health reforms implemented in France and Italy reflect a long history of turbulence between the state (or its agencies) and the unions. However, throughout this history, one thing has remained clear: the national level is perceived by all the industrial relations actors as the most efficient at which to pursue simultaneously both efficiency and fairness. This perception is now changing, but only rather slowly.

The key dynamics that underpin this change have something to do with information, not only its quality but also its distribution among the principal industrial relations actors. Theoretically speaking, a decentralized decision-making process has to be based on a widescale and fair distribution of information among the actors involved. The perfectly competitive market is merely the illustration of this axiom. Of course, we are aware that, in fact, such an axiom is an academic dream (or nightmare): in the real world, markets need institutions. However, in terms of trends, one may assume that decentralization goes hand in hand with a fairer distribution of information about prices, resources, options, futures and so on. However, this is obviously not the case in the health-care market and all attempts to transform it into a 'quasi market' have failed in one way or another. The British experiment is, from this point of view, very enlightening (France, 1998). Many examples can be given of the discrepancies between the role that devolved actors are expected to play on the one hand and the information they require for this purpose on the other.

In Italy, there is such a discrepancy between the information held by the Italian *aziende* and the data they need to define their own strategies. In fact, data on population needs in terms of public health are not available for a given hospital. As a result performance indicators deal mainly with internal, if not financial, aspects of hospital activity. As far as direct participation is concerned, the problem is as difficult, though it is rather different. Direct participation is now implemented through management instruments (such as quality assurance) and pay individualization. However, the traditional unions do not see it as a step towards joint management. Indeed, hospital staff, who are actually involved in direct participation, see it rather as a way for managers to carry out changes required for economic reasons.

Furthermore, in 2000, a reform of the methods for allocating resources for health care among regions and urban areas took place in Italy. Following the launch of this fourth reform, the regions have to spend on health care what the state defines as being an 'essential and uniform level of care for all citizens', using regional resources from special taxes. To sustain the poorest regions certain redistributive procedures have been introduced. Hence the real challenge for the Italian unions, if they want to be simultaneously responsible and active, is to enter into the difficult and hazardous negotiation processes aimed at specifying what should be defined as appropriate, relevant and indeed essential for inclusion in the basket of health consumption indices.

In France, the information asymmetry centres mainly on the negotiations between each hospital and the regional hospital agency (ARH). In many respects, and at first sight, the regional agency, which is in charge of allocating the resources among hospitals, has more information and power than the individual hospital. However, the situation is actually not so simple. First, hospital managers and medical staff can hide information about performance. By dealing with the rather complex links between treated diagnosis and operating costs, hospital managers control the basis of the whole information system. Second, hospital actors may discover extra resources, for example, from private or 'para-public' activities such as clinical trials or private ventures. In this way, they may purchase resources exceeding the global budget they receive through the formal procedures. As the agency theory predicts, given the lack of efficient incentives, information asymmetries may well benefit the hospital.

In this game, union representatives are facing a classic dilemma in both France and Italy. If they adopt a strategy consisting of being involved in routine, daily management, they will gain access to relevant information but, at the same time, they will risk being seen by their members as no longer fully involved in protecting their immediate interests. This cooperative position will be even more uncomfortable if tough decisions have to be taken, such as the closure of certain activities or lay-offs. However, if unions decide not to get into the management game, they will be seen as marginal actors in hospitals that are increasingly considered to be market driven. Facing such health-care reforms, unions have to evolve.

At a confederal level, in Italy as well as in France, the way the welfare state is changing is a real issue. Here, many dimensions of union philosophy and activity are concerned, which spread well beyond the boundaries of health care alone. Indeed, unions are aware of two major changes: the relationships between unions are changing and in some cases new unions have arisen. For instance, with respect to the former point, in Italy, a restructuring of public sector unions has occurred within the CISL. The health-care sector now forms part of the new organization that embraces all public services. This new organization has been created to manage the restructuring process of the entire public sector more efficiently and also to promote general interest in those public companies within which the processes of individualization and competition are becoming more acute.

In France, the historical divisions between the major union confederations (CGT, FO and CFDT) have been intensified during the reform process. Following the strikes and demonstrations that occurred in 1995, CGT and FO joined efforts to fight against the reforms. In fact, this strange alliance was merely tactical and therefore proved transitory. At the same time, because their national executive and most representatives were mainly in favour of the Juppé plan (launched in April 1996), CFDT was seen as helping the then right-wing government to attack the French welfare state. However, CFDT opinion with respect to the reform plan was more complex than attributed by its opponents. In fact, the economic reform and policy of decentralization were believed to be an efficient weapon to delay the entry of private commercial actors into the health-care market and to improve the role of local levels. In the area of hospital management, the reform was also seen as a good way to challenge the power of doctors, and thereby increasing the decision power of other professionals, such as nurses and managers, who are closer to the CFDT.

In this process, new trade unions were created using the claims submitted by civil servants on pensions and wages and opponents inside the CFDT as a lever. At first sight, these groups are little more than pseudo-unions created on a very narrow and corporatist basis. However, while it is true that in terms of votes they do not have much strength, the new collective behaviour they represent is more sophisticated. In fact, these new unions (syndicats solidaires, unitaires et démocratiques, or SUD) challenge the traditional unions in two ways. First, they benefit from clear professional identities within the hospital sector and, second, they have gained legitimacy, at least in some areas where CFDT used to be strong.

Union Representation

If the crisis in trade unionism is assessed against quantitative indicators such as the turnout in elections or the proportion of votes cast for the traditional and multi-sector unions, it would seem that it has not really affected the Italian and French hospital sectors. In the French health sector staff, for example, turnout in works council elections is very high. During the 1999 elections, 449,886 of the 702,021 people registered did, indeed, vote (70 per cent). In Italy, the voting turnout in 1997 was even higher (75 per cent).

During the last elections in French and Italian hospitals, the breakdown of votes between the main unions was as follows:

Table 6.1   Breakdown of works council votes in French and Italian hospitals

France (1999)   CGT: 30.59%   CFDT: 28.63% FO: 23.69%   Others: 15%

Italy (1997)   CGIL: 27.61% CISL: 31.9 % UIL: 15.17%   Others: 25.31%

In both countries we observe a similar breakdown of votes by representative union. Despite fairly small numbers of members, these results seem to show that the bodies taking part in bargaining are representative of the 'grass roots'. Voting among managers, however, was very different. In France, managers voted largely for the majority and multi-sector trade unions. Employees such as nurses, clerical or technical staff, similarly generally voted for one of the three main unions. In Italy, however, most managers (76 per cent) voted for managers' trade unions whose main feature is that they are occupational rather than sectoral.

In France, each union decides what stance to take according to its traditional background and views. There is no joint forum for debating particular issues in an attempt to reach a common union position. At both local and national levels, therefore, each union adopts its own specific position. The RSU provides Italy, however, with an industrial relations system whose local focus is to find a consensus or at least some kind of reconciliation based on compromise among the unions. The French culture of conflict therefore seems to contrast markedly with the Italian culture of consensus.

Reduction of Working Time, Efficiency and Participation: Contrasting France and Italy

The aim of the comparative study[1] launched in February 1999 was precisely to analyse how these two contrasting industrial relations systems have in practice responded in the light of the reforms taking place in hospitals across France and Italy. For this purpose, three hospitals were chosen in each of the two countries.

The methods used have been shaped by two requirements. Firstly, it was necessary to involve hospital trade unionists in the study as it was taking place and, secondly, the co-researchers from France and Italy had to be able to compare analyses and results as they were being processed. The research team included some 20 or so people answering to a steering group of eight (French and Italian trade unionists and researchers).

From an empirical point of view, the study makes use of two sets of data. The first includes national statistics and information on the French and Italian hospital sectors (on areas like the structure and development of the supply of health resources, staffing, changes in the methods of regulation, financing and operations). The data available were used to build up a general picture of the economic and social circumstances of hospitals in the two countries. The second data set includes chiefly monographs that were drawn up on three establishments in each country and refined throughout the study. For this purpose 'objective' data (on for example patient and staff profiles) were compared with qualitative data drawn from interviews with the main players in the hospital and health-care services (such as administrators, care staff and trade unionists).

As we have seen, the health systems of the countries covered by the study, and in particular their hospital systems, have undergone far-reaching change. Past investigations carried out by researchers working with trade unionists[2] show that these changes can be classified in four key dimensions defining the framework of problems to be addressed by the study.

- The first dimension is the *opening up* of hospitals to their environments. Whether this involves partnerships, networks or other forms of cooperation, this openness is now a key feature of hospital organization.
- The second key dimension revealed by the study is that of the *cohesion* of hospital organization. This is both a variable and a strategic issue that may be in conflict with the economic imperatives of flexibility and competition.

- This leads on to a third dimension of hospital activity, which is at the core of the study: professional *legitimacy and expertise*. Mandarin-style (or feudal) behaviour is far from having disappeared from the hospital world. With technical and legislative reforms, however, the 'nature' of power in hospitals is changing to provide scope for a wider range of actors.
- Lastly, located in some ways at the crossroads of occupational practices and the industrial relations system, is the rise of *corporatism* as a key factor in the current dynamics of organizational change – a challenge for all the established players.

In each hospital, one important and recent organizational change was studied, such as the implementation of a quality approach and/or a reorganization of activities accompanying a reorganization, and often a reduction, of working time.

In order to structure the analysis, a composite selection of answers to 30 of the questions felt to be the most important from the point of view of the research hypotheses and the main themes addressed was drawn up:

- the impact of change on work organization;
- relationships with the external environment;
- the quality and organization of work; and
- the place of the trade unions in the changes.

Three main findings emerged from this initial analysis. In overall terms, they characterize the changes observed in the 14 departments (or units), and the perceptions that hospital workers have of them.

Increased workload In the six hospitals taken as a whole, 42 per cent of workers considered that their work had increased since the organizational change had been implemented. Furthermore, data on hospital activity reveal in all hospitals but one a reduction in the average length of patient stay. As a fall in length of stay automatically results in a heavier work load (because of an increase in patient turnover), it is not surprising that 70 per cent of the staff felt that the change had done little to improve their working conditions, given that staff numbers had remained the same.

Few changes in work practices This tendency was illustrated by the fact that 60 per cent of the respondents felt that their external environment had remained unchanged; a similar proportion (65 per cent) felt that their tasks had not 'really' changed. Thus it seems that for a majority of staff members, the main outcome of the change has been to increase average productivity without much benefit for them.

A relative trade union presence Only 50 per cent of respondents felt that the trade unions had been informed of the changes and only between 30 per cent and 40 per cent of the respondents felt, depending on the question, that the trade unions had been involved in decision making.

Cross-matching was also carried out to highlight differences in responses by hospital department, occupation and country. The *hospital department* variable was significant in 84 per cent of cases. Depending on the variables, the types of department responsible for the differences were not the same. Generally, surgical and casualty departments differed from other departments, especially with respect to the external environment. Laboratories also gave different answers. As far as the trade unions were concerned there were few differences, although workers in ophthalmology and paediatrics (who also mentioned change less frequently) more often judged the roles of the trade unions in a more positive light. Fairly surprisingly, as far as *occupations* were concerned, the differences in the responses were often insignificant between for instance nurses and others. When differences could be noted, it appeared that managers and doctors gave more optimistic opinions than nurses about the impact of change. Overall, the *country* variable was often very discriminating: the differences in the responses between French and Italian respondents were statistically significant for 58 per cent of the questions. For instance, changes leading to more intensive work were mentioned more often by Italians. More of the French respondents felt that the situation had not changed or had improved. The French considered that the trade unions were generally active and favourable, whereas the Italians felt them to be less involved or more inconsistent.

Conclusions

The role and behaviour of the trade unions are modifying in several ways as a result of economic and social change. As far as health-care reforms are concerned in France and Italy, the main challenge to the unions has something to do with the boundaries or frontiers issue. First, the location of power is shifting from the central to the regional level. Second, hospitals are themselves breaking down boundaries and increasingly dealing directly with social services, primary health-care agencies, such as family doctors, and other hospitals. Health-care networks are the future frameworks for professional activities. These new developments require workers with the specialisms and status necessary to facilitate professional mobility and flexibility. However, the unions are not yet prepared for such a cultural revolution. As a result, they have to adapt their organization as well as their way of thinking about the reforms themselves.

With this in mind, the ongoing research has already cast some insights into the way in which similar issues are tackled in different contexts. Two examples of such differences between the ways in which French and Italian unionists regard the near future of their respective hospital systems can be given by reference to the research methodology itself.

Perceptions of the Relationships between Unions

When the survey and the questionnaire were initially being drawn up, researchers formulated one of the questions as follows: 'What is the position of the trade union on the change in question?'. From this functionalist point of view, the trade union is seen as a single player whose aim is to maximize its influence by increasing its density of membership. The French trade union delegates proposed that the term 'trade union' should be used in the plural, since the use of the singular for all unions seemed to them to reflect an old view of trade unionism. For the Italians, the singular was less of a problem since the RSU made it possible to assimilate the unions into a single body, which is pluralist by nature. In Italy, where there is an apparent culture of consensus, it might be expected that the RSU occupies a position of strength. In France, by contrast, conflicts between unions at local level should make their influence more fragile. Discussions in the research group showed, however, that the themes actually addressed were perhaps not so different.

Professional Identity of Nurses

In several of the research questions, the term 'paramedical', widely used in French, was used to designate non-medical care workers. However, the Italian members of the research group felt that this term could be seen as pejorative (FIST Report, 1999), though it did not raise any particular problems for the French union representatives.

In France, the demand for overall responsibility for patients has to some extent been met by the new definition of the nursing function (law of 31 April 1978). Work under medical prescription is undoubtedly still paramount (such as caring, performance of prescribed tasks and operation of equipment). Alongside, however, there is also a 'personal role', which complements the preceding role, where patients are perceived as a whole and not just from the point of view of their pathology (Acker, 1991; Michelangeli et al., 1993). In France, as in Italy, the status of nurses is following the same path somewhere between corporatism on the one side (having their own professional organizations) and unionism on the other (defending their rights alongside those of other occupations). However, only in Italy have nurses obtained improvements in their training programmes, which are now more closely linked than in France to the universities. The ratio between nurses and care assistants is four times higher in favour of nurses in the three Italian hospitals than in the three French hospitals.

As far as the Scenario 21 propositions are concerned, the hospital sector example shows that the problems unions are facing are rather similar in both countries in terms of level of activity, areas of intervention and balance between direct and indirect participation. However, one of the main issues and future challenges will be to combine national characteristics based on historical trajectories with the process of European integration that will lead, to a greater or lesser extent, to international strategies at a supranational level.

Notes

1   This study, known by the acronym Refipar (for 'Recherche France-Italie sur la Participation'), was funded by the Commission of the European Communities (DGXII) under the TSER (Targeted Socio-Economic Research) programme. It started in February 1999 and finished in February 2002. For further information about the study and health reforms in France and Italy, see working document LEST CNRS, 2000.

2   This research was conducted under the Scenario 21 programme thanks to assistance from the Commission of the European Communities (DGV). It brought researchers and trade unionists together from various economic sectors to work on the question of direct participation in France, Germany and Italy. The aim was to demonstrate whether, and under what social, economic and occupational conditions, this form of involvement had, on the one hand, become necessary for enterprise efficiency and, on the other, enhanced or weakened the power and the role of the trade unions (Pinaud, 1997).

References

Acker, F. (1991), 'La fonction de l'infirmière. L'imaginaire nécessaire', *Sciences Sociales et Santé*, Vol. 9, No. 2, June, pp. 123–43.

Bordogna, L., Dell'Aringa, C. and Della Rocca, G. (1999), 'Italy: A Case of Co-ordinated Decentralization', in Bach, S., Bordogna, L., Della Rocca, G. and Winchester, D. (eds), *Public Service Employment Relations in Europe*, Routledge, London, pp. 94–129.

Dunlop, J. (1958), *Industrial Relations Systems*, Holt, New York.

FIST Report (1999), *Materiale a cura di D.ssa Filanino Cristina*, November, CISL, Rome.

France, G. (1998), 'Health-care Quasi-Markets in a Decentralized System of Government', in Bartlett, W., Roberts, J. and Le Grand, J. (eds), *A Revolution in Social Policy. Quasi-Market Reforms in the 1990s*, Policy Press, Bristol, pp. 155–73.

Guégan, L. (1995), *Le contractuel: un moyen ou une stratégie pour la CFDT*, working paper, Paris, CFDT.

Kester, G. and Pinaud, H. (eds) (1996), *Trade Unions and Democratic Participation in Europe*, Avebury, Aldershot.

LEST CNRS (2000), *Refipar: un an déjà*, April, Aix en Provence.

Michelangeli, C., Branciard, A. and Mossé, P. (1993), 'L'infirmière: de la gratitude à la reconnaissance', *Revue Etudes*, March, pp. 317–26.

Mossé, P. (1997), 'Le lit de Procuste; l'hôpital: impératifs économiques et missions sociales', Editions ERES, Ramonville.

Mossé, P., Gervasoni, N. and Kerleau, M. (1999), 'Les restructurations hospitalières; enjeux, acteurs, stratégies', September, Lest/MiRe, Paris.

Pinaud, H. (1997), 'La coopération syndicats/recherche', *Education Permanente*, Vol. 131, No. 2, pp. 173–81.

Pinaud, H., Le Tron, M. and Chouraqui, A. (eds) (1999), *Syndicalisme et démocratie dans l'entreprise*, L'Harmattan, Paris.

Chapter 7

New Management Systems and Worthwhile Work: the Swedish Experience[1]

Christofer Edling and Åke Sandberg

In this chapter we intend first to analyse 'new management' as a concept, and break it down into a certain number of elements as regularly found in the discourse of both popular books on management and more research-oriented texts on new forms of management, work practices and flexible organization. Second, we investigate the extent to which we find those different elements in practice in Swedish firms, and third we analyse the relationship between new forms of management and outcomes in terms of competitiveness and quality of work or worthwhile jobs. These perspectives and data present essential preconditions for trade unions and democratic participation in 'the new working life'. The underlying thesis of this chapter is that 'new management' is spreading widely and comes with promises of new forms of work organization, worthwhile jobs and greater influence for workers.

New Management is Spreading ...

Management and work organization are being transformed. Flat and flexible organizations, decentralization and richer job content in companies managed by means of corporate culture and goals are replacing pyramid-shaped companies with their Taylorist division of labour and detailed control systems. The background to these developments is a competitive, world product market that requires adaptation to the various demands from customers, and a labour market with employees demanding quality of work. Fordist standardized mass production for mass markets belongs to history. Through such transformations, the goals of employees – good jobs – can be achieved alongside the goals of management – good business. This apparent harmony between goals and interests provides a basis for cooperative labour relations, because we find ourselves in a win/win situation. This seems to put an end to conflicts of interest and an end to the history of industrial relations.

This is – in a condensed form – the narrative or discourse that we frequently encounter in popular management literature and debate, among consultants and in policy documents from the social partners and governments. It is a discourse that centres on de-bureaucratization and on an ongoing shift from Taylorism, Fordism and centralized hierarchies in the direction of flexible organization, post-Fordism, flattened pyramids and networking among firms. Local adaptation takes place within goals and standards set in benchmarking processes that are to a growing extent international in scope. The 'new forms of management' bring with them and require new forms of work organization with more demanding jobs and the 'empowerment' of employees. Overall, then, the assumption is that new jobs are good jobs.

... and Creating a Win/Win Situation

Of special interest is the postulation of a win/win situation with the new forms of work and organization simultaneously meeting the goals of employers and employees. To us, the latter means having worthwhile jobs, that is, jobs requiring good qualifications, a high degree of control and social support. We want to test this relationship empirically rather than take it for granted as a piece of rhetoric regarding a 'new era in work' and 'innovation'. For example, group or teamwork may be 'worthwhile work' provided that there is, among other things, a high degree of employee control over pace and tasks – otherwise the result may be negative group pressure, stress and health problems.

In many of the popular management texts, it is unclear whether they are intended to represent a description of the current situation in the economy and working life, or a possible and desired future, and if the latter, what the necessary preconditions would be for its realization. It is also unclear to what extent the ideas and elements of 'new management' really are new. Be that as it may, the massive bombardment of those ideas makes it important to test them empirically for both practical and theoretical reasons, over and above the selected case studies generally drawn on by their exponents.

Does New Management bring Participation at Work?

We are also interested in the relationship between new forms of management with employee involvement, 'empowerment', participation and strategic dialogue on the one hand, and with democratic participation in working life and the economy on the other. Democratic participation presupposes an articulation between levels, with links between the individual, the workplace and the wider economy, in short a multi-level integrated system of industrial relations (Sandberg, 2002b). There is a need for representative democratic institutions – that is trade unions, works councils and other associations – that contribute to creating conditions for participation by all workers in decision making at all levels from daily work routines to company matters. There is a similar need for a form of work organization that enhances the development of skills and control for everyone and not just the few. We are far from such a situation today. New management does not automatically or generally generate worthwhile jobs for all, nor democratic participation. Other studies show that representative participation can go hand in hand very well with direct employee involvement in for instance group work (EPOC, 1997; Sisson, 2000). We find that the situation in today's working life, like that of yesterday's, is contradictory and full of ambiguities as developments are uneven. Taylor and hierarchies are indeed still found in the network society.

The Origins of the 'New': Scandinavian Working Life and US Management

In discussing the thesis of a radical breach with Taylorism and Fordism, we shall be referring to Swedish cases, but also to international material. There are reasons for the weight given here to Swedish experience. Swedish working life in general and Volvo in particular have been icons of 'the new working life'. Among researchers, politicians and trade unionists, and also among many managers in Europe and internationally, Sweden has been seen as an avant garde example of how to create human and productive organizations. In both sociological and management texts, the Volvo Kalmar and Uddevalla plants have been used to illustrate that 'something different' is possible.

Today, however, Sweden and its image as a pioneer in social and working life have been 'normalized' as a result of international pressures and benchmarking, slower economic growth and a subsequent loss of self-confidence, as the models, both national and workplace, lost part of their attractiveness. There are, however, still differences due to the inertia of institutional divergences which are also maintained by the mechanism of international companies making full use of such differences when localizing production. In another domain Sweden has been heralded over the last couple of years as the information and communications technology and internet industry hub of Europe (for an empirical survey of the Swedish internet sector, see Sandberg and Augustsson, 2002).

As a rule, we write 'companies' even though perhaps we should use the more general term 'organizations' as our data also cover governmental and voluntary organizations. The choice of words reflects the origins of the managerial thinking that dominates today, essentially that of major US consultancy companies. In Sweden today nine out of the 10 largest management consultancy firms are US owned, most of them originating from the Boston area (Björkman, 2002). 'New management' is not just a question of words, but concepts that are traded by major consultants in an effort to implement them across all sectors of the economy, including the public sector. The quality of, for example, health care and education are threatened when professional values and expertise are completely subordinated to economic goals within a neo-liberal framework through the introduction of new business concepts. In the public sector at least it should be the other way around (Gustafsson, 1994; von Otter, 2002). Henceforth we shall refer to new management (without quotation marks). But how new, and how great its impact, will be kept open for a while.

New Management and Work Organization: Elements of a Discourse

Our previous work (Edling and Sandberg, 1996; Sandberg et al., 1992; Sandberg, 1995; 2002a), together with a survey of theoretical and empirical studies (Sandberg, forthcoming), provide sufficient ground for us to elaborate concepts and systematize what we mean by new forms of management, new work organization and new labour relations. A vast number of the features of these terms recur in various management texts. As is common in this genre, they reflect both observations on what has already taken place and prescriptive recommendations to companies. Be that as it may. The empirical foundation for management philosophies and instruments is often unclear, yet this does not prevent us from studying the actual existence of managerial forms that are generally believed to have an impact on actual management practices.

Below we group together a number of elements and features that we have come across in the literature on new management. The main novelty is the emphasis on management through ideas as well as precisely defined economic objectives, rather than management through narrowly defined jobs and managers exercising direct and close control of work performance. Ideological control could be exercised by attempts to inculcate new ideas amongst the employees, but also indirectly through for instance performance-related pay systems. The 'soft' profile of new managerial methods thus also has a 'hard' side to it: the systematic monitoring of the achievement of economic targets and their related pay forms. We distinguish the following characteristics.

New Management according to Management Literature

- *The organization is flat* and has few levels. Intermediate levels are removed or reduced and major decisions are centralized while routine decisions are decentralized; the centralization aspect is not always made explicit.
- The organization is divided into *independent units oriented towards achieving explicit goals.* These units are often profit centres, that is, they are themselves responsible for contributions to company profits. The units may exist at several different levels and in various organizational forms, such as divisions, regions, departments and work teams.
- One way of controlling these units is by measuring their results and other target achievements. These *control systems* are often computer supported. The contributions of the units or profit centres are followed up by means of decentralized economic controls (including planning, budgeting and accounting systems). Other targets are also monitored: quantity and quality of products or orders, their safe delivery and so on, as well as absenteeism, staff turnover and employees' attitudes towards the company.
- *Ideological control* is particularly emphasized as the new way of controlling individuals and groups. It is essential that the 'culture' and values of management are internalized by the workers. A number of methods are usually recommended. Goals, values and entire 'corporate cultures' are conveyed and inculcated amongst the employees by inspiring and charismatic leaders, through quality circles and development groups, meetings, conferences, direct contacts between managers and subordinates, campaigns, marketing and other appearances in the mass media. In addition, on the job training and staff development may, besides contributing to an upgrading of the individual's skills and competences, serve as an instrument of motivation. Team spirit is a value but it may also create strong group pressures. Successful ideological control results in commitment to the company, its goals and activity.
- *New pay and reward structures,* which for the individual or the work team are directly related to the achievement of the company's targets or to their contribution to company profits, are also instruments of control. Examples

are payment by results, payment by competence, gratuities and bonuses, profit sharing and stock options.

An additional element is the *breaking up of the traditional relationship between the employer and the employee* through new forms of organizing production such as franchising, outsourcing, subcontracting and agency work. In our empirical study, however, there are no data on this aspect. This aspect is related to numerical flexibility of the workforce, whereas we, in the next section, focus on functional or task flexibility.

The Character of Work and Labour Relations

Among forms of new work organization may be counted teamwork, career ladders within a job (as distinct from careers leading to other generally management jobs), on the job training, decentralization of decisions concerning routine operations, and the workers' own control of pace and intensity. Qualification requirements and the distribution of training activities are signs of whether there are, or whether there is the intention is to create, jobs with development potential for *everyone* within the company. One of the results of the integration of work tasks, especially vertical integration, could be small and decreasing differences between blue-collar and white-collar jobs, respectively.

A general hypothesis in management literature is that with new management there follow more *cooperative relations* between employers and union organizations, above all in questions concerning the company's general operations. Wage negotiations remain but become more decentralized and individualized.

Under which Conditions do we find New Management?

As a rule, both in the management and social science literature, the emergence of new forms of management and organization are explained by conditions in the product and labour markets. A product market with intensive competition and varied demand, which makes customer orientation necessary, is thought to promote new forms of management and possibly also new forms of work organization. A labour market reflecting high expectations from a well-trained workforce is also assumed to contribute to similar transformations. Swedish debates have also indicated full employment and an active labour market policy as driving forces for developments in work organization (Meidner,

1991). Meanwhile, decentralized decision making, the broadening of work tasks and the delegation of work to groups have been strong and consistent demands from the unions. However, the unions have been sceptical about a number of the new forms of managerial control, such as individualized wages determined at management's discretion and quality circles and other sorts of off-line problem-solving groups.

Empirical Analysis and Results

Studies of new management strategies in Sweden have often been conducted as case studies (see, for example, Alvesson, 1989; Beckérus et al., 1988; Bélanger et al., 1999; Edström et al., 1989). We shall now proceed to investigate this area by means of the Workplace Survey's interviews with managers in a cross-sectional survey of all workplaces in Sweden (see Appendix to this chapter for further details of methods). The nature of this kind of data forces us to be less fine-tuned in our analysis than is usual in case studies. The benefit of the data from the Workplace Survey is that they help us to gauge the extent to which new managerial forms are in practice distributed across working life in Sweden, as well as to assess their relationship to the quality of work of the employees concerned. Until the follow-up study carried out in 2001 and 2002 has been reported, we are unable to study change over time in the managerial patterns found, nor can we discover the moment at which such patterns break through. It may be that we are here dealing simply with ideas that still, at the time of the survey, had not yet had the level of impact expected. If we do not find a breakthrough for new management practices, then another interpretation may be that the discourse of new management is based on a number of specific companies that have received disproportionate attention in previous research and popular management literature, and that we have been misled by a few well-publicized cases (see also Osterman, 1994). There may be a tendency in popular discourse, and especially in that of management consultants, to exaggerate the degree of change and to set rather low criteria for evaluating change (Ahrne and Papakostas, forthcoming; Ahrne and Sandberg, 2000).

In the literature, the engineering industry is often said to be at the forefront of new management, and within the public sector, health care is under pressure to become customer- and market-oriented. Apart from these two sectors, we shall also investigate 'other sectors of industry' (manufacturing, except for engineering and construction), commerce/trade, banking and insurance, and public administration. We now proceed to describe each element of new management individually and then in combination, and finally in relation to outcomes in terms of competitiveness and quality at work.

Re-erecting the Pyramids?

A basic idea within new management writings is the desirability of a flat organizational structure. Management by objectives replaces direct control. Should we wish to, we could read these texts as manifestos against all kinds of bureaucratization, including hierarchical, vertical divisions of labour. And flattening the pyramids accompanies the creation of more satisfying work, according to the proponents (Carlzon, 1989; Edström et al., 1989).

Empirically, however, hierarchical organization seems to offer at the same time both better potential for development *within* the job and a greater number of *career* ladders towards other, more advanced jobs (le Grand, 1993; Perrow, 1986). It would seem that – somewhat surprisingly – several positive motivational incentives risk disappearing with the flat organization. An alternative interpretation could be that with the vertical and horizontal integration of work tasks, continuous development takes place within the job itself, a development which is not seen and perceived as 'real change' since workers feel that they are still in the 'same job'.

Ideology and Corporate Culture

Making the employees embrace management's picture of reality, goals and values constitutes one important feature of managerial thinking. However, measuring the final outcome of attempts at ideological influence requires studies of individual workers' attitudes. In the Workplace Survey we do not have such data, but we are able to trace methods designed to involve workers in the ideas and performance of the company (and we can then relate those and other methods to outcomes in terms of efficiency and work quality). A number of methods are usually recommended to create commitment: charismatic leadership, quality circles and other 'off-line' problem-solving groups, meetings at various organizational levels, induction courses, conferences, more direct interaction between managers and subordinates, campaigns and so on. Skills training may also serve as an instrument of motivation. Group spirit is a positive value, which may however also foster intense group pressures. These methods may be viewed as central to new forms of ideological control, but may also provide useful information to new employees as well as the development of competences.

However, methods entirely different from those directly aimed at ideological control may also contribute to workers' commitment to the company. One example is marketing and media appearances, which not only influence consumers but may also create positive attitudes among workers towards the company. Another example is methods of economic control that may help to mould attitudes towards the company and its profits, such as stock options and other such types of remuneration.

Within the public sector, quality circles and other such groups exist in 62 per cent of workplaces, as compared with 53 per cent in the private sector. Within individual sectors, quality circles exist in less than half the establishments in commerce (41 per cent) and public administration (44 per cent). The engineering industry has quality circles in over half of its workplaces (56 per cent), whereas the health-care sector is at the forefront, with quality circles or development groups in two thirds of its establishments. Quality circles and the like are therefore fairly common in Swedish establishments, and this can be taken as a sign of the impact of new management type ideas.

Another form of contact between management and workers is human resource planning and staff development interviews. Class-oriented differences are greatest within the private sector, where some 95 per cent of the companies use staff development interviews for high-ranking white-collar workers, as compared with 65 per cent for blue-collar workers. Within the public sector, this disproportion is considerably less with a difference of approximately five percentage points between white-collar and blue-collar workers. For the latter category, staff development interviews are found in over 80 per cent of workplaces.

Figure 7.1 shows the existence of induction courses lasting one day or more. Major differences exist between the private and public sectors. At private-sector workplaces, white-collar workers enjoy most of the induction training whereas mainly blue-collar workers attend such courses in the public sector. This could perhaps be explained by the fact that the percentage of white-collar workers with professional skills is higher in the public sector (above all in health care) and that they do not require any particular induction as their work tasks have already been clearly defined in their training. Close to 60 per cent of workplaces in the health-care sector lay on induction courses for blue-collar workers, while the corresponding figure for the engineering industry is over 30 per cent.

If induction courses were used as a means of inculcating company goals and ideology into workers in accordance with new management thinking, then they ought to be more evenly distributed between blue- and white-collar workers

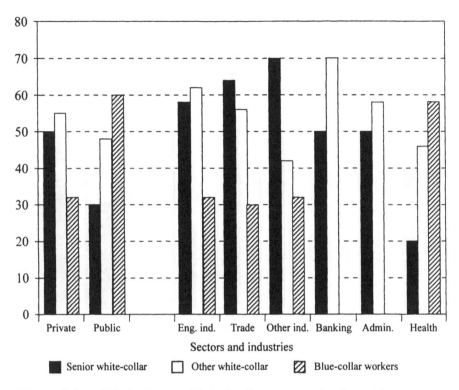

Figure 7.1   Workplaces with induction courses lasting at least one day (percentages)

in the private sector. Induction training alone could not therefore be seen as an indicator of new management. To qualify as indicators of ideological control, quality circles, induction courses and on-the-job training should in our view take place together at the same workplace. They also prove to be positively correlated, but only at a moderately high level.

Elements of Economic Control

The existence of independent units at all levels of the organizational hierarchy – usually profit centres but always results-oriented – constitutes an important feature of the new managerial thinking. We are able to illustrate the problem with the question: 'Is there any unit or person below the level of top management with responsibility for profits?' Such responsibility is found in not quite two-thirds of all workplaces. The variation in this share between sectors and industries is shown in Figure 7.2.

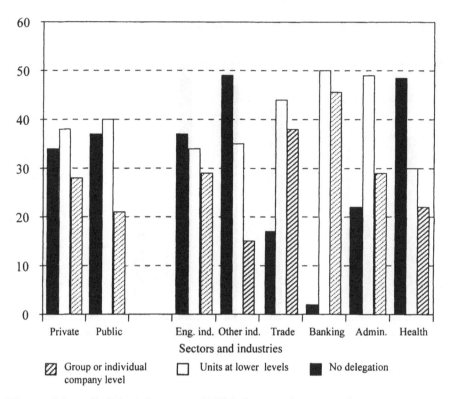

Figure 7.2   Delegated responsibility for results or profits (percentages)

Delegated responsibility for results or profits is somewhat more common within the private sector but, as we can see, the difference is small. Within the public sector, almost 40 per cent the establishments do not have such delegated responsibility. Surprisingly enough, the engineering industry is also strongly centralized in this respect. The engineering industry locates responsibility for results at group level in 18 per cent of its workplaces and at the individual company level in 11 per cent, as compared with 12 and 4 per cent respectively within 'other industry'. The difference between industrial sectors is small but nevertheless it lies in the direction that would be expected, with the engineering industry at the forefront in this respect. Within banking and insurance, nearly all workplaces have a certain degree of responsibility for results allocated to some level below top management. This is also the industry where such responsibility at group level is most common.

Performance-related pay and reward systems, together with control over results and goals (measured as contributions to company profits, quality, safety of delivery, productivity and so on), make up a central core of instruments of economic control within the new managerial thinking. Profit sharing, convertible bonds and stock options are much discussed today, but profit sharing has existed for a long time and not only in companies with new managerial ideas. These methods could be regarded as ways of securing workers' commitment to the company's overall goals, and could therefore be viewed as part of the attempt to win ideological control. Profit sharing is most frequent within banking and insurance, followed closely by commerce. Within the industrial sector, as expected, the engineering industry comes top.

The motives behind, for instance, stock options are meanwhile the same as those for profit sharing: increased productivity as a result of increased commitment to the company. With respect to stock options in particular, we conducted a study based on interviews with management and questionnaires to employees in three companies. The results demonstrate a positive correlation between employee ownership of stock options and commitment to the company. However, when keeping constant the degree to which the workers think they have a job with development potential, this correlation disappears.

Such a job with potential, rather than ownership of stock options, thus co-varies with a feeling of commitment to the company (see Figure 7.3). Stock options, convertibles and the like could by contrast be expected to contribute to an instrumental attitude: ownership as a means of making a profit on the capital markets rather than as a commitment to a specific company and its activities (Gelin et al., 1991). This example shows the importance of supplementing our study of the extent of the forms of control as reported by managers with surveys of the resulting, actual behaviour and attitudes among employees.

The question whether the workplace operates some degree of individualized pay determination according to the adaptability of the worker is used as an indicator of a new form of pay formation. The traditional view is that white-collar workers have always had individualized pay determination, characterized by negotiations or talks between individual employees and the employer based on the employee's performance, and often with considerable influence on the part of the employer over the whole process. The wages of blue-collar workers, however, have always been typically subject to collective bargaining, and here union influence has been strong at both national and workplace levels. Nevertheless, individual workers have been able to influence their actual pay, for example through piece-rates, which are performance-related but based on general, nationally negotiated rules.

As expected, individualized flexible pay setting is most common within the private sector and is used mostly for white-collar workers. This is seen in Figure

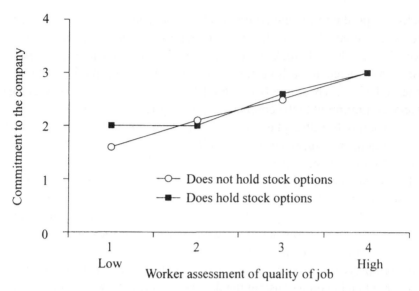

Figure 7.3   Correlation between commitment to the company, ownership of stock options, and jobs with potential

Source: Gelin et al., 1991

7.4, where we show the extent of flexible pay across sectors and industries. At 15 per cent of workplaces in health care, wages of blue-collar workers were at least to some extent influenced by flexible arrangements. Since then, further, more individualized pay determination systems have been introduced across parts of the health-care sector. Within the engineering industry, a good 70 per cent of workplaces use such wage structures for blue-collar workers. In this respect the engineering industry differs considerably from other industries.

Worthwhile Jobs

In the popular management literature, it is common to assume a harmonious relationship between new management and worthwhile jobs, and also between new management and good business. Le Grand's (1996) analysis of career prospects and development potentials within companies' internal labour markets shows that, within the individual job, they are greatest within the private sector. Coming top with respect to job development are the engineering industry and banking and insurance.

New forms of work organization imply that employees take decisions concerning routine work quite often in a team. Teamwork and integration of

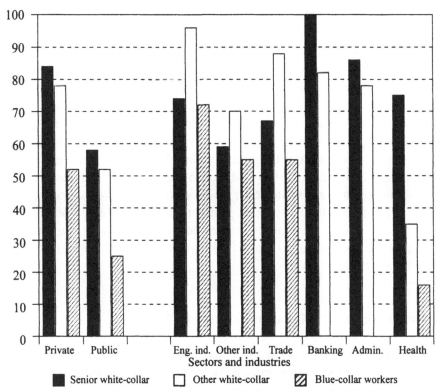

| | | Senior white-collar | | | Other white-collar | | | Blue-collar workers |

Figure 7.4   Workplaces with systems for flexible wage setting (percentages)

work tasks are expected to reduce differences between blue-collar and white-collar workers' jobs. In aggregate, 34 per cent of workplaces report that these differences have decreased. On average, only 5 per cent report an increase in the differences. The differences have decreased to a larger extent within the private sector, and again the engineering industry stands out as the most obvious exponent of new management (see, for example, Mahon, 1994 on co-worker agreements within ABB). The engineering sector is also leading in the trend towards closer cooperation between blue-collar and white-collar unions in various sectors, partly to the detriment of cooperation within the union confederations themselves, such as LO for blue-collar workers (Göransson and Holmgren, 2000).

This reduction in the differences in work content, however, is not necessarily equivalent to a development of worthwhile jobs. Reduced differences between blue- and white-collar workers should primarily favour the blue-collared, even though one result could be that important traditions of the exercise of skills might decrease in value. For white-collar workers it is by no means certain that less definite demarcation with respect to blue-collar jobs is itself equivalent to worthwhile jobs. The changes could imply that more white-collar workers will be working with broader, but less skilled, work tasks, closer to direct production and not infrequently with heavier performance pressures than for more detached staff. On the other hand, more broadly defined tasks for those working directly in the production process could mean greater support and training, and a reduced role for traditional, disciplinary supervision and control functions. While this process continues, it has in some cases become more difficult to draw the traditional demarcation lines between blue- and white-collar workers. Blue-collar workers sometimes have a relationship to management similar to that white-collar workers used to have, but in only some of those cases do they have a work situation and competence level equal to that of white-collar workers (Göransson and Holmgren, 2000).

New Management: A Coherent Strategy In Practice?

So far we have been able to show that some of the cornerstones in new management are fairly widespread in Swedish working life. In this section we shall examine whether those elements might appear simultaneously in various kinds of workplaces and market conditions and thereby indicate the existence of a new integrated management strategy. We identify nine conditions that characterize new management.

The Nine Conditions

The first four conditions are related to ideology and corporate culture. The next two cover what we have called elements of economic control. The last three conditions concern new forms of work organization. All of them relate to workplaces with at least 50 employees, due in part to the fact that some of the questions have been put to management only in the large workplaces.

We have refrained from including 'flattened pyramids' among the nine conditions. Keeping hierarchical structure outside the conditions enables us to test later on the relationship between organizational structure and the application of new managerial methods. With these nine conditions as a basis, we have constructed an index that also serves as our operational definition of new management. As already mentioned, the extent to which these elements are really new is an issue we do not investigate here; they are part of 'new management' in the sense that they are presented in management literature as such.

Workplaces should have the following ideological control elements:

1　quality circles or other 'off-line' problem-solving and development groups;
2　induction courses lasting more than one whole day;
3　on-the-job training for at least a small number of employees over the previous year;
4　staff development interviews.

In addition, the following elements of economic control must exist:

5　responsibility for results located below top management level;
6　flexible pay determination (to some extent).

Work should further be organized so that:

7　decisions concerning work tasks to be performed are to some extent taken by workers themselves;
8　decisions on how to perform tasks are to some extent taken by workers themselves;
9　differences between blue- and white-collar workers are reduced.

How Common is a New Management Strategy?

By summing up these conditions we have generated an index that we claim indicates the use of methods of new company management and work organization. This index will be interpreted so that the larger the number of conditions met, the higher the degree of new management at the workplace. Table 7.1 and Figure 7.5 show the distribution of conditions fulfilled for new management by sector, industry and workplace size. Purely at random, 1.7 per cent of all workplaces should meet all nine conditions – in fact, a few more do so. As the table indicates, the observed percentage of workplaces fulfilling all nine conditions is somewhat higher (2.2 per cent). It is also obvious that there are large variations between different types of workplace.

The new management strategy is most common within the private sector, where over one-quarter of the establishments meet seven or more conditions.

Table 7.1 Number of conditions fulfilled by sector, type of industry, and workplace size (N=668)

Conditions	Private	Public	Eng.	Other	Trade	Health	All	50–99	100–499 employees	500+
0–3	17.6	14.2	13.8	12.2	26.4	14.0	15.9	27.0	16.4	5.0
4–6	52.2	64.1	43.7	60.9	56.8	68.2	58.0	54.9	60.9	55.9
7	19.0	12.6	21.4	18.9	12.6	13.4	15.9	12.7	15.2	20.1
8	7.6	8.3	13.9	5.0	4.1	4.4	7.9	5.4	5.1	15.1
9	3.6	0.8	7.1	3.0	0.0	0.0	2.2	0.0	2.4	3.9
Total	100.0%	100.0%	100.0%	100.0%	100.0%	100.0%	100.0%	100.0%	100.0%	100.0%

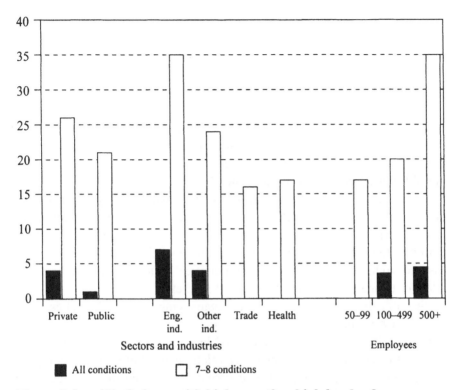

Figure 7.5   **Workplaces with high or rather high levels of new management (percentage of companies)**

The corresponding figure for establishments within the public sector is around 20 per cent. A closer look at the distribution between different industries reveals that the engineering industry is at the very top, which is perfectly in line with the expectations arising from the debates on new management. Within the engineering industry, 7 per cent of workplaces have met all nine conditions and a good 35 per cent fulfil seven or more. Other manufacturing, which has met nine conditions in 3 per cent of establishments, ends up at a level lower than engineering but higher than commerce/trade, which has no establishment at all that reaches nine on our index. Within the health-care sector, as in commerce, there is no establishment meeting all conditions, and not quite 20 per cent that meet seven or more.

To sum up, new management as an integrated and implemented strategy does not yet seem to be particularly widespread across the Swedish labour market. Table 7.1, however, indicates that a coordinated set of control methods described as new management can be observed in some workplaces. This combined strategy is found above all in large workplaces in the private sector in the engineering industry.

The 'Causes and Effects' of New Management and Flexibility

Let us by way of conclusion examine the pattern of relationships described in theory. We shall use our data to analyse certain central relationships between the market conditions underpinning new management on the one hand, and possible causes and effects on the other. First, market conditions are alleged to be causes for changes in management styles and work organization. It is claimed that a product market, characterized by customer orientation and heavy competition, leads to new forms of company management. A labour market with high employment, highly skilled job seekers and strong unions is assumed to have the same effect. Our empirical material does not, however, allow us to analyse the role of the labour market.

Second, the development of new management allegedly takes place alongside a deconstruction of the hierarchical division of labour, that is, a decrease in the number of managerial levels. Third, new management is assumed to co-vary with cooperative relationships between the company and union. Fourth, a frequently recurring idea is that new management produces two positive outcomes: on the one hand worthwhile jobs for the workers and on the other improved efficiency and profits for the company. These four statements could be said to constitute the core of our theoretical hypotheses.

We would thus expect a correlation between these factors in accordance with the model in Figure 7.6. As a result of market conditions characterized by customer-tailored production and heavy competition, we would expect to find new management. This test can be made only for business establishments, as the questions regarding market conditions were put only to these. The fact that signs of new management are noted within the tax-financed public sector may be due to increased financing through service charges and to the introduction of competition between different public establishments as a result of the citizens' right to choose, for example, schools and hospitals. Another background factor is the process of ongoing privatization, especially in Stockholm, of everything from health care and child care to public housing and transport. A further explanation could be the ideological climate over the past couple of decades, with its tendency to favour the trendsetters in managerial thinking and practice. These are generally major private companies within industry

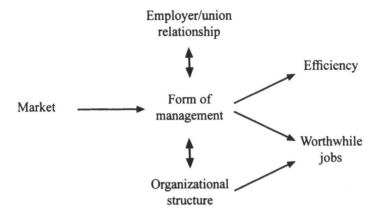

Figure 7.6   Model of analysis: new management and its context

and services, with many of the consultancy firms, and the concepts they use, having a US background. It is also apparent how many ideas within new management fit very well into trends towards deregulation and neo-liberal thinking in general.

The Importance of Market Pressures

The first hypothesis, on the market/company management relationship, is tested through regression analysis, where we control for type of industry, workplace size, and class composition (that is, the balance between blue- and white-collar work).[2] Our analysis shows that new management can in fact be an effect of the market conditions described in the literature. There is a positive and clearly significant correlation between new company management and high market pressures, defined as a situation characterized by both customer-oriented production and intense competition (by customer orientation, we mean that the workplace tailors its products and services to a high degree to the customer's demands). It would seem that precisely this combination is important. Exposure to competition and the degree of customer-tailored products and services, analysed as separate variables, do not generate the same effects on new management. Competition by itself yields no significant effect on new management and only customer orientation by itself yields a weaker effect than market pressure, in the direction expected.

Another result of the analysis is that new management, as expected, tends to be positively correlated with workplace size. Moreover, the proportion of blue- and white-collar workers is similarly correlated with the existence of new management. The higher the proportion of white-collar workers, the higher the extent of new management.

Decentralized Hierarchies

As indicated earlier, we have found no correlation between new management and a flat organizational structure. Bearing the theoretical discussion in mind, this means that we have to reject the hypothesis that flattened pyramids are a feature of new company management. Those establishments where we find new management do not tend to be flat. In and of itself, this fact does not exclude the possibility that at some earlier stage they were actually more hierarchical than at the time of the data collection. We do, however, find a positive correlation between decentralization and new management, which is possibly in line with the theory. The fact that decisions are decentralized means in this case that they are allocated to some level below the highest establishment level. The decisions in question concern the introduction of new products/services, pricing, pay increases and promotions of subordinates, and minor increases in staff numbers. Overall, this means that a high degree of hierarchical division of labour still remains but that decision making has to a larger extent been transferred to lower levels. The extent to which centralized decision making has been reinforced at the same time has not been directly examined, but the new forms of management may be seen as instruments for ensuring such central control under new conditions.

Industrial Relations

It is somewhat unclear how labour relations are related to new management. Should a cooperative relationship between employer and union be viewed as a contributory factor to, or as a consequence of, new management? Or should changing labour relations be understood as a subelement of the total management strategy? The literature provides little guidance to the answers to these questions but makes it clear that new management and changing labour relations are related. One could further suspect that when it comes to influence at the workplace, union strength is both affected by and itself affects the existence of new management. The primary direction of these correlations is not immediately obvious. In managerial thinking it is claimed that relationships between employer and union in establishments with new management are characterized by consensus over questions concerning the company's operations. Yet it may be argued that the union could perceive new management as a threat, something which could lead to a more pronounced conflict between the parties.

We use two indices, one of which measures the relationship between employer and union in terms of cooperation or antagonism while the other measures union strength at the establishment level as an indicator of the degree of union influence over important questions. The great majority of establishments report that relationships at the workplace are characterized by cooperation and that union influence is fairly strong. In view of the problems involved in unscrambling the effects of management styles on labour relations, we have carried out here only a correlation analysis, and a causal regression analysis. We note that union influence tends to be somewhat stronger in establishments with new management, but that no correlation exists between cooperation between the parties and the new management strategy. These results also remain the same when not controlling for class composition and workplace hierarchy. The correlations are also valid when we control for type of industry.

It therefore looks as if labour relations are not affected by the workplace's management strategy. Yet, as mentioned, there is a tendency for strong unions to be found within establishments with new management. With respect to the order of events, however, we have no information – whether new management entails increased influence for the union or whether a strong union contributes to the growth of new management. Our results are at odds with the conventional hypotheses that new management could entail a weakening of the union organizations. Yet it should be noted that these variables, like others, reflect the views of workplace managers, and do not necessarily accord with those of the union representatives. Owing to limited resources, we were unable to ask the union representatives about this.

Outcome: Efficiency?

We have few means to illustrate the relationship between company efficiency and new management. The best we can offer is to use the workplace managers' own opinions of their workplace performance in relation to others engaged in similar activity, an admittedly uncertain indicator. Efficiency measured in this way proves to be positively related to new management – that is, at workplaces with a high degree of new management, the manager estimates that his/her company has an edge over the competitors. This result is in line with the alleged effects of new management. Other interesting outcomes, for which, however, we have no data, might be the organization's adaptability and level of sustainable production.

Outcome: Quality of Work?

In our view, one of the most interesting relationships in the theoretical model (Figure 7.6 above) is that between type of company management and worthwhile jobs. We use two indicators of worthwhile jobs. The first of these is the development potential within the individual job as reported by *managers* in interviews (see le Grand, 1996). The second indicator is a measure of worthwhile jobs constructed on the basis of data for individuals from the Level of Living Survey.[3] The latter measure builds on *employees' self-reported* degree of, on the one hand, demands to learn and be creative at work and, on the other hand, their control over their work – the so-called demand-control model (Karasek and Theorell, 1990). The result of our analysis shows that there is a clear, positive correlation between new forms of management and job development potential as perceived by managers. This is perhaps not surprising, since a question on job development should be positively correlated with our measure of new management, as this contains questions on training and workers' influence. Given the discussion nowadays of 'employability', the chance to develop competences may be seen as an essential aspect of worthwhile work.

However, we find no significant correlation between new management and the Level of Living Survey's measure of self-reported worthwhile jobs. On the other hand, the correlation is close to significant and pointing in the 'right' direction – that is, worthwhile jobs tend to be somewhat more common in workplaces with a high degree of new management. When controlling for new company management, the workplace's hierarchical structure is not linked with either worthwhile work or job development. Thus, it would seem that hierarchical form is of little significance for the presence of worthwhile work. We also find that such work is most frequently found at workplaces with a predominance of white-collar workers.

Other Swedish Surveys

A couple of years after our study, Karlsson and Eriksson (1995) and Karlsson (2002) carried out a survey on working conditions of a representative sample of working Swedes, linked to a survey of managers, using an operationalization of

Atkinson's model of the 'flexible firm' (1984). In short, their results reveal that there are very few flexible workplaces and, in fact, on a strong interpretation of Atkinson, only 4 per cent of workplaces are flexible. Karlsson and Eriksson also investigated the quality of work in flexible and traditional workplaces, and like us they found that there were very small, insignificant differences (based on the demand-control model). On the other hand, they found that women and blue-collar workers experienced systematically lower quality of work than men and white-collar employees. In the worst types of job (with high demands, isolation and little control), blue-collar workers and women figure prominently. Class and gender explain differences in quality of work among individuals, differences that are not explained by the degree of flexibility or new management of the workplace.

In another Swedish survey of flexibility, the so-called Flex-1, about one-quarter of companies were found to be flexible, using a weaker definition involving two characteristics, namely improvement in skills and delegated responsibility (Nutek, 1996). That result is on the same level as in our survey when using our weaker definition (seven out of nine elements located). In a second survey of a sample of around 5,000 Swedish workplaces in 1997 designed to analyse strategies of change (Flex-2), Wikman (2001) found that among companies with more than 50 employees, roughly 30 per cent use a 'functionally flexible' strategy. However, about 15 per cent cluster around each of 'numerically flexible' and 'outsourcing change' strategies. The survey also found high and growing levels of employee influence and development of competences, higher than those in, for example, Southern European countries (Wikman et al., 2000). The Flex-2 study found only a weak correlation between the degree and type of flexibility of the firm and the working environment as reported by employees. More important factors determining working conditions seem to include the nature of the job, training and position in the organization. The weak correlation may be interpreted as a result of methodological difficulties in measuring company structure and work environment (Wikman, 2001).

Conclusions

In this chapter we have tried to construct, on the basis of our own work and literature surveys, a general picture of what is usually meant by a new model of management, work organization and labour relations. In our own empirical study we grouped together a number of features (forms of control and organization) into comprehensive categories. Empirically, we find that the various elements of new management do exist within Swedish working life. As we noted in the introductory discussion, the engineering industry often employs new managerial methods.

With our consolidated measure of new management, we find that workplaces exhibiting a high proportion of the elements are fairly uncommon. Within the private sector, barely a third of workplaces meet even seven of the nine conditions we had established as measures of new management, while the same goes for about 20 per cent of public sector workplaces. New management is most common in large workplaces within the private sector; the engineering industry comes top, as expected. The higher the proportion of white-collar workers among the employees, the higher the extent of new management. Our findings are supported by other Swedish and international studies that are reviewed elsewhere (Sandberg, forthcoming).

We find no correlation between new management (new forms of control and organization) and flat organizational structures. We therefore have to reject the thesis that flattened pyramids constitute an important element of new management. However, a decentralization of overall policy decisions to levels below top management at the establishment is indeed linked to the practice of new management.

With respect to labour relations at the workplace, a vast majority of the managers interviewed reported that employer/union relationships are characterized by cooperation and that the degree of cooperation is not related to the existence of new management. Union influence is fairly strong, and – surprisingly considering the views and theories presented in the management literature – somewhat stronger at establishments with new forms of management.

The relationship between new company management and the prospects for worthwhile jobs is also a core question in the context of this book. Our results both confirm and contradict the propositions brought forward in the debates on new management and worthwhile work. Our aggregate measure of new management, which does not include a flat organization, has a positive correlation with the potential for job development as reported by our respondents, namely managers. On the other hand we find no significant correlation between the employees' own reports on the quality of their jobs, but the correlation is close to significant and positive.

To sum up, our analysis indicates that it might make sense to speak of new management, not only at the ideological level but also to a limited extent in real working life. Flattened pyramids do not seem to constitute an integrated element of new management, nor do they seem to contribute to worthwhile work for employees. Other elements of new management are nevertheless widely spread, although not very often found together in a coherent strategy, and only weakly or not at all related to worthwhile work.

Acknowledgements

We should like to thank our three colleagues responsible for the Swedish Workplace Survey (APU): Carl le Grand, Ryszard Szulkin and Mikael Tåhlin at the Stockholm University Department of Sociology and Institute for Social Research. Thanks also to Aina Godenius Berntsson for translating an earlier version of this chapter. At the National Institute for Working Life our colleagues Fredrik Augustsson, Klas Levinsson, Birger Viklund and Anders Wikman gave valuable comments on a draft version of this chapter.

Notes

1   This chapter is to a large extent based on an earlier version entitled 'Är Taylor död och pyramiderna rivna?' by Edling and Sandberg in the final report of the Swedish workplace survey (APU) (le Grand et al., 1996). To a smaller extent it also derives from a chapter by the same authors in a Swedish textbook reflecting critical perspectives on management (Sandberg, 2002). It has been translated by Aina Godenius Berntsson, but quotations from texts published in languages other than English have been translated by the authors.

2   By controlling for type of industry, we eliminate differences between sectors with respect to the extent of new management. The aim is to reveal differences based on market pressures, which may vary widely between industries. We also find it practical to control for possible effects of workplace size, as this seems to be related to new company management, as well as for 'class composition' at the workplace, assuming that the elements found within new management are most common at workplaces characterized by a high white-collar density.

3   A measure of the individual's psycho-social work environment has been cross-tabulated for 37 industries and three 'classes' of employees based on data from the Level of Living Survey. Each workplace in the Workplace Survey has, dependent on type of industry and class composition, been given a mean value for this measure. The links between the two surveys are described in more detail in the 'technical' appendix to le Grand et al., 1993.

References

Ahrne, G. and Papakostas, A. (forthcoming), *Organisationer, samhälle och globalisering Tröghetens mekanismer och förnyelsens förutsättningar*, University of Stockholm (manuscript).

Ahrne, G. and Sandberg, Å. (2000), *New Management, ICT and the New Working Life*, report from a workshop within the Worklife 2000 Programme, Arbetslivsinstitutet, Stockholm.

Alvesson, M. (1989), *Ledning av kunskapsföretag*, Norstedts, Stockholm.

Atkinson, J. (1984), 'Manpower Strategies for Flexible Organizations', *Personnel Management*, August, pp. 28–31.

Beckérus, Å. and Edström, A. together with Edlund, C., Ekvall, G., Forslin, J. and Rendahl, J.E. (1988), *Doktrinskiftet. Nya ideal i svenskt ledarskap*, Svenska Dagbladets Förlag, Stockholm.

Bélanger, J., Berggren, C., Björkman, T. and Köhler, C (1999), *Being Local Worldwide. ABB and the Challenge of Global Management*, ILR Press, Ithaca Press.

Björkman, T. (2002), '"Management" – en modeindustri', in Sandberg, Å. (ed.), *Ledning för alla?*, SNS Förlag, Stockholm.

Carlzon, J. (1989), *Moments of Truth. New Strategies for Today's Customer-driven Economy*, Harpers & Row, New York.

Edling, C. and Sandberg, Å. (1996), 'Är Taylor död och pyramiderna rivna?', in le Grand, C., Szulkin, R. and Tåhlin, M. (eds), *Sveriges arbetsplatser. Organisation, personalutveckling, styrning*, SNS Förlag (2nd edn), Stockholm.

Edström, A., Norbäck, L.E. and Rendahl, J.E. (1989), *Förnyelsens ledarskap. SAS' utveckling från flygbolag till reseföretag*, Norstedts, Stockholm.

EPOC (1997), *New Forms of Work Organization*, European Foundation for the Improvement of Living and Working Conditions, Dublin.

Fritzell, J. and Lundberg, O. (1993a), *Ett förlorat eller förlovat årtionde? Välfärdsutvecklingen mellan 1981 och 1991*, Institutet för social forskning (Institute for Social Research), Stockholm.

Fritzell, J. and Lundberg, O. (1993b), *Vardagens villkor*, Brombergs, Stockholm.

Gelin, G., Sundström, L. and Sandberg, Å. (1991), *Sanna ägare. Engagemang genom arbete eller konvertibler*, Swedish Centre for Working Life, Stockholm.

Göransson, I. and Holmgren, A. (2000), *Löftet. Löntagarna och makten på arbetets marknad*, Bilda, Stockholm.

Gustafsson, R. (1994), *Köp och sälj, var god svälj*, Arbetsmiljöfonden, Stockholm.

Karasek, R. and Theorell, T. (1990), *Healthy Work: Stress, Productivity and the Reconstruction of Working Life*, Basic Books, New York.

Karlsson, J.C. (2002), 'Flexibilitet i praktiken', in Sandberg, Å. (ed.), *Ledning för alla?*, SNS Förlag, Stockholm.

Karlsson, J.C. and Eriksson, B. (1995), *Flexibla arbetsplatser och arbetsvillkor*, Arkiv Förlag, Lund.

le Grand, C. (1993; revised 1996), 'Karriär- och utvecklingsmöjligheter på de interna arbetsmarknaderna', in le Grand, C., Szulkin, R. and Tåhlin, M. (eds), *Sveriges arbetsplatser. Organisation, personalutveckling, styrning*, SNS Förlag (2nd edn), Stockholm.

le Grand, C., Szulkin, R. and Tåhlin, M. (1993; revised 1996) (eds), *Sveriges arbetsplatser. Organisation, personalutveckling, styrning*, SNS Förlag (2nd edn), Stockholm.

Mahon, R. (1994), 'Wage-earners and/or Co-workers? Contested identities', *Economic and Industrial Democracy*, Vol. 15, No. 3: also in Clement, W. and Mahon, R. (eds) (1994), *Swedish Social Democracy*, Canadian Scholars' Press, Toronto.

Meidner, R. (1991), 'Makropolitik som stöd för det utvecklande arbetet', in *Efter Taylor*, Produktivitetsdelegationen and Arbetslivsfonden, Stockholm.

Nutek (1996), *Towards Flexible Work Organizations*, Stockholm.

Osterman, P. (1994), 'How Common is Workplace Transformation and Who Adopts It?', *Industrial and Labour Relations Review*, Vol. 47, No. 2, pp. 173–8.

Perrow, Charles (1986), *Complex Organizations: a Critical Essay*, McGraw-Hill, New York.

Sandberg, Å. (1994), 'Justice at Work: Solidaristic Work Policy as a Renewal of the Swedish Labour Market Model', *Market Economy and Social Justice*, Institute of Social Sciences, Chuo University, Tokyo.

Sandberg, Å. (ed.) (1995), *Enriching Production. Perspectives on Volvo's Uddevalla Plant as an Alternative to Lean Production*, Avebury, Aldershot.

Sandberg, Å. (ed.) (2002a), *Ledning för alla?*, SNS Förlag, Stockholm.

Sandberg, Å. (2002b), 'New Management – New Democratic Participation?' in *Essays in Honour of Litsa Nicolaou*, University of Piraeus, Piraeus.

Sandberg, Å (forthcoming), *Taylor in the Network Society*, working paper (Mitior project), Arbetslivsinstitutet/ NIWL, Stockholm.

Sandberg, Å. and Augustsson, F. (2002), *Interactive Media in Sweden*, Arbetslivsinstitutet/ NIWL, Stockholm.

Sandberg, Å., Broms, G., Grip, A., Steen, J., Sundström, L. and Ullmark, P. (1992), *Technological Change and Co-Determination in Sweden*, Temple University Press, Philadelphia.

Sisson, K. (2000), *Direct Participation and the Modernization of Work Organization*, European Foundation for the Improvement of Living and Working Conditions, Dublin.

Von Otter, C. (2002), 'Inte bara vinster', in *Ledning för alla?*, in Sandberg, Å. (ed.), *Ledning för alla?*, SNS Förlag, Stockholm.

Wikman, A. (2001), *Internationalisering, flexibilitet och förändrade företagsformer*, Arbetslivsinstitutet/NIWL, Stockholm.

Wikman, A., Eklund, I. and Englund, A. (2000), 'Arbetsförhållanden i Sverige och Europaä', in Marklund, S. (ed.), *Arbetsliv och hälsa 2000*, Arbetslivsinstitutet/Arbetsskyddsstyrelsen, Stockholm.

Appendix: the Swedish Workplace Survey (APU)

The 1991 Swedish Workplace or Establishment Survey (APU) was conducted as an extension of the Swedish Level of Living Survey of 1991 and carried out at the Institute of Social Research (Sofi) and the Department of Sociology at Stockholm University. The Level of Living Survey (LNU) consists of a nationally representative sample of individuals aged 18 to 75 (Fritzell and Lundberg, 1993a; 1993b). Those who worked at a workplace with more than 10 employees and agreed to contribute to the Workplace Survey were asked for the name and address of their employers. Managers (and personnel managers at workplaces with 50 or more employees) at the 2,135 workplaces were contacted and interviewed over the telephone by Statistics Sweden (SCB). The response rate was a remarkable 93 per cent. We know of only a few other similar data sets. Le Grand et al. (1993) gives full technical and statistical details and defines the indices used.

It should be noted, however, that the Workplace Survey was not tailored to study new forms of management (like Osterman, 1994, and Karlsson and Eriksson, 1995) but to develop a comprehensive database of workplaces to be used for analyzing a number of different characteristics. This has two consequences. First, the questions were not formulated in the context of only one specific research question, so some of our indicators have limitations, but they may, on the other hand, be related to a broad array of characteristics of the organization. Second, the respondent did not know in which context his or her answer would finally be interpreted.

A second Workplace Survey is presently being carried out, but no results are as yet available. The 1991 study however is still of great interest, and the results of our analysis of the incidence of new management and its relationship with quality of work have so far been available only in Swedish. The idea of a breakthrough for 'new management' had been circulating for a decade even in 1991. If anything has changed since then, the incidence today would have probably been yet greater. Studies five years later than ours, however, found a level of new management about the same as ours, and a similarly weak correlation with the quality of work.

Chapter 8

New Concepts in Work Organization: a Case from the Norwegian Offshore Petroleum Industry[1]

Thoralf Ulrik Qvale

Introduction

The context for trade union and employee participation in decision making at the enterprise level has been changing quite rapidly over the last two decades. On the surface, in Central Europe and the USA, the power of the unions seems to have diminished for a number of reasons. These include neo-liberal politics, changes in labour laws, rising unemployment, restructuring and globalization of markets and industry, new technology and new ways of organizing work. Union membership has tended to go down both in relative and absolute terms, at least partly because newcomers to the labour market with higher education do not tend to join unions. Individualism seems to be replacing the collective orientation of earlier generations of workers. The traditional power base of unions seems therefore to be eroding. It is rather common to say that solidarity among workers is waning, and it is relatively easy to draft a negative scenario for unions and their influence on working life. Liberals may claim that employees are better off without unions and that in the new, emerging forms of working life they can take care of their own interests without union membership. Such ideas and perspectives also appear in Norway. For example in a recent government White Paper on working life legislation in the future (NOU, 1999), there are predictions about dramatic decentralization and individualization in negotiations and labour contracts as a consequence of – or precondition for – the flexibility necessary in the organization of the future. One of its principal messages, albeit a somewhat exaggerated one, is that highly skilled employees will need to negotiate for themselves in a context of shifting employers and the rapid turnaround of projects and tasks in emerging knowledge-based network organizations.

The general perspective of this chapter, however, is more optimistic. We accept that profound changes are taking place at the workplace and on the labour market. But rather than assuming that they will bring unequivocal consequences for individual employees and unions, we shall discuss the possibilities for managing these changes in ways that secure both the collective and individual interests of employees and the competitiveness of their enterprises. This chapter deals with one large enterprise and the changes that have taken place there. However, this enterprise is not unique in its participative approach to organizational development and greenfield site design. On the contrary, although it is making a greater and more systematic effort than many other major Norwegian corporations, most are somewhere along the same track.

Managers of more advanced enterprises strongly feel the need for much faster development of competence, capacity, innovation and productivity in view of increasing international competition. At the same time, working together with the local unions on planning and implementing organizational change comes naturally to many professional managers. We assume that this approach reflects the combined effect of a number of factors. These include a long series of working life reforms over more than 50 years, positive joint experiences from working together on research and development projects over the last 30 years and changes in curriculum and teaching methods inspired by such projects at universities. Finally, it has been repeatedly argued that Norwegian society has a relatively strong egalitarian culture, which probably supports this collaborative approach to changes in working life (Emery and Thorsrud, 1969, 1976; Qvale, 1998b).

At the macro-level, we also have the interesting situation that countries like Sweden and Norway, and probably Finland, have tended not to reflect the same negative trends as other European countries in terms of union membership. It stands at an all time high in both Sweden and Norway, although both countries have been exposed to the same general conditions, including periods with high unemployment, as other industrialized Western nations.

Changes on the European Scene

In terms of formal employee participation, the EU directive adopted in 1994 on European works councils (EWCs) seems to have proved a success from the point of view of its advocates. This is certainly the case in Nordic corporations, but also in British ones (Didier, 1997; Qvale and Serck-Hanssen, 1999; see also chapter 3 in this book). The directive came into force in 1996. Eligible British companies, which are active across many European countries, have largely established EWCs despite strong opposition to the directive from Conservative political circles and the Confederation of British Industry (CBI). The directive did not become compulsory for British companies until December 1999, but they have nevertheless become leading lights in Europe with respect to setting up EWCs. Trade unions and employees in Eastern Europe seem also to have benefited from the directive since some West European companies have invited employees from their Eastern European plants to elect representatives to the EWC. This is, at least, the case in Poland (Rudolf, 1999). Similarly, in one Norwegian corporation we have studied in some detail (Qvale and Serck-Hanssen, 1999), the EWC is seen by top management as an important body for discussing and developing the corporation's strategy. So there are signs overall that large companies really do want a dialogue with representatives of their employees. Otherwise they would hardly be over-fulfilling the terms of the directive in the way they are doing.

There is also a relatively clear trend in advanced sectors of working life towards more and deeper involvement of individuals through forms of direct participation. New, decentralized, flexible, cross-disciplinary forms of work organization are spreading quite rapidly in some industrial sectors. In principle this can be seen as an obvious choice by enterprises because their competitive edge depends more and more on their ability to develop and utilize knowledge (Qvale, 1996a). The EU Green Paper on work organization is significant in this respect (Commission, 1997). On the other hand, the picture is blurred by parallel developments like sudden outsourcing, lean production, enforced control of the individual, or else little change inside the enterprise at all. So the 'empowerment' necessary to make decentralized, more flexible forms of work organization operate to the advantage of the employees is frequently missing, certainly in the USA. A similar argument is presented by Falkum (2000) based on his more general studies of the implementation of new productivity concepts in Norwegian industry. He claims that such 'concept driven' organizational developments are, in most cases, part of a top-down management strategy to enforce control of the individual. He makes an exception only for workplace changes conducted within the 'Tavistock tradition'. In other words, he argues that concepts like Total Quality Management, Just-in-Time and Business Process Re-engineering are being implemented mainly within the confines of the bureaucratic, scientific management paradigm.

However, there are cases where participation, 'empowerment' and organizational design go together in a holistic way as indeed discussed in the Green Paper. The case of a greenfield site design project (the creation of an entirely new industrial plant with new technology and new organization) related in this chapter may be included amongst these. The project is actually being conducted within the current Norwegian version of the Tavistock tradition. We shall return later to the question as to whether such developments may be interpreted as signs of an emerging general trend, or whether they merely represent exceptions, perhaps even short-lived ones, from the general rule.

But even if the employees, individually and collectively, benefit in such advanced cases, the issue of union outcomes is more open. If enterprises want to promote both formal, indirect, employee participation and direct participation in decision making in daily work situations, we might predict that there would be little or no room for the local or central unions. This is the well-known American union criticism to some greenfield site design projects similar to the one being presented here: 'It is being done to keep unions out'.

The positive union perspective, however, which is outlined by the Scenario 21 group (Kester and Pinaud, 1996), is that existing unions may be able to adapt in line with these changes in working life. This is not something we may expect to come automatically, but is more likely to follow conscious strategies from the unions, possibly with the support of legislation at national and supranational (EU) levels. This is the alternative discussed in this chapter.

There is yet another possibility. New unions may form and gradually replace the old ones. There may be signs in some countries that this is indeed happening, for example in the British telecommunications sector. Local unions for professional and managerial staff in hi-tech industries may grow, win recognition and influence at the enterprise level, and then amalgamate into larger federations (Qvale, 1998a). We shall not, however, pursue the discussion of this possibility, which in Norway – so far – seems of less relevance.

The case presented here is the first large-scale attempt in Norway to coordinate representative forms of participation with direct forms. The system of site-level works councils reporting to one corporate council is expected to initiate, support and monitor parallel development of such organizations across the corporation's many production sites. The action plan has been decided by the board of directors of the corporation, in which the employees hold one-third of the seats. Deliberations between management and the unions then led to the formalization of a new production philosophy, which spells out the values and ground rules for the changes.

The particular feature of this action research project in industry – besides the use of the works council system as the main vehicle for corporate turnaround – is the extensive application of organizational and management development methods in the preparatory phases.

Background and Role of the Unions

Historically, in Norway, the central trade union federation (LO) has frequently initiated efforts to promote industrial democracy. Together with the employers' confederation (NHO), LO has promoted research and development and has taken part in the planning and execution of reforms on working parties and committees exploring this field. As argued elsewhere (Qvale 1998b), this policy of cooperation over 30 years on issues which have, to some degree, been contentious is probably one important explanation why the labour market organizations are still able to work together on important national matters. This does not mean that the relationship between the parties is entirely harmonious and idyllic. The employers have, however, largely taken the position that there is more to gain by being involved than by standing outside protesting when controversial matters like board representation are being proposed. For their part, the unions have been involved in joint productivity drives since the 1950s. Hence there has been some degree of joint learning and reflection in the leadership of both employers and unions at national level in connection with all major working life reforms over recent decades.

Through the recession and consequent unemployment in the late 1980s, the unions and their members also learnt that representative systems for industrial democracy do not necessarily secure employment. Furthermore, the belief in government-owned enterprise as a vehicle for employment had already vanished from the labour movement. It has also become clear that employment in the public sector is no guarantee against redundancy. Partly for these reasons, the recession did not lead to union demands for increased board representation (beyond the 33 per cent already available). The trend towards strengthening the codetermination side of industrial democracy also seems to have halted. At the same time, however, there have been no initiatives to reduce the unions' and workers' formal rights to participate in decision making. Employees' formal security of employment remains unchanged. However, union rhetoric, interest and energy have turned rather to issues like learning at work, training and further education – that is, promoting employability among their members.

Some decentralization and restructuring have taken place in the industrial relations system over the last 20 years, though. The number of national unions has been reduced and the opportunities for concluding local and enterprise level agreements are better than ever before. If the local parties agree, and the terms are within a general, national framework, the industry level unions and employers' federations will normally accept. Over the last decade, the general context for enterprise-level collaboration has dramatically improved.

In local projects concerned with organizational change and development, however, many of the well-known obstacles from earlier 'experiments' and projects reappear. These include: resistance to change among middle managers; workers' and shop stewards' fear of new challenges; supervisors' fear of loss of power; administrative inabilities to support new ways of working; and fear of senior management of loss of control and corporate synergies. Such issues, of course, receive considerable attention and are dealt with in various ways. One of the main problems, however, is that few realize that the transition from a traditional, hierarchic/bureaucratic organizational form to a participative, team-based and flexible, learning organization in most cases represents a turnaround – that is, a new organizational paradigm (Eijnatten, 1993; Emery, 1978; Trist, 1981). A piecemeal, incremental change procedure normally does not work. As Borgen (1995) points out, most enterprises in Norway still lack a coherent strategy, that is, a systematic way to deal with a variety of issues and at the same time to manage a changing environment. They are therefore vulnerable to fads and fashions and present their workers with inconsistent policies and initiatives, which makes participation risky for the union leaders. While managements are gradually realizing this, and in relatively advanced enterprises are prepared to devote considerable time and resources to strategy development and organizational change, less systematic efforts have been devoted to the changes required within the union system.

The optimistic perspective, of course, is that the unions will learn and change more or less automatically as they move along. This assumption is frequently combined with the view that a multi-union situation will be more common in those enterprises reflecting the changing composition of employees. The pessimistic scenario is that the 'empowered' members in the workplace of the future may find that the unions no longer serve their interests and hence leave them.

Certainly we know less about the consequences for the trade unions with respect to the successful development of workers' democratic participation in modern industrial settings than we do with respect to the same factors from the enterprise's side. What might the new trade union paradigm be to match the new paradigm of work? The case presented in this chapter addresses this very issue. It deals with workers' participation in a greenfield site design project, and a parallel development and implementation of a more general process of change across all production facilities of a large corporation. The local joint management/union design team reports to the works council of the particular plant in question. Furthermore, the local site-level works council, on which all the trade unions are represented, relates to the corporate-level works council where top management and the local union leaders are members. The system of site-level works councils and corporate works council is expected to have the strategic role in securing coordinated development across the enterprise under the auspices of a newly agreed corporate-wide philosophy of production.

Industrial Relations in Offshore Petroleum

The offshore petroleum industry in Norway has a somewhat idiosyncratic pattern of industrial relations. Although the government decided quite early that national legislation should apply to aspects like industrial relations, health and safety and the working environment (as opposed to the UK system under which the continental shelf is seen as lying outside the national labour market), a more varied union structure in fact emerged. In the company in question there are now five acknowledged trade unions representing the employees.[2]

However, strong national pressures to harmonize developments offshore with the national labour market and institutions seem gradually to have paid off. The largest offshore unions are now affiliated to national federations, and the traditional land-based unions have gained a strong foothold offshore. Hence they have to consider the national context when bargaining. Strikes and other disputes have become less frequent, and competition between the unions less visible and problematic over the last few years.

For a number of reasons the offshore petroleum industry has itself become quite bureaucratic, and more so than comparable industries onshore (Qvale, 1993). Specifications, documentation and prescribed, formal procedures during the 1980s controlled an increasing part of the activities and the individual's working day. The industrial relations system also reflected this high degree of formalization. Therefore the companies find themselves in a double bind. On the one hand, they want to change the organization to improve performance, but on the other, they find that collective agreements, union structures and norms on staffing and qualifications related to safety are tightly interwoven with their own traditional structures and procedures. Because of the industry's centrality for the national economy, its high profitability, high-risk potential and its safety requirements, the local unions are very powerful. Unless the unions are involved and positive towards change, the chances to make necessary progress are rather slim, and change can become quite costly. So when the company in this case decided formally to link all development work to the works council system, some rather important pragmatic reasons also featured.

The Company

The company in question is one of the largest operating oil companies active on the Norwegian continental shelf, and it is also increasing its international involvement. On the international scene, however, it is of moderate size. Current employment is around 17,000.

From the very outset, the company's policy has been to build on the Norwegian tradition of democracy in working life, work constructively with the unions, provide high standards in its working environment and offer the best possible opportunities for learning and development to its employees. The company has expanded fast, opening up new production facilities almost every year for the last 15 years. It has therefore, in principle, also had unusually good opportunities for systematizing operating experience and bringing it to bear on the design and development of new units. From the start, however, the ability to utilize such 'greenfield site design' opportunities was seen by the international offshore petroleum industry, on its arrival in Norway in the early 1970s, as one of its weakest points (Thorsrud, 1978).

Falling oil prices in 1986, and the generally lower and more uncertain levels afterwards, led to mounting pressure for improved productivity. By 1995 several cost reduction campaigns had been pushed through, and considerable savings had been obtained. Most of these related to renegotiating contracts with suppliers, improving logistics and reducing stocks, but the way in which production units were operated remained largely unchanged and hence quite costly. Furthermore, there was limited flexibility in the organization, with little mobility from offshore to onshore work. There also was a growing need to increase mobility between old fields, which were being phased out, and new fields coming on-stream in different regions. However, the various campaigns to improve productivity and reduce costs had also created resentment amongst both individuals and the unions.

The company had, however, firmly adhered to the *formal* side of employee and union rights to participate in joint information, consultation and decision making bodies through the established procedures. So formal decisions in the relevant areas were not made by management, unless the works council, the working environment committee or the local union leadership had been involved and consulted in accordance with the rules. But the same bureaucratic way of working was also a major cause of frustration and dissatisfaction among employees and managers.

Developing the New Corporate Strategy

The research on which this chapter is based resulted from an initiative by the company-level works council early in 1996. At this stage, the company's board of directors and top management were concerned about the problematic relationship with their offshore workers and unions. A routine attitude survey revealed in 1995 that a high proportion (65 per cent) of those working offshore had little or no trust in top management. The board of directors instructed top management to explore the factors that lay behind this result and to propose a plan to improve the situation, *Rebuilding Co-operation and Trust*. The board made it clear that it expected the established channels for participation to be used for this purpose.

All leaders of the local unions with members in the company's offshore production facilities were invited to meet, form a working party and discuss the situation with top management and so develop a plan. The Work Research Institute (WRI) was invited to help structure the discussions, amongst other tasks.

At the meeting the union leaders expressed their dissatisfaction with the way the company dealt with organizational development and change. They referred to a recent sudden management decision to outsource maintenance and modification work on some of the production facilities, against a background of campaigns for cost cutting and management change that had repeatedly created frustration among their members. Union participation in these campaigns had been limited to making comments on the implementation of fully worked out packages of measures at formal works council or working environment committee meetings. By that stage, it was difficult to influence the content of the plans. Union leaders had frequently been put into embarrassing situations when the new campaign had unpredicted and negative consequences for their members' working conditions. The unions also were sceptical about the economic benefits of the various campaigns, and claimed that they were never evaluated in a way that the company could learn from them. They felt they could involve themselves in organizational transformation only if the company was consistent in its actions and developed an open strategy towards solving problems.

One outcome of the meeting was an agreement to do some joint fact finding. They did not use the usual method, namely finding consultants who could conduct a survey on their behalf. Rather, they agreed to a suggestion that the members of the committee should make personal contact with management and the union representatives of each of the more than 20 works councils covering the various production units. The works council members were to be interviewed on what they thought could be done to improve collaboration and develop trust.

The results, analysed by WRI, showed a very positive, general attitude towards the works councils both amongst management and local union members. The overwhelming majority of both management and unions (96 per cent) said they generally cooperated well – at least in a formal sense – and they all thought the works council could play an important role in promoting collaboration and the development of trust. But it also became clear that the works councils were not, in fact, being used as a channel for these purposes. And there were also fairly large discrepancies between the various works councils and how they operated. The oldest, and most experienced, were well established and followed all the relevant rules, while some operated mainly in bargaining mode and other, newer ones barely knew the rules and were uncertain about how to work together. A few managers used the works council actively for joint consultation, but most tended to see the meetings as necessary rituals and put little time or effort into them.

The working party agreed on the following plan:

- to develop a package of documentation and offer training/induction courses to new works council members;
- to offer support in the form of organizational development expertise to help works council members better work together;
- to develop a corporate strategy for the implementation of greenfield site design and redesign of existing production units. This new production philosophy heralded union and employee participation from the outset. The works council should have a key role in planning and coordinating activities at site level;
- to agree that the company-level works council was the appropriate body to oversee company-level developments;
- to discuss this plan at a meeting for all chairs, deputy chairs and secretaries for the works councils in question.

At the meeting in question, the general ideas were positively received. This was mainly because the top manager and local union leader of each production unit now felt that they were being offered support to develop their own organization, rather than merely being told in detail what to do by management consultants who had been hired in.

The outline corporate plan for the new design/redesign, however, created some resentment, the basis of which was not easy to grasp. Clearly any idea of undertaking a 'pilot' in the form of demonstration projects or showcases was met with hostility. Managers and union leaders both seemed to think in terms of standard, corporate-wide solutions, and found it hard to imagine that the various sites could develop organizationally in line with their own situation and resources. If that were to happen, many seemed convinced that either all corporate synergies would disappear, or else the single pilot scheme would determine the kind of solutions that all the others should implement. The outcome was a rethinking of the general plan designed to implement the new production philosophy. Although the policy to use the works council system was not changed, top management was clearly uncertain about how to achieve coordinated site-level development without recourse to standardized organizational solutions promoted through a central campaign. The offers of practical support for the works councils and for the development of the production organization for the Hermod field were, however, being upheld.

Over the following year, the WRI was invited by four different works councils to help them improve their ability to work together and to start a discussion on more general local change strategies. At the same time, the WRI was invited to work with the Hermod team (see below), and top management stated clearly that the Hermod project should be the first case of employee and union involvement from the first day of planning. Though there was considerable financial and technological risk associated with this project, management nevertheless opted for the participative approach.

In parallel, the joint management/union working parties continued to discuss change strategy across all production facilities. They also visited a number of advanced enterprises in Norway and abroad, sometimes with the Hermod team and sometimes on their own, and drafted a set of reports, which were finally accepted by all parties. This work also fed into the ongoing debate about redesigning the collective agreement for offshore employees. The existing agreement was structured by job classification, formal qualifications and length of service. Hence it reflected and reinforced the existing form of work organization. The feeling was that there was a need to reward learning at work more explicitly and also to create a better bridge from offshore to onshore work.

Developing a New Manufacturing Philosophy

Parallel to the discussions on the company works council, the company had also commissioned a benchmarking process, comparing itself to other oil and gas producers and processors. In the area of offshore petroleum production, the study revealed that although this particular enterprise was among the largest in the world, its productivity was only mediocre. It had not (yet) shown itself able to benefit financially from its size and from having most of its production facilities located in the same region.

A working party consisting of the relevant local union leaders and managers from offshore production was established to work on a plan to improve performance and efficiency. Towards the end of 1996, it produced a document that dealt with a number of the issues that had led to disputes and low trust in management. It spelt out the vision for the production part of the company and the main principles underpinning work organization, management, personnel issues, and health, safety and environmental policy. The unions particularly welcomed the explicit policies on outsourcing and redundancies. The company went far in stating policies that would ensure security of employment for its workers, while at the same time laying down that the conditions for doing so were that the workers should be willing and interested in being flexible, taking more responsibility and improving their skills and competencies. During the final phase of drafting this document, special joint working parties began to deal more specifically with the questions of greenfield site design and brownfield redesign.

The company is, of course, a longstanding user of advanced information and communications technology (ICT). By the end of 2000, computer systems had taken over most communication and documentation functions. Letters, fax and hard copies are no longer much in use. In line with the new production philosophy, computer networks, along with functional and professional networks between people, had delayered much of the hierarchical corporate structure and opened up very decentralized ways of operating the production facilities, reducing data entry to a minimum.

Throughout the years 1997–2000, the brownfield redesign activities got under way on the approximately 20 production units offshore. Most of these are rather large facilities with up to 200 people on board at any one time. The oldest came on-stream just before 1980. The WRI was invited by the management of most of these units to help design start-up seminars, provide information, lecture, and in some cases to become quite deeply involved in designing strategy and the change process. These activities have run alongside the implementation of SAP software, in which there was heavy involvement of external consultants. Organizational development activities, however, are mostly undertaken by the local parties through the works council, with some support from WRI researchers working with the company's own organizational design specialists. 'Integrated teams' or 'self-managed teams' have been guiding local efforts in redesigning work organization, although the concept 'participative redesign' probably covers the realities better. It was the first time that the company had left such development to local management within a rather broadly stated philosophy.

Indeed, union leaders, workers and managers at all levels have been involved in the implementation process, and the plans for transition have been formally approved by the local works councils. The production and maintenance workers, who will constitute the new teams, will carry most administrative functions (such as budgeting, ordering tools and spares, financial and inventory control and planning training) as part of their daily routine. Workers and managers from Hermod have participated in start-up seminars for most of the other units throughout the year 2000. Most production units have also made the first moves away from the old craft-based forms of work organization towards more integrated versions. A modified pay system gives an extra allowance for multi-skilling and working in teams.

Formal organization has so far become flatter (the supervisory level has gone). Coordination between teams, and between the integrated teams and the team of managers, takes place through sets of scheduled meetings on a daily and weekly basis. Functional and professional networks have been defined and each member of the organization has been tied into them. These networks now formally constitute a web linking the other dividing lines in the organization. Some network-building activities have been initiated, but the networks are still at an early stage of development.

The Production Ship: Hermod Alpha

Oil production on the Hermod field started from a production ship ('Alpha') early in 1999, while the second unit ('Beta'), a semi-submersible gas production platform, came on-stream in October 2000 together with 'Charlie', a storage tanker permanently moored on the field. Total investments, covering the offshore production facilities, the drilling of wells, underwater systems, pipelines and land-based processing plants and bases, amounted to between US\$ 5 and 6 billion.

Hermod is seen as an important example of the new corporate strategy in practice. The concept of 'pilot project' is not being used, because the new general strategy and policies have already been decided in the company. However, Hermod is the first opportunity for a greenfield site design to appear after the new policies had been approved. It is commonly assumed that it is easier to create a state of the art production system when starting from scratch than modifying an existing plant and organization. As a result, expectations about Hermod within the company were very high and certainly higher than in the case of older units.

The technical design of the ship started early in 1996. The ship was built in Japan and came to Norway early in 1998 for completion. The director for production, who was appointed early in 1996, was concerned that operating staff should be involved in the early design phase so that they could bring in the 'user perspective' as soon as possible. This involved making the design team consider – and if necessary, modify or change – the technical aspects of productivity, health and safety and the working and living environment in the production phase. The director seriously endorsed the newly emerging philosophy of the company, and was quite aware that its implementation would constitute a turnaround in relation to existing practices – a major and profound change.

At this stage in the company's development, staff with experience of both the design and operation of production systems were on hand. So it was possible to put together a team which could effectively influence the design process ('design for operability'). Earlier research in this field had identified the availability of such staff as a key factor in the successful use of greenfield site design opportunities (Qvale and Hanssen-Bauer, 1990; Qvale, 1993).

Recruitment of key staff for operations started in the second half of 1996 through internal advertising. To reach the target of 20 per cent women, vacancies were also announced in the company's land-based petrochemical plants. Initially, the Hermod operations team was not sufficiently large to allow it to constitute its own works council and work environment committee. Therefore, the corporate-level unions nominated representatives to liaise with Hermod management and to participate in the interim works council and the Hermod design process.

An initial two-day meeting in September 1996 for the 20 delegates, who at that time had been assigned to Hermod Production, laid out the following principles for building up the organization:

- organizing a process among Hermod employees to identify the core values on which the organization should be built (*Defining the Hermod Culture*);
- multi-skilled, integrated teams to take care of all routine operations and maintenance tasks on board the ship;
- extensive use of computer networks and data systems to make the teams self-managing;
- involving the unions and all employees in the design and development process, through a joint team and working parties, plus regular meetings and team-building activities involving all those working for Hermod Production;
- starting joint fact finding activities, particularly visits to advanced manufacturers in Norway and other countries;
- limited use of external consultants.

Discussions revealed considerable disagreement and scepticism in relation to both the visionary statements of the director and the company's willingness and ability to follow up the policies. 'Isn't this just another campaign or fad?' and 'How can we trust the company to follow up all its fine words?' were amongst the questions asked. On the other hand, all those present expressed strong interest in developing an organization that would be different from the company's traditional, bureaucratic and centralized forms of decision making. The local union leaders expressed their satisfaction with the opportunity to participate in all phases of the development of the new organization, but also said that they expected it would be difficult to create something radically new and better within the (unchanged) context of the rest of the company.

A joint management/union team formed the interim works council that was to be main body for planning the development. Two joint working groups were also established, one to work on 'the Hermod culture' and the other to work on implementing the integrated team idea.

Their work included joint visits to advanced manufacturers in several sectors and countries abroad. From these visits, they realized there were no fixed *a priori* ready-made solutions and that they would have to find their own. The most important effect, however, was the acquisition of shared experience against which they could test their own values and assumptions. For example, when on occasion confronted by certain management and union ideas and attitudes on a visit abroad, there was often a clear convergence of Norwegian management and union representatives' views about what was desirable.

Over this period the company also had two new plants in their final phase of completion. One was a shore-based petrochemical plant with an innovative organizational design inspired by a Canadian plant (DuPont), and the other was an oil production ship with organizational design more directly linked to the company's new manufacturing philosophy. Both were radical in relation to the company's past but generally in tune with the new production philosophy. However, Hermod production facilities were to be even more radical, both in terms of involving the workers and unions deeply in the design and development process and in terms of the work environment created through the end design. At Hermod there would, for instance, be *no* supervisors, while the other two facilities still included such roles in their work organization in the start-up and early production phases, with the possibility of removing them later.

Within an open socio-technical systems perspective, the working group on culture undertook measures to identify core organizational values and a code of conduct. The well-known problem of linking values and practices then appeared. Discussions about 'what is important for you besides pay, health and safety and security of employment', however, gradually brought forth a set of criteria and values. These included freedom, truth, honesty, learning and development, compassion, well-being, a sense of belonging and trust.

A brief summary was printed and distributed to all Hermod employees. However, there were some strong negative reactions from the corporate level. Here some managers saw it as a 'unilateral declaration of independence' from Hermod. Heated discussions emerged about possible inconsistencies between Hermod's policies and the company's (that is, between the general management philosophy of the company and the production philosophy). In the end, the dispute was resolved or died out, because formally speaking there were no significant contradictions between the documents and because Hermod's need to operationalize and attach meanings to its own concepts had to be accepted.

Consolidation of the 'integrated team concept' on board the Alpha ship gradually led to a solution with four teams, each having responsibility for all systems and tasks within a geographical section of the ship, one catering/ service team and a management team of three. A further team of varying size to be staffed by maintenance contractors was also included. Despite criticisms from elsewhere in the company about the degree of union involvement, the proposed solution, with integrated teams covering all the main skills, resulted in a staffing level below any other comparable production unit. It was also considerably lower than early management estimates for Hermod. Acceptance of the proposal within the various unions involved followed more or less automatically from their participation in the process. Regular team-building activities were organized to induct newcomers and to help the team develop a common understanding of values, purpose and procedures.

One year before the planned start-up of production, all the employees (managers and workers) who were to operate the new unit had been recruited, and some key staff for the Beta platform had been identified. The dedicated Hermod operating organization had grown to around 140 members spread across three shift groups of 35 workers each and a shore-based support organization of around 30. The level of qualifications and experience was high for all groups of employees.

When the ship came to Norway for its final fitting out one year before production was due to start, the Hermod production organization took key roles in the testing and commissioning of all systems, including the new work organization. Sorting out new roles, responsibilities and relationships turned out a demanding process but generally systems worked well. The ship then sailed out and entered service as planned. The first year was difficult because of equipment failures and technical design errors, which caused production stoppages and the need to replace major units and redesign systems. Despite the extra workloads that resulted, however, there was no wish to return to ordinary ways of working. The system with integrated teams became well established and is being continuously improved and extended into new areas. Efforts to develop the relationship with the support teams in the shore-based part of Hermod Production have also been successful and may signify the first steps in creating the network organization that is part of the corporate vision.

Meanwhile, production on Hermod B, which is the world's largest semi-submersible offshore production unit, started on schedule in October 2000. Its organizational design is based on the same principles as those on Hermod A, and some core staff were relocated from A to B to help transfer experience. The start-up went well overall and the organizational development processes have been designed the same way. However, serious design faults and other problems with the technology also appeared and had to be put right. Commitment to the new way of working is still strong, and it would appear that developments are more or less following the same pattern as on A.

Summary of Methods Applied

The following summarizes the nature of the innovations in participatory practices at Hermod.

1   Joint consultation and the development of agreement on general policies in important areas and their formalization into a statement on company philosophy. This is less binding than a collective agreement, but was seen by the unions as good enough as a platform for collaboration on organizational development.

2   Utilizing the works councils at company and site levels as the main forums for participation in the planning, initiation and evaluation of the enterprise's development. This is a rather dramatic change from common practice in the company and in Norwegian industry in general. These bodies, and particularly the works councils, tend to be reactive, rather than proactive, in joint consultation and information disclosure.

3   Joint working parties to develop strategy and proposals for solutions and report back to the works councils. Central union representatives acted on behalf of the local unit until local representatives could be elected.

4   Joint site visits abroad. These acted both as fact-finding and discussion/ clarification activities. It was the first time that union representatives had travelled together with management in this way. These activities had the indirect consequence of securing the understanding and continuing support of the union leadership at company level.

5   Employee involvement from day one. When the employees through their unions became involved in the organizational design process, no decisions had yet been made.

6   Broad involvement in recruitment, planning, training, evaluation and organization. Reports from the working groups, management and local unions were presented and discussed in larger meetings to which all employees were invited.

7   Utilizing the organizational principles applicable in the production phase from the outset in the preparatory stages. Teamwork was the main organizing principle in the initial planning stage as well as in the design of administrative systems and in commissioning the production unit itself. The purpose was to work with a consistent set of principles all the way through.

8   Systematic review of experiences against agreed values and principles. Action researchers had a role in helping to highlight experiences and propose remedial action when problems were identified.

9   Extra responsibilities for all team members in addition to their main production and maintenance tasks. These extra roles were distributed according to task needs and special skills and interests. For example, the coordinator role is rotated among all team members, because they all need to learn to cover this function.

10 Utilizing action researchers and organizational development resources from the company to help with the process. Such resources were made available to all groups, and gradually they learnt to use them. The strategy from the researchers' side was to collaborate with the various working parties, meetings, workshops and works councils in helping them with methods for joint problem solving. All Hermod employees were also given a short course in group-work methods based on Total Quality Management thinking.

11 Regular participation of the Hermod Production team with the other members of the WRI's Forum for Advanced Manufacturing for the Process Industry. Here joint management/union teams from Norway's largest enterprises meet twice a year to share experiences.

Concluding Remarks: the Unfinished Process

The challenge of Hermod was to ensure the parallel development of its work organization, its system of management and union relations and its application of technology, while at the same remaining aware of the boundaries, that is, its relationship to the external environment and particularly to top management.

We assume that the external environment today is much more conducive to organizational redesign and development than in earlier phases of the democratization of working life in Norway. So relatively more resources can be spent on the company's internal processes, and the chances for succeeding are in general much better than before. Success would then mean a total transformation of the company's way of organizing itself and developing its production facilities from the traditional hierarchical, functionally divided form towards an integrated, flexible, participative form.

A breakthrough happened in the year 2000 when all existing offshore production units of the company initiated participative redesign processes and invited Hermod team members to help in the start-up phase of their discussion and planning sessions. Earlier animosity between the different units has been sharply reduced, and there are now signs of constructive exchange between them rather than competition and suspicion. Initially we assumed that managing the relationship with company top management would represent the most serious long-term challenge faced by our action research methods. Indeed, it is still open whether support from company headquarters will be sustained. It is partly a challenge to the leaders of the production units to bring headquarters along with them. So far, however, the process has been relatively smooth. The shareholders replaced the board of directors and chief executive officer (CEO) in 1999, but this did not lead to any change in policy in this field, rather the opposite. The new CEO did, however, set some tough cost reduction targets to be met from 2001, which constitute the backdrop for the changes in the organization.

After four years of systematic activities, it seems that the social partners in Hermod have learnt to manage the development of their own internal, systems, including involving external organizational development resources when needed. Consultation has created an understanding that each production unit has to find its own solutions within the terms of a common policy or philosophy. The introduction of SAP so far seems generally to support the decentralization process, but whether this will remain so in the future is uncertain.

One very central positive result, which cuts across all production units, is that the trust between top management and offshore workers/local unions seems to have been re-established. This, we believe, is mainly because top management is committed to the decision to involve the local unions, the works councils and the workers in general from 'day one' when new initiatives are being considered. For the unions, new forms of work organization are no longer a contentious issue, and all the local unions support this development. In other areas they have different policies and tactics and their leaders may have quite different attitudes to the company and its leadership. The unions have also, so far, seemed to manage the growing pluralism in work organization across the different units. The same collective agreement still applies to all units.

The other side of democratic participation – that individual workers and teams of workers increase their involvement and learning at work, and hence become more autonomous and innovative – can also be observed at Hermod, and is certainly valued by workers and managers alike. For them this is the most important aspect of the changes in the company. We can, however, only speculate with respect to the likely long-term effects of these changes on their commitment to their various unions.

Over the four years of participating in Hermod, the central and local shop stewards have shifted away from a rather sceptical bargaining mode in their dealings with its management. They have, on the whole, learnt to work openly on defining problems, and then searching for and trying out solutions against the agreed criteria. One side effect, however, is that workers in Hermod – which is rather small – have learnt about each others' strong and weak points, and have therefore become better in selecting people for the various task assignments that emerge. Consensus on such issues runs across union affiliations. Therefore, in elections for the works council and work environment committee, candidates are proposed and elected to some degree independently of their union membership. Hence the composition of these bodies may not always reflect the relative strength of the unions present. This phenomenon illustrates the need for adjusting union thinking and practices in line with the requirements of this kind of local development.

So far the experience from the works councils, which have brought in action research support, seems positive. However, continual monitoring is needed. Serious efforts are required to bring important issues to the attention of the works councils if they are to remain alert and active. Rapid turnover of managers and shop stewards makes this process all the more difficult.

In view of the current development of more flexible, participative and integrated forms of work organization, the traditional, complex system of representative democracy within the enterprise may seem a bit out of date. It rather reflects the bureaucratic, hierarchical concept of the organization of the past. To quote Eijnatten (1993), the trend in working life is away from complex organizations and simple jobs and towards simple organizations and complex jobs. On this basis we *could* argue that the formal arrangements for workers' indirect participation could be removed or simplified because the need for participation is now taken care of through other mechanisms in the course of routine work organization. Alternatively, we might argue along the lines of this chapter, namely that the bodies for joint consultation and decision making could be mobilized to take a key role in coordinating the process of organizational transformation. They could, for example, take the role normally assigned to special bipartite task groups and steering committees, which tend to be set up when major organizational change is on the agenda. This argument would also be consistent with the view that workers and their representatives have to be involved both in developing work organization and in their daily routines in order to be able to participate actively in discussions and negotiations in representative bodies at board level (Emery and Thorsrud, 1969).

We have listed above some of the more obviously unsettled issues. Others will appear and some have been looming for a while. The need for a new reward system at Hermod has been announced, but so far this kind of issue has been dealt with at company and industry levels. We might also expect that the notion of a career and our approaches towards further education could also take a new twist. In principle, offshore working with its particular shift patterns opens up completely new ways of balancing family and work, and work and education in the context of gender issues. And if new bridges between offshore and onshore work are being constructed, then even more options become apparent. One challenge will be to create an environment that supports such changes. For the company, the development of tolerance towards diversity across its various production units is a part of that challenge. To succeed, the company will have to accept that these units must construct their own realities within the general framework of general policies and some common understanding of direction.

A second implication is that the policies, roles and functions of unions and their local representatives will have to develop alongside one another for the unions to remain viable. So far, we can argue that the bottom-up, participative, self-organizing process in Hermod has opened up for its employees the chance to make their values explicit and then to use these as criteria for assessing the socio-technical solutions they have designed. But the bottom-up process is partly preceded by and partly runs in parallel with a top-down participative process linked to the hierarchy of works councils across the company, themselves based on collective agreements and legislation. This means that the union leaders transcend the traditional boundaries of union participation and influence. They operate far beyond bargaining over pay and conditions and working hours through joint consultation in the works council. Rankin (1990), on the basis of Canadian experience, argues that participation in this type of process is the best way to develop the kind of local union representation needed in the future. Through representative democracy in the company, local union representatives also have mechanisms for taking fresh looks at the bottom-up system. It may be that we are indeed witnessing aspects of a new trade union paradigm in this complex pattern of bargaining, participation in joint decision making and involvement in workplace development.

In the multi-union setting of this company, it can also be argued that the active utilization of the works council system could create joint learning and development processes across production units and local unions. After only four years of experience, however, it is still too early to conclude whether the parties have actually been able to make use of this system as a vehicle for a necessary turnaround of the company. For the unions it was important to prevent 'fads and fashions' and the widespread use of special project teams with worker 'representatives' handpicked by management. As long as top management is committed to the decision to utilize the works council system, works councils may indeed act as a joint learning arena for the different unions as well.

The experiences with democratic participation in this company are in principle valid only for this single case. However, all the other advanced manufacturers in this sector are on the same track towards decentralized, integrated, participative and flexible forms of participation, and they all involve their local unions and employees in various ways. The attempt to utilize the works council system so extensively is, as far as we know, unique to this company. In the process industry in Norway in general, however, we see the same general trend towards enhanced participation as in the case presented here. The radical redesign of the organization at Hermod has been an inspiration for the redesign of older organizations in a number of other companies. For the last five years or so, a forum for new production concepts in the process industry – which brings together operations managers and union leaders from all the major process industries in Norway – has supported this kind of transfer of experience.

Similar developments are reported from other countries, even though there are differences in union densities and legislation on formal participation, and clear signs that union membership is declining in virtually all but the Scandinavian countries. Within the confines of the process industry in Norway, however, we would argue that the existing framework for formal participation and the mutual level of trust developed over decades has created a platform for further democratization of the workplace. In this context, the local unions will remain legitimate partners and probably retain their membership.

Notes

1   I am indebted to my colleagues in the WRI team of researchers involved in this large-scale project, notably Beate Karlsen, Øystein Fossen, Fredrik Winther and Kathrine Holstad, and to our partners in the management and unions of the company involved. The background to the complex process of change in this company can be found partly in the long-standing research that has been taking place since the 1960s into Norwegian working life, workers' democratic participation and industrial democracy (Emery and Thorsrud, 1969, 1976; Qvale, 1976; Gustavsen, 1992). These research activities have been organized in the form of bi- and tripartite programmes, mainly at the national level, and have led both to a number of remarkable changes in working life and to interesting research results. The objective of these changes was initially to create work organizations *(a new design)*, which gave the workers greater scope for decision making and learning in the job than the traditional scientific management/bureaucratic solutions. Improved productivity was not in itself an objective, although productivity increases did follow (Gulowsen, 1975). Gradually, in the 1970s and 1980s, the approach became more *process oriented* and hence shifted to direct participation in redesigning work organization. Broad involvement of the employees in the change process through various forms of discussion came into focus. Then finally, since the 1990s, efforts have been directed towards the promotion of both a participative redesign and enterprise development process, and the provision of more concrete tools and concepts, which the partners can use to create better organizational solutions.

2   An independent federation consisting of the workers employed by the operating companies emerged early. It is still the largest union for offshore oil company employees, and most of it recently joined a national confederation. Workers employed by the most common offshore contractors (such as construction, maintenance, drilling, catering, supplies, helicopter links, well-services and underwater operations) are spread across a large number of unions. Two older national federations are also firmly established. LO in the 1970s formed its own union for petroleum workers, which targets all groups including academics. It had a slow start, but has grown considerably over the last 10 years. Another independent national federation has recruited some of the production operators. This multi-union structure, and the competition between the various unions, have historically created a complex and turbulent situation. Pay levels offshore are about 50 per cent higher than for comparable work onshore. Therefore national pressures to keep wage drift offshore under control have been high and have led to many cases of compulsory arbitration connected with collective bargaining.

References

Borgen, S.O. (1995), 'Samarbeid om bedriftsutvikling. Hvilke krav stilles til lokale fagforeninger?', in Olberg, D. (ed.), *Endringer i Arbeidslivets Organizering*, FAFO, Oslo.

Commission of the EC (1997), *Partnership for a New Organization of Work*, Green Paper, April, Directorate-General V, Brussels.

Didier, J.M. (1997), *European Works Councils. A Comparative Analysis of National Implementing Measures of the European Directive 94/95/EC of 22 September 1994*, Club de Bruxelles, Brussels.

Eijnatten, F.M. (1993), *The Paradigm that Changed the Work Place*, Van Gorcum, Assen.

Eikeland, O. and Henrik, F.D. (eds) (1995), *Forskning og handling, Søkelys på aksjonsforskning*, Work Research Institute, Oslo.

Emery, F.E. (1978), *The Emergence of a New Paradigm of Work*, Centre for Continuing Education, Australian National University, Canberra.

Emery, F.E. and Thorsrud, E. (1969), *Form and Content in Industrial Democracy*, Tavistock, London.

Emery, F.E. and Thorsrud, E. (1976), *Democracy at Work*, Nijhoff, Leiden.

Engelstad, P.H. (1996), 'The Development Organization as Communicative Instrumentation: Experiences from the Karlstad Program', in Toulmin, S. and Gustavsen, B. (eds), *Beyond Theory. Changing Organizations through Participation*, John Benjamins, Amsterdam.

Falkum, E. (2000), 'Når partssamarbeidet setter dagsorden', in Pålshaugen, Ø. and Qvale, T.U. (eds), *Forskning og Bedriftsutvikling – Nye Samarbeidsforsøk*, Publication Series 9/2000, Work Research Institute, Oslo.

Gulowsen, J. (1975), *Arbeidervilkår*, Et tilbakeblikk på Samarbeidsprosjektet LO/NAF, Tanum-Norli, Oslo.

Gustavsen, B. (1992), *Dialogue and Development*, Van Gorcum, Assen.

Gustavsen, B., Colbjørnsen, T. and Pålshaugen, Ø. (1998), *Development Coalitions in Working Life. The Enterprise 2000 Program in Norway*, John Benjamins, Amsterdam.

Kester, G. and Pinaud, H. (eds) (1996), *Trade Unions and Democratic Participation in Europe: A Scenario for the 21st Century*, Avebury, Aldershot.

Lange, K. (1968), *Samarbeidsprosjektet LO/NAF og fagforeningsforhold*, Work Research Institute, Oslo.

NOU (1999), *Nytt Millenium, Nytt Arbeidsliv. Trygghet og verdiskapning i et fleksibelt arbeidsliv. Utredning fra et utvalg oppnevnt ved kongelig resolusjon av 19.mars 1999* ('New Millenium, New Working Life. Security and the Creation of Wealth in a Flexible Working Life. Recommendations from a Commission appointed by the Government 19 March 1999'), NOU 1999, No. 34, Ministry of Municipal and Regional Affairs, Oslo.

Pålshaugen, Ø. (1998), *The End of the Theory of Organization?*, John Benjamins, Amsterdam.

Qvale, T.U. (1976), 'A Norwegian Strategy for the Democratization of Industry', *Human Relations*, Vol. 29, No. 5, pp. 453–69.

Qvale, T.U. (1993), 'Design for Safety in Large-scale Industrial Projects: the Case of the Norwegian Offshore Oil Development', in Wilpert, B. and Qvale, T.U. (eds), *Safety and Reliability in Hazardous Work Systems*, Lawrence Erlbaum, Hove.

Qvale, T.U. (1996a), 'Direct Participation in Scandinavia: From Workers' Rights to Economic Necessity', in Kester, G. and Pinaud, H. (eds), *Trade Unions and Democratic Participation in Europe: A Scenario for the 21st Century*, Avebury, Aldershot, pp. 135–48.

Qvale, T.U. (1996b), 'Local Development and Institutional Change: Experience from a "Fifth Generation" National Programme for the Democratization of Work Life', in Drenth, P.J.D., Koopman, P.L. and Wilpert. B. (eds), *Organizational Decision Making under Different Economic and Political Conditions*, North Holland, Amsterdam.

Qvale, T.U. (1998a), 'Background Report: Inquiry on Flexibility', Eurocadres Symposium on Work Organization, New Technology and Flexibility. Challenges for Professional and Managerial Staff, Vienna, October, *Eurocadres*, Brussels.

Qvale, T.U. (1998b), 'Past, Present and Future of Quality of Work Life in Norway: Some Reflections after 30 Years of National Reforms and Research Programs', 24th International Congress of Applied Psychology, San Francisco, 9–14 August.

Qvale, T.U. and Hanssen-Bauer, J. (1990), 'Implementing QWL in Large Scale Project Organizations: Blue Water Site Design in the Norwegian Offshore Oil Industry', in Meadow, H.L. and Sirgy, M.J. (eds), *Quality of Life Studies in Marketing and Management*, Proceedings: The Third Quality of Life/Marketing Conference, Virginia Polytechnic Institute and State University, Blacksburg, Virginia.

Qvale, T.U. and Serck-Hanssen, C. (1999), 'The European Works Council: Demokratisering av arbeidslivet på internasjonalt nivå?', in Falkum, E., Eldring, L. and Colbjørnsen, T. (eds), *Medbestemmelse og medvirkning*, Forskningsstiftelsen FAFO, Oslo.

Rankin, T. (1990), *New Forms of Work Organization – the Challenge for North American Unions*, The University of Toronto Press, Toronto.

Rudolf, S. (1999), *Polish Representatives of Company Employees in European Works Councils*. Report, Institute of Economics, University of Lodz, Poland.

Thorsrud, E. (1978), *Reflections on the Lysebu Conference on Oil Activities*, AI.Doc 1/1978, Work Research Institute, Oslo.

Trist, E.L. (1981), *The Evolution of Socio-Technical Systems*, Occasional Paper No. 2, Ontario Quality of Working Life Center, Toronto.

PART III
THEMATIC ASPECTS

Chapter 9

Social Transformation, Self-organization at Work and Participation in Germany

Helmut Martens

Introduction

Questions about the future of industrial democracy lie at the heart of the issues under discussion here. This chapter outlines first of all the general background to these questions, a globalized economy, and – in common with many contemporary observers – we shall be assuming that we are currently on the cusp of a new epoch that can most readily be compared with the radical changes of the early nineteenth century (Fricke, 2001; Hutton and Giddens, 2000; Martens et al., 2001). It is possible, then, to speak in terms of the end of the Fordist model of regulation (Dörre, 2001b) as well as of a closely related and deep crisis in the institutions of the former, Fordist labour-based society. The argument is therefore posited on acceptance of a real and profound crisis of the old labour society as seen in institutional terms and determined by Fordism. It cannot be assumed that the Fordist model of regulation that we previously knew will ever re-emerge.

The institutionally rooted forms of this old labour society seem to be especially stable in Germany and, indeed, were arguably transferred particularly successfully to the former East Germany in the early 1990s (Martens, 1996; Hoffmann et al., 1994). However, this is a rather superficial view. The old institutional forms of codetermination now provide a framework for negotiation of radically different issues. 'Cooperation' as it used to be defined is not necessarily what we now understand by 'cooperation'. In the heyday of Fordism, bargaining centred on the extent of the partial decoupling of wage labour from market risk; now, in the era of the 'labour entrepreneur', it centres rather on re-establishing a link between employment and market risk (Dörre, 2001a).

The debates now are no longer about the major alternatives to capitalism: utopian alternatives are no longer on the agenda. And nobody argues that the market is anything other than an institutional achievement. The major faultline now is between attempts at regulation of a new welfare state on the one hand and concepts of radical, neo-liberal deregulation on the other. Objective observers are able to reach realistic assessments of the potential for social change only if they take this changed subjectivity into consideration. The key terms now are 'labour entrepreneur' (Voss and Pongratz, 1998), new, individual members of 'civil society' (Wolf, 2001) and 'subjectivization of labour' (Moldaschl, 2001). The term 'labour entrepreneur' (Arbeitskraftunternehmer) is a neologism which refers to those self-motivated workers who, engaged in various forms of team or project work, benefit from high degrees of autonomy at work. However, because they are likely to work in profit centres, they also develop entrepreneurial ways of thinking along with their employer.

Even then, though, the scope for change can be assessed either optimistically or pessimistically. The ultimate decision will depend less on criteria assumed to be 'objective' and more on the personality of the person reaching the assessment. It is interesting to note, though, that an observer as perceptive and, usually, optimistic as Anthony Giddens has most recently presented a critical view of developments.[1] I freely admit that I am more inclined to Gramsci's 'pessimism of the intelligence', but at the same time, I endorse the view that we should seek 'optimism of the will'. The general image of trade unions, codetermination and involvement offered by expert observers in Germany could be summarized as follows: the unions in Germany have had a decade of grappling with far-reaching changes, such as dwindling membership, mergers and organizational development processes (Martens, 2001) and now, after their hopes for a 'new politics' after the general elections of 1998 were dashed, they are debating the future in a search for new directions (IG Metall, 2001). I believe, however, that they are still very much 'children of Fordism' and have still to deal with the worst of the adaptation crisis. In the view of a number of prominent observers in the 1990s, the debates are about the 'sclerosis and decay of the old institutions' (Glotz, 1998), the 'successful failure' of the organizational reform of trade unions (Alemann and Schmid, 1998), the inevitable adaptation to the role of 'social monitor' (Streeck, 1999) and the 'danger of de-unionization' (Streeck, 1996). According to Hutton, however (Hutton and Giddens, 2000), it is too early to write the unions' obituary.

There is no question that the unions in Germany continue to lose members and are assuming in their planning that these losses will continue at the rate of three per cent a year. Their former core constituency, skilled workers from the major sectors of industry, is dwindling, and the unions have a long way to go in opening up to employees in the new knowledge economy, whether mainstream or on the periphery. What seems relatively stable in Germany is, therefore, actually being constantly and substantially eroded. It should, however, be clear that a further 10 years of 'successful failure' of organizational reform will ultimately no longer be successful.

The strongest defining features of German industrial relations have been works councils and codetermination, which contrast deeply with the Anglo-Saxon model (Kotthof, 1994), and even today these features still seem particularly stable. In the wake of the ascendancy of managerial participation models in the 1990s, a significant number of expert observers have referred to powerful new impetus for codetermination (Müller-Jentsch, 1993; Hilbert and Schmid, 1994). I argued against this from the outset and take a very different view (Martens, 1994; Martens, 1995; Martens, 2002).

Institutionalized codetermination as it was instigated in post-war Germany was part of the tradition of older concepts of economic democracy and could be seen as a pragmatic manifestation of some of their key notions in the specific social constellations of power of the post-war period (Borsdorf, 1982). This was, however, also true of the advance of managerial models of participation in the 1990s, prompted initially by controversy surrounding Japanese methods; many observers thought this would similarly provide impetus for codetermination but under a very different set of conditions. Under the pressure of globalization, both the trade unions and the concept of codetermination went on the defensive.

Two things can be observed: in institutional terms, strong codetermination rights have been weakened at the operative level; and already weak rights at the strategic decision making level have been further weakened while demands have been stepped up at the same level. Forms of direct participation have probably been strengthened overall, albeit in a thoroughly contradictory fashion, but it is clear that codetermination is still an issue only in the company and workplace arena and that it is assessed virtually exclusively in terms of its efficiency (Kommission Mitbestimmung, 1998). This Commission also noted growth in what it called 'codetermination-free zones'. However, it should not be forgotten that even weak codetermination rights have been extended by European works councils (see chapter 3 of this book), and that what management offers by way of worker involvement also includes prospects for participation and emancipation that reflect greater expectations and/or needs on the part of workers, thereby creating substantial potential for democratization. What follows focuses mainly on this issue.

Self-organization at Work and Participation – 10 Arguments

1   The whole debate about the future of work is probably the most revealing of all those covered in the survey carried out by IG Metall for its report on its own future. Workers taking part in the survey really represented an 'expert view' of their own positions. I detect a high degree of realism in their comments on the future shape of work, alongside notions of 'new work' and 'subjectivization of work', and of the 'labour entrepreneur' 'between self-determination and self-exploitation'; these are clearly emerging trends, and no longer distant concepts.

IG Metall, the German metalworking union, comments in its report (IG Metall, 2001) that elements of the future of work, such as workers taking responsibility for their own skills, for organizing their own work and for results, are increasingly becoming elements of employment, for example in conjunction with team- or group-working and new working time patterns. Its empirical findings suggest that in some respects, the concept meets with workers' approval, for example their views on skills training or on working time arrangements, or the fact that respondents took a value-based approach to vocational labour and had generally high levels of job satisfaction more or less across the board.

With respect to the 'new members of civil society' – workers as citizens, whom the trade unions seek to recruit and, indeed, must recruit if they are to remain viable in future – the evidence lies in support of a fundamental change (Martens, Peter and Wolf, 2001): Fordism is in its death throes. I also see here evidence that workers' hopes and aspirations are bound up with the changing shape of labour (Voss and Pongratz, 1998; Martens, Peter and Wolf, 2001; Moldaschl, 2001). The question that then arises is whether neo-liberal promises of new work and new concepts of work (Deckstein and Felixberger, 2000) are really the actual successors to Fordism.

2   Among the promises of the neo-liberal revolution are managerial models of participation. These became popular particularly with the focus on Japan in the early 1990s but are to be found in all entrepreneurial models of modernization. Total Quality Management and continuous improvement processes are just two of the key concepts in the debate. Learning organizations, flat hierarchies, networks, management of change, learning and dialogue also characterize the literature, and some of these concepts can be seen as modern myths that drive the process of modernization.

All these concepts form part of human experience and are reflected in the expectations of new labour entrepreneurs. However, a modest overall view is taken of the development of labour in IG Metall's survey. Not only do respondents expect and welcome the prospect of greater use of teamwork in future, but there is also an expectation, viewed critically, that casual labour, overtime and poorly paid service jobs will increase.

These perspectives have already been thrown up as IG Metall has engaged with organizational development as part of its 'participation-oriented trade union company policy' project. In the wake of participation initiatives, demands have been constructed and consolidated, even in cases where participation came about 'with its back to the wall' – that is, aimed ultimately at rationalization (Martens and Frerichs, 1999) – and succeeded in developing further around such processes. I shall return to this point below.

3   First, though, I should like to consider one or two conceptual points that, in my view, demonstrate the extent to which and the reason why participation and codetermination carries high importance for the emerging new type of labour entrepreneur. The clearest illustration of this is, perhaps, to be seen in what is termed the 'new economy'.[2] The 'new economy' is, moreover, not a peripheral phenomenon that will disappear now the NEMAX (the new technology share index) bubble has burst but, as a 'knowledge economy' (Castel, 2000), it is intimately bound up with the 'old economy', maybe even inextricably (Hack, 2001) and is gaining steadily in influence. With trends emerging in differing time frames, here is a particularly clear present example of what we can all expect in the future.

A 'labour entrepreneur' fluctuates between self-determination and self-exploitation. The demands and challenges of self-organization at work, of 'doing it yourself' (Wolf, 2001; Peters, 2001), produce a fundamentally changed form of labour. These workers operate in teams with partial autonomy and on a networking basis, and are directly confronted with the requirements of the market; the old hierarchies, meanwhile, are becoming flatter and waning in importance. As consumers and citizens, these new representatives of a different form of highly skilled worker perceive their work as meeting a long-term need for employment with social demands, or else they articulate such demands themselves, often in relation to themes and issues that are raised in public discourse (such as environmental concerns and so on).

As a result, the dream of self-determined but also socially responsible work is evolving rapidly, but there is a danger that it may also rapidly turn into a nightmare of consistent dependence on markets. Old institutional structures that promoted social integration and solidarity are now eroding, to be replaced by what Sennet (1998) called 'the corrosion of character'. The images of man (and the labour entrepreneur is, in fact, a thoroughly male concept) that are now prevalent are those of the winners in the struggle to compete.[3]

We need to take seriously this tension between new promises and the ensuing positive and negative experiences. It is no longer enough simply to assert that people are not aware that new false promises, or ideology, are leading them increasingly to exploit themselves. Nor will it be enough simply to tell people that they are under an illusion. We need instead to identify with the way in which individuals understand and interpret their own situations when they work in radically altered conditions, and to create new space for dialogue and policy alternatives that are tailored to new problems and to those individuals' needs and interests. In short, we need to develop projects or experiments (Wolf, 2001) that connect with the 'primary' labour policy of the new labour entrepreneurs, open up new opportunities for negotiation and use new institutionalization processes in the shape of 'secondary' labour policy to exploit these opportunities.[4]

4   In relation to my theme of 'industrial democracy', the central argument is now that the experience of 'doing it yourself' brings with it far-reaching potential and demands for greater democracy. Moreover, these indicate future trends that are radically different from the narrow field of industrial democracy that characterized Fordism. However, those employees who formulated demands for participation and lived through all the tensions when those demands were met in the 1990s also lived through continuous business reorganization that substantially frustrated their demands in response to the need to break down demarcations within work and to increase shareholder value. They were confronted with trade unions and institutional codetermination practices that did not always reflect their own perceptions of participation or at least did not have the appropriate solutions to offer. Let us first, though, take a look at companies.

The first half of the 1990s was the heyday of entrepreneurial models of participation, such as quality circles, now long since past. What we see today are forms of guided and highly selective participation (Dörre, 2001a; Jürgenhake et al., 1999), with instances of 'co-entrepreneurship' and encouragement of real dialogue in everyday company situations, including now in companies within the much-vaunted 'new economy'.

Simultaneously, the demand for greater self-organization at work has strengthened both demands for participation (and not just in manufacturing) and the potential that employees bring to such participative processes. It is, then, no coincidence that the issue of direct participation took off in the early 1990s, having long been a focus of trade union policy and practice yet never having been fully developed there. However, the unions failed to make direct participation a broad topic of employment policy even where they had the actors to do so at company level (Frerichs and Bundesmann-Jansen, 1995; Martens and Frerichs, 1999).

Since unemployment has, broadly speaking, remained high, issues of sustainability of both natural and human resources have slipped down the agenda. However, since use of resources is an ongoing issue, these arguments are tending to increase in importance and to be brought to the fore by occasional social crises, such as the BSE crisis.

5   In newcomer and start-up companies in what is called the 'new economy', two features are observable. First, there is company practice where management considers it important to avoid claims by the unions for participation under law (Works Constitution Act); here, employees often think they have to manage alone and in line with company practices. Second, after the bubble of speculation on the NEMAX share index burst in March 2000, many more works councils were formed and trade union pilot schemes achieved some successes.

An up-to-date (2001) study on the scope and forms of worker participation in the new economy in 225 of the 344 companies then listed on the new German equities listing, the *neuer Markt*, found that 39 per cent of those companies – and as many as 48 per cent of the companies with more than 500 employees – had some organized form of worker participation (www.politik-digital.de). In 26 per cent, it was a works council, while 13 per cent had some kind of customized form of participation. In half of all cases, statutory or alternative forms of participation had been in place for more than three years. In the case of start-ups, which made up 38 of the 225 companies in the sample, 20 per cent of these companies said they had some organized form of participation but not a works council. The study's authors hypothesize that forms of organized worker participation will probably increase further over the coming months, that the role-determined differences between employee and employer in the current situation are clear to all those involved, and that it is a marker of the potential for innovation within the new economy that these companies are not restricting themselves to the conventional forms of participation, even though – as the authors acknowledge – the traditional works council remains the best form in many cases.

Meanwhile, the first reports from trade union pilot schemes show that when contact is established, both material interests and issues of transparency in company decision-making take centre stage along with management/staff relations. It also emerges that while there is an abstract acknowledgement of the need for trade unions, companies will in practice put distance between themselves and the unions, fearing 'remote control'. The Siemens project found that IG Metall in particular has an image problem. Participation also focuses the spotlight on the policy services of trade unions, in some cases against a benchmarking model whereby a newly constituted works council will critically evaluate the services offered by various trade unions.

6   There is as yet rather little empirical information about labour relations in the information economy and about the expectations of both employees and management as to their future shape.[5] The empirical data we do have, however, support conceptual models of the ideal of a labour entrepreneur. Yet if these models are relevant to a new subjectivity both created by and creating a metamorphosis in work, then how do employees in the new economy see trade unions?

I stress above the promises of, demands for and potential of emancipation that go hand in hand with rising demands for and ability to deliver highly efficient work and work-related dealings. On the other hand, I also point to the contradictions inherent in experiences with globalization: when the market has such a pervading influence and the boundaries around work are removed, massive new loads can emerge, expectations of greater freedom are thwarted and productivist expectations (economic performance as the basis for social participation) or even stereotypical masculine ideals, such as that of the 'lone wolf', gain new force. At least, this can be the case where the conflicting experiences are dealt with in isolation against a backdrop of keener market competition.

The question, then, is what collective debate is going on and whether (and how) trade unions may succeed in finding ways of overcoming the contradictions and using and developing the new potential. It is clear from the findings of trade union pilot schemes that workers who to some extent match the stereotype of the labour entrepreneur are sceptical about (their current perceptions of) both unions and participation. This prejudice, but also justified criticism, makes for a formidable obstacle to overcome.[6]

7   The fact that trade unions and institutionalized participation gain support mostly, or only, in the abstract and in practice meet great resistance is not the result of deep-rooted prejudice from either workers or political opponents. It has more to do with the fact that the unions as 'large bureaucratic organizations' and codetermination as an 'inefficient bureaucratic structure' are strongly characteristic of the old Fordist model of regulation, having been part of that model for many decades.

The old image of trade unions derives from Fordism and is most strongly typified by IG Metall, a classic pioneer trade union representing skilled workers and fulfilling a collective bargaining role. In this image, trade unions equate with hierarchical and bureaucratic structures, cumbersome procedures, a closed mind, standardization and out-of-date ritual that leave no room for cultural diversity, experimentation and innovation. Participation – that is, creating scope for 'doing it yourself' – along with concrete services, transparency, a customer orientation and efficiency are expectations and demands that trade unions frequently failed to meet in the eyes of the new 'labour entrepreneurs'. Old images are so often borne out in practice, and it is easy for the fear of 'remote control' cited above to emerge. These organizations appear to have difficulty in moving with the times and 'daring to be more democratic'.

Much the same is true of institutionalized codetermination. Codetermination was seen as a basic concept for 'economic democracy' in its incarnation as a model for regaining social control of the economy against the backdrop of a fundamental clash of interests between labour and capital and with its aim of using public ownership to counter ownership of labour. It was, and remained after 1945, the brainchild of the Fordist model of regulation with typically downplayed direct participation and largely without precautions against externalization, such as the cost to the environment.

The result is that institutionalized participation encounters substantial reservations specifically among those working in the new economy. It has not succeeded in solving all the problems of control and efficiency, and scandals around failure of supervisory board scrutiny in the 1980s are just part of the problem. The truth is that, even where company-level participation worked relatively well, it was always an instrument for social policy support of decisions made on economic grounds. Such stakeholder interests, especially with strong emphasis of external control demands by national or regional union officials, have come to be challenged in a later era of shareholder value and in the light of codetermination practice. In the 1990s, every new, spectacular instance of mismanagement in private industry triggered questions about the role of the supervisors and, at least implicitly, criticism of codetermination.[7] The current debate around 'corporate governance' appears to focus on technical adequacy but is really solely about economic efficiency. This statement is of course an oversimplification, and the label itself smacks of ideology, yet there is no sign at all that the unions are in any position to initiate a new debate around participation policy on this basis.

Indeed, no active discussion is taking place around the tension between the need for efficiency on the one hand and transparency and scrutiny of entrepreneurial activity on the other, and the fact that the issue of ownership and classic models of social ownership will not deliver solutions. A whole series of issues is simply not adequately covered in debates held or initiated in union circles: the continued need for social supervision of economic activity even under the changed circumstances of a global economy; the need to take the interests of 'living labour' into account; the scope for long-term planning and for protection of environmental interests; recognition that costs cannot simply be externalized; and whether and how, aside from the challenge of international networks within the framework of European or transnational works councils, the fraught issues of globalization and localization can be transformed into a union focus on labour-oriented modernization within regional structural policy.[8]

There are, of course, networks actively debating these issues (see, for example, www.weltwoche.de or a 'network for socially responsible business' created by a group of Swiss university lecturers). What I am not aware of is any intensive dialogue between them and the trade unions. I see no evidence of active discussion within new alliances and coalitions of issues such as the future shape of institutional developments, including the (still crucial) topic of economic efficiency but also the (equally crucial) topic of workers' interests, consumer interests, gender issues and so on. The issues of environmental protection and long-term planning cut right across the debate around an innovative and innovation-promoting development of participation. It begins with rights to participation at company level over environmental protection and extends into corporate participation, where institutional anchoring of environmental interests is still worthy of debate. It is therefore of crucial importance within the framework of regional economic and structural policy (Agenda 21) where, under the banner of citizen involvement in issues to do with living and working in a region, further-reaching issues around the organization of involvement (for example, a debate around the best way to assess the impact of technology)[9] will be crucial for the future development of a living democracy.

8   As work has changed in the wake of the end of the Fordist model of regulation, analysis of the future trends in democratic structures too has had to be debated. There is both objective and subjective scope for democratization, the former including such factors as the internet, various kinds of network and non-governmental organizations (NGOs) and the latter taking the form of new subjectivity in work. This scope has to be seen against the backdrop of a loss of meaning and function on the part of the old institutional arrangements as well as of the organizations and institutions embodying them. Those who now wish to make meaningful use of such scope must be aware that the key issue is a potential for democratization arising from the subjectivization and the 'boundarylessness' of work that goes beyond the conventional framework of 'industrial democracy'.

These new calls, and scope, for democratization have so far been problematic because the existing institutions, including not only, for instance, the trade unions but also political institutions, have not yet come up with the right solutions. It is scant comfort for the unions and for institutional participation that other traditional institutions, like welfare associations, training bodies and so on, are faring little better and that even the political parties themselves now have a negative image. Much will depend on how the labour organizations and institutions, which have always stood particularly for the democratization of social and economic processes, are able to tailor their own models to exploit the new potential that labour entrepreneurs bring with them. If they cannot do this, they will continue to decline in both their significance and their scope for action; ultimately, even their past achievements towards social democratization could be eclipsed if new social movements do not emerge that are capable of identifying and progressing towards new democratization processes and achieving new institutional forms.

9   There is a risk that the traditional labour institutions cannot successfully adapt themselves in their efforts to come to grips with the new confusions that surround them, and that the old labour society's new knowledge of itself and its scope cannot be fully exploited. This 'new confusion' is nowhere near as extensive as when Habermas first developed the concept (neue Unübersichtlichkeit) in the mid-1980s, but top-down analysis – of the overview of processes of change – must be accompanied by a bottom-

up approach to the primary employment policy now unfolding against the backdrop of 'new work'. The issue here will be to develop an understanding of contexts and of real opportunities that increasingly operate outside the traditional work/life divide. This will need a critical analysis of emerging new 'objective' structures as well as acknowledgement of the way in which they have been overtaken by the individual civil social subjects who work and articulate their work-related interests under these new circumstances. There are huge challenges here for political education processes in the trade unions.

There are now calls for an unbiased bottom-up approach to these experiences and initiatives towards integration so that new knowledge can emerge from the welter of dialogues; this would require new thinking but there are practical starting points for this both in IG Metall's most recent organizational development and in the old traditions of trade union education.

IG Metall has built on the encouraging experiences of part 2.1 of its organizational development project on 'participation-oriented social company policy' (Martens and Frerichs, 1999) to develop skills within its education and consultancy activities in areas such as process support, project management, team development, conflict consultancy, supervision and coaching (IG Metall, 2000). Trade union educational activity is thus focusing on tapping into innovative approaches to a changing economic reality. By mobilizing participation potential for employees, the aim is to strengthen the scope for works council activity, and this may mean that the contradictory participation models offered by management become the forum for practical opposition in the company and for political reflection in trade union education.

IG Metall has also been able to make use of important experience from its past development of political education in the 1960s. If the experience of those participating in union-sponsored political education is any indication, then there was broad discussion and practice at that time of what was known as 'exemplary learning' (Negt 1967) and the use of experience. In many cases, however, this has translated into a view that all that was needed was to carry over existing solutions and the right understanding to these experiences ('primary' labour policy).

The question arises, however, of the guiding influences. In the early 1960s, when Voss and Pongratz's twentieth-century vocationalized worker (1998) was centre stage as Fordism reached its heyday, IG Metall's very open and experience-oriented education work was focused primarily on whether the concept of the 'working class' still meant anything meaningful for the reality of members' lives. It seems probable that the answer was both 'yes' and 'no', but in any case, it was not a Marxist concept of class since the issue was not whether codetermination would point the way out of the capitalist class society and towards a socialist society. The experience demonstrates the extent to which pictures of the past condition thinking, even in an open and undogmatic approach to everyday realities.[10] Although the vocationalized workers of Fordism had not yet emerged at that time, the discussion in union circles focused for policy and practical purposes on the consolidation and extension of the labour institutions that secured them a place in society. Indeed, the situation today is the same. Labour entrepreneurs occupy the same space, but the processes of understanding and modelling are still focused on defending the old position of the vocationalized workers of the past. Codetermination, which met their needs patchily and sometimes inadequately but always with enthusiasm, is still at the heart of such debates. However, its future can be secured only if the scope for democratization now opening up to individuals within civil society can be coupled with a practical form which achieves an institutional balance between shareholder and stakeholder interests against the neo-liberal hegemony that still dominates the modernization process and which matches institutional changes to the new demands for self-organization at work, participation and emancipation.

It has been argued that what is needed is to 'strengthen the individual and bring clarity to the issues', and this was, and still is, the case. In this context, then, the changing experiences of work and the expectations and hopes that it arouses – and thwarts – could be said to be the raw material that can and must be appropriated by trade union political education. Above all, it is a social space for 'practical research' as described above which is not solely, or even largely, accessible to privileged scientific investigation. Institutionalized knowledge can make its best contribution where it too engages in what has been described as the 'rough and tumble of dialogic encounters'.

10 My theme is 'participation and democratization', and this final argument is reserved for some general conclusions. Here, as above, the issue is that political education in trade union activity should relate to the experiences of change in working life and in everyday life, to provide understanding based on members' everyday experiences. We have already considered the need to 'strengthen the individual and bring clarity to the issues'; to do this, we need to re-express the viability of our own organizational and institutional models and to make an active contribution to developing new and viable models and inspirations.

If workers' expectations – and especially those of the new 'labour entrepreneurs' – are refocusing as a result of an all-pervasive and directly market-mediated shaping of the economy on the issues of how they can achieve their demands and potential for wider participation against the backdrop of contradictory company-level and social experiences, and how those representing their interests in companies may reflect this in their activity, then a key priority for trade unions' educational work will be to make this a policy priority for both activists and officials. Politicization of the often fragmented experiences of participation within companies may then be understood as, for example, a process in which demands for individual participation, but also wider scope for development at work and the expectations and disappointments linked with it, may be articulated and incorporated in some cases into proposals for new standards.

The debate around wider-ranging demands for participation and influence could be linked with that. There are points of contact with the communicative processes of labour entrepreneurs in the field of primary labour policy in 'new work' or of their nature as clients in old and new markets. And what has been called a 'reflected individualism' would be easier to achieve in the communication of labour entrepreneurs within their decentralized and networked structures if the old labour organizations and institutions entered into the 'rough and tumble of dialogic encounters' entirely without prejudice and with humility so that new understandings could emerge – for them as for others.

The existing accounts of experiences indicate that there are further challenges ahead for the old, outdated organizational and institutional structures within trade unions. They are stamped through with Fordism, the key movement of the time they were developing, and they are still geared to the relatively homogenous experiences of mass industrial labour and influenced by the corresponding social milieu and the styles of representation and politics these represent. They have never managed even to achieve greater openness to a white-collar environment. Yet the challenges facing unions today in achieving cultural diversity within an organizational and institutional environment of integration are infinitely greater. They have not yet found the inspiration to help them meet these challenges and to link in convincingly with the sheer diversity of workers' everyday experience. This, too, is an area that needs urgent attention in political education, especially now and – I assume – not only as far as union officials are concerned.

Conclusions

Codetermination as an institution has had a lasting influence in shaping the relations between capital and labour, particularly in Germany, but it cannot be understood as a post-war phenomenon without the concerted efforts and evolution of powers in the old labour movement dating as far back as the late 1880s and during the Weimar Republic. Nor can it be detached from the broad social consensus that emerged, at least in relation to this aspect of a new economic order, after the defeat of the German labour movement in 1933 and the public disavowal of the previously dominant capital groups that occurred at the end of the Reich. The experience of history shows that there had to be lengthy learning processes after a period of profound upheaval and catastrophic events before an institutional framework emerged that could be described as a historic achievement in relation to the highs and lows of its own history, notwithstanding the remaining areas of confusion and tension in its key ideas as well as in those of other institutionalization processes.

It is worth remembering this in our time of profound upheaval set about with huge risks but also huge opportunities as Fordism dies, a time that is justifiably compared by serious commentators with the upheavals of the early 19th century. The current period demonstrates what a social asset achievements like codetermination are. As Fordism comes to an end against the backdrop of the rise of post-industrial society, the labour society will not disappear but will be transformed. Only dogmatic neo-liberals could believe that the labour society of the future could be based solely on market institutions and its 'labour entrepreneurs' whose role in the abstract fiction of *homo economici* is entirely geared to the market's requirements. A stable future for society requires stable institutional change in many of the key institutions of the old labour society.

There may also be new institutionalization processes and, perhaps, also new and less rigid forms of communication and of delivery of economic and social services, such as are often highlighted in discussions of networking. If these are to be achieved, though, the labour entrepreneur has to be seen as a new individual member of civil society, organizing him- or herself and 'doing it him- or herself'. This offers huge potential for greater economic efficiency in transactions of all kinds as well as for codetermination and a form of participation and democratization. However, achieving these goals will also continue to require institutional frameworks so that, against far-reaching market domination and globalization, models of and conditions for participation are not stripped of all the promises of emancipation that the neo-liberal revolution currently holds out. The concept of codetermination can today be reformulated as both meeting the demands of new individual members of civil society for participation and presenting with new authority its old, but now once again topical, aims of social control and legitimation of economic dealings. Against this backdrop, its future in the new era we are now entering after the death of Fordism has just dawned. Neo-liberalism may be present at this dawning but it is not of itself the successor to Fordism.

Notes

1 'After all, the most analogous period of growth, technological change and global reach was that between 1880 and 1914 when urbanization exploded, trade boomed and Europeans migrated in their millions to the New World. But it ended in war and recession; the dynamism of the underlying economy released ungovernable tensions over inequality and social injustice. Today could equally be the high water mark of a second wave of globalization for which the world has not yet acquired the political, cultural and social equipment to handle – and a relapse is possible.' (Hutton and Giddens, 2000, p. 215).

2 I am, however, explicitly leaving aside here specific issues of the representation of interests in the new economy. These focus on such areas as forms of 'boundaryless working' and 'family-friendly working hours', and even in the new economy, individuals marry and age. I am not here dealing with the full spectrum of representation of interests.

3 Schnack and Gesterkamp (1998) write 'In an individualized society in which traditional social relationships and contexts are fragmenting, values such as solidarity and brotherhood necessarily play a smaller part than they used to. Individuals who do not want to be among the losers of modernization have to act more rapidly, more selfishly and more powerfully than their direct counterparts. They must be as alert and as responsive as a wolf if they are to prevent anyone taking an option on their job, for example. The portrait of the solitary fighter may seem archetypal but more significantly, it is highly current' [translation].

4 'Primary labour policy' is the independent and direct action taken by working people with a view to articulating and protecting their work-related interests. Such policy should not be confused with spontaneous action, as it may be organized. At IBM Düsseldorf, for example, the works council initiated a debate amongst employees through the intranet focused on removing boundaries on working time. 'Secondary labour policy' then builds on this action and develops it. It also covers the ways in which the interests of social movements are represented and the organizations that emerge as a result.

5 This focuses primarily on highly skilled labour entrepreneurs, who can position themselves with relative stability at the centre of the employment system, rather than on those who find precarious positions on its periphery such as in call centres, in logistics and in pseudo-self-employment.

6 There are no reliable statistics on levels of union density in the new economy in Germany, although observers sometimes quote between 2 and 4 per cent. An employers' research body (iwd, 2001) provides no figures for Germany but quotes remarkably high rates of 85 per cent for Denmark, up to 70 per cent for Belgium, 58 per cent for Sweden and 57 per cent for Greece. There are also figures for the proportion of employees in the new

economy covered by collective agreements: this is 20 per cent in Germany and a range from 60 to 100 per cent elsewhere, with no figures quoted for Greece.

7   The aim of this line of argument is to construct a feasible and critical external view from the perspective of the ideal type of the labour entrepreneur. The subjective truth of this kind of actor, who for example developed the full potential of codetermination in the coal and steel industry by interpreting the call from earlier times to 'dare more democracy' (Hindrichs et al., 2000) is, of course, rather different and any retrospective expert analysis will therefore have to make a careful balance between the glory and the failure of codetermination (Martens, 2002).

8   An empirical research project raising issues about the scope for trade union involvement in regional modernization coalitions is currently under way at the German Institute for Worker Training (FIAB) in Recklinghausen (FIAB, 2001). See also Flocken et al. (2001) on the more limited role of trade unions in 'coevolutionary cooperation alliances' that resulted from projects on employment-oriented modernization cofinanced by the European Union.

9   Instruments such as Jungk's 'future workshops' and Dienel's 'planning cells' from the debates of the 1960s and 1970s are available to be further developed in this context (Dienel, 1977; Dienel, 1997).

10   In my view, this is what is happening with the 'experience approach' to education taken by IG Metall at that time. This is in contrast to the subsequent path of supported training activity in the 1970s which was aimed at assisting with implementing correct versus false consciousness and was also designed to orient company-level representatives to of centralized trade union policy.

References

Alemann, U.v. and Schmid, J. (eds) (1998), *Die Gewerkschaft ÖTV. Reformen im Dickicht gewerkschaftlicher Organizationspolitik*, Baden-Baden.

Borsdorf, U. (1982), *Hans Böckler. Arbeit und Leben eines Gewerkschafters von 1875 bis 1945*, Cologne.

Castel, R. (2000), *Die Metamorphosen der sozialen Frage. Eine Chronik der Lohnarbeit*, Konstanz.

Deckstein, D. and Felixberger, P. (2000), *Arbeit neu denken. Wie wir die Chancen der New Economy nutzen können*, Frankfurt/New York.

Dienel, P. (1977), 'Versuche mit neuen Beteiligungsverfahren', in Jungk, R. and Weyer, A. (eds), *Die Grenzen der Resignation*, Wuppertal, pp. 97–112.

Dienel, P. (1997), *Die Planungszelle. Eine Alternative zur Establishment-Demokratie*, Opladen.

Dörre, K. (2001a), *Das deutsche Produktionsmodell unter dem Druck des Shareholder Value*, unpublished paper given at conference on 'Shareholder Value and Globalization', Bad Homburg, 10–12 May.

Dörre, K. (2001b), 'Gibt es ein nachfordistisches Produktionsmodell? Managementprinzipien, Firmenorganisation und Arbeitsorganisation im flexiblen Kapitalismus', in Candius, M. and Deppe, R. (eds), *Akkumulationsregime – Shareholder Society – Neoliberalismus und neue Sozialdemokratie*, Hamburg, pp. 83–107.

FIAB (2001), *Globalisierung, Industriepolitik und mikrosoziale Regulation. Die Akteure der industriellen Beziehungen als Kooperationspartner in regionalen Entwicklungskoalitionen*, project application, Recklinghausen.

Flocken, P., Howaldt, J. and Kopp, R. (eds.) (2001), Conference proceedings: *Kooperationsverbünde und gesellschaftliche Modernisierung – Theorie und Praxis der Netzwerkarbeit*, Gabler-Verlag, Wiesbaden.

Frerichs, J. and Bundesmann-Jansen, J. (1995), *Betriebspolitik und Organizationswandel. Neuansätze gewerkschaftlicher Politik zwischen Delegation und Partizipation*, Münster.

Fricke, W. (ed.) (2001), *Jahrbuch Arbeit und Technik 2001*, Bonn.

Glotz, P. (1998), 'Flucht vor der Wirklichkeit. Über Erstarrung und Zerfall deutscher Institutionen', special issue of *Spiegel*, September, p. 178ff.

Hack, L. (2001), 'Die "New Economy" als neue Formation der Unternehmensorganization', in Fricke, W. (ed.) (2001), *Jahrbuch Arbeit und Technik 2001*, Bonn.

Hilbert, J. and Schmid, J. (1994), *Wirtschaftsstandort und Zukunft des Sozialstaates*, Marburg.

Hindrichs, W., Jürgenhake, U., Kleinschmidt, C., Kruse, W., Lichte, R. and Martens, H. (eds) (2000), *Der lange Abschied vom Malocher. Sozialer Umbruch in der Stahlindustrie und die Rolle der Betriebsräte von 1960 bis in die neunziger Jahre*, Essen.

Hoffmann, R., Kluge, N., Linne, G. and Metzger, E. (eds.) (1994), *Problemstart: Politischer und Sozialer Wandel in den neuen Bundesländern*, Cologne.

Howaldt, J., Kopp, R. and Martens, H. (2000), 'Koevolutionäre Kooperationsverbünde als regionales Innovationsmanagement', in Naegele, G. and Peter, G. (eds), *Arbeit – Alter – Region. Zur Debatte um die Zukunft der Arbeit, um die demographische Entwicklung und die Chance regionalpolitischer Gestaltung*, Münster, pp. 239–69.

Hutton, W. and Giddens, A. (eds) (2000), *On the Edge: Living with Global Capitalism*, Vintage Books.

IG Metall (ed.) (2000), *Bildung und Beratung im Bereich Prozessbegleitung, Projektmanagement, Teamentwicklung, Konfliktberatung, Supervision und Coaching. Ein Angebot der IG Metall*, project documentation, Frankfurt/Main.

IG Metall (ed.) (2001), *IG Metall – Zukunftsreport. Ergebnissse im Überblick, Zuspitzungen und Diskussionsanreize*, Frankfurt/Main.

iwd (Informationsdienst der deutschen Wirtschaft) (2001), *New Economy. Arbeitsbeziehungen im Umbruch*, issue 47, 22 November, Cologne.

Jürgenhake, U., Lichte, R., Martens, H. and Sczesny, C. with Hessling, A. (1999), *Bestandsaufnahme der Beteiligungsverfahren bei TKS. Einschätzungen und Meinungen von Führungskräften verschiedener Ebenen und betrieblichen Experten* (research report), Dortmund.

Kommission Mitbestimmung (1998), *Mitbestimmung und neue Unternehmenskulturen – Bilanz und Perspektiven*, Verlag Bertelsmann Stiftung, Gütersloh.

Kotthoff, H. (1994), *Betriebsräte und Bürgerstatus*, Munich/Mering.

Martens, H. (1994), 'Empirische Institutionsforschung – theoretische und methodologische Aspekte am Beispiel der Mitbestimmungsforschung', in Göhler, G. (ed.), *Die Eigenart der Institutionen. Zum Profil politischer Institutionentheorie*, Baden-Baden, pp. 237–300.

Martens, H. (1995), 'Mitbestimmung als intermediäre Institution. Ein empirisches Projekt in theoretischer Absicht. Vorläufig resümierende Überlegungen aus Anlass des 5. Kolloquiums zum DFG-Schwerpunktprogramm "Theorie politischer Institutionen" vom 28.–30.10.1994 in Bonn', in Martens, H. (ed.), *Beiträge zur gewerkschaftlichen Reformdebatte. Sfs-Materialen aus der Forschung*, Vol. 27, pp. 19–31.

Martens, H. (1996), 'Zur Institutionalisierung von Mitbestimmung in Ostdeutschland im Kontext der Modernisierung der industriellen Beziehungen in der Bundesrepublik Deutschland', in Kollmorgen, R., Reissig, R. and Weiss, J. (eds), *Sozialer Wandel und Akteure in Ostdeutschland*, Opladen, pp. 165–78.

Martens, H. and Frerichs, J. (1999), *Betriebsräte und Beteiligung*, Dortmund.

Martens, H. (2001), *Vom Verschwinden der Politik und dem verschämten Umgang mit Macht. Exemplifiziert am Mitbestimmungsdiskurs und der darin ausgeklammerten Figur des Arbeitsdirektors. Beitrag zum Forschungskolloquium des FIAB*, 28 November, Recklinghausen.

Martens, H. (2002), *Die Zukunft der Mitbestimmung beginnt gerade neu: Empirische und konzeptionelle Beiträge zur aktuellen mitbestimmungspolitischen Diskussion*, LIT-Verlag, Münster/Hamburg/London.

Martens, H., Peter, G. and Wolf, F.O. (eds) (2001), *Zwischen Selbstbestimmung und Selbstausbeutung. Gesellschaftlicher Umbruch und neue Arbeit*, Campus Verlag, Frankfurt/ New York.

Moldaschl, M. (2001), 'Subjektivierung. Eine neue Stufe der Entwicklung der Arbeitswissenschaften', in Moldaschl, M. and Voss, G.G. (eds), *Subjektivierung von Arbeit*, Munich and Mering, pp. 23–51.

Müller-Jentsch, W. (1993), 'Organization und Mitbestimmung. Evolution einer diffizilen Synthese', in Müller-Jentsch, W. (ed.), *Profitable Ethik, effiziente Kultur. Neue Sinnstiftungen durch das Management?*, Munich and Mering.

Negt, O. (1967), *Soziologische Phantasie und Exemplarisches Lernen. Zur Theorie und Praxis der Arbeiterbildung*, Frankfurt/Main.

Peters, K. (2001), 'Individuelle Autonomie und Reorganization von Unternehmen', in Fricke, W. (ed.), *Jahrbuch Arbeit und Technik 2001*, pp. 371–88.

Schnack, D. and Gersterkamp, K. (1998), *Hauptsache Arbeit?*, Reinbeck bei Hamburg.

Sennet, R. (1998), *Corrosion of Character, the Culture of New Capitalism*, New York.

Streeck, W. (1996), 'Industrielle Beziehungen in einer internationalisierten Wirtschaft', in FESt (ed.), *Globalisierung der Wirtschaft, Standortwettbewerb und Mitbestimmung*, Gesprächskreis Arbeit und Soziales, No. 70, Bonn.

Streeck, W. (1999), 'Mitbestimmung in der Marktwirtschaft: Geht das?', in *Gewerkschaftliche Monatshefte*, No. 3/1999, pp. 158–66.

Streeck, W. (2000), *Zwei Seelen wohnen, ach, in der staatsfreien Brust. Der Kanzler und sein Lernziel von der zivilen Bürgergesellschaft. Anmerkungen zu einer neuen politischen Formel*, FR 10 July 2000.

Voss, J. and Pongratz, J. (1998), 'Der Arbeitskraftunternehmer. Eine neue Grundform der Ware Arbeitskraft', *Kölner Zeitschrift für Soziologie und Sozialpsychologie*, Vol. 1, pp. 131–58.

Wolf, F. O. (2001), 'Selbersausbeutung im Übergang wohin? Überlegungen zur "Neuen Arbeit" im Hinblick auf ihre Gestaltungsmöglichkeiten', in Martens, H., Peter, G. and Wolf, F.O. (eds), *Zwischen Selbstbestimmung und Selbstausbeutung. Gesellschaftlicher Umbruch und Neue Arbeit*, Campus Verlag, Frankfurt/New York, pp. 208–38.

www.politik-digital.de (2001), *'Are we family?' Umfang und Formen der Mitarbeiter-Mitbestimmung in der New Economy*.

Chapter 10

Worker Participation in the Reduction of Working Hours in France[1]

Henri Pinaud

Introduction

The reduction of working hours has a twofold impact on workers, both in their working lives and in their social, family and private lives.[2] The current debate in France revolves around the number of jobs generated by the legislation and agreements involved. However, there is also a second debate, which has attracted little attention but which has arisen in disputes over the application of the 35-hour week, about the reasons why a reduction in working hours does not always meet workers' expectations either at or outside work. There are two aspects of this second debate that are worth examining: the position and the role of workers in the process, and the fact that the reduction in working hours has come at a time of weakened trade union influence.

The Role of Workers in Reducing Working Hours

Let us look first at the position and role which the law and the social partners have given workers in the process of reducing working hours (RWH): negotiating, implementing, monitoring and evaluating. Alongside their traditional indirect participation through the trade unions and elected staff representation bodies, there are many different forms of direct involvement in France. Such involvement may be individual or collective, informal or institutionalized. It may be initiated by a law, left to the initiative of the social partners or regulated between workers and management. It may concern many different aspects of working life. It may simply take the form of oral or written information or consultation (discussion groups, quality-control groups), but some (semi-independent) groups technically have powers of self-management.

As far as the trade unions are concerned, the direct involvement of workers corresponds to long-standing demands for the right of expression made by two of the major French union confederations, the French Democratic Confederation of Labour (Confédération Française Démocratique du Travail, CFDT) in 1973 and the General Confederation of Labour (Confédération Générale du Travail, CGT) in 1978. These demands were based on the assumption that workers are the main experts on working conditions and work organization, and they led to workers being given the right of expression on working conditions and the organization and content of work under laws introduced in 1982, 1983 and 1986. By contrast, the third main confederation, CGT-Force Ouvrière, has always vigorously opposed direct expression for workers, which it regards as dangerous for the trade union movement and elected staff representatives in undertakings.

The demands reflected the theory that trade unions are experienced and skilled in defending workers' 'quantitative' collective interests, but that they need to rely on workers' knowledge for the 'qualitative' aspects of working life, and at the time they formed part of a trend towards self-management. The delay between the making and the implementation of these demands, together with opposition from employers, trade union weakness burdened with an outmoded method of managing collective action, and middle-management hostility, all combined to produce a general inertia, which meant that direct expression failed to take off in the legal context, even though more than 20,000 agreements were signed between 1986 and 1993 (though few with any real effect). However, worker involvement has often come up in the recent trade union debate on negotiating the reduction in working hours:

> A successful agreement is constructed together with the workers, and effective negotiations require their support, simply because they are the first people affected by RWH, by developments in how their work and their life outside work is organized and by the effects of RWH on employment... Prepare an information sheet for the workers in your company ... Use the scope which the law gives you to organize information meetings ... (CFDT, 1997, p. 12).

> [The negotiations] placed permanently under the responsibility of the workers must cover demands which have been established with them and by them, they must progress in a manner which is totally transparent for those concerned, and the final decision must be taken together with them ... (CGT, 1998, p. 16).

The participative policies pursued by employers – 'man management/ motivation' (Martin, 1999, p. 58) – also use the direct involvement of workers. They rely on the belief that there is 'a supposed convergence between democracy and effectiveness in response to new market constraints' (Gautrat,

1999, p.198). Participative discussion could develop into new methods for the social partners to develop and implement RWH.

So we already have a legal framework, valid reasons, the will among the trade unions and employers and practices which can be used as the basis for organizing, justifying and encouraging the direct expression/involvement of workers in the RWH process. Direct involvement has, admittedly, never up to now been one of the demands made at grass roots level, where there are fears of unemployment and exclusion. However, a number of studies of the experience of direct involvement show that this is a latent need and something that workers seek to attain as soon as the conditions are right (Kester and Pinaud, 1995; Heller et al., 1998).

Approaches to Working Hours

Working hours may be considered from the point of view of *duration* (number of time units and their distribution and regularity) and *content* (what workers actually do during their working hours). The worker population is not homogeneous and working time does not have the same meaning or the same consequences for everyone, as it depends on their socio-professional characteristics and the content, organization and conditions of their work. Plans to reduce working hours must therefore take account of the links between these two components of duration and content. Furthermore, the duration and organization of working hours have a direct bearing on free time outside work, and the reduction of working hours includes an element of flexibility which, from the workers' point of view, needs to link up with the other elements of life outside work, so that the periods of time worked are more in harmony with other non-work requirements. The duration and conditions of working life are also directly connected with life expectancy among different categories of workers. This link concerns society as a whole, in terms of the potential upheavals it could cause.

Alongside this systemic view there is another approach in which the components of working hours are organized according to political or trade union priorities (such as reducing unemployment). It is, admittedly, the role of the legislature and the trade unions to make choices and fix priorities, but this classification according to different objectives and frames of reference tends to obscure the systemic links; the impact on the RWH process and on its effects will not be the same. The priority given to employment, for example, as the main aim of RWH can have serious implications. First of all, it tends to reduce working hours to the duration component and to mask the links with the content component. Then it may also lead to an undifferentiated view of the workforce and weaken the link between time at work and time outside work. This tendency to concentrate almost exclusively on reducing unemployment also tends to entrench the trade unions in their traditional practices.

The fact is that in a situation where the trade unions are losing power, collective 'quantitative' demands tend to take precedence over 'qualitative' demands such as work organization and working conditions. In the trade union tradition, such 'unifying' demands are meant to attract maximum worker support and thus to be more effective. Indeed, as Grinsmir has pointed out: 'Such a situation reflects an old French tradition that trade unions should not get involved in work organization other than in making demands against "the system", but never, or almost never, in negotiating' (Grinsmir, 2000, p. 30). This tends to bolster a type of trade unionism in which decisions are taken mainly by a small nucleus of militants who are often both union activists and elected representatives. The workers are then often consulted only in order to rubber-stamp the trade union's decisions. Wildcat industrial action becomes the only occasion for trade union democracy.

Trade Unionism, Worker Involvement and Reducing Working Hours

The fairly considerable loss of trade union influence among workers appears to be a clear indication of their disenchantment with the traditional forms of indirect involvement in the undertaking through unions and representatives on the staff representation bodies (Regini et al., 1992; Bunel and Thuderoz, 1999). The sort of trade unionism that used to be based on the collective is increasingly coming into confrontation with the individualized and varied interests of workers, as we can see from its efforts to drum up solidarity and support for a return to unifying issues (Reynaud, 1998). It is having increasing difficulty in integrating the workers' point of view in measures linking the reorganization and reduction of working hours/the organization of work/working and living conditions. We are currently moving away from a model that aimed to make working and employment conditions homogeneous, towards a more fragmented, individual approach. But even if the social link between activist and worker has grown wider, and if some authors talk about 'the increasingly externalized relationship between trade unionism and the workers, which has now become part and parcel of industrial life' (Bunel and Thuderoz, 1999, p. 137), the legitimacy and usefulness of trade unionism are certainly not being challenged, particularly not by those aged over 40. Quite simply, trade union activities, particularly negotiations, are things that happen a long way away from workers, and direct expression does not appeal to them. 'Hands-on trade unionism' is dying out.

The results of the second CNRS-CFDT research programme, PAROLES 2^3 (1991–95), on trade unionism and participation, confirm the problems which the unions are facing in overcoming the divide between direct and indirect involvement. The authors link this divide to the fact that it is being increasingly left to employers to satisfy workers' demands regarding conditions at work and particularly work organization, while the unions are once again focusing on collective bargaining rather than other forms of union action, and therefore have little interest in the staff representation bodies (Le Tron and Pinaud, 1999).

Trade union reactions to recent laws (Robien, 1996; Aubry, 1998) proposing or introducing a reduction in working hours can vary. Let us consider three different but not exclusive scenarios. The first involves a return to traditional union attitudes and practices, with the emphasis on traditional collective bargaining, branches monopolized by small groups of activists, a focus on disputes and so on. In situations and/or at times when union negotiating teams find themselves in difficult circumstances because of various structural or cyclical factors (such as the economic situation, the state of industrial relations, the level of union membership or problems of union effectiveness), there may be a strong temptation not to enter into the qualitative aspects of negotiations, which may be felt to be too risky, too fragmented or likely to result in a corporatist orientation. Instead, unions are likely to stick to the quantitative aspects (such as the number of jobs created or saved, general rules for organizing new working time schedules, the maintenance of wage levels and so on), taking a fairly undifferentiated view of the workforce. They may also adopt a relaxed approach to management implementation and monitoring strategies, without ensuring any methods for checking or guiding them.

The second scenario is based on the theory that union members play an active part in constructing collective action. This is a recurrent theme in France's trade union organizations and has resurfaced since negotiations started on working hours. As a strategy, it is first of all an attempt to arrest the trend away from unionization, which began in the early 1980s and had reached dramatic proportions by the end of the decade, thus reflecting a cultural development. The traditional model of the union branch was based on a hard core of activists (often also holding posts as elected staff representatives), surrounded by an inner circle with fewer responsibilities and then other more passive members. Finally there came the workers, who were called on only if a show of strength were needed or when there were elections. However, various factors including the development of participative management have promoted the emergence of a new model of the union branch in undertakings, demanding more democratic practices in order to adapt to changes in firms. According to the unions' way of thinking, if trade unionism encourages members to take an active part in negotiations then, when it comes to formulating demands, a policy can be developed which is better able to incorporate the various occupational requirements in a firm. This should result in a return to hands-on practices and a better, more diverse collectivity can be created. This member-led unionism, which is also referred to as 'participative', can sit happily alongside, or may even replace, calls for workers to have direct expression/involvement. However, member-led unionism, and militant unionism, often still share the same fear that the direct involvement of workers will lead to a loss of union identity, watered down by individual and corporatist demands. Furthermore, union distrust of involvement is often distrust of its own weakness and fear that, once the negotiations or the dispute is over, the wave on which the union was carried along will ebb away (Reynaud, 1998).

There is a third possible scenario based on the use of 'democratic participation' procedures (Kester and Pinaud, 1996). This attempts to find new ways of linking the various forms of indirect participation (such as collective bargaining and information/consultation procedures) with direct participation in decision making (through advisory bodies like discussion groups or through decision-making bodies like autonomous groups) in the various stages of the process of securing shorter hours. These stages include negotiation of an agreement, implementation, monitoring and evaluation. Such procedures could provide fuller, more relevant information on workers' expectations and proposals, the situation in the work units and the linkage between working hours and time outside work. They are therefore likely to provide results better suited to working situations, and to improve firms' performance. They could facilitate the changes that need to be made in a process of adaptation. Workers might also be expected to be more supportive of innovation if it takes account of their concerns. The involvement of the grass roots is not just a democratic requirement: it is a prerequisite for success, as Mossé et al. (1999) stress in relation to another top-down reform concerning hospital restructuring. Strauss (1998) maintains that the trade unions and elected representation bodies are becoming oligarchies and will never fully represent workers' interests or give them opportunities to participate individually; direct participation is needed for this. Furthermore, according to Kester and Pinaud (1996), those involved in the processes of change need to be differentiated and the various participative approaches, both direct and indirect, within the undertaking and beyond, are not always contradictory or incompatible. Pinaud argues that indeed:

> [t]he various forms of participation ... can be cumulative. When applied individually they lose both their meaning and their effect. Democratic participation is to be found within them as a dynamic whole. There is a need for a systematic approach to greater democratic participation... Trade unions are best placed to take up the challenge that democratic participation represents by integrating its diverse manifestations into a coherent strategy ... (Pinaud, 1996a, p. 24).

Heller et al. (1998) also emphasise that where there is a trade union, participative structures tend to be much more effective and longer lived as a result of comanagement with the hierarchy. These results have been confirmed by the European Foundation's EPOC study (Sisson, 1996; Sisson, 1997).

It is fundamentally useful to assess the forms and effects of worker participation in developing and monitoring agreements; the RWH process can reveal complete changes in union strategy and practice, highlighting the problems presented by the influence of and the direction taken by French trade unionism. An analysis of the first studies of the negotiation and implementation of agreements following the Robien and Aubry laws in France gives us some idea of the nature and degree of worker involvement in the RWH process. It also gives us a better understanding of the aims and forms of union action and the roles of the various actors in the undertaking.

The Robien Law

In June 1996, the French Parliament adopted a law known as the Robien law, named after its author. It allowed the reduction of working hours in firms in the private sector, with state aid in the form of exemption from social security contributions, in order to promote job saving or the recruitment of new workers. The law provided that the reduction in working hours and the number of jobs created should be strictly in proportion, so that, for example, a 10 per cent reduction in working hours should create 10 per cent more jobs, or at least save them. There was also one notable innovation in this law. In view of the low level of unionization in France, and the almost total absence of unions in the small and medium-sized enterprise (SME) sector, it provided for a so-called mandating procedure for firms without union representation. According to this procedure, management in such firms is required to find a worker among the staff who agrees to be mandated by an outside trade union to negotiate the agreement. The Robien law was repealed in June 1998 by the Aubry law. However, in 18 months it produced a total of just over 3,000 agreements covering 350,000 workers who moved to a 35- or 32-hour working week. Some 42,000 jobs were classified as having been created or saved.

Negotiations

According to a survey of 12 small and medium-sized businesses conducted in the first half of 1998 (Bloch-London et al., 1999), negotiations were initiated primarily by the employers. There was some initial reticence among the workers, who sometimes interpreted such moves as a sign of decline, with the company attempting to use redundancies to improve its situation. They feared, for example, that the Robien law – and later the Aubry law – might precipitate a decision by the company to lay off some of its workers and get compensation for them. Workers also feared that their wages would be frozen or reduced. Management often therefore had to go through a lengthy information and explanation exercise in advance among the workforce. According to an opinion poll carried out in June 1999 among 526 workers whose working hours had been reduced for one year under a Robien agreement, eight out of 10 declared that they had been consulted before RWH, half by referendum.[4] On the whole, half the workers considered that this form of consultation made it possible for their opinions to be taken into account (Doisneau, 2000).

   For management, the stated objectives were: 1) to reduce unproductive, 'underoccupied' time in the face of widely fluctuating markets; 2) to react more efficiently when orders are received; 3) to extend the range of working hours; and 4) to reduce the wage bill, both by freezing wages and by taking on less well paid workers. The main objective as far as the trade unions were concerned was to defend 'the cause of employment'. In SMEs where there was little union representation, mandating was often used, but did not appear to pave the way for union development.

   A more global analysis of the agreements concluded as a result of the Robien law indicates that in exchange for the annualization of working time, working hours were reduced and jobs were safeguarded or created. Making jobs less insecure was an additional objective in some agreements. In addition, 'sufficient account was not taken of the views of the workers before the measure was taken and as one of its objectives, and not enough consideration was given to the effects on work organization' (Boisard and Charpentier, 1997, p. 117). Links with time outside work were hardly mentioned.

Implementation of the Agreements

A number of problems emerged in the implementation of the agreements, mainly as a result of the annualization of working time. The complex nature of the new ways of arranging working time meant that discussions had to be held with workers and explanations provided, often until long after the agreement was signed. The introduction of a system for creating flexible working time ('modulation') also undermines the whole idea of extra pay for overtime and is eliminating this formerly very widespread source of internal flexibility. According to Boisard and Charpentier 'Perhaps the main advantage [of modulation] is not that it increases the overall flexibility of working time, but that it reduces the cost of it while at the same time eliminating paid unproductive time and overtime paid at a higher rate' (1997, p. 112).

As regards the reorganization of work, a number of effects were observed: skills were redeployed because the structure of the workforce was remodelled as a result of recruitment, and various forms of multi-skilling were sometimes developed, which the staff accepted more or less happily. According to Boisard and Dalle (1997), the effects on employment were very different: there was a marked reduction or slower growth in the number of insecure jobs, but there was little effect on the overall number of jobs. It was as if the reduction in working hours was intended to reduce insecurity rather than to increase the volume of employment. Insecurity is falling, but external flexibility is on the increase again (including fixed-term contracts, temporary contracts and subcontracting).

> Thus, in some firms, the organization of the planning departments had to be constantly adjusted and renegotiated with the staff concerned ... In most firms reorganizations were the subject of proper negotiation and/or informal adjustments when they were carried out (Bloch-London et al., 1999, p. 104).

It is at this point in the process that forms of direct worker participation appear to have been used in informal agreements between management and workers, without any indication as to whether there was any intervention from the trade unions or the staff representatives.

Doisneau makes the following comment on the opinion poll among 526 workers:

A majority of the workers seems satisfied [with RWH] but nearly half (46 per cent) have mixed feelings, and 20 per cent are clearly unhappy ... The success of RWH rests on the success of the adjustments to their working time, while respecting, and even improving their working conditions (Doisneau, 2000, p. 65).

The First Aubry Law

On 18 June 1998 a new law (called the Aubry law after the then Minister of Employment and Solidarity), providing for a reduction in the working week to 35 hours, was adopted by the French Parliament. It encouraged the social partners to negotiate at sector and company level, and it provided state aid for firms saving or creating jobs. A report on the agreements concluded was put before parliament for debate in the autumn of 1999, before the definitive version of the law was adopted on 19 January 2000.

According to the Ministry of Employment and Solidarity (September 2001), more than 70,000 agreements had been signed by 16 August 2001. They covered seven million workers (out of a potential 12 million) and included pledges to create (87 per cent) or save (13 per cent) 364,000 jobs. Neither this first law nor the second applied to the civil service (4.8 million workers). The date of the RWH for civil servants was determined by decree at 1,600 hours per year from 1 January 2002 (Ministry of Employment and Solidarity, 2001).

The law provoked enormous hostility among French employers, who resent any interference by the state. It also led to the departure of the chairman of the National Council of French Employers (Conseil National du Patronat Français, CNPF), which subsequently became the Movement of French Enterprises (Mouvement des Entreprises de France, MEDEF), nor was it universally welcomed by the trade unions. The CFDT, one of whose main demands over a number of years had been a reduction in working hours and which had been behind most of the Robien agreements, broadly supported the new law, while the CGT and especially the CGT-Force Ouvrière were more reticent.[5]

Preliminary Studies

The first Aubry law was the subject of a number of studies, most of them commissioned by the Minister of Employment and Solidarity herself to accompany the report she drew up in September 1999, and all were designed to assist parliament's debate on the second law, which was adopted on 19 January 2000. The studies were based on monographs, and were generally carried out between late 1998 and early 1999, when DARES (the Directorate of Research, Studies and Statistics at the Ministry of Employment and Solidarity) noted that more than 90 per cent of the agreements had been concluded in firms with fewer than 200 workers, and 40 per cent in firms with fewer than 20. The nature of the studies and the small scale of the firms concerned – implying a low trade union presence – should be taken into account when drawing any preliminary conclusions.

Role of the Actors

Direct worker participation In its report on the lessons to be learnt from the agreements, the ministry states that 'the support of all categories of workers [is] one of the conditions for success' (1999, p. 34). However, it does not suggest any methods for achieving this. The second Aubry law makes it compulsory for workers to be consulted and to give their approval in order to validate a company agreement negotiated with one or more trade unions. The consultation exercise must be held during working hours, by secret ballot in sealed envelopes, and the practical organization is the responsibility of the employer.

The Ministry document gives the results of an opinion poll showing that eight out of 10 workers were consulted 'about RWH' in 53 per cent of cases by the management, in 36 per cent by the unions and in 27 per cent by the staff representatives. In 43 per cent of cases there was a vote or referendum on RWH. According to other opinion polls carried out by the CFDT (in 1998 and 1999, among 10,000 workers in 150 companies in various sectors), workers simply voted to say what they thought about the agreement (45 per cent), or they were informed and consulted (34 per cent), or not informed and consulted at all (17 per cent). The poll does not mention any other form of direct involvement in the negotiations.

The issue of participation is also covered in a study of managers and the 35-hour week, which involved nine companies: 'Negotiations are not the right time to be considering the activities of managers and how their work is organized, much less to be launching the collective involvement of those concerned in such an exercise' (Bouffartigue and Bouteiller, 2000, p. 49). An article published in September 1999 by the National Institute for the Improvement of Working Conditions (Agence Nationale pour l'Amélioration des Conditions de Travail, ANACT) underlines the need to:

make it easier for workers to say what they think about RWH ... The impact of RWH on individuals will vary greatly depending on whether they adopt a passive, accepting attitude or, by contrast, if they are given the opportunity to become personally involved in the process with a feeling that this genuinely serves some purpose (Masson and Roland, 1999, p. 15).

According to Boisard and Pelisse (2000, p. 2), it took a long time for workers to say what they wanted '... because the framework for RWH had already been decided by the management', yet in most cases the negotiators took account of their wishes (often extra days off), which were collectively expressed. For Rocca (2000, p.88), 'the workers mistrusted the implementation of RWH ... individuals were at the very least worried, if not downright suspicious. This also explains the small number of cases where workers initiated the discussions'. Following their study of 14 companies in the Île-de-France region, Charpentier et al. (2000) argued that the negotiation process had stimulated various forms of workers' participation:

> through working groups that made possible a progressive working out of RWH in the various departments, or through consulting the workers (by questionnaires, referendums and so on) ... this participation being out of the control of the trade unions ... [or through strikes] when working conditions and life outside work are homogeneous in large groups, and a dispute may promote the emergence of a collective actor (Charpentier et al., 2000, p. 31).

Renewed social dialogue? The insistence on the trade unions' monopoly on negotiations is designed to strengthen their role at every level, but especially within undertakings. RWH negotiations thus mark an important point in the legitimation of trade union action among management and workers. The appointment of a mandated representative in firms where there is no union presence may also be seen as likely to lead to new support for the unions.

The Ministry (1999, p. 39) considers that 'social dialogue is renewed and regenerated' by means of RWH negotiations. However, other commentators remain sceptical about this: 'We still doubt whether industrial relations will be profoundly changed once this enormous exercise is over' (Boisard and Pelisse, 2000, p. 12). Research by the Institute for Economic and Social Research (Institut de Recherches Economiques et Sociales, IRES) on mandating a worker to represent staff in small and medium-sized enterprises without union representation also found that it was usually preceded by an in-house compromise, either directly with the workers or, usually, with non-affiliated representatives. This very much restricted the scope of the negotiations.

IRES concluded that 'mandating – which is an occasion for contacts – is not spontaneously a route into unionization'. Moreover, the trade unions often claim to have doubts about the mandating procedure:

> After all, there are actually very few demands ... The effects in terms of trade union support are uncertain ... People need to avoid falling into the trap of rubber-stamping a draft agreement that has been written at the employer's behest, but without letting down any workers who are prepared to accept it ... (Dufour et al., 1999, p. 37).

Staff representation bodies The question of the representativeness of these bodies is also examined in the IRES study, which covers only small and medium-sized businesses. It was found that a number of works councils had more work to do and a wider role to play, while some staff representatives felt that their role had been legitimated by the end of the consultation phase. Other authors, such as Boisard and Pelisse (2000), remain sceptical as to how long this resurgence will last.

A number of CFDT trade union federations found that the staff representation bodies were rarely consulted and their proposals were rarely supported, and that negotiations usually remained in the hands of a few activists.

> The elected health and safety committee (comité d'hygiène, sécurité et conditions de travail, CHSCT), which was most affected by the introduction of RWH and the creation of new jobs – elements which will change working conditions and the way in which work is organized – was not involved, yet these are two of its specific tasks (CFDT-Santé-Sociaux, 1999, p. 4).

According to Jean-Paul Peulet, Confederation Political Secretary of the CFDT:

> Three years ago the relationship between RWH and working conditions was not universally obvious ... The reality is that, when it comes to working conditions, as in other fields, it is not always easy or even possible to make employers and workers understand what you mean. This is why the CHSCT representatives must not give up if they cannot get their point of view across when the agreement is being negotiated (*Célidé Magazine*, 2000, p. 10).

Organization of work and working conditions Most of the studies agree that the organization of work and working conditions 'are the main gaps in the agreements ... We even believe that this situation did not, as you might think, come about because the employers deliberately wanted to keep those issues out of the negotiations, but, more prosaically, because the unions themselves do not usually automatically include them in the discussions' (Grinsmir, 2000, p. 30). ANACT even found that 'the consultation and negotiation processes between management and staff representatives tend to underestimate or even to ignore matters relating to the impact of planned reorganizations on health and working conditions' (Masson and Roland, 1999, p. 9).

Innovations relate mainly to how working time is organized, and less to how work is organized. According to a study by DARES (Doisneau and Fournier, 1999) of almost 18,000 agreements covering 2.46 million workers, the main issues were: arrangements for adapting to fluctuations in activity, such as flexibilization of collective duration of work, overtime and part-time work (68 per cent of agreements); extra holidays (31 per cent); and arrangements for intensifying the time for which equipment is in use (15 per cent). Meyer noted that in Alsace, flexibilization of shift arrangements was associated with RWH in 80 per cent of agreements (Meyer, 2000).

Staff diversity Finally, a number of studies looked at how the agreements affected specific categories of workers, especially women, managers and part-time staff.

The findings for women were fairly negative:

> ... From its very conception the law on the 35-hour week, despite being very authoritative on matters of labour law, has never concerned itself with issues of male/female equality. The change in opening hours in service industries involving direct contact with customers, in which there are a considerable number of female workers, is a perfect illustration of some of the 'hidden' or 'unexpected' aspects of RWH ... If they conceal this dimension, the negotiators are, whether consciously or unconsciously, blurring the real situation of such workers ... (Séhili, 2000).

Another study noted that '... there are no examples of female managers being collectively involved in the development of RWH arrangements' (Bloch-London et al., 1999, p. 92).

On the subject of managers, 'an analysis of the texts of the agreements shows that managers as a specific group are given little consideration ... Negotiations are not the right time to be considering the activities of managers and how their work is organized ...' (Bouffartigue and Bouteiller, 2000, p. 51).

Part-time workers (whose working week is below the statutory or agreed duration) account for 18 per cent of all workers, a figure that has doubled since 1982. According to the Ministry of Employment and Solidarity (1999), RWH agreements also covered these workers, yet there is no indication that they were consulted any more or less than the other categories of workers in the negotiation phase.

Finally, it should be emphasized that in the agreements 'wage restraint' measures (often taking the form of wage freezes for one or several years) were applied indiscriminately to all workers, without taking into account any criteria relating for instance to the level of remuneration or family situation. According to the DARES study, variations in basic pay rises are of the order of one per cent for two years when comparing companies involved in Robien/Aubry RWH processes with other companies (Boisard and Pelisse, 2000, p. 14).

Workers and the Initial Effects of the Agreements

Workers have scarcely been studied as actors in the RWH process, or where they have been, they seem to have made only a small contribution, except perhaps in micro-businesses and small and medium-sized enterprises, mainly in one-to-one talks with the management and the hierarchy. Their role in applying the agreements has, to all intents and purposes, not been analyzed. The impact of RWH on their lives at work and outside, on the other hand, has attracted more interest.

According to the CFDT opinion poll mentioned above (1999, p. 3), workers have reacted fairly positively to the application of RWH: 'For 71 per cent the new working hours do not present a problem, 52 per cent were able to choose (either individually or as part of a team) the type of RWH they wanted (half-day, day and so on), and for 52 per cent work has not changed.' However, '45 per cent said that they were working fewer hours but doing as much as before, and 19 per cent said that they stayed on after normal hours in order to finish their work [64 per cent in total]' (CFDT, 1999, p. 3).

According to the Ministry of Employment and Solidarity, workers feel that 'RWH is effective, even if the workload is not always proportionately reduced' and as a result they have 'genuinely free time, but without any dramatic change in lifestyle'. The Ministry felt that 'the overall assessment was generally positive for the company and the workers' personal lives, but slightly less positive for working conditions', since 40 per cent of workers felt that RWH is bad for working rhythms (Ministry of Employment and Solidarity, 1999, p. 124).

The other studies paint a more varied picture of the first applications, but two main points emerge.

Threat of deterioration in conditions at work and outside work Observers' fears about the deterioration of working conditions relate to two aspects.

First, there is the question of the flexibility of the new shift periods and the workload:

> RWH goes hand in hand with the development of atypical working hours whose health effects are well known: digestive problems, difficulty in sleeping, cardiovascular and nervous disorders, etc. The main issue is still the 'predictability' of free time (Masson and Roland, 1999, p. 12).

The same fear is expressed about the workload of managers: 'Increased tensions and new contradictions for managers. Stress and guilt are the new working conditions ... At long last the message is being forced home that, in subordinating themselves to the economic aims of the company, managers are being delegated by employers into self-exploitation' (Bouffartigue and Bouteiller, 2000, p. 50). Moreover: 'One questions the relative hypocrisy of agreements that procure them RWH without taking into account the fact that they work considerably over legal working time and that they will have to reach more ambitious objectives within a theoretically lesser time' (Charpentier et al., 2000, p. 35). According to Pina (2000, p. 12), although 75 per cent of workers take a fairly positive view of their situation, 21 per cent have seen their workload increase. Moreover, between 1984 and 1993 the number of workers whose working rhythm is determined by the client or by the public has grown from 39 per cent to 58 per cent. The recruitment of new workers might limit the intensification of work, but a number of studies have pointed to disagreements on the number, work rate, type and, above all, distribution of recruits (for managers, see Bouffartigue and Bouteiller, 2000; more generally, see Boisard and Pelisse, 2000 and Charpentier et al., 2000). These fears have been more or less confirmed by the CFDT in an update to its 'work in questions' opinion poll: '44 per cent of workers have the impression that work is intensifying' (CFDT, 1999, p. 3).

However, according to the survey by the Ministry of Employment and Solidarity referred to earlier (1999, p. 135) and in contrast to the figures given above, 79 per cent of workers feel that their working conditions have remained the same or have improved.

Secondly, there is the question of the failure to link working time and time outside work:

> Workers appreciate the free time gained, provided that it fits in with the general structure of their social life ... The two spheres are permanently connected;

the real problem stems from the almost total lack of discussion on this point in undertakings ... Flexibility necessarily brings changes in personal routines and can cause upheaval in family life and friendships ... In future, we can expect better linkage between work and social rhythms to become one of the main elements of social dialogue in undertakings ... (Masson and Roland, 1999, p. 12).

This is also Grumbach's analysis: 'A new clash of approaches is developing between the right to work and the right to rest. The conflict is not about R for reduction, but about A for adjustment' (Grumbach, 2000, p. 237).

The Ministry would like to see:

better harmonization of leisure time ... The collective reduction in working time and the wide range of different working hours naturally prompts us to try to improve the harmonization of leisure time, school or university hours and the opening hours for local public administration and services (1999, p. 139).

According to the survey quoted by the Ministry (1999, p. 139), for three quarters of individuals 'the new distribution of working hours has not caused any particular problems in relations with colleagues, bosses, clients or families'.

Flexible working hours rather than work reorganization The reorganization of working hours is widespread, takes very different forms and does not always go hand in hand with the reorganization of work. It may include fluctuating working hours or a wider range of opening hours, equipment may be in use for longer periods, and a fifth shift may be introduced, with the disappearance of the one-dimensional view of the company schedule and the emergence of a situation in which a whole range of different arrangements are available (Boisard and Pelisse, 2000; Charpentier et al. 2000).

Changes in the organization of work include: broader multi-tasking, sometimes only among new recruits or the less skilled; the refocusing of work on the main added value and the transfer of the least skilled tasks to other jobs. In other words, it includes the redeployment of workers' skills; the creation of job-sharing or small teams to make substitution easier; the development of new duties; computerization and the development of websites (Boisard and Pelisse, 2000; Masson and Roland, 1999; Bloch-London et al., 1999; Ministry of Employment and Solidarity, 1999). According to the CFDT survey, only 16 per cent of workers feel that 'work has been significantly reorganized' (1999, p. 3). The authors of the study in Île-de-France consider that: 'Work organization changes only when time is a central variable of the activity. Hence it is not the result of the will or of a pertinent judgement by management of the company' (Charpentier et al., 2000, p. 32). They also hit on unexpected features of changes in work organization: 'Many workers are brought in to develop forms of co-operation that until then were neither requested nor necessary ... The individualization of the rules brings more co-operation not run by the company but more often originated by the workers themselves' (Charpentier et al., 2000, p. 33).

Monitoring and Evaluation

The law sets out the rules for evaluating the implementation of RWH. Agreements must include a monitoring committee, and the works council must be kept informed of the results of its work. The importance of monitoring is underlined by ANACT, which recommends 'a detailed report after 12 or 18 months' (Masson and Roland, 1999, p. 18). The studies mentioned do not provide any information on whether monitoring is referred to in the agreements or on the role, methods and operation of any committees. Boisard and Pelisse note 'the weakness of the checks provided for' (2000, p. 7). A study by ANACT gives a critical view of the situation:

> In the companies [surveyed], the situation is paradoxical: most of the agreements make provisions for monitoring committees, but we see that they are often phantoms: meetings scheduled every three months are not held, assessments are not made ... the monitoring committee is then an empty shell ... One is struck by the way in which managements lose interest in monitoring the results of RWH ... and by the attitude of the social partners (who might feel dispossessed of RWH by the management which conducted its implementation) (Masson and Pépin, 2000, p. 52).

The studies carried out under the PAROLES programme had already pointed out that the unions 'demonstrated their poor ability to administer an agreement, as if they did not feel morally or practically involved in its application' (Bunel and Thuderoz, 1999, p. 121).

Conclusions

There are currently still relatively few studies on the reduction in working hours following the Robien law and the Aubry law, and they lack detachment.

They fall into the categories of statistical studies on the agreements, opinion polls and qualitative studies in the form of monographs on the negotiations and their effects.

The statistical results and the opinion polls presented by the Ministry of Employment and Solidarity, particularly in its publication (1999), *The Reduction of Working Hours – Lessons to be Learnt from the Agreements (Summer 1998–Summer 1999)*, were heavily criticized,[6] particularly with respect to the effects of RWH on employment.[7] The statistics on the number of sectoral and company agreements seem to indicate a major resurgence in negotiations, although a number of authors have pointed out that the mandating process has led to very little increase in trade union membership, and that there is a risk that the recovery will be short-lived. The qualitative studies have focused mainly on micro-businesses and small and medium-sized firms where there is little union representation, and they have not been able to stand back and assess the ways in which the agreements have been implemented and their effects. They have shown little interest in the direct involvement of workers or the role of the staff representation bodies, and none at all in union democracy.

So it is very difficult to draw any conclusions at present, and we must be careful about interpreting incomplete data. However, most of the studies and statements have produced sufficiently similar findings to provide a provisional response to the questions we raised at the beginning.

The priority which politicians and trade unions have given to employment has tended to weigh heavily on RWH and has actually bolstered the position of militant unionism, which would otherwise, because of its traditions and its current lack of representation, have found it very difficult to mobilize supporters and workers.[8] Yet it seems that the instructions issued by the unions have merely served to inhibit this mobilization. In defence of the unions' workplace branches, it should be said that those instructions could be paradoxical. They required branches to appeal to their members or even all the staff in the firm, yet at the same time they asked the branches to make extremely general quantitative and collective demands the formulation of which did not actually involve the members or staff. Is it therefore any surprise that there was so little direct involvement in the negotiating phase in the form of information and/or consultation about draft agreements that were almost complete? Or that working conditions, work organization (as distinct from the organization of working hours) and the link with time outside work were almost totally absent from the negotiations, and that the wide variety of socio-occupational situations were not taken into account? It was only in micro-businesses and small and medium-sized enterprises where there was no previous union presence and where mandating had not yet been introduced that there were forms of direct worker participation in informal negotiations with management, and the staff representation bodies gained a certain renewed influence. Due to the size of the companies where the surveys were carried out, we lack information about the use of institutionalized working groups, whether consultative (such as quality circles or expression groups) or decision making, in the RWH process.

The widespread flexibility identified here indicates the risk that conditions at work may deteriorate, that there is no consistency between working patterns and social patterns outside work, and finally that there is even greater emphasis on the individual, which could break up work teams and make collective action and organization even more difficult. The gap between the satisfaction which workers generally feel according to certain opinion polls, and the more detailed findings of studies on the ground, calls for further study over the longer term, in particular to shed light on the causes of the current industrial disputes that are developing over the implementation of RWH. Until March 2000 the ministry tried to play down the significance of these conflicts.[9] But in November 2000, DARES, its Directorate of Research, Studies and Statistics, pointed out that the number of days of strikes in both semi-public and private sectors had risen in 1999 by more than 60 per cent over the corresponding figure for 1998. The first cause of the strikes (27 per cent) concerned pay claims, and the second (25 per cent) was related to the adjustment and reduction of working time. In companies with more than 200 workers, claims related to working time were the main cause of disputes in 1999.

The process of reducing working hours appears to be well and truly off the launch pad and a retreat seems quite unlikely, though the policy of the new centre-right government elected in June 2002 on this topic remains to be seen. Meanwhile, the importance of the state in the production of new social norms has been confirmed, along with a standardization effect on negotiations and agreements, as was the case in the 1982 law on the workers' right of expression (Pinaud, 1996b). The negotiation phase has passed in the traditional way of industrial relations in France, without workers being any more or less involved than usual, without the trade unions changing their views or practices and without employers seeing it as an opportunity to introduce or increase participative practices. Direct participation is still considered by the employers as a management tool. Industrial democracy seems kept by unions mostly for the purposes of industrial action.

The initial impact of the agreements produced is still ambiguous, varied and much debated. The gap between the potential effect of the reform on the active role of the workers themselves on decisions which concern them, and the top-down conformist way in which it is being managed, augurs badly for a revival of ideas and practices of self-management in France. One of the challenges for the unions was to combat the usual technocratic top-down method used to elaborate and implement social change. In the long run, the fact that it was not taken up by the trade unions that represent one of the main actors of industrial democracy might well lead to a stagnation or weakening of its influence and credibility among workers in France.

Notes

1   An abridged version of this chapter, dated June 2000, was presented to the Congrès de l'association internationale des sociologues de langue française (Congress of the International Association of French-speaking Sociologists) Québec, 3–8 July 2000.

2   Since 1900 the statutory working week has been amended four times in France: in 1919 (eight hours a day × six days = 48 hours a week); 1936 (40 hours); 1982 (39 hours); and 1998 (35 hours). The organization of working time was for a long time governed by the law of 1936 which prohibited any variation in the duration of the working week. A series of laws in 1982, 1986, 1987 and 1993 gave firms increasing scope by allowing them, under certain conditions, to introduce flexibility into the working week as part of a sectoral or company agreement, and possibly reduce working hours at the same time. An incentive to promote part-time work, introduced in 1992, in the form of a partial exemption from payment of social security contributions by employers (if they created or converted an existing job into a part-time post) was fairly successful, with 200,000 extra jobs in two years. However, these laws were not as successful as expected with either firms or workers (Boisard and Charpentier, 1997). As far as the trade unions were concerned, the CGT and FO were against the adaptation of working time, fearing annualized and compulsory part-time working, modulations in working hours, excessive flexibility and a drop in wages. The CFDT and the CFE-CGC were more equivocal, agreeing to accept a certain degree of flexibility while at the same time condemning excessive flexibility and its effects on workers.

There are several points to note about the negotiations held after these laws were introduced. First, they did not cover the area of work organization. Second, workers rarely and hardly contributed to the debate on how their working time should be adapted. They also often disputed whether flexibility made sense, either technically or socially, caught as they were between economic constraints and employment considerations. Finally, workers on annualized part-time felt confused and insecure compared with other workers. In October 1995 a national intersectoral agreement on working time was signed between trade unions and employers. This was to lead to sectoral and then company agreements. It has as yet had no notable effect. It was in 1996, with the introduction of the Robien law, and in 1998, with the first Aubry law, that we began to see significant negotiations at sectoral and company level on reducing working hours.

3   CNRS-CFDT scientific cooperation programmes PAROLES 1 and 2: Analytical programme of research and observation concerning freedom of expression for workers.

4   Out of the total number of workers consulted, management took the initiative for 50 per cent, unions for 30 per cent and staff representatives for 20 per cent. The bigger the company, the more often unions are quoted as having organized the consultation. In the smaller companies, management is more often quoted as having initiated the consultation.

5   The CGT-FO's criticisms were spelled out by Michelle Biagi, the union's secretary: '... collective agreements are the best way to ensure that all workers in the same occupational sector have the same guarantees ... Unfortunately this situation has now come under serious threat from the law on the 35-hour week, which has returned negotiations to company level, totally demolishing collective agreements and neutralising the Labour Code. Confronted with the dangers of seeing collective agreements terminated, flexibility in firms, wage restraint and insecure jobs, the CGT-Force Ouvrière continues to give its full support to the contractual system introduced by the law of 11 February 1950', in 'Mieux que la loi', CGT-FO Hebdo, 7 October 1998, p. 4.

6   'To supplement its report on the law on the 35-hour week, Aubry's office commissioned polling institutes (IPSOS and IFOP) to carry out surveys among firms and workers who had adopted the 35-hour week. The results of those surveys show the many advantages of reducing working hours, but no explanation is given about the methods ... DARES (the Directorate of Research, Studies and Statistics) worked very hard to produce a report on the initial progress in reducing working hours, but was unable to publish it ... The work was made public in September [1999] not by DARES, but by Aubry's office, and attached to an obviously "political" report ...'. Quoted in an 'Open letter to the Bureau of the National Statistics Council (Conseil National de l'Information Statistique)' CFDT-CGT et al. (1999).

7   'How can we evaluate ... the effect of the law on employment ... No economist would dare. The breakdown produced by the Ministry of Employment and Solidarity cannot claim to be a rigorous analysis of the effects of RWH on employment ... It merely records, with a certain margin of error, the employment commitments made in the agreements ... What is being recorded today is not how the transition to a 35-hour week affects firms, but the cumulative effect of RWH and the reduction in social contributions' (Boisard and Pelisse, 2000, p. 1).

8   After the recommendation in the CFDT's *Guide for RWH Negotiators* to 'exchange flexibility in the organization of working time for RWH and recruitment' (1998), J.P. Peulet, the Confederation's General Secretary, wrote that 'the absence of the working conditions variable from the negotiations [particularly after the Robien law] reflected the hierarchy's choice of priorities. RWH is above all about employment' (*Célidé Magazine*, 2000, p. 12).

9   The Ministry of Employment and Solidarity wrote in its document, 'Press release – The reduction of working hours', dated 15 March 2000, p. 10: 'The implementation of the 35-hour week has not led to an increase in industrial disputes. On the contrary, the number of industrial disputes is continuing to fall ... The same applies to the number of workers on strike'. The figures quoted by the Ministry relate to the first eight months of 1999.

References

Aznar, G. (1993), *Travailler moins pour travailler tous*, Syros, Paris.

Bélier, G. (2000), 'Sur le forfait en heures pour les cadres et le contingent annuel', *Semaine Sociale Lamy*, No. 964.

Bloch-London, C., Coutrot, T., Didry, C. and Michon, F. (1999), 'Découvrir la réduction et l'aménagement des temps de travail, la mise en œuvre des accords Robien dans douze petites et moyennes entreprises', *Travail et Emploi*, No. 79, pp. 89–106.

Boisard, P. and Charpentier, P. (1997), 'Négocier le temps de travail', in *Des relations professionelles en mouvement, séminaire du GIP Mutations Industrielles*, pp. 97–117.

Boisard, P. and Dalle, B. (1997), 'Bilan critique de la loi Robien', *Problèmes économiques*, La Documentation française, Paris, pp. 29–40.

Boisard, P. and Pelisse, J. (2000), 'Analyse des premiers accords conventionnés de passage à 35 heures – Etude monographique de 12 accords', *DARES document d'études*, No. 37.

Bouffartigue, P. and Bouteiller, J. (2000), 'Réduire le temps sans réduire la charge ? Les cadres et les 35 heures', *Travail et Emploi*, No. 82, pp. 37–52.

Bunel, J. and Thuderoz, C. (1999), 'Le syndicalisme entre participation et institutionnalisation', in Le Tron, M., Pinaud, H. and Chouraqui, A. (eds), *Syndicalisme et démocratie dans l'entreprise*, L'Harmattan, Paris, pp. 117–46.

Célidé Magazine (2000), No. 7, March.

Cette, G. and Couprie, H. (2000), 'La modulation des horaires de travail dans les accords 35 heures: quelques caractéristiques', *Travail et Emploi*, No. 83, p. 17.

CFDT- Syndicalisme-Hebdo (1997), No. 2629, 2 January.

CFDT (1998), *Réduction du temps de travail – Le guide du négociateur*, CFDT productions, Paris.

CFDT (1999), 'Une grande enquête de la CFDT', *Le temps de travail en questions*, No. 6.

CFDT-Santé-Sociaux (1999), *Les cahiers de la fédé – Revue trimestrielle de la Fédération des syndicats Santé-Sociaux*, No. 5, Autumn.

CFDT-CGT syndicats, INSEE, DPD (Education nationale), Administration centrale du Ministère de l'emploi et la solidarité (1999), 'Lettre ouverte au bureau du Conseil national de l'information statistique', p. 4.

CGT (1998), 'La bataille des 35 heures', *La Vie Ouvrière*, No. 2786, pp. 14–21.

CGT (1999), 'Propositions 2ème loi 35 heures', Maryse Dumas, conférence de presse, leaflet.

CGT (2000), '35 heures, comment se servir de la loi?', *La Vie Ouvrière*, No. 2889, pp. 11–41.

CGT-Force Ouvrière (1998), 'Mieux que la loi', in *FO-Hebdo*, 7 October, pp. 1–4.

CGT-Force Ouvrière (1999), 'Loi relative à la réduction du temps de travail', leaflet.

Charpentier, P. (1985), 'Incidences économiques et coût de la réduction du temps de travail. L'exemple de Thomson grand public', *Travail et Emploi*, No. 25, pp. 7–20.

Charpentier, P., Moisan, A. and Pigeyre, F. (2000), *La négociation sur les 35 heures – Enquête auprès de 14 entreprises de l'Ile-de-France*, Préfecture Ile-de-France/Conseil Régional Ile-de-France.

DARES (1998), *La réduction de la durée du travail dans le cadre de la loi de Robien , bilan d'une année de conventions*, 03.1, Directorate of Research, Studies and Statistics, Ministry of Employment, Paris.

Doisneau, L. (2000), 'Les accords Robien, un an après: l'expérience des salariés', *Travail et Emploi*, No. 83, July, pp. 61–78.

Doisneau, L. and Fournier, B. (1999), 'Le passage au 35 heures: situation à la fin juin 1999', DARES, Premières synthèses, 99.12 (week 52, part 1), Directorate of Research, Studies and Statistics, Ministry of Employment, Paris, pp. 1–8.

Dubrac, M-D. (1997), 'Expérience d'entreprise', *Semaine Sociale Lamy*, No. 831, pp. 3–6.

Dufour, C., Adelheid, H., Vincent, C. and Viprey, M. (1999), 'Le mandatement dans le cadre de la loi du 13 juin 1998', *La revue de l'IRES*, No. 31, pp. 2–40.

Dumas, M. (1998), 'Les négociations sur la RTT à 35 heures: chance et défi pour le syndicalisme et la CGT', *Syndicalisme et société*, No. 2, pp. 217–35.

Fermanian, J.-D. (1999), 'Le temps de travail des cadres', *INSEE*, No. 671.

Fiole, M., Passeron, V. and Roger, M. (2000), 'Premières évaluations quantitatives des réductions collectives du temps de travail', *Document d'études DARES*, No. 35.

Freyssinet, J. (1997), 'La loi Robien: rupture qualitative ou aubaine éphémère', *La revue de l'IRES*, No. 23, pp. 5–34.

Gautrat, J. (1999), 'Le statut de l'expression', in Le Tron, M., Pinaud, H. and Chouraqui, A. (eds), *Syndicalisme et démocratie dans l'entreprise*, L'Harmattan, Paris, pp. 187–206.

Gorz, A. (1998), 'Le travail perd sa centralité dans la vie des gens', *Alternatives économiques*, No. 157, pp. 61–5.

Grinsmir, J. (2000), 'Innover en négociant, négocier en innovant', in Grumbach, T. and Pina, L. (eds), *35 heures, négocier les conditions de travail*, Les Editions de l'Atelier, Paris, pp. 17–30.

Grumbach, T. (2000), 'Conclusion', in Grumbach, T. and Pina, L. (eds), *35 heures, négocier les conditions de travail*, Les Editions de l'Atelier, Paris, pp. 225–37.

Grumbach, T. and Pina, L. (eds) (2000), *35 heures, négocier les conditions de travail*, Les Editions de l'Atelier, Paris.

Heller, F., Pusic, E., Strauss, G. and Wilpert, B. (1998), *Organizational Participation – Myth and Reality*, Oxford University Press, Oxford.

Kapp, T. (1999), 'Vers les 35 heures en agriculture ? Durée du travail dans le secteur agricole et réduction du temps de travail', *Droit ouvrier*, pp. 317–21.

Kester, G. and Pinaud, H. (1996), 'Introduction: Democratic Participation : a Challenge for Democracy', in Kester, G. and Pinaud, H. (eds), *Trade Unions and Democratic Participation in Europe: A Scenario for the 21st Century*, Avebury, Aldershot, pp. 1–9.

Labbe, C. (1997), 'Secteur sanitaire et social – Loi Robien: l'épreuve de force', *Espace social européen*, No. 376.

Le Tron, M. and Pinaud, H. (1999), 'Introduction générale', in Le Tron, M., Pinaud, H. and Chouraqui, A. (eds), *Syndicalisme et démocratie dans l'entreprise*, L'Harmattan, Paris, pp. 7–50.

Martin, D. (1994), *La démocratie industrielle – La participation directe dans les entreprises*, PUF, Paris.

Martin, D. with Farmakidès, A.M. (1999), 'Participation des salariés et modernisation des entreprises', in Le Tron, M., Pinaud, H. and Chouraqui, A. (eds), *Syndicalisme et démocratie dans l'entreprise*, L'Harmattan, Paris, pp. 51–88.

Masson, A. and Pépin, M. (2000), 'Réduction du temps de travail et enjeux organisationnels', *Travail et Emploi*, No. 83, pp. 47–59.

Masson, A. and Roland, T. (1999), 'Retour d'expérience – Les 35 heures, un an après', *Travail et Changements – Revue de l'Anact*, No. 249, pp. 7–16.

Meyer, F. (2000), 'Analyse de 200 accords en Alsace', in Grumbach, T. and Pina, L. (eds), *35 heures, négocier les conditions de travail*, Les Editions de l'Atelier, Paris, pp. 47–64.

Ministry of Employment and Solidarity (Ministère de l'Emploi et de la Solidarité) (1999), *La réduction du temps de travail – Les enseignements des accords (été 1998–été 1999)*, La documentation française, Paris.

Ministry of Employment and Solidarity (Ministère de l'Emploi et de la Solidarité) (2000), *Dossier de presse – La réduction du temps de travail*, 15 March.

Ministry of Employment and Solidarity (Ministère de l'Emploi et de la Solidarité) (2001), Website: www.35h.travail.gouv.fr.

Mossé, P., Gervasoni, N. and Kerleau, M. (1999), 'Les restructurations hospitalières; acteurs, enjeux et stratégies', *Convention MiRe*, 6.

Niel, S. (2000), 'Qui sont les cadres exclus des 35 heures?', *Semaine Sociale Lamy*, No. 963.

Pina, L. (2000), 'Introduction', in Grumbach, T. and Pina, L. (eds), *35 heures, négocier les conditions de travail*, Les Editions de l'Atelier, Paris, pp. 9–16.

Pinaud, H. (1996a), 'The Role of Social Actors during Recent Developments in Worker Participation in Ten Countries of Western Europe', in Kester, G. and Pinaud, H. (eds) (1996), *Trade Unions and Democratic Participation in Europe: A Scenario for the 21st Century*, Avebury, Aldershot, pp. 11–25.

Pinaud, H. (1996b), 'Direct Participation in France', in Kester, G. and Pinaud, H. (eds), *Trade Unions and Democratic Participation in Europe: A Scenario for the 21st Century*, Avebury, Aldershot, pp. 22–46.

Regalia, I. (1995), *Humanize Work and Increase Profitability? – Direct Participation in Organizational Change viewed by the Social Partners in Europe*, European Foundation for the Improvement of Living and Working Conditions, Dublin.

Regini, M. et al. (eds) (1992), *The Future of Labour Movements*, SAGE Studies in International Sociology, No. 43, London.

Reynaud, J.-D. (1998), *Le conflit, la négociation et la règle*, second expanded edition, Octares, Toulouse, France.

Rocca, M. (2000), 'L'expérience de l'appui conseil', in Grumbach, T. and Pina, L. (eds), *35 heures, négocier les conditions de travail*, Les Editions de l'Atelier, Paris, pp. 83–96.

Sisson, K. (1996), *Se mettre d'accord – Idées et pratiques. La participation directe dans le changement organisationnel*, European Foundation for the Improvement of Living and Working Conditions, Dublin.

Sisson, K. (ed.) (1997), *First Results of Establishment Survey*, European Foundation for the Improvement of Living and Working Conditions, Dublin.

Séhili, D. (2000), 'Construire l'égalité femmes/hommes', in Grumbach, T. and Pina, L. (eds), *35 heures, négocier les conditions de travail*, Les Editions de l'Atelier, Paris, pp. 185–200.

Semaine Sociale Lamy (1999), '35 heures – Le projet de loi – Réactions syndicales', No. 945, August, pp. 41–7.

Strauss, G. (1998), 'Collective Bargaining, Unions and Participation', in Heller, F., Pusic, E., Strauss, G. and Wilpert, B. (eds), *Organizational Participation – Myth and Reality*, Oxford University Press, Oxford.

Chapter 11

Worker Participation in Negotiating Working Time in Italy

Anna M. Ponzellini

Introduction

Working time is currently high on the collective bargaining agenda in Italy. However, with the passing of time, both the specific issues under discussion and the bargaining levels have changed. For a long period – at least for the whole of the 1980s – negotiation centred on the 'generalized reduction of working hours' under the slogan 'lavorare meno per lavorare tutti' ('work less so that everyone can work') launched by Pierre Carniti, secretary of the CISL trade union confederation. The results were marginal, however: the working week still amounted to 40 hours and the modest reduction in working hours was mainly achieved by increasing the number of days off.

Over the last 10 years, though in some sectors for even longer and generally as a result of pressure applied by employers, the focus of bargaining has progressively shifted towards 'working hours flexibilization'. This gives rise to a wide variety of plant utilization schemes and differentiated working hours schedules, almost always tied to the specific nature of the technology and product market concerned. This growing destandardization of working hours has increased the importance of company-level bargaining: indeed, in recent years this issue has been the most frequent subject of bargaining after pay.

Latterly, moreover, interesting new forms of bargaining have arisen which seek to combine the granting of 'flexible hours according to firms' needs' with 'flexible hours according to employees' needs' and in particular to promote arrangements that enable workers to balance work with their family and personal commitments more easily. The interesting feature of this new wave of bargaining on working hours is that it is driven from the bottom up – by the specific everyday needs of workers (especially women workers) – rather than by the long-term strategies devised by the union confederations at central level.

This chapter will examine bargaining on working time in Italy over the last 10 years, dealing in particular with flexible working arrangements negotiated at company level. The first section will discuss the evolution of trade union policies in recent years as part of the dialectic between the 'generalized reduction' and the 'flexibilization' of working hours. It will also examine the impact of those policies on industrial relations and on bargaining structures (and especially the emergence of the company level as the main arena of negotiations on working hours). The second section will concentrate on the different – and sometimes conflicting – meanings implied by the term 'working time flexibility', depending to whether it is used by employers or by workers. It will also analyse the organizational implications of the destandardization of working hours from the point of view of both the organization of production (or of the service provided) and the working conditions of the employees. The third and final section will focus on the new policies for reconciling work with family life promoted by both the trade unions and a number of family-friendly firms. Examples will be given of interesting company experiments in the organization of working hours designed to harmonize the firm's needs with the work/life balance of its workers.

Reduction or Flexibility?

In Italy, as in all European countries, the debate on reducing working hours and its possible effects in terms of employment seems to have come to a standstill (Bosch, 1999). Between the end of the 1970s and the second half of the 1980s the policy of 'work less so that everyone can work' aroused great interest, especially within one of the trade union confederations (CISL). However, after that, the issue was largely set aside for a number of years, during which time industry collective bargaining achieved minor benefits in the form of extra days of paid leave but left the official working week substantially unchanged at 40 hours, except in the public sector where employees generally work a 36-hour week. Compared with the target of 35 hours – amounting to a 12 per cent decrease in average working time – the reduction actually achieved during the 1980s and 1990s in the private sector did not amount to more than between 5 and 6 per cent. This was a modest result which, with respect to industrial workers, was annulled by a simultaneous and more than proportional increase in overtime (Olini, 1994). A similar phenomenon, by the way, took place in the UK at the same time (Rubery, 1998).

The half-failure of the strategy to reduce working hours over that period was due in part to the opposition raised by employers, and perhaps also in part to the scant impetus given by the unions to the policy, which was never popular with workers. The unions' decision to advance moderate and incremental claims (instead of one big campaign) for reduced working hours found little consensus among workers, who were reluctant to give up their potential pay increases in a period of wage restraint in exchange for a reduction of a few minutes in their working day. And the meagre results were also due in part – at least for some years – to splits in the trade union front, with the CGIL unwilling to make working-time reduction the central issue of bargaining when national industry agreements were renewed.[1]

Furthermore, throughout the 1970s and 1980s, the unions clearly preferred to increase employment through early retirement and the replacement recruitment of young people rather than through a substantial reduction of working time (although, from many points of view, early retirement can be considered a form of working-time reduction).

The issue of a generalized reduction in working time returned, however, to the agenda in 1997 when the Italian government pledged, following the French example, to introduce a law restricting the statutory working week to 35 hours. Somewhat surprisingly (and unlike in France), this undertaking – prompted by the government coalition's need to placate its most radical left-wing component, Communist Reconstruction (Rifondazione Comunista) – provoked the opposition not only of the employers' associations (traditionally hostile to reductions in working hours) but also of the trade unions themselves. Their opposition was grounded on reasons of method rather than on reasons of substance, given that they had declared themselves in favour of a progressive reduction of working hours. The most important reason of method was the reluctance of the unions to cede an area that had always been within the purview of the social partners to the executive and to the political parties. It was probably more because of the stance taken up by the unions, rather than events within the coalition, that the government's pledge to reduce working hours was eventually shelved.

It may also be that this episode can be interpreted – after years of discussion between the social partners and also internally within the unions themselves – as resulting from general scepticism over the employment creation potential of generalized policies for working-time reduction. Various Italian commentators have pointed out that, although working-time reduction is undeniably a means to improve the living conditions of workers and to protect jobs, the ways in which it can be generally implemented in practice remain unclear (Leonardi, 2000). Practical problems include increasing costs and therefore reducing the competitiveness of firms, the possibility of increasing overtime by skilled personnel, and generating labour-market tensions in areas of full employment, with the attendant risk of exacerbating, rather than resolving, the traditional north/south dualism of the Italian economy.

Some commentators have also emphasized that Italy is characterized by the large-scale presence of small and very small firms to which a law introducing an across-the-board reduction of working hours would be inapplicable, by a large amount of irregular employment and by a public administration in which the working week has been 36 hours or less for years. In such a country, they maintain, the number of workers affected by the reduction would be too small to produce significant results in terms of new employment (Olini, 2000).

In practical terms, with the passage of time, it has grown increasingly clear that an automatic and undifferentiated reduction of working time could once have been achieved easily in a Fordist organization, with its predictable production flows and high interchangeability of labour. However, it is much more difficult to implement today, in conditions of flexible production, consumer-driven markets, and the increasing differentiation of skills.

Interesting light is shed on this aspect by studies on the application of 'solidarity contracts' (agreements reached in cases of company crisis and financed out of a public funds). The attempt to redistribute work in accordance with the law, by applying the same reduction in hours to all workers in the company, has failed in the majority of cases. It has clashed, in fact, with the existence in internal labour markets of a demand for highly specific labour in terms of the tasks to be performed and, conversely, with the scant substitutability of skills present in the company (Cesos, 1994).

With the option of a statutory reduction in working hours discarded at least for the time being, the goal of job creation together with favouring female employment has been partially resumed by the Italian government – following the example of the Netherlands – by providing incentives for part-time contracts. In all EU countries, the increasing importance of part-time work has been interpreted as a shift from collective to individual working-time reductions (Lehndorff, 1998). It should, in any case, be pointed out that part time has been traditionally little used in Italy. Like all Southern European countries, Italy is characterized by the low participation of women in the labour market. This is, however, offset by the absence of the male/female polarization in terms of working hours that generally marks out the Nordic countries and gives rise to some concern among commentators (Rubery, 1999). Following these recent government measures, part-time employment has increased markedly in the services sector and, to some extent, in public administration, though the overall percentage of part-time workers is still rather low (just over 10 per cent).

Reduction plus Flexibility: the Emergence of an 'Italian Way'?

Two phenomena have led to renewed bargaining on working time since the end of the 1980s, taking the place of the original objective of a generalized reduction in working hours.

The first consists of the new market and production requirements generated by the advent of the so-called 'post-Fordist' economy and the onset of globalization, factors which have compelled firms to intensify the use of plant and to adjust their production and service rates to the exigencies of their customers. The second phenomenon – to date the less evident of the two – is the emergence and legitimation, in a period of relative affluence and increasing female participation in the labour market, of the need for male and female workers to achieve a better balance between their work and their personal and family lives, by means of flexible working-time arrangements, amongst other things.

Both these phenomena (which are discussed in detail in the next section) have shifted the focus of bargaining towards flexibility – albeit often in different directions – rather than towards a wholesale reduction in working hours. However, the Italian experience of the last 15 years has shown that working-time flexibility and working-time reduction are not incompatible. Nor are flexibility and new employment.

This is also the case with regard to 'more difficult' flexibility, or the flexibility required by the needs of production or services. Actually, acceptance of working-time flexibility by the unions has also entailed their acceptance that working-hours policies may be appropriated by firms. In fact, whilst the policy of reduction of working time has a markedly social connotation, that of flexibility requires close attention to the costs and organizational concerns of firms, and therefore to the technical solutions proposed by management. On the other hand, the unions' agreement to negotiate on differentiated and flexible working hours has opened the possibility of resuming a policy of working-time reduction in a more viable form, if it is true – as a European Commission report declared 10 years ago – that 'policies to reduce working time can be effective only if they are closely linked with the reorganization of production'.[2] The entitlement acquired by worker representatives through the negotiation of flexibility to involve themselves in the technical aspects of various working-hours arrangements, and to choose the one best suited to a particular plant or market, enables them to advance proposals for reductions in working time which firms find acceptable in terms of costs.

Accordingly, the Italian model of bargaining on working time in recent years can be regarded as positive. In Italy, in fact, bargaining on production flexibility – especially in the form of extra shifts, an extension of production schedules to include the weekend and variable weekly working hours according to the production cycle – has been under way since the early 1980s, and therefore began earlier in Italy than in other countries (CNEL, 1993). In a period when the generalized reduction of working time produced mediocre results, the Italian unions negotiated hundreds of agreements in the manufacturing sector. These conceded production flexibility in exchange for reductions in working hours, which in numerous companies fell to 36 – or even 32 – hours a week on average for shift workers, and worker autonomy in the use of rest days by means of the 'hours account system' (Piazza et al., 1998). In short, these developments constituted a working-time policy which combined flexibility with reductions in hours.

With respect to what has been depicted as the European trend in working hours over the last 20 years – the shift from 'collective' reduction to 'individual' reductions of working time in the form of part-time work (Lehndorff, 1998; Sanne, 1998) – the Italian case seems somewhat different, and perhaps intermediate between the two instances. And this is not only because the incidence of part time is still low in Italy, which may prove to be only a phase. It is also because a great deal of the working-time flexibility that has been negotiated has received collective reductions in working time in return, although these have been restricted to certain companies and/or occupational groups (and are therefore not 'generalized'). The Italian experience also highlights the importance of the company level for bargaining on working time. It is in fact at this level that it is possible to define the working hours schedules and their duration (which cannot be standardized) best suited to the technology, the type of market and the needs of the customer.[3] At company level, moreover, it is easier to identify the differing needs of male and female workers and to obtain a more beneficial exchange between the demand and supply of working-time flexibility.

What Flexibility? Company Needs versus Workers' Needs

Negative Connotations of 'Flexibility'

When, in the mid-1980s, talk began in Italy on 'flexibility' – of working hours but also more generally of employment relationships – between unions and employers, but also among workers themselves, there ensued what was sometimes a heated debate. The notion of flexibility that began to spread soon acquired a political significance – the relaxing of union rigidities – and only subsequently did attention shift to its technical aspect, namely that firms must adapt their organization in order to respond rapidly to changing markets. As for the quality of workers' lives – an aspect obviously affected by the flexibilization of working hours – this was seen by unions in only negative terms as a possible worsening of working conditions, and not as a possible improvement in the relationship between work and the rest of a person's life.

That period was rather difficult for the unions. Whilst companies discarded, albeit slowly, the bureaucratic model of corporate organization, the unions found it difficult to imagine a model of work other than the standard one: permanent employment for 40 hours a week, for 11 months a year, for the entire period stretching from completion of school to retirement.

For their part, firms sought to monopolize the flexibilization of working hours, giving overriding priority to their technical and commercial needs. This forced the unions on the defensive as they sought to keep their control over labour, despite the fact that the labour market was becoming enormously differentiated, especially as a result of entry by women and highly skilled workers, two categories which demanded new forms of employment. The stubborn resistance mounted by the Italian unions against part-time work over the entire 1970s and 1980s is indicative of how they failed to understand the changes then in progress. By the end of the 1990s, however, the attitude of the unions to flexibility had shifted considerably and in recent years 'flexibility bargaining' has become one of the main issues in collective agreements and labour market policies.

Firms' Flexibility: Cost Cutting, Customer Orientation and Just-in-Time

Until the mid-1980s, there were two main means available to Italian companies when obliged to introduce flexible hours in order to adjust to changing markets: overtime and the temporary redundancy fund (cassa integrazione guadagni). Requested by companies in periods of surplus demand, overtime – very well paid and therefore welcomed by a large part of workers, especially men – became a practice that the unions found increasingly difficult to control. By contrast, when production declined because of crises (but also and increasingly because of seasonal trends in output), companies could rely on a typically Italian arrangement: the temporary redundancy fund, which permitted large-scale temporary lay-offs of workers, who received supplementary benefit. In this way contractual ('theoretical') working hours were still rigidly applied, so that the principle was preserved, while the hours actually worked tended to differ substantially between workers. It should be pointed out, however, that in the 1980s the use of another flexibility measure – rotating shifts, often including night work – was already more frequent in Italy than in the rest of Europe (CNEL, 1993).

Over time, this traditional model of flexibility in the Italian production system has changed, mainly because of the restrictions imposed on the use of the temporary redundancy fund by public finances, but also because of the proliferation and increasing complexity of flexibility needs brought about by the changing operation of markets and the fierce competition provoked by globalization. What, therefore, are the factors that currently induce firms to pursue flexible working time arrangements, and what have been the responses forthcoming from collective bargaining?

There are three main organizational objectives, sometimes tied specifically to the product/service and sometimes coexisting in the same type of production:

1 optimization of the use of plant in order to reduce costs;
2 extension of opening hours to the public or of the service, as a customer-orientation strategy (for companies in private and public services);
3 the modularization of production in order to cope with seasonal trends or as a strategy to respond rapidly to fluctuations in the demand for certain products (just-in-time production).

The first objective is typical of a manufacturing firm seeking to optimize the use of plant, especially, as increasingly happens, when the latter requires large-scale investment. Being unable or unwilling to increase its technological capital, the firm tries to increase output by increasing daytime shifts, and sometimes by introducing night shifts as well. In some sectors, at least during certain months of the year, the production schedule requires Saturday and even Sunday working. This tendency to intensify daytime shifts now involves almost all manufacturing sectors in Italy. The extension of work into the night, and into the weekends, is especially common among large textile firms (which were the first to introduce the so-called 'six days × six hours system'), metalworking and, to a lesser extent, food companies as well as chemical plants, which traditionally work on a continuous cycle. Once the technical needs of production had been recognized, company-level bargaining in the 1990s was principally aimed at obtaining benefits for workers. The most recent trend has been to exchange pay increases for reduced working hours: in plants where work is organized into daytime shifts, fewer than 38 hours per week are usually worked; in those with night shifts and weekend working, this amount falls in some cases to 32 hours per week (Piazza et al., 1998).

More unusual, but rapidly increasing, is the trend towards shift work in commercial or service sector companies. This is the second set of objectives relating to working hours noted above. Recent years, in fact, have witnessed increasing pressure in workplaces – supermarkets, banks, data processing centres, mail and telephone companies, public offices, call centres and so on – for front-office hours to be prolonged into the afternoon, evening, or Saturdays and Sundays in order to satisfy customer demands. Afternoon opening to the public is still relatively rare in the case of public offices in Italy, where the traditional hours of 08.00 to 14.00 have favoured employees, many of whom are women. The recently liberalized shop hours – with opening on Sundays and in the evenings – have sparked debate among workers worried about a worsening of their employment conditions and across the country as a whole (even the Catholic Church has pronounced against the innovation). However, the trend towards longer opening hours, and therefore to new working time arrangements, by now seems unstoppable. In some cases, the extension of hours does not correspond to an entirely new shift, and this may lead to the creation of part-time jobs. The combination of full-time and part-time arrangements in large retail outlets has made shift work superfluous almost everywhere.

The first two cases of production/service reorganization have led, then, to working time changes in terms of shift patterns, schedules and the introduction of part time. The third objective, by contrast, involves changes in the seasonal, or more generally period-based, rhythm of work, in the sense that workers are asked to work more hours (or more days) during certain periods and fewer hours (or days) in others. This is traditionally the case in sectors with seasonal products – food, fashion or tourism, for example – which require more intensive productive effort in certain periods of the year. In this case, basic working time is no longer weekly but multi-weekly, and the pattern of alternating periods of long and short working hours is very similar – and therefore predictable – year after year. But even a non-seasonal product may require adjustments of the production flow. Many companies have shifted towards a strategy of rapid response to the market that entails the flexible adjustment of production to fluctuations in sales. This is increasingly the case with mass-produced consumer goods like cars or domestic appliances. Once again, working time must be modularized across the weeks/months of the year. But unlike the case of seasonal production, it is probable that production changes are less predictable, and the consequent announcements of increases (or decreases) in weekly working hours are made at shorter notice, which causes problems for workers, who cannot properly plan their lives outside work. For this reason, the introduction of productive flexibility over the course of the year has often been negotiated in exchange for the right of workers to choose when they will take hours/days off work, the purpose being to balance the advantages and disadvantages to the firm and its workers. Almost all collective agreements in manufacturing now provide for multi-period working time; indeed, the practice is so widespread that the most recent renegotiations in the chemicals and metalworking sectors have gone a step further by introducing annualized hours.

Workers' Flexibility: New (and Old) Social Needs for Time

What sort of working hours do male and female workers want? Do they envisage an 'ideal' system? Surveys conducted mainly among female workers, but also analysis of bargaining agendas (CNEL, 1993), show that there are three main patterns in the needs expressed by workers with respect to the reconciliation of working time and family or leisure time:

1　more time available for family life or other personal activities (the need to act on the 'duration' of working time);
2　more choice as to when to work, while performing the normal number of hours, so that work does not overlap with other commitments (the need to act on the 'distribution' of working hours over the day or week); and
3　the right to take time off in specific circumstances (for example, maternity leave, care of small children or other family members, in-service training, university examinations and so on).

In all three cases, the requests of workers differ markedly by gender, age of children, household income, training programmes, the place of work in individual strategies and so on. This finding tells us two things. The first is that in the future the standard pattern of working (that is, eight hours a day for five days a week) will be little more than a benchmark. The second is that it will be impossible to identify specific working hours for groups of workers (for 'mothers', 'for young people', and so on) because the possible combinations of work and personal circumstances/choices have proliferated so much in contemporary society.

Having more *time available* for oneself and for one's family is an aspiration that has always driven the female labour force's demand for a better quality of life. Historically, it has most frequently taken the form of pressure for the reduction of working hours for all workers. This is a fundamental need, of which workers' representatives have always been aware, and it is shared by both people who have specific family commitments and those who do not. The rate at which working hours have diminished, however, has not been sufficient to meet objective personal/family circumstances, nor has it been sufficient to support the strategies adopted by couples to combine income and the amount of time to devote to family responsibilities. For this reason, the aspiration to have more time for family care, for training or for other personal matters has given rise to pressure for individual reductions: part-time arrangements amounting to one-half, two-thirds, three-quarters and so on of full-time hours, with a proportional reduction in pay.

In Italy, part-time employment spread slowly, largely because of the initial hostility raised by the trade unions, for which reason company-level bargaining was long dominated by the so-called 'maximum quota' clauses. Until a few years ago, part-time work was available almost only in the large-scale retail sector, and it was almost entirely women who requested it. More recently, the situation has changed somewhat, mainly as a result of new hirings and the growth of more innovative sectors like telecommunications, and the percentage of males (young and newly-hired) has risen slightly. The civil service and the public services (transport, health and so on) also now accept part-time workers. The most recent bargaining round has concentrated mainly on the modularization of part-time: that is, the introduction of diversified bands of hours instead of the classic half-time arrangement. It has thus been possible to observe that workers requesting part-time employment prefer longer working hours, because this enables them to avoid excessive reductions in income (Regione Lombardia, 1998). Contrary to the expectations of the unions, which made great efforts to ensure the right to 'return to full time', in the majority of cases the decision to switch to part-time employment is definitive (or at least long lasting).

Reductions of daily or weekly hour bands are particularly welcomed by workers, because they increase free time without affecting income. Numerous agreements, especially for white-collar workers, have introduced shorter lunch breaks (which in the Southern European countries are traditionally long), enabling employees to leave work earlier in the evening. Still rare in Italy, however, are the agreements on the 'short week' (four days) introduced in other European countries, where commuting is probably more difficult.

However, for many workers the problem is not 'how much' work they do but *'when'*. There are people willing to put in their eight hours provided they can choose to work in the morning rather than the afternoon, only some months in the year rather than the whole year round, many hours in a few days or a few hours every day, and so on. This is the most interesting aspect of the flexibilization of working time, because by maintaining income unchanged, it prevents the labour-market dualism between full-time male work and part-time female work that characterizes many countries. Unfortunately, however, it is the most complicated direction in which to move, because it presupposes a match – difficult to achieve – between workers' needs and the technical constraints on companies. The bargaining that has created opportunities for employees to choose the distribution of their working hours covers mainly daily in/out flexibility: in both the private and public sectors, many agreements have been signed which allow employees to choose when to clock on and off, except for a time-band during the day when their presence in the workplace is obligatory. In many cases, daily balance is not necessary, but may be only weekly or even monthly or annual, a system which gives even greater freedom to workers. In some cases, the time card has been replaced by a monthly signing-in sheet managed personally by the worker. This type of flexibility is obviously more difficult to introduce in production, where work is constrained by teams and machinery: in these cases, the only form of flexibility granted is the swapping of shifts among workers. One innovation that has instead been introduced in almost all medium to large companies is the annual negotiation of holidays and individual leave (obtained partly in the form of reduced hours) and of collective stoppages, which enable workers to plan their non-work activities better. As we have seen, the chance for workers to take days off as and when they want has become common in production units with multi-period or annualized hours. In these cases, the unions have often negotiated 'hours accounts' which enable workers to take time off, at short notice, by 'cashing in' hours previously accumulated through overtime work.

Finally, the right to paid leave is becoming increasingly common, with workers being entitled to take a 'break' from work for *social and personal reasons*. In Italy there are numerous laws and contractual provisions which grant leave for social needs: the law on maternity leave, of course, the recently introduced law on parental leave or leave for training purposes and the law on voluntary work are all examples. Sectoral agreements also cover the right to have time off to study, the right to have time to care for handicapped or sick family members, and so on. The focus of company-level bargaining is usually on increasing the hours or days of leave envisaged by the law, and especially on their remuneration: most leave of absence, in fact, is remunerated only in part or not at all. Numerous company agreements grant full pay in the case of maternity leave (rather than the 80 per cent stipulated by the law), extra paid leave for parents (up to 150 hours in the first three years of the child's life), paid paternity leave or benefits for workers caring for sick family members.

It is evident, therefore, that male and female workers have very different requirements with respect to working time, and their needs change as their circumstances or life strategies change. Accordingly, the most innovative aspect of the present phase of negotiation on working hours is that it is no longer possible to assume that there is one working time that applies to all workers indiscriminately, like the traditional standard schedule of eight hours a day, five days a week, until retirement.

Work/Life Balance: Best Practice in Bargained Flexibility

Working Time, Free Time, Time for Caring

The idea of working time used to be very clear, while that of 'free time' (or, as intellectuals of the left prefer, 'freed time') was rather vague. It evoked some sort of no man's land that might be filled with pastimes (preferably popular ones like fishing), with vocational retraining (although this preferably took place during working time and was paid for by employers), or by social relations (in the generic sense), but which should be principally devoted to resting. There is no doubt that as long as the amount of time that workers could devote to rest appeared insufficient, social policies targeted at the progressive reduction of working hours enjoyed their greatest success. But thereafter – as testified by dozens of surveys, both in Italy and other European countries, on the preferences of workers between reduced working hours and pay rises (Lehndorff, 1998) – the policy of a generalized reduction in working hours went into critical decline, always subordinate to the more impelling demand for increased remuneration.

However, a further change of scenario can be discerned. In recent decades, growing in parallel with the increased labour-market participation by women, free time has assumed a more precise connotation, being identified – to a large extent even if not totally – with 'time to care' (Balbo, 1987), or time devoted to family activities and relations, which includes caring for children, the elderly and the ill. Unlike free time, 'caring time' is more rigid and more difficult to compress. And it may also be less easy to barter for pay increases.

This need for time has increased alongside the growth of female employment, because the time that women traditionally devoted to taking care of their families must in some way be replaced. However, it does actually concern both female and male workers: in fact, the progressive redistribution between women and men of 'work for the market' also makes the redistribution of 'work for the family' necessary – as well as fair.

The social demand for caring time is first and foremost a demand for reduced working hours. But it also expresses the desire of male and female workers for greater power to decide 'when' to work: during the day, during the year and, indeed, across the course of their entire lives. In this sense it concerns the autonomy of work.

Bargaining Shifts Focus back to Male and Female Workers

As we saw in the previous section, the flexibility requirements of companies are often quite different from those of its workers. Harmonizing these two types of requirement is desirable but by no means easy. Analysis of company-level bargaining in Italy over the last 10 years has shown that – at least to date – the most frequent reasons for the destandardization of working hours have centred on the technical-productive needs of companies. As a result, they have not always, and not necessarily, been to the advantage of workers. Indeed, in the case of increased shift working, weekend work and the greater use of overtime, it may be that the working conditions of the latter have worsened.

However, in some cases, the changes in working hours desired by companies for their own ends have had the 'indirect' outcome of being advantageous to workers, especially when their introduction has been negotiated by the trade union in exchange for specific concessions in terms of reduced working time for the workers rather than monetary benefits, like increased overtime rates and shift allowances. As we have seen, the most typical exchange in such cases of 'bargained flexibility' has been between the introduction of new shifts and the reduction of weekly working hours (down to 32 hours in cases where work has been extended to Sundays). Also of great interest is the negotiated exchange of flexible annual hours for increases in weekly working time according to the pace of production determined by the company – under which arrangement workers may themselves decide when to recoup the hours (the well-known system of the 'hours bank').

However, certain innovations in working hours have been 'invented' for the express purpose of improving the quality of working life, making it easier for employees to reconcile their jobs with family commitments. For the moment there is only a limited number of such cases – a few but valuable ones – but they appear to be increasing, for two distinct reasons. Firstly, the unions are growing more sensitive to the issue of reconciling work and the family (whereas until only a short while ago union bargaining was concerned solely with job protection and wages). Secondly, firms are paying closer attention to the social dimension and to the living conditions of their employees, given that this is also a means to obtain greater commitment to work and closer identification with company goals. These experiences are discussed in the next section.

A Survey of Corporate Working-time Experiments on Work/Life Balance

Electrolux-Zanussi: 'Rosa al lavoro'

Electrolux-Zanussi has several plants manufacturing domestic appliances in Italy. One of them is the Susegana factory at Treviso, near Venice, where this experiment was launched.

The agreement is known as 'Rosa al lavoro' – 'Rose at work' – named after a typical female worker in the factory. It is perhaps the first case in Italy of an agreement intended to help women workers reconcile their working time with their 'caring time'. The case is well known and has been widely discussed, not least because – although the solution found by the company was technically unobjectionable – the company's female employees initially showed little interest in the innovation, or indeed were hostile to it.

The flexibility scheme was introduced in a department where employees worked an average of 38.3 hours a week on three six-hour shifts for six days a week. Before the agreement, rotation through the three shifts was compulsory, so that a worker spent one week on the first shift (from 05.45 to 12.00), one week on the second (from 12.00 to 18.15), and one week on the third (from 18.15 to 01.00).

The new agreement, signed in 1996, offers two possible arrangements:

1   'fixed shifts' – the worker may choose a shift and work only that shift henceforth (always in the morning or in the afternoon or in the evening). Shifts may be exchanged for one day, one week or one year, but only provided that there are two other people willing to accept the changeover;

2   'rearranging the shift duration' – apart from total weekly working hours
    (which cannot vary), women workers may agree among themselves to
    adjust their shifts. For example, one of them may work one hour fewer per
    day, while two of her colleagues on the other two shifts work for an extra
    half hour. A worker may work less for a day, a week or a year as long as
    there are other workers willing to make up the hours not covered.

It should be noted that, although very liberal, these innovations were
not initially greeted with any great enthusiasm by female workers, who
commented 'Besides doing the work, now we've got to organize it as well!'
Only subsequently did the agreement begin to work, but its implementation has
shown that, although the self-management of working hours is still an important
objective, it causes difficulties for workers. These include new organizational
duties, the assumption of responsibility, and the mediation of disputes not only
between firm and workforce but also among workers with different needs.

The Zanussi agreement has introduced the principle that a worker is entitled
to decide on his/her own both the duration and scheduling of his/her work,
albeit under certain constraints. It will be seen, in fact, that the second form
of working-hours self-management focuses on flexibility of duration, while
the first focuses on the flexible scheduling of working hours.

From the point of view of reconciling work with family commitments,
arrangements which give workers greater freedom to schedule their working
hours are more significant, and they mark an important innovation – one, for
that matter, central to debate on working hours in numerous countries. The
social objective of giving workers greater leeway in deciding their working
hours is no longer restricted solely to 'how many hours' to work – a possibility
often previously granted to women in the form of part-time employment. It
now also extends to the possibility of rearranging (in qualitative as well as
quantitative terms) all their various 'times' in order to attenuate conflicts
among them. Working time is no longer the independent variable around
which a person's organization of his/her time rotates; rather, it is only one of
the variables in play.

Banca Commerciale Italiana: 'Long Part-time and Emergency Part-time'

The Banca Commerciale Italiana (BCI) is an important banking group with
branches in every part of the country. In June 1995, the trade union signed an
agreement on part-time work that has served as a model for numerous other
agreements in the banking sector.

It should be pointed out that, until the mid-1990s, part-time employment was relatively rare in Italy (even today the country records one of the lowest percentages in Europe). In the banking sector too, despite its high level of feminization, part-time employment was possible only for a limited number of workers until a few years ago. Indeed, it was not permitted for middle and senior managers.

The new company agreement has introduced substantial innovations and highly articulated forms of part-time work, both 'horizontal' (certain hours a week) and 'vertical' (certain days a week). It is also possible to obtain part-time jobs of differing durations, and which are therefore as individualized as possible: from a minimum of 15 hours a week to a maximum of 32.5.

The agreement has the merit of addressing a number of issues of major concern to people who choose part time. The first is that working a reduced number of hours may overly compromise a person's income. Numerous empirical studies were carried out in Italy into this subject in the 1980s and are quoted by Nerb (1986) and Tempia (1988). These showed, in fact, that the majority of female workers with family problems who opt for part time would prefer the so-called 'long part time' arrangement of between 30 and 40 hours a week. More specifically, 25 per cent of Italian workers (with 17 per cent as the European average) preferred to work 30–34 hours a week (Nerb, 1986). The standard system of half time, in fact, significantly reduces a worker's earnings. It is now possible to work 32.5 hours a week at Banca Commerciale – thereby solving problems to do with child care, for instance being at home during the afternoons – while still earning 86 per cent of a full salary.

The second issue is that of obtaining an immediate and substantial reduction in working hours in order to deal with an unexpected personal or family problem (for example, the illness of a family member). The 15 hours a week solution – dubbed 'emergency part time' – meets this need very well for, at very short notice, it allows employees to work only five hours a day for three days a week if necessary. The arrangement is automatically reversible (after six months) unless the employee asks for an extension (in other cases of part time, by contrast, the law states that the return to full time is not automatically guaranteed but is subordinate to the company's requirements).

This new system has been a great success: more than one thousand employees out of some 16,000 eligible opted for these forms of employment in the first year of its implementation. Moreover, the proportion of male employees who have asked to switch to part time is substantially above the national average (17 per cent).

Tim: 'Tim-Mamma'

Tim is one of the largest mobile telephone companies in Italy with around 10,000 employees. Since its creation only a few years ago, the company has applied all possible forms of flexibility to its deployment of workers including shift systems, part time, telework and temporary agency work. The declared aim of the company's management is to deliver customer services around the clock, but also to have a satisfied workforce, because – as the head of human resources put it – 'If you're going to be good on the phone, you've got to be satisfied with your job'.

Tim has a very young workforce (the average age is 31), and the proportion of parents with small children is particularly high. For this reason, among various projects of a social nature – including those for handicapped employees, working students, ex-prisoner cooperatives and women aged over 40 wanting to return to work – the company has set up a project for working mothers known as 'Tim-Mamma'. This project, negotiated with the unions in 1997, divides into two levels. The first provides on-line updates (or in the form of a periodic newsletter) for women workers on maternity leave. The aim is to keep them constantly abreast of events in the company – changes in organization charts, introduction of new computer programmes, contract renewals and so on – so that even while they are absent they feel involved in the corporate climate.

The second level consists of working-hours facilitation for parents with children under the age of eight. It should be pointed out that, at the time of the agreement, Italy did not yet have a law on parental leave, only one (later extended to fathers) which allowed mothers to take time off work to care for children only in the case of illness, and only until the child was three years old. The Tim agreement is therefore a major step forward, and it has in some ways served as a stimulus for the enactment of the recent law on parental leave (law no. 53/2000).

The agreement introduces a package of 14 hours a month (around 150 hours a year) – unpaid, but which can be recouped in the form of overtime – for employees so that they can deal with urgent or less urgent problems concerning their children's welfare. Certificates do not have to be produced to justify leave for this purpose, and permission can be granted at very short notice. The 'hours credit' can be used even for minimal periods of time, such as half an hour. The 'hours debt' must be redeemed within three months. Time 'transactions' are recorded on a sort of personal current account possessed by all the workers covered by the agreement.

The system does not give rise to direct costs for the company apart from the minor problem of organizing substitutions, and it considerably enhances the workers' quality of life. As a female worker said, 'You're more relaxed in your work: every so often I can go and pick up my son from school, and that makes a big difference'.

This agreement – like the one at Zanussi – has also introduced the innovative principle that individual workers themselves may organize their working time, whereas working hours were previously the same for all workers and regulated externally by means of the law or the employment contract, which imposed their uniform application.

Whirlpool Italia: 'Evening Part-time'

Whirlpool Italia manufactures domestic appliances and has several plants in Italy, with a total workforce of around 3,500 employees. This case is interesting because, unlike the previous ones, it concerns not a working-hours arrangement introduced for the benefit of workers but rather (as more frequently happens) a form of flexibility to meet specific technical and production needs of the company (Fondazione Regionale Pietro Seveso, 1998). Nevertheless, the agreement was welcomed by the workers and is now considered to be a good example of flexible working hours harmonized with the needs of employees.

It should be pointed out that Whirlpool is a company that is unconventional in its work organization and that it has introduced a variety of atypical forms in its plants such as weekend contracts, fixed-term contracts, highly diversified shift schedules, niche working hours and multi-period time schedules. But it is also a company that has traditionally taken pains to provide decent working conditions and a positive corporate climate for its employees, and it has always been sensitive to the social issue of reconciling work and family life. Every plant has a joint company-union committee, consisting of supervisors and union representatives, which manages the 'new working hours schedules' and seeks to ensure that they work efficiently by finding an appropriate match between individual needs and production requirements.

The working time schedules presented here involve two forms of part-time evening work. The first operates at the company's plant in Cassinetta and consists of 20 hours per week organized into four hours a day for five days a week worked from 20.00 to 24.00. The second, in operation at the Siena factory, consists of 30 hours per week organized into six hours a day for five days, from 17.00 to 23.00. Under both schemes, employees work on fixed shifts at non-standard times of the day (what used to be called 'antisocial hours'). By this means, the company has achieved its objective of raising production without increasing the number of shifts, which would have generated extra costs owing to the bonuses paid to shift workers.

A survey of the company's employees, however, has shown that the majority of them like – or at least do not dislike – these atypical working hours (atypical in terms of both duration and, in particular, scheduling). Evening work is particularly suited to university students (who can attend lectures during the day), to female workers with small children (who alternate with their husbands), workers caring for elderly and sick family members and workers with other jobs (for example, in small-scale retailing). Those who find late-evening work most burdensome are the parents of school-age children (because they almost never see them), or people for whom social relations are important (because it is usually in the evening that people go out with friends or partners).

These atypical working hours are assigned to newly recruited employees because they are willing to accept any schedule in order to obtain a job. Some of them, however, even when they could have switched to the normal pattern of eight hours on alternating shifts, have preferred to continue working in the evenings, because they regard this arrangement as a better fit – in terms of number of hours as well as scheduling – with the organization of their lives.

Commentary

The four experiments described above are among the best known and most closely studied in Italy, and it is to be hoped that they will not remain isolated cases. Some of these new types of working-time schedule have been in operation for a number of years, and it is probable that it is in their quality as 'good practice' that they are spreading to other workplaces as well. However, in the meantime, they remain largely symbolic and highlight a number of features.

Firstly, the experiments discussed reveal that the working-time needs of workers can be satisfied at even zero cost to companies: as with many innovations, the only cost consists in the effort required to devise and introduce them. Secondly, they show that certain categories of worker are willing to accept non-standard working hours if these enable them to reconcile certain personal and family needs with work more satisfactorily than was the case with traditional working-time schedules. They also confirm that company-level bargaining is the best arena in which to achieve positive results in the flexibilization of working hours. It is at this level that better account can be taken of the firm's specific 'compatibilities' and also of the differing needs of the workforce as not all solutions are applicable, or necessary, everywhere. Finally, the fact that these experiments have met considerable consensus among workers highlights that it is crucial for trade union action to start from the everyday needs – personal and diversified – of workers themselves.

Conclusions

The End of Standard Working Hours

In recent years, working hours – to an even greater extent than wages – have become one of the major components in the redefinition of work. There are by now significant differences – in income, quality of life and the significance of work – between full-time workers and part-time workers, between daytime workers and shift workers, between workers who do overtime and workers who do not, and between workers on fixed schedules and those able, at least to some extent, to decide their own working hours.

The most interesting aspect is undoubtedly the fact that many jobs no longer require the physical presence of the worker – as evidenced by the increasingly intense debate on telework – and this, albeit gradually, is occasioning a shift from 'time-based' managerial systems of work assessment to ones based on 'results'. On the other hand, an increasing number of occupations, especially in services, require work to be performed at non-traditional times of the day, even at times which used to be called 'antisocial', like evenings, nights or weekends. These changes are coming about when increasing labour-market participation by women, and also the slow but steady redistribution of family tasks within the couple, induce many people – both men and women – to advance specific demands with respect to both the duration and scheduling of their working time, so that they can better reconcile their work and family responsibilities.

All this is exerting increasing influence on the organization of working hours in companies, both in manufacturing and services, both private and public. These changes, moreover, have revived the unions' interest in the issue of working hours from a standpoint different from the more traditional one of their generalized overall reduction. The next few years will probably see the end of the standardized work schedule. The rigid timetable envisaged by the traditional model – what we may call the 'Fordist-union-male' system – no longer suits the requirements of firms; neither, it seems, is it in the best interests of the workers. This radical change may cause some problems for the unions by hampering their representational status (as is also happening with the spread of other forms of atypical work), but it will enhance company-level bargaining and its ability to provide individualized responses to workers' needs.

The reduction of working hours across the board is still the goal of trade union action, but it should not be set in opposition to the flexibilization and destandardization demanded by companies and workers. And for the trade unions in any case, accepting and promoting the 'positive' flexibility of working hours – flexibility, that is, which enables the balancing of family and work responsibilities – is by no means at odds with their objective of employment growth. Indeed, it is the best means available to encourage women to enter the world of work.

Working Time as a Social Issue

Striking a new work/life balance is one of the most important problems that the advanced countries are called upon to solve. Certain social models, like those of the Nordic countries, were long based on the belief that it was possible to respond to care needs through the public services. In other countries, like those of Southern Europe, response to the dilemma has taken the form of scant labour-market participation by women. However, it has grown increasingly clear not only that labour-market entry by women on an equal footing with men is a certainty for all the European countries, but also that more advanced social services – even in the countries that can afford them – cannot entirely substitute for relational and care activities, some of which will continue to bear upon individuals as parents, children, relatives or even simply as friends and neighbours.

It therefore becomes important to enhance the integration of people's work and non-work lives through diversified solutions that take account of changing needs over the course of an entire life, and also of individual choices and styles with respect to working and living.

This is an objective to be pursued by both firms, which are often worried about an increase in costs, and by the unions, which in the past have not shown much attention to the problem. It is important, however, not to commit the error of thinking that there are only 'technical' solutions, ones which operate solely at the level of industrial relations. Rather, care needs are also essentially social needs, which must engage with responses that are far more wide-ranging than those forthcoming from bargaining between a firm and its workers.

When examined from a sufficiently broad perspective – that of the alternation and contradiction between working time and caring time and between economy and society – working hours will inevitably assume the importance of a fully-fledged social issue. There is consequently evident need for action on working hours which is also institutional in form. Such action must help to reconcile company policies on working time with the welfare system by offering incentives for firms to reduce working hours, support for the creation of company services to families, allowances for workers who devote part of their time to caring responsibilities, support for experiments in new working time arrangements and so on.

Notes

1   The CGIL changed its position after its 1989 Congress, when it set the introduction of a 35-hour working week within the next 15 years as one of its objectives (supported by the Italian Communist Party).
2   Taddei (1989) points out that 'a reduction in working time cannot be generalized and undifferentiated; rather, it should be tied to the reorganization of production. It this way the saving deriving to the firm from better use of its capital can be exchanged for greater wage stability'.
3   That company-level negotiation is the most appropriate has also emerged from the debate on the application of reduced working time in other countries: see, for example on France, Boulin and Cette (1999) and Freyssinet (1998).

References

Accornero, A. and Di Nicola, P. (1996), 'La flessibilità degli orari di lavoro', in Galli, G. (ed.) *La mobilità nella società italiana*, Edizioni Confindustria.
Balbo, L. (1987), *Time to Care. Politiche del tempo e diritti quotidiani*, Angeli.
Bettio, F. and Villa, P. (1997), *Changing Patterns of Work and Working Time for Men and Women in Italy*, Manchester School of Management Editions.
Bordogna, L. (1998), 'La contrattazione decentrata nell'industria', in Cesos (ed.), *Le relazioni sindacali in Italia. Rapporto 1996–97*, Rome.
Boulin, J.Y. and Cette, G. (1999), 'Temps de travail et emploi en France: entre production reglementaire et innovations dans l'entreprise', paper presented at the conference *Working Time in Europe*, 10–11 October, Helsinki.
Bosch, G. (1999), 'Working Time: Trends and New Issues', *Revue Internationale du Travail*, Vol. 138, No. 2.
Cesos (ed.) (1994), *L'esperienza dei contratti di solidarietà: costi e benefici sul piano economico, occupazionale, organizzativo*, mimeo, Rome.
Chiesi, A.M. (1995), 'Le trasformazioni dei contenuti del lavoro', in Chiesi, A.M., Regalia, I. and Regini, M. (eds), *Lavoro e Relazioni Industriali in Europa*, NIS, Rome.
CNEL (1993), 'Tempo di lavoro e flessibilità dell'orario', *Documenti Cnel*, No. 29, Rome.

de Lange, W. (1999), 'Working Organization and Working Time', paper presented at the conference *Working Time in Europe*, 10–11 October, Helsinki.

Esping Andersen, G. (1990), *The Three Worlds of Welfare Capitalism*, Polity Press, Oxford

Fondazione Regionale Pietro Seveso (1998), *Il Caso Whirlpool*, mimeo, Milan.

Freyssinet, J. (1998), 'France: A Recurrent Aim, Repeated Near-failures and a New Law', *Transfer*, Vol. 4, No. 4, pp. 641–56.

Gauvin, A. and Silveira, R. (1999), 'La flexibilité du temps de travail au féminin', in Bosch, G., Meulders, D. and Michon, F. (eds), *Working Time: New Issues, New Norms, New Measures*, Edition du Dulbea.

Lehndorff, S. (1998) 'From "Collective" to "Individual" Reduction in Working Time? Trends and Experience with Working Time in the European Union', *Transfer*, Vol. 4, No. 4, pp. 598–620.

Leonardi, S. (2000), 'La contrattazione interconfederale', in Cesos (ed.), *Le relazioni sindacali in Italia. Rapporto 1997–8*, Rome.

Nerb, G. (1986), 'Resultati di un'inchiesta della Commissione Europea su alcuni aspetti del mercato del lavoro, dal punto di vista dei datori di lavoro e dei dipendenti', *Economia Europea*, No. 27, March.

Olini, G. (1994), 'Anni ottanta, lavorando meno solo sulla carta', *Politica ed Economia*, No. 1.

Olini, G. (2000), 'La questione delle 35 ore: tra politica e dibattito culturale', in Cesos (ed.), *Le Relazioni Sindacali in Italia. Rapporto 1997–98*.

Piazza, M., Ponzellini, A.M., Provenzano, E. and Tempia, A. (1998), *Riprogettare il tempo. Manuale per la progettazione degli orari di lavoro*, Edizioni Lavoro.

Ponzellini, A.M. (1996), 'Riduzione degli orari e sistemi di solidarietà nelle crisi aziendali. L'esperienza italiana', paper presented at the conference *Orario di lavoro ed organizzazione sociale del tempo in Europa*, 17 September, Milan.

Ponzellini, A.M. (1997), 'Tempo di lavoro: dalle donne una soluzione per tutti', *Il Progetto*, No. 17, September/October.

Regione Lombardia (1998), Survey on Worker Expectations from Part-time Working.

Rubery, J. (1998), 'Working Time in the UK', *Transfer*, Vol. 4, No. 4, pp. 657–77.

Sanne, C. (1998), 'The Working Hours Issue in Sweden', *Transfer*, Vol. 4, No. 4, pp. 715–28.

Taddei, D. (1989), 'Conseguenze economiche e sociali del tempo di lavoro nella comunità', quoted by Olini, G. (1991), 'L'orario di lavoro', in Cesos (ed.), *Le Relazioni Sindacali in Italia. Rapporto 1989–90*.

Tempia, A. (1988), 'Riduzione ed articolazione degli orari di lavoro: le ricerche empiriche sul tempo di lavoro in Italia', in Valli, V. (ed.), *Tempo di lavoro ed occupazione. Il caso Italiano*, NIS, Rome.

Tempia, A. (1993), *Ricomporre i tempi*, Ediesse.

Chapter 12

Worker Participation in Central and Eastern Europe: Union Strategies

Daniel Vaughan-Whitehead[1]

Introduction

Since the beginning of the transition from communist to capitalist economies, trade unions in Central and Eastern Europe have been confronted by a need to restructure on many fronts: at the national level, trying to get involved in the reforms and improving – or at least maintaining – living standards; at intermediate levels, building and strengthening their own regional and sectoral structures; and finally, at enterprise level, retaining their membership and influence over management policies despite harsh restructuring and privatization. Trade unions have also progressively realized the importance of the relationship between these different levels to build up their representativeness and acquire greater independence from political parties, which is particularly important in the transition process. Trade unions now also have to prepare themselves to enter the European Union (EU) and assume the role which is expected of them within it.

Faced with such multi-lateral and multi-dimensional policy requirements, and in a context characterized by a general lack of human and financial resources, what policies have trade unions in Central and Eastern Europe developed with regard to workers' democratic participation at enterprise level? Compared with their colleagues in Western countries, who often viewed direct forms of workers' participation with suspicion before coming to play a more positive role in their implementation (Kester and Pinaud, 1996), have trade unions in Central and Eastern Europe been more positive about workers' participation from the start of the reforms? And what are the challenges, but also problems they are encountering in this field? What action are they taking to implement the *acquis communautaire* in this area? These are some of the questions addressed in this chapter.

In Central and Eastern European countries, workers can influence the decision-making process in various ways: first in an indirect way, as members of trade union organizations; secondly, through works councils and other forms of participation in decision making; and thirdly, through their shares in the ownership of their enterprise, which gives them some power as shareholders.

We shall focus here on two main forms of workers' participation:

- employee ownership, that is, workers' participation in the capital of their enterprise, which has rapidly grown to become an important feature of transition in the region; and
- works councils, a form of participation in decision making particularly relevant for Central and Eastern Europe, and one which also represents an important element emphasized by the EU.

These two forms of workers' participation have not followed the same path since they have evolved rather independently from each other, which explains why here we clearly address the two issues in a distinct way. The purpose of this chapter is therefore not to provide evidence and details about the views of all trade union organizations in the region on all possible forms of workers' participation (forms of organizational participation, for instance, are not addressed here). Rather, through the use of significant examples, the chapter aims to highlight some of the challenges but also problems that trade unions meet in this area. It seeks thereby to induce others to provide more evidence on this rather poorly researched area. On the basis of this first assessment, we shall then try in the third section to identify the necessary strategies that trade unions may elaborate in this area.

Employee Ownership: the Role of the Unions in Privatization

Emergent Employee Ownership on an Unprecedented Scale

The reform process in Central and Eastern Europe has been accompanied by the widespread introduction of employee ownership. Indeed, in many countries of the region employee ownership has rapidly become a dominant form of property, and insider owners – namely employees and managers – have become major owners.

For many, the scope and persistence of the employee ownership phenomenon has been an unwelcome surprise. Employee ownership was never intended to develop on a large scale. For many experts advising governments from this region on their first steps towards a market economy, this form of property could only lead to bad corporate governance. For instance, for the World Bank:

> employee-owned firms may weaken corporate governance; insiders are generally not able to bring new skills and new capital to the company, and they may deter outsiders with skills and capital from investing. Managers and employees may simply prevent outsiders from buying shares. Moreover, insiders may vote to pay higher salaries even if that reduces profits (World Bank, 1996, pp. 54–5).

Despite this initial aversion, often ideologically driven, employee ownership as a method of privatization has taken place extensively, mainly by default, generally because of the difficulties encountered in the course of mass privatization or other privatization routes, and the shortage of foreign and domestic capital. In all Central and Eastern European countries, with the exception of the Czech Republic, a significant proportion of enterprise assets so far privatized has ended up being transferred to insiders.

This process has been observed on a large scale in Russia and Ukraine, but also in the Baltic countries, especially in Lithuania, where nearly all privatized enterprises have had an element of employee ownership and where majority employee ownership was found in more than half of the enterprises privatized (ILO, 1998). The same phenomenon, although to a lesser degree, has been observed in Latvia. In Romania, most commercial companies have been privatized through the management/employee buy-out method. In Slovenia, no fewer than 80 per cent of privatized Slovenian enterprises chose internal buy-out as a privatization method (Prasnikar and Gregoric, 2000).

Even in Central and Eastern European countries in which employee ownership is not generally believed to be widespread we can find surprising instances of employee ownership. For example, in Estonia, where foreigners own more than half of private industry, it was estimated that majority insider ownership covered around 36 per cent of newly privatized enterprises. Of these, about half are owned mainly by the management and the other half by a broader group of employees (Mygind, 1997, p. 57).

Minority employee ownership has also developed in other Central and Eastern European countries, such as Hungary, Poland, and Bulgaria. In Hungary, it is estimated that there have been nearly 300 cases of privatization through employee share-ownership programmes (ESOPs), in which at least 40 per cent of the employees were involved. In Poland, all privatization routes have included, often to a considerable degree, some form of employee ownership. As a result, there have been a number of employee and management buy-outs there, often taking the form of a lease-purchase agreement. By the end of 1995, 788 enterprises had taken this course, representing 68.8 per cent of directly privatized enterprises (Nuti, 1997b, pp. 169–70).

This experience in Central and Eastern Europe contrasts with experiences in the West – for instance in the UK and France which have developed employee ownership in the most extensive way – where only a small percentage of the capital of public companies has been privatized through employee ownership. Considering the place of employee ownership as a property and organizational form, and the large number of workers with shares, it is particularly important to analyse trade union behaviour with regard to this form of participation.

The Unions' Innovative Role: Helping Workers to Become Owners

Trade unions have contributed to this movement in different ways. In the privatization process, while foreign experts were mainly advising reliance on private capital – especially through foreign investment – or mass privatization (through investment funds), trade unions have supported employee ownership as an alternative way of privatization. Employee share-ownership was often found in the programmes of trade unions (see the example of the Hungarian trade union MSZOSZ in Galgoczi and Hovorka, 1998). The promotion of these schemes was generally presented as part of their views in favour of democratic participation, especially in countries with a tradition in self-management as in Slovenia. In other cases, their support was more pragmatic and corresponded to a means of avoiding the domination of the ownership by an external buyer, as well as the restructuring and massive lay-offs to be expected in this process. Trade unions have tried to be active at different levels.

At the *national* level, they have often managed to get involved in direct negotiations with the national privatization agency. In this way, employees have been deeply involved in the privatization process.

We should mention the essential role that trade unions played, for instance, in Romania or Hungary in encouraging the creation of ESOPs. In Poland, trade unions also contributed to the decision to distribute to employees 20 per cent of capital privatized through the direct sales process and 15 per cent in companies in the mass privatization programme.[2] Similarly in Bulgaria, employees were offered 20 per cent of their firm's shares at a reduced price. The involvement of employees in the privatization process, also with the support of trade unions, was most significant in Russia, with a combination of gift-equity to employees (25 per cent of shares in a corporatized enterprise), opportunities to purchase stock at reduced prices (10 per cent of shares) and concessions to managers (allowed to buy a further 5 per cent).

Trade unions also succeeded in some cases in resisting the policy of many governments in the region which consisted in privatizing through employee ownership only those enterprises on the verge of bankruptcy – also those that did not attract foreign investment – and where heavy restructuring was needed. Trade unions also demanded workers' participation in the best performing enterprises: for instance, in Slovakia and other countries (Brzica, 1998, p. 12).

At the *enterprise* level, trade unions have also played a role in helping employees to get involved in the privatization of their enterprise, and in defending employees' interests in this process. For instance, trade unions in Ukraine have been actively involved in the privatization process, and have helped workers to become owners of their enterprise. In Estonia, the local trade unions have sometimes used their own resources to help workers to buy shares during the privatization of the company (Laja and Terk, 1996).

In Slovakia, where the trade unions enjoy good relations with the banks, lobbying by trade unions also convinced banks to provide credit facilities to employees to buy back their company and operate it. This is particularly important in light of the unwillingness of banks to provide credits to employee-owned enterprises (ILO, 1998).

Trade unions have also contributed to influence not only the scale but also the kind of employee share-ownership schemes adopted by the company. In fact, employee ownership can lead to very different – often unfair – distributions of shares among insiders: in some cases, shares can be bought mainly by the management, thus leading to more management buy-out schemes; in other cases, all categories of employees are entitled to participate and decide to acquire shares. By systematically favouring this latter scheme, trade unions have helped to safeguard employee share-ownership against management domination. In Slovakia, for instance (Brzica, 1998), but also Romania (Munteanu, 1997), trade unions have often helped workers to prepare a buy-out scheme involving an employee joint-stock company in an employee buy-out (EBO). This was designed to counter the management's initiative in acquiring the enterprise through a management buy-out and the establishment of a limited liability company.

This promotion of employee ownership has enabled workers to obtain more influence over key policy areas. In Poland, trade unions have contributed to the development of ESOPs in regions in crisis, for instance in the Katowice region, upper Silesia (Schliva, 1997). This allowed workers to have a say in enterprise restructuring programmes.

In some enterprises in Estonia, trade unions have managed to use the new ownership structure to influence employment decisions and to limit the number of dismissals (Elenurm, 1996). In Slovakia, trade unions have seen employee ownership as a way to develop workers' participation in key decisions, and to avoid an increase in unemployment.

The attitude of the trade unions has not been supportive in all countries. In Hungary, despite initial support, different parties and trade unions progressively reduced their enthusiasm not only for employee share-ownership, but also for works councils and self-management principles in general (Cox and Mason, 2000, p. 101). In the former Yugoslavia, the unions have opposed employee share-ownership in reaction to the imposition of employee ownership under socialism (Uvalic, 1997). Similarly, Russian trade unions have done little to develop new institutions to protect employee shareholders, despite their policy intentions to support a wide extension of employee ownership.

Trade Union Failure to Ensure the Survival of Employee Ownership

Despite the trade unions' initial support for employee ownership in the privatization process, a number of drawbacks have emerged as this form of property has developed.

Lack of shareholders' participation rights   First, the evidence suggests that there has been only a loose relationship between formal structures of ownership, formal structures of control and real decision-making power (Blasi et al., 1997; Jones and Weisskopf, 1996). In general, share-ownership should be accompanied by voting rights on a 'one share/one vote' basis. The more shares that employees have, the more say they should have in company governance. This employee control can be exercised individually by employee owners, with proportional voting on the basis of the number of shares. This system may be considered as the fairest and most efficient.

However, the 'one share/one vote' rule has not generally been adopted in other countries in Central and Eastern Europe, with the exception of the Baltic states, particularly Estonia. In Bulgaria, for example, employee ownership was introduced without giving employees any right to participate in decision making. Meanwhile in Russia the first privatization option led to the free distribution of shares, but without voting rights; the second and third options, on the other hand, introduced the possibility of distributing to the workers a majority of voting shares. Non-voting shares were also distributed in Lithuania. But even in the countries where employee ownership was accompanied by voting rights, thus leading to a great number of enterprises with majority worker ownership, in many cases this did not enable employees to exercise a controlling stake on account of the dispersal or lack of interest by the employee owners. At the same time, although in theory minority employee share ownership could also lead to control if the remaining shares were dispersed among a number of outside shareholders (Nuti, 1997a), in practice outside owners were found to be much less dispersed than the workers.

The absence of real influence in the decision-making process has led many employees to lose interest in ownership and has discouraged them from keeping their shares.

The dilution of employee ownership In most Central and Eastern European countries, employee ownership seems to be evolving along the same lines. After an initial phase during which the management succeeds in keeping the enterprise through insider privatization in partnership with the workers, the management changes behaviour in a second phase, and rather looks for full control of the capital or for a partnership with an external investor. The manager, by buying back the shares of the workers, generally succeeds in marginalizing them in terms of both ownership and decision making. Another way to dilute employee share-ownership consists in issuing new shares to allow an external investor to come in. This broadening of enterprise assets has proved to be an easier and quicker way to change ownership for the management than the re-purchase of employees' shares. This is where trade unions as workers' representatives have not always played the monitoring and assisting role they might have done. By not playing a more active role in informing the workers of their shareholders' rights and by providing them with little support to keep their shares, they have generally not helped employees to maintain a significant degree of employee ownership in the enterprise. For instance, they have not always opposed augmentation of enterprise capital and have not seemed much concerned by the progressive dilution of employee ownership.

Was this a conscious policy on the part of trade unions, in the belief either that external capital would improve corporate governance, or that the dilution of employee ownership would increase trade union power within the enterprise? Or was it only a 'failure' on their side to take into account the possible detrimental effects of this trend on workers as shareholders, but also, by means of an indirect 'boomerang' effect, on trade unions in the long run?

Whatever its reasons, this 'laissez-faire' attitude contrasted with the efforts generally made by the same trade unions to impose employee share-ownership in the privatization process. For instance, the largest trade union (OK Kovo) in Slovakia has been very active in promoting employee share-ownership in the privatization process, by negotiating with the privatization agency and the Ministry of Privatization, and even organizing internal training and seminars on employee ownership. Between the two waves of privatization, in 1995–96, it organized meetings with trade union members from enterprises that had already been privatized by employee ownership and employees from enterprises that were starting the same process. Nevertheless, its activity in this field has always focused on the creation and social control of legislation on privatization. As a result it stopped as soon as the statutory bodies of employee joint-stock companies were created. At that point, trade unions reverted to their traditional role, that is, mainly collective bargaining and in particular negotiating for higher wages (Brzica, 1998, pp. 12–13). Other trade unions in the region, after their involvement in the privatization process, limited their initiatives to the traditional labour-management relationship under the threat of lay-offs or real wage reductions without trying to modify the decision-making process through employee share ownership.

In Bulgaria, although trade unions supported management-employee buy-outs (MEBO) in the privatization process, this technique turned out to be a way of selling state assets to friends (more generous offers from external buyers have often been refused) on the most advantageous conditions.[3] This privatization did not induce the new owners to carry out restructuring, but rather led to liquidation or – when the devalued shares of the employees could be bought back by the management at good price – to the selling of the enterprise or part of it to an external buyer at a much higher price. As a result of this trend, and despite the fact that employee ownership was found to have a number of net economic advantages, both in terms of speed in the privatization process and of corporate governance – exemplary cases were found in Ukraine (Vaughan-Whitehead, 1997), Hungary (MRP, 1997), Romania (Munteanu, 1997) and Lithuania (Mygind, 1997) – it has progressively declined in importance over the last few years.

Contrasting Views on Participation: the Case of Works Councils

In contrast to the experience in EU countries, works councils have not been much developed in Central and Eastern Europe. Until the year 2000, only two countries, Slovenia and Hungary, had introduced legislative provisions for promoting this type of workers' involvement in the company. They were therefore the only two countries where a dual system of workers' representation prevailed, indirect through the trade unions and direct through the works councils.[4] Among the factors that explain the poor development of works councils in Central and Eastern Europe, trade unions' policy towards this form of participation has undoubtedly played a role, to a different extent though according to the countries.

Trade unions in Central and Eastern Europe have had different reactions with regard to the development of works councils, from fierce opposition for instance in Poland, Hungary, Romania or even Slovakia, to more nuanced positions in Bulgaria or the Czech Republic and a clearly positive attitude in Slovenia.

From Self-management to Diversity: Poland and Slovenia

In many countries of Central and Eastern Europe, works councils and trade unions have developed in an uneasy relationship. In some cases, it evolved over time, as for instance in *Poland*, where there was a strong tradition of self-management and employee councils and a very close historical relationship between trade unions and employee councils. In the 1980s, when the trade union Solidarnosc was still illegal, many trade union activists utilized these structures to promote free trade unionism. Later on, employee councils clearly provided important institutional support to the trade unions. However, a shift of trade union policy vis-à-vis employee councils appeared in the early 1980s.

Although the trade union Solidarnosc's 1980–81 economic reform programme was strongly based on self-management, works councils, self-financing and autonomy of the firm, between 1982 and 1989 its leaders committed themselves to an economic reform strategy premised on privatization and the creation of competitive markets. From 1989, the first Solidarnosc-supported government implemented a neo-liberal economic reform programme, also known as 'shock therapy' policy, led by L. Balcerowicz. The message from the government at that time was clear: 'The long-term strategic aim of this government is to return to Poland old and tested economic institutions. Poles cannot afford ideological experimentation' (quotation from Tadeusz Mazowiecki in 1989, a member of Solidarnosc and close adviser of Lech Wałesa, reported in Weinstein, 2000). The Solidarnosc leadership supported the basic direction of the government's economic reform strategy, which also included the dissolution of employee councils (as works councils were known during the communist period). In February 1993, both trade unions – Solidarnosc and OPZZ – signed a pact with the government on the elimination of works councils in companies going through the privatization process. The subsequent new law meant that trade unions remained the only representatives of workers' interests at enterprise level, and that an indirect form of workers' representation replaced direct workers' representation which had developed in the self-management period. The trade unions succeeded, however, as we saw in the previous section, in promoting employee ownership in the privatization process.

Polish trade union leaders tried to explain their position with regard to the new legislation on works councils by referring to their fear of seeing them circumvent the trade unions' role, and becoming dominated by management. But according to Weinstein (2000, p. 61), who studied Solidarnosc's programmes over the years, this position directly reflected the 'conventional conception that Solidarnosc leaders had of property rights'. They believed that co-governance rights would be contradictory to private management, which was expected to be the only driver of economic growth. This view was confirmed by econometric results from different surveys carried out at different periods among trade union leaders: while they continued to support employee councils in state enterprises, they did not support their establishment in privatized companies (Weinstein, 2000).

The new law – and especially the distinction it created between the state and private sectors with regard to the representation of workers' interests – clearly had direct effects at enterprise level. While there is the obligatory presence of works councils in state enterprises, where these councils enjoy significant rights, especially with regard to the management of the enterprise – even the appointment of the manager – and its eventual privatization, the law implies the suppression of works councils once the enterprise is privatized. As a result, a sort of dual system of workers' representation developed in Poland, with (i) works councils with extended rights and strong trade unions in state enterprises; and (ii) the absence of works councils in privatized enterprises where workers' interests can be covered only by their trade unions, whose strength and membership continues to decline. In new private enterprises, the situation is even worse, with the absence of any form of workers' representation. In this type of enterprise, not only are trade unions not present, but there are no works councils either, partly because national trade unions rejected such participation.

This opposition to works councils in the long term may well lead to a growing gap between trade union policy and workers' expectations at enterprise level, and potentially lead to a further weakening of union membership. Trade unions in the future may well have a high price to pay for such a policy.

By contrast, trade unions in *Slovenia*, on the basis of a strong self-management tradition, have supported government steps to keep an extensive framework for workers' participation in enterprise management. Different forms of participation have developed. Workers were first given some influence in decision making through their participation in supervisory boards and management boards (Worker Participation in Management Act, 1993). In enterprises with up to 1,000 employees, at least one-third of the members of the supervisory boards – and half in those with 1,000 or more employees – have to be workers' representatives elected by the works council. This law was supported by the trade unions, which also fought to keep its content. On two occasions, under pressure from the employers' organization, the government proposed amendments to parliament in order to tone down this law, but without success because of massive trade union protests. The most recent attempt was in September 1999, when the government adopted and sent to parliament, without prior tripartite consultation, a proposed amendment to article 264 of the Companies Act, aimed at reducing the percentage of workers' representatives on supervisory boards. It aimed at reducing this participation to 'at most one third of all members' (Article 45 of the proposal) thus contradicting article 79 of the Worker Participation in Management Act. Once again, the fierce opposition of trade unions, which officially complained and also attracted the attention of international organizations (such as the European Trade Union Confederation and the European Commission), well illustrates the importance that the trade unions currently attach to the preservation of institutionalized forms of direct workers' representation in Slovenian enterprises.

Workers' participation was also promoted in Slovenia through works councils, which were mainly adopted following the main features of the German codetermination model. The system was defined through various legislative instruments in 1993, but mainly through the law on codetermination with other specific issues being covered by the law on commercial companies. It was supported by the trade unions from the beginning. The implementation of the law in the workplace is optional, and is left to the collective initiative of employees. This type of workers' representation exists in around one fifth of Slovenian companies (Stanojevic, 2000).

This may, at least partly, be explained by the tradition of Yugoslav self-management and workers' collectives or works councils, where not only were the workers closely involved in the enterprise, but also trade unions were very close to the workers. At the end of the 1980s and beginning of the

1990s, when the old works councils were losing their power, trade unions took over their function of representing workers' interests. They saw the new law on codetermination of 1993 as an additional way to stabilize their new role, and in particular, to acquire more control over the privatization process. For Stanojevic (2000), it is not certain that this strategy has paid off for the unions since in practice trade unions and works councils are not very close, and often develop separate contacts with the management. Moreover, works councils would have pushed trade unions to focus primarily on wage negotiations; in a country in which wages are already the highest in the region, and are mainly determined at higher – multi-employer – level, this process would have significantly reduced trade union influence and radicalized their position at enterprise level.

What is certain, however, is that trade unions have constituted a key factor in the formation of works councils in Slovenian enterprises. Paradoxically, this has led to the double representation of workers' interests in unionized enterprises – that is, mainly state companies – while workers in other non-unionized companies (all new private enterprises), also because of the optional nature of the law, suffered from the absence of any form of worker representation. This chapter analyses in its section on policy below the implications that such differentiation could have for trade unions and discusses what strategies they may elaborate in this regard.

The Influence of Government Strategy: Hungary and the Czech Republic

In *Hungary*, having been marginalized in the 1970s and 1980s, works councils were promoted by the government at the beginning of the transition. New works councils were defined within the new Labour Code of 1992. Works councils became obligatory in enterprises employing 51 and more workers, while workers' representatives could be elected in enterprises employing between 15 and 50 workers inclusive. Trade unions first viewed works councils rather suspiciously, as a potential threat to their already weaker position at enterprise level. Nevertheless, after the new law came into force, trade unions and works councils learnt to work together in order to protect workers' rights in the transition.

Employers on their side were rather opposed to any further rights given to their employees, and repeatedly stated their preference for dealing with the trade unions only, a position that may be explained by the rather weak and fragmented position of trade unions, and their difficulty for instance in mobilizing the labour force and organizing a strike.

Trade unions accepted the presence of works councils, which had no bargaining rights, only consultation and information rights. Trade unions continued to negotiate and sign collective agreements with the management – on wages and other working conditions – and to play a role in social welfare at plant level. Works councils performed their task of information and consultation, and became particularly active in protecting jobs in the restructuring process, often with the support of trade unions. Trade union representativeness was defined through works council election results. And in many cases, trade unions at enterprise level were interested in setting up works councils in order to initiate council elections, which were held for the first time in early summer 1993. In many cases, works councils helped trade unions to institutionalize their influence at enterprise level, with many works councils representatives also being trade union members (Lado and Tóth, 1996; Tóth, 1997). This overlapping at the workplace minimized the possible tensions between the two institutions, something which should be viewed as a positive outcome. On the other hand, it also reflects the fact that works councils were dominated by trade unions and therefore did not represent a real alternative channel for employee representation and participation.

The relationship between trade unions and works councils became tense again when the new government that came into power in 1998, inspired by neo-liberal theories, decided to give works councils the right to sign collective agreements in enterprises where there was no trade union present. A first attempt in 1992 had already been rejected. It should be noted that, in a first draft of Labour Code amendments, the new government, which has not proved to be very committed to social dialogue (ESC, 2000), even raised the possibility of giving works councils the right to sign collective agreements in enterprises where trade unions were indeed already present. The government, however, had to withdraw this amendment following strong opposition from trade unions and political parties. The same government ejected trade unions from the social security and social insurance boards, and progressively removed the role that the social partners had acquired in all other areas (such as minimum pay, employment, the public sector and so on).

The consequent amendments to the Labour Code, accepted in 1999, brought serious tensions at enterprise level. In many small private or newly privatized enterprises, it gave an incentive to management to eliminate trade unions from the enterprise and to have works councils signing collective agreements, since they do not enjoy other trade union rights, especially the right to strike. Similar behaviour was also observed among multinational companies located in Hungary, which tried to circumvent trade unions through the development of works councils. It is in this rather tense context that European works councils will have to be set up in accordance with the EU directive.

Similarly in *Slovakia*, the government recently proposed that works councils could sign collective agreements where trade unions are absent. This proposal also led to trade union criticism of the law and rejection of works councils altogether.

In the *Czech Republic*, as part of the neo-liberal policy of the government after 1989, works councils were disbanded, while trade unions had to counter repeated attempts to reduce their influence at national and local levels. A solid presence at plant level inherited from the previous regime allowed the unions to protect workers' interests in the transition process, but did not lead to developments of direct forms of workers' participation. Moreover, the two main national trade unions, the Trade Union Association of Bohemia and Moravia and CSKOS, expressed radically opposed positions: the former favoured the promotion of works councils, while the latter opposed it in order to avoid further deterioration of its influence at enterprise level. The introduction of works councils under a new law in 2000, resulting from a change in government, could erase such contrasts at the local level since both union associations will have to adapt to the new situation. They will have to ensure, however, that the new law, which took effect from January 2001, is not used by government or employers to circumvent trade unions at the local level.

Works Councils as an Employer's Tool? Trade Union Fears in Bulgaria and Romania

Different trade unions within the same country do not always have the same policy with respect to workers' participation. In *Bulgaria*, for instance, while the national leaders of the Confederation of Independent Trade Unions in Bulgaria (CITUB) generally supported the idea of having works councils, the support of CITUB representatives at industry level was much weaker. Meanwhile, the other national trade union, the Confederation of Labour (Podkrepa) also clearly rejected works councils and on many occasions emphasized that they did not really have a place within the Bulgarian industrial relations system. Despite this rather weak support for works councils on the part of high-ranking trade union leaders, survey results have shown that a majority of trade union leaders at company level, in both the public and the private sector, favour the introduction of works councils and see them as a useful tool to influence management decisions further (ITUSR, 1997). Despite this, no law on works councils has yet been promulgated in Bulgaria, where workers nevertheless have a say in the general assembly scheme inherited from the self-management tradition. A new law on works councils should soon be brought before parliament.

Possible attempts on the part of employer representatives to use works councils as a way of circumventing the trade unions' role, however, may well lead trade unions in Bulgaria to modify their positive position vis-à-vis works councils. The new Union of Employers of Bulgaria (a dissident faction of the Bulgarian Industrial Association), for instance, has clearly expressed a wish to see works councils empowered to sign collective agreements.

Similarly in *Romania*, it is mainly to avoid the introduction of works councils and their development by management to bypass trade unions that Romanian trade unions have very strongly rejected this form of participation. The leaders of different national trade unions have expressed their fears of progressive erosion of their collective bargaining rights at company level.

For a Coherent and Transparent Trade Union Policy

We have seen that different forms of participation in decision making have emerged in enterprises in most Central and Eastern European countries: indirectly through trade union membership, but also directly through works councils and employee share ownership.

Trade Unions and the Survival of Employee Share-ownership

In several transition economies, trade unions welcomed employee ownership and played a positive role in its development at enterprise level (ILO, 1998). However, they do not seem to have done much to avoid its dilution and progressive disappearance in enterprises. No doubt a more ambitious policy should be designed by trade unions to make it possible for this form of property to survive and demonstrate its viability in the long run.

Trade unions should organize their action well beyond their traditional mandate. They could, for instance, participate in promoting institutions to develop employee share-ownership within the enterprise, or in designing centres of expertise for employee share-ownership. But they could also become much more effective in this area by simply helping workers to behave as shareholders: employees often do not play an active role in shareholders' general meetings because they have yet to acquire a full understanding of their status as owner – they know neither their rights nor responsibilities. Such a policy could help to achieve a better balance between the managerial board and the shareholders' meeting. Furthermore, the lack of interest often exhibited by employees is also frequently related to their lack of information concerning future returns on the company's investments and so their own future dividends; trade unions could redouble their efforts to obtain the relevant information from the management and pass it on to the employees. This could motivate workers to remain the coowners of the firm. The trade unions should in this way seek to extend rather than to abandon their traditional activities in the enterprise. Results have shown that employee share-ownership seems neither to lessen trade union influence nor to limit collective bargaining (ILO, 1998).

At the same time, however, workers as shareholders should integrate their interests within the more general goals of the trade unions. In many cases, workers after having acquired part of their enterprise's assets, considered trade union policy as of secondary importance, even superfluous, and tried to increase their influence on the decision-making process outside traditional trade union structures. An effort must be made in the future by both workers as shareholders and by trade unions to reinforce this close relationship, whose disappearance would be detrimental for both sides and certainly workers' interests in general.

For a More Constructive Stance on Works Councils

We have seen that the relationship between trade unions and works councils can be influenced by different circumstances. We can expect the degree of opposition of trade unions at first to vary according to their strength and situation at enterprise level: the greater their fragmentation, the lower their capacity to mobilize (to call a strike, for instance); and the lower their unionization, the greater their opposition will be to works councils, because of their fear of seeing their own position marginalized within the enterprise.

To note also is that trade union leaders operating at the branch and sectoral level were often found to be the most fiercely opposed to the introduction of works councils at enterprise level. Here trade unions should start a debate among themselves for modifying such attitudes, and explain why and how such different types of actor and level of operation could be complementary rather than mutually exclusive.

The strategies of the two other main actors – that is, employers and the government – will also influence the trade union position. Management's attempts to use works councils to marginalize trade unions inexorably lead to tensions between the two institutions. By contrast, it is interesting to observe that employers are less keen on introducing works councils in a context in which trade unions, as in Hungary, found themselves to be relatively weak and thus not in a position significantly to counter management decisions. In this case, trade unions should view works councils as a way to strengthen their influence within the enterprise rather than the opposite.

The way in which the government adopts a law on works councils also influences trade union attitudes. Trade union involvement in the preparation of the law is crucial, and trade unions should fight to ensure it. In this way, they could ensure that their previous prerogatives with regard to collective bargaining – such as negotiating and signing collective agreements – would not be given to works councils.

Trade unions should also be consulted on the obligatory nature of the law. While the optional nature of the law in Slovenia contributed to a positive reaction from trade unions, in Hungary the obligatory implementation of works councils, combined with the latter's new rights (such as signing collective agreements) which had so far been assigned to trade unions, only led the unions to oppose the whole idea of works councils. Nevertheless, trade unions should not reject the principle of promoting such forms of worker participation. This is because their reaction could be used by governments to emphasize the 'non-democratic nature of trade unions', and emphasize the basic antagonism between the demand to involve workers' representatives and the implementation of the Community *acquis* in this area. This situation would certainly give the wrong image of trade unions to the public, and would not be well understood by workers themselves. This policy of 'non-rejection' should also be applied to other participatory forms. For instance, in Slovenia, while trade unions legitimately rejected a first draft of the law on profit sharing that aimed at constraining wage increases and would have thus interfered with wage bargaining, we may regret that trade unions did not propose any other alternative. As a result, no law on profit sharing has yet been retained in Slovenia. In cases of this type, trade unions should show that they are not against such forms of workers' participation, but rather against the specific form in which they are proposed.

For a Better Combination of Participatory Forms

Although the trade unions have at some point supported one form of direct workers' participation or another, in no country in the region do they seem to have defined a coherent and comprehensive policy on the efficient *combination* of all the different forms of workers' participation. We have seen that, too often, the progressive dilution of workers' share-ownership was due to an absence or under-utilization of works councils and/or lack of trade union monitoring of developments in employee ownership. Despite being shareholders, the workers could not get the appropriate information on enterprise performance. In this context – also characterized by increased unemployment – the workers rapidly lost interest in keeping their shares or became the easy victims of management attempts to buy back their shares at a price below their face value. Works councils or other mechanisms of participation must be promoted more systematically alongside employee share ownership, especially in cases where voting rights have been restricted. At the same time, it would be worth supplementing workers' participation in decision making with forms of workers' involvement in the financial performance of the enterprise.

It is therefore with regard to their overall strategy vis-à-vis these different but complementary forms of workers' participation that we must assess trade unions' strategies and analyse possible improvements, especially with regard to key variables for the workers, such as working conditions, incomes, and employment.

Slovenia provides a good example of an efficient combination of at least employee ownership and works councils. In the 1992 law on privatization (which allocated 20 per cent of the shares to the workers, 20 per cent to the Development Fund that auctioned the shares to investment funds, 10 per cent to the National Pension Fund and 10 per cent to the Restitution Fund), the works council in each enterprise was empowered to allocate the remaining 40 per cent of company shares for sale to insiders (the workers) or outsiders (through a public tender). The proximity between trade unions and the workers obviously often led to common trade union and works council strategies on privatization and employee ownership, something which also explains the positive attitude of trade unions with regard to direct forms of worker participation such as works councils or employee share-ownership. According to Stanojevic (2000) this combination of participatory forms may explain why a higher level of worker-management cooperation was observed in Slovenia compared with Hungary, where similar works councils had been introduced on the basis of the German model.

Extending Workers' Participation to Small Private Enterprises

We have seen that many Central and Eastern European countries are facing the same pattern of participatory practices at enterprise level, mainly strong trade unionization and workers' participation in state and/or large enterprises, and the absence of any form of worker interest representation in private enterprises, especially in small firms, although this similar outcome has been generated by different processes. In Poland, for instance, the dismantling of workers' participation in privatized enterprises was due to government initiative supported by the trade unions. In Slovenia, however, it is rather the support of works councils by trade unions that led the two forms to coexist in state enterprises where trade union influence was the strongest and led to its absence in small private enterprises. A similar outcome is also observed in Hungary, where the works councils rarely operate in non-union enterprises or otherwise seem to be dominated by trade unions. Only multi-national enterprises seem to have clearly pushed out trade unions in order to favour the less adversarial system of works councils.

This shows that there is common ground for trade unions in Central and Eastern Europe, despite their different ideological positions on worker participation. This consists in the urgent need to represent workers' interests in private enterprises more effectively, especially in small businesses. Here, trade unions should see works councils or other forms of workers' participation as effective instruments with which to respond to this goal, and thus influence legislation on works councils to extend it to small businesses.

Conclusions

Restructuring and privatization in the early years of reform has clearly had tremendous effects on the trade union presence at enterprise level in the countries reviewed in this chapter. While privatization has brought massive restructuring and lay-off programmes, the early years of reform have also been characterized by a dramatic fall in real wages and living standards. At the same time, the emergence of the private sector has brought the mushrooming of small private enterprises, which often do not recognize trade unions or sign collective agreements, if they sign individual labour contracts at all. These trends have combined to bring a rapid decline in trade union membership at enterprise level.

EU membership requires the development of forms of worker participation at enterprise level. The main challenge for the trade unions thus seems to lie in countering the reduction of their influence at enterprise level, while also developing direct forms of workers' participation. This requires trade unions to identify clearly the strategies that could reinforce these two movements, and even make them reinforce each other.

The evidence shows that trade unions in the region have so far focused on protecting their position and maintaining their influence in policy making at both national and enterprise level. It is in terms of this global policy that we should trace trade union attitudes towards workers' participation; it explains why the two forms of participation analysed in this chapter – that is, employee ownership and works councils – have taken radically opposing directions. Trade unions have generally supported employee share-ownership, which made it possible to ensure workers' participation in the privatization process and to avoid the domination of this process by external buyers (private domestic or foreign investor), something which could have turned out to be detrimental for trade union survival. Conversely, in this first phase, trade unions did not support works councils, which they viewed as an additional factor weakening their precarious position at enterprise level. Only in those countries with a strong self-management tradition and a trade union movement relatively self-confident in its possible interaction with works councils, such as Slovenia, could this form of participation enjoy trade union support.

Paradoxically, trade union positions on these two forms of participation have now taken two opposing directions. A lack of clear long-term strategy on the part of trade unions has led to a progressive dilution of employee share ownership despite initial union support in the early stages of privatization. On the other hand, trade unions, despite their initial opposition, have turned out to be much more positive with regard to works councils. Either they learnt to live with works councils when put in place by the authorities, or they started to work out a strategy for introducing this form of participation within the framework of the legal harmonization demanded by the European Union.

These differences clearly reveal the need for a more supportive and coherent policy strategy in this area. In the long run, this could only be beneficial for the trade union movements in these countries, despite the adjustments that will be needed in the short run.

Notes

1   The author is responsible for social dialogue in EU enlargement at the European Commission. His opinions do not necessarily reflect those of the European Commission.
2   The direct sales process represents the process by which enterprises are sold on the market, everybody being generally able to buy. This contrasts with other processes of privatization, where certain actors are given preference, priority or even exclusivity in the buying process. Other processes include mass privatization (vouchers to citizens), employee buy-outs (shares to employees) and strategic privatization (selling to strategic investors, generally foreign).

3   Compared with employee buy-outs, which represent a process through which employees buy out their company generally through bank loans, in the management-employee buy-out, management is also involved. Management generally forms a coalition with the employees to prevent another investor, possibly foreign, from taking over the company. The trade unions in Bulgaria favoured this type of solution, but were sometimes disappointed by the policy adopted by management at a subsequent stage, since it did not always follow the restructuring and employment plans that it had agreed with the workers. Furthermore, management would then sometimes try to buy back all the shares from the employees rather than ensuring the long-term survival of employee ownership.

4   Editor's note: while all other contributors to this book see works councils as a form of *indirect* worker representation, Daniel Vaughan-Whitehead argues that they are a form of *direct* economic democracy at enterprise level, comparable with others such as financial participation. In his view, indirect participation takes place through the medium of trade unions.

References

Blasi, J.R, Kroumova, M. and Kruse, D.L. (1997), *Kremlin Capitalism*, Cornell, ILR Press, Ithaca.

Brzica, D. (1998), 'Privatization in Slovakia: The Role of Employee and Management Participation', working paper IPPRED-12, Interdepartmental Action Programme on Privatization, Restructuring and Economic Democracy, International Labour Office, Geneva.

Cox, T. and Mason, B. (2000), 'Trends and Developments in East Central European Industrial Relations', *Industrial Relations Journal*, Vol. 31, No. 2, pp. 97–114.

Earle, J. S., and Estrin, S. (1996), 'Employee Ownership in Transition', in Frydman, R., Gray, C. and Rapaczynski, A. (eds), *Corporate Governance in Central Europe and Russia*, Vol. 2, CEU Press, Budapest.

ESC (2000), *Hungary on the Way to Accession*, Economic and Social Committee, Brussels.

Elenurm, T. (1996), 'NORMA : An Employee Owned Company in the Metal Industry', in Mygind, N. and Norgaard Pedersen, P. (eds), *Privatization and Financial Participation in the Baltic Countries: Case Studies*, Copenhagen Business School, Copenhagen.

Galgoczi, B. and Hovorka, J. (1998), 'Employee Ownership in Hungary: The Role of Employers' and Workers' Organizations', working paper IPPRED–11, Interdepartmental Action Programme on Privatization, Restructuring and Economic Democracy, International Labour Office, Geneva.

ILO (1998), *Experts' Policy Report – Employee Ownership in Privatization: Lessons from Central and Eastern Europe*, International Labour Office-CEET, Budapest.

ITUSR (1997), 'Industrial Democracy and Participation in Management', Institute for Trade Unions and Social Research, CITUB.

Jones, D. and Weisskopf, T. (1996), 'Employee Ownership and Control: Evidence from Russia'. Proceedings of the 48th Meeting of the Industrial Relations Research Association.

Kester, G. and Pinaud, H. (eds) (1996), *Trade Unions and Democratic Participation: A Scenario for the 21st Century*, Avebury, Aldershot.

Lado, M. and Tóth, F. (1996), *Helyzetkép az érdekegyeztetésröl. 1990–1994*, Erdekegyeztetö Tanacs Titkarsaga-Phare Tarsadalmi Parbeszéd Projekt, Budapest.

Laja, T. and Terk, E. (1996), 'ESTRE: Ownership Dominated by a Core Group of Employees', in Mygind, N. and Norgaard Pedersen, P. (eds), *Privatization and Financial Participation in the Baltic Countries: Case Studies*, Copenhagen Business School, Copenhagen.

MRP (Employee Stock Ownership Plan, Hungary) (1997), Figures on ESOPs in Hungary, MRP, Budapest.

Munteanu, C. (1997), 'Employee Share-ownership in Romania: The Main Path to Privatization', in Uvalic, M. and Vaughan-Whitehead, D. (eds), *Privatization Surprises in Transition Economies: Employee Ownership in Central and Eastern Europe*, Edward Elgar, Cheltenham.

Mygind, N. (1997), 'Employee Ownership in the Baltic Countries', in Uvalic, M. and Vaughan-Whitehead, D. (eds), *Privatization Surprises in Transition Economies: Employee Ownership in Central and Eastern Europe*, Edward Elgar, Cheltenham.

Nuti, M. (1997a), 'Employeeism: Corporate Governance and Employee Share-ownership in Transition Economies', in Blejer, M.I. and Skreb, M. (eds), *Macro-economic Stabilization in Transition Economies*, Central European University Press, Budapest/London/New York.

Nuti, M. (1997b), 'Employee Ownership in Polish Privatizations', in Uvalic, M. and Vaughan-Whitehead, D. (eds) (1997) *Privatization Surprises in Transition Economies: Employee Ownership in Central and Eastern Europe*, Edward Elgar, Cheltenham.

Prasnikar, J. and Gregoric, A. (2000), 'Workers' Participation in Slovenian Enterprises Ten Years Later', paper presented at the 10th Conference of the International Association for the Economics of Participation, Trento-Arco, 6–8 July.

Schliva, R. (1997), 'Enterprise Privatization and Employee Buy-outs in Poland: An Analysis of the Process', ILO working paper, Interdepartmental Action Programme on Privatization, Restructuring and Economic Democracy, International Labour Office, Geneva.

Stanojevic, M. (2000), 'The German Model of Industrial Relations in Post-Communism: Workplace Co-operation in Hungary and Slovenia', paper presented at the 10th Conference of the International Association for the Economics of Participation, Trento-Arco, 6–8 July

Tóth, A. (1997), 'The Invention of Works Councils in Hungary', *European Journal of Industrial Relations*, Vol. 3, No. 2, pp. 161–81.

Uvalic, M. (1997), 'Privatization in the Yugoslav Successor States: Converting Self-management into Property Rights', in Uvalic, M. and Vaughan-Whitehead, D. (eds), *Privatization Surprises in Transition Economies: Employee Ownership in Central and Eastern Europe*, Edward Elgar, Cheltenham.

Uvalic, M. and Vaughan-Whitehead, D. (eds) (1997), *Privatization Surprises in Transition Economies: Employee Ownership in Central and Eastern Europe*, Edward Elgar, Cheltenham.

Vaughan-Whitehead, D. (1997), 'Employee Ownership alongside Hyper-stagflation in Ukraine: Enterprise Survey Results for 1993–95', in Uvalic, M. and Vaughan-Whitehead, D. (eds), *Privatization Surprises in Transition Economies: Employee Ownership in Central and Eastern Europe*, Edward Elgar, Cheltenham.

Weinstein, M. (2000), 'Solidarity's Abandonment of Worker Councils: Redefining Employee Stakeholder Rights in Post-socialist Poland', *British Journal of Industrial Relations*, Vol. 38, No. 1, March, pp. 49–73.

World Bank (1996), *World Development Report: From Plan to Market*, World Bank, Washington DC.

Chapter 13

Trade Union Education and Democratic Participation: the Case of Malta[1]

Edward Zammit, Saviour Rizzo and Joseph Vancell

Introduction

The link between education and democratization is well established. A minimum level of education is clearly necessary for citizens to be able to exercise meaningfully their democratic rights. In the process of development towards democratic workers' participation,[2] workers' and trade union education (TUE) is an essential tool for enabling workers to overcome their culture of dependence, subordination and passivity which is traditionally embedded in their work roles. Furthermore, the technical complexity of the modern work organization demands that decisions are made by well-informed and highly qualified people. Undoubtedly, those who for their own reasons are against the introduction of workers' participation may sometimes use the 'low level of the workers' [formal] education' as a delaying technique behind which to hide their real intentions. The existing level of workers' education may thus be depicted as being perennially inadequate for the responsibilities of participation. Though it may be promoted to serve different interests, the principle of workers' education is however nowadays universally accepted. Despite their different agendas, the leaders of industry, trade unions and, of course, governments have a common interest in promoting workers' education. In today's globalized labour-market conditions, lifelong workers' education is widely recognized as an essential condition for employability (Commission, 1997). Many adults today are returning to education to acquire credentials that may serve them as an insurance against any possible adversities at work. TUE – as a special branch of workers' education – is equally necessary for the survival of trade unions which, in addition to militating against the workers' traditional culture of subordination to managerial authority and know-how, rallies members on the principle of solidarity in an era of widespread individualism. Just as employers are resorting to staff training or human resources development to enhance the skills, knowledge and commitment of their employees, so trade unions should resort to TUE as a mechanism for their own organizational development. TUE is equally necessary to enable workers to undertake the responsibilities of participation for which they need to be prepared technically and psychologically. In the process of achieving these aims, workers are likely to rely on their natural allies and representatives – the trade unions.

In addition to its contribution to personal growth and functionality, education theorists usually identify two divergent objectives of education in general, namely that of 'cultural reproduction' and 'cultural transformation'. The survival of organizations like trade unions, their effectiveness and development require the realization of both sets of objectives. In their efforts to change the prevailing situation in industry, trade unions have always recognized the importance of TUE. This is required by workers and unions to acquire the competence for the furtherance of their roles. By their very nature, trade unions are concerned with the management of cultural change and TUE forms an important part of their strategy to bring about change. Trade unions acknowledge the value of TUE in carrying out their traditional collective bargaining role, in rallying their members and instilling in them appropriate values, and in implementing direct forms of workers' participation. However, TUE activities do not seem to have generated too much interest in the literature of industrial relations. Indeed, as Holford states: 'To students of industrial relations, union education has been a side issue, a peripheral activity of institutions which are properly to be judged by their bargaining capacity' (Holford, 1994, p. 247). In recent years, on an international level, the interest at universities and research institutes in subjects like TUE and worker participation has generally waned (Welton, 1997; Spencer, 1998; and Kester and Sidibe, 1998).

This chapter explores empirically one concrete application of the third proposition outlined in the introduction to this book. This is the condition that the sustained spread of democratic participation is possible only in the presence of 'a framework to provide facilities for research, information, education ... and legal advice, as well as an institutionalized framework of trade union-university/research cooperation'. Likewise the fourth proposition states that democratic participation 'poses a particular challenge to the trade union movement to provide the necessary support [for appropriate innovative approaches]'. In order to do this, TUE must perform a 'culturally transformative' role, systematically, formally and informally.

This chapter reports on a longitudinal survey[3] of the TUE programmes organized by Malta's largest trade union – the General Workers' Union (GWU) – over the years since its establishment. It is argued that, while partially reflecting the traditional 'paternalist' culture, TUE was 'transformative' to the extent that it aimed at overcoming the traditional workers' subculture of 'compliance with paternalism'. Furthermore, transformative TUE does not simply substitute a fatalistic mentality with a new set of attitudes, but also creates concrete alternatives where these attitudes could operate. In other words, an education intended to transform 'has to be grounded in present or emerging events or organization with a vision of the future' (Heaney and Horton, 1990, p. 92). To what extent were the GWU's TUE activities designed with such a vision? It will be argued that, though some success was achieved, TUE fell short of implanting the values of democratic participation and social partnership at the appropriate historical epochs. Instead, the TUE objectives have generally tended to reflect the changing trade union agendas – as perceived by the leadership – in which they played a supportive role. TUE has thus played a mainly 'reproductive' and a subsidiary 'transformative' role. This established TUE pattern may have served the union and its members well enough in the past, according to the exigencies and circumstances prevailing at the time. However, this chapter also suggests that the future development and effectiveness of the trade union require a more proactive and 'transformative' TUE role to be played. This agenda should be enshrined and guided by the results of policy research carried out by independent and sympathetic researchers working in an autonomous capacity. Through their empirical data and scientific analysis they can identify the strategy upon which TUE can be planned and executed.

It has been argued elsewhere that the present and future challenge to TUE strategy lies in an unreserved and systematic commitment to democratic worker participation (Kester and Pinaud, 1996). Failing this, the union may itself end up adopting a narrow, 'reproductive' outlook, effectively leading to the adoption of a restrictive, backward-looking role and a lack of innovation when confronting new situations. At present, when major initiatives for workplace participation are emerging from the employers' side – under their schemes for 'employee involvement' from which the unions are usually excluded – union leaders would do well to reassess their TUE policy towards direct participation. They might well conclude that the traditional, indirect forms of democratic participation through collective bargaining and the direct forms are indeed complementary and mutually reinforcing.

TUE Methodology

According to the principles established by Paolo Freire (1972), TUE should ideally be organized around the concept of cooperative learning. Experience shows that people learn better when working together with others in a cooperative atmosphere. Some adult worker educators are pioneering the techniques of cooperative learning now making their way in the formal primary, secondary and even higher education systems (Mayo, 1999). In practice, however, most educational institutions – including those offering TUE – generally mirror the dominating managerial concept of organizational hierarchy, control from the top, dependency of the pupil on the instructor, and paternalist patterns of interaction. The organization of schools, discipline and the teacher's control is more reminiscent of the supervisor in a plant than of Freire's cooperative pedagogy.

One main characteristic of TUE methodology should be the use of both a formal and informal learning context and strategy. Formal learning opportunities may be unavailable or unfeasible for many adult workers. Hence TUE organizers may impart knowledge in accessible formats outside the formal classroom pattern. In fact, apprenticeship schemes have always relied on the role of the work experience itself as a necessary ingredient of the learning process and as a further stimulant to workers' interests in further learning and qualification development.

TUE should also lead to a greater acceptance and appreciation of diversity and tolerance, thus giving a wider meaning to the 'historically restricted' concept of working class solidarity (Hyman, 1994). Because trade union membership is becoming increasingly heterogeneous the need is being felt by worker educators to develop educational strategies for teaching individuals from different gender, religious, class and ethnic backgrounds. This again contributes towards the development and consolidation of democratic institutions in pluralist societies.

However, as trade unions pursue their objectives in a social-cultural context, their effectiveness has to be measured within such parameters. Precisely because they act as agencies of change in a particular social landscape, both their initial interventions and their subsequent success or failure must always be assessed against the historically specific background in which they emerge and operate.

Trade Union Organization

When compared with most countries, the present state of Maltese trade unionism appears healthy. Evidence includes the relatively high level of union density (60 per cent), which has been continuously increasing, as well as the social visibility and influence of the unions on public and private decision making. The movement is Eurocentric and its roots lie in its British counterpart. Nevertheless, the Maltese trade union movement is best understood and analysed within Malta's general cultural and historical experience of colonialism and post-colonialism. Indeed, up to this day, the history of the Maltese labour movement has reflected local political and economic developments and cultural characteristics. Likewise, TUE efforts have historically reflected the unions' current agenda as perceived by the leadership. These include the members' responses to the changing challenges confronting the unions from time to time.

Maltese trade unions are currently organized in two opposing camps. The GWU, whose members amount to 57 per cent of trade union members, is traditionally close to the Malta Labour Party (MLP) and upholds a left wing, social-democratic ideology. Its members are organized in 10 different sections, each representing specific industrial sectors. Its strength lies among manual labourers in the public and private sectors. By contrast, the Confederation of Malta Trade Unions (CMTU) consists of a looser confederation of a number of unions, chief among which are the Union of United Workers (UHM, in its Maltese acronym), the Malta Union of Teachers (MUT) and the Malta Union of Bank Employees (MUBE). Collectively, their members amount to 41 per cent of Malta's total trade union membership.

The main union in the CMTU is the UHM. Like the GWU, this is a general union, organized in seven different sections, with its main strength lying among clerical workers in the public sector. The CMTU's affiliates generally uphold an ideology based on the traditional social teachings of the Catholic Church.

The following section of this chapter presents some data about the cultural background. The subsequent sections present an analysis of the changing TUE objectives over time, which are compared with the main issues confronting the union leadership at different historical epochs.

The Cultural Background

The GWU was founded in 1943, during World War II. At that time, Malta was an integral part of the British Empire and playing an important part in the allied war strategy in the Mediterranean and North Africa. A siege mentality prevailed, as it had for many years in varying degrees. In fact, Malta had been a colony since Roman times and had been dominated by a succession of foreign rulers who controlled its part of the world. As a result, the Maltese people traditionally experienced a condition of national 'powerlessness' and fatalism. A series of patterned responses or adaptations to their situation were developed by the people to this condition, which will briefly be described below in view of their bearing on TUE.[4]

Compliance with Paternalism

Compliance with paternalism is the most traditional response, and is deeply ingrained in a culture of submission and helplessness when dealing with a superior power. It legitimizes the subordinate position by invoking 'paternalist-filial' relations with the implied mutual obligations, which normally accompany such relations in a family context. This response is reinforced by religious traditions and, when applied to ideal 'employer/employee' relations, militates against the 'oppositional' values required for trade union action.

Patronage and Clientelism

Patronage and clientelism as a response constitute a realistic but concealed manipulation of power by individuals who seek to secure for themselves advantages or benefits from someone in a superior position. He acts as their 'patron' in preference to others, while they become 'his clients'. This response militates both against the 'paternalist' ideology and the values of collective consciousness and solidarity on which trade unionism is based.

Localism

Localism constitutes a strategic retreat from the national arena of decision making particularly on economic and political matters. It is accompanied by social and political involvement at the local level. Here villagers establish their own standards and symbols of identification, and are better placed to compete for prestige and power at the local 'parish/village' level. This may lead to local rivalries and factions, which militate against the development of 'national', working class solidarity, consciousness and action.

This chapter reviews the various TUE strategies adopted by the GWU throughout its half century of existence showing mainly how it aimed at recasting the traditional cultural responses described above. At the same time, TUE has also sought to provide the training required by its officials to fulfil their roles adequately. Even here, however, the focus of attention will be on the ways through which the appropriate ideas, values, norms and feelings accompanying the roles were imparted rather than on the technical aspects of the roles themselves.

It should be further noted that TUE includes not only the formal educational programmes presented by the union through its education section, but also the other activities performed by the union to communicate its ideas and perceptions to its members and others. These include particularly the speeches and exhortations by its leaders to officials and members, which are invariably and faithfully reported in its popular newspapers. The GWU publishes two of the leading popular papers in Malta: *L-Orizzont* on weekdays and *It-Torca* on Sundays, both in Maltese (*It-Torca* was formerly published as *The Torch*, in both English and Maltese). These papers, as well as most of the Union's other publications, are published by its own printing press, and are widely circulated among all sections of the working class.

The main epochs in the union's history, other related developments that took place from time to time and its TUE objectives are summarized in Table 13.1. These are followed by a commentary in which the relevant data illustrating the main arguments are presented. For the sake of brevity, the commentary will be restricted to Epochs I and III.

Epoch I (1943–52): Post-war Reconstruction and Labour Mobilization

The initial period is characterized by the establishment of the GWU and its integration and consolidation into Maltese society. Almost from the start this union became a formidable ally of the Malta Labour Party and together they constituted the Maltese Labour Movement (MLM). Over the years, the two organizations worked towards the creation of a social welfare state based on socialist ideas tempered with a dose of traditional paternalism. The leaders' inspiration was partly derived from the British labour movement with whom they maintained regular contacts. The militant drydocks workers played a prominent role in the organization and throughout the years significantly influenced union policy.

Table 13.1 Developmental epochs and strategies towards trade union education

Epochs	Main Developments		TUE Strategy
I (1943–52)	• Malta is a colony of strategic military importance for the British Empire	⇒	Mobilization and organization of workers behind leadership
	• The defence and post-war reconstruction industries provide substantial employment. However, the number of jobs is threatened by cuts in Britain's defence expenditure	⇒	Recruitment and training of promising young workers in trade union leadership
	• The Maltese Labour Movement (MLM) is organized into two flanks: the industrial (GWU) and the political (MLP)		
	• Trade union and political goals overlap and reinforce each other		
II (1953–70)	• Emigration is promoted as safety valve for unemployment	⇑	Familiarization and reproduction of British trade union practices of collective bargaining
	• First run-down of British military base	⇑	Training leadership core
	• Confrontation between the Malta Labour Movement and the traditional dominant groups (including the Church and professional classes)	⇑	Instilling discipline and loyalty to union and Party leadership
		⇑	Propagating vision of a better future

III (1971–86)	• Prolonged period of Labour Party in government • Amalgamation (fusion) between GWU and MLP; full cooperation of GWU with the government's political, social and economic policies, in exchange for the union's involvement in planning and execution of policies (including industrial relations and education) • Collaboration with government for the achievement of two overriding political objectives: 1 economic independence (despite a tightly closed economy and high unemployment); 2 establishment of welfare state (national minimum wage, social housing, social services, pensions, unemployment assistance, etc.)	⟹ Justification of union policy of collaboration with government in terms of social justice, welfare state, workers' dignity and workers' participation ⟹ Union promotes the establishment of the Workers' Participation Development Centre at the University ⟹ 'Worker participation' as an ideological support legitimizing the policy of 'union participation in government'; union espousal of national objectives and its fusion with the MLP
IV (1987–2000)	• Nationalist Party in government: neo-liberal and pro-European agenda • GWU searches for an autonomous trade union identity • Formal detachment from political leadership (after the resignation of Mintoff from the MLP helm) • Facing new challenges from Europeanization (and globalization), post-Fordism and a weak economy	⟹ Autonomy, militancy and responsibility ⟹ Recruitment of the new, emergent workforce (women, services, small and medium-sized enterprises and youth) ⟹ Balance sought between social partnership and confrontation ⟹ Inter-union rivalry

During the GWU's first 15 years of existence, Malta was still a fortress-colony of considerable importance to the defence strategy of Britain and its allies. The defence industry provided substantial employment in Malta even in peacetime. From time to time, the local economy was adversely affected by cuts in Britain's defence budgets. These caused widespread poverty and hardships. The British economic strategy additionally created a culture of dependence and powerlessness (Zammit, 1984) within the Maltese working class who rarely questioned or challenged decisions coming from either their colonial masters or the Maltese political elite (Boissevain, 1969).

Almost from its establishment in 1943, the GWU became the strongest union on the island. Its numbers gave it the strength to address problems created by the dependence of the local labour market on British interests and needs. Indeed, the dismantling of the British base during the 1950s led to thousands of dismissals. Successive Maltese governments resorted to mass emigration as a solution for the growing population and heavy unemployment. On the other hand, workers started to reap the benefits of a strong union and labour movement. Wages gradually improved and emigration was regulated and assisted. This contrasted with post-World War I days, when workers were offered some help only through benefit societies. All that time, the trade union movement had been rudimentary and fragmented, often dominated by politicians or clerics and engulfed by political intrigues.

The GWU pressed the government to pass important legislation safeguarding the interests of the workers and the union. The Trade Union Act of 1945 recognized the right to strike and protected trade union funds, while the Conciliation and Arbitration Act of 1948 provided the machinery to solve industrial disputes. Furthermore, the Conditions of Employment (Regulation) Act of 1952 regulated employment in the private sector.

TUE Initiatives

The first leaders of the GWU, particularly its founder, Reggie Miller, saw in education a very important tool for democratization, recruitment and mobilization of the masses within its ranks. One of the first and perhaps most important informal educational initiatives was the establishment of the union's weekly paper, *The Torch*. According to Attard Bezzina, one of the founding members of the GWU, the objectives of this newspaper were:

> To teach with detailed meaning the vague words [the worker] often hears that he must live a decent life, and earn a decent wage for his livelihood and the

maintenance of his family. Above all, it will urge him to be united with his fellow workers, in order to safeguard his own rights and that of his country.[5]

The bilingual weekly publication was used as a platform to propagate the union's political, moral, educational and even gender policies and actions among its membership. It also served as a forum of discussion among members and non-members.

A topical issue that featured in *The Torch* during the early period under review concerned the right of women to work. The GWU's spokesmen at that time disapproved of women who wanted to maintain the jobs they had procured during the war years. Economic, moral, ethical, sexist and all sorts of other reasons – all smacking of paternalism and male chauvinism – were cited by certain officials to justify their claim for the retreat of women from the workforce. Here are some of the most provocative statements that appeared in *The Torch* over this period:

> ... much of the wages earned by them [women] are being spent on the purchase of lipstick and powder[6]

> ... women present a serious threat ... not only because employers prefer those who work for lower pay but also, even more importantly, because they have an added sexual appeal[7]

> ... a man works for a woman, so she does not need to work[8]

> ... the inferior wage [of women] is keeping down the wages of men[9]

Even at that time, these ideas and policies were seen by some as paternalistic and divisive. Female members (particularly dockyard workers) accused their union of instilling 'sexual hostility' among the male labour force and for this reason they threatened to leave the union. Indeed the union, under the threat of this early and dangerous exit of members, pleaded with the women to reconsider the possible consequences of such a decision – pointing out that 'their skirts' were much less important 'to the [drydocks'] management than to the GWU'.[10]

Over this period, the union's TUE initiatives were of two kinds: one was formal and in-house and directed towards its members while the other was a national campaign criticizing the national state-controlled educational system. Its strategy was aimed at reaching two distinct groups: the first group comprised shop stewards and union officers while the other group was made up of the general GWU members. The primary objective of the formal TUE initiatives for shop stewards and officers was to teach trade union principles and to promulgate information about the union's policies and activities.

The educational activities for the young members of the GWU were more informal. They relied less on formal lectures and more on social and cultural activities. The Youth Movement of the GWU was very active in this regard and organized various activities for its members including art exhibitions, film shows, weekend camps and tours to various localities of archaeological importance and industrial complexes, such as the dockyards and the power station. These activities were aimed at fostering the young member's loyalty and motivation towards the GWU.

From its earliest days, the GWU was highly critical of the state educational provision for both children and adults (particularly workers). Indeed, during the second half of the 1940s, with the prospects of self-government on the horizon, the union insisted that the masses 'should be educated in the right way … and taught to attach importance to such vital matters on which the future of these islands largely depended'.[11]

For the union, education was also a top priority in the reconstruction of war-torn Malta. It criticized strongly, through its weekly newspaper and in many of its public meetings, the educational system, which was seen as serving the colonial needs. The union demanded a schooling structure that catered for the more urgent technical needs of the nation. It was argued that:

> The whole basis and direction of our education has been to produce, apart from the professions, a surplus of clerical labour, definitely ornamental but not so definitely useful or usable … The solution is to go for a less academic or classical instruction, for less veneer if you like, and instead for a more rational, more practical curriculum. We could do with fewer blackcoats and more tradesmen, more technicians, more skilled workers... When the artisan is no longer despised, education will become more rational. Schools will be divided between the textbook and the lathe. Only then can we talk of reconstruction with a degree of sense in our words.[12]

The GWU also insisted that the teaching of English should take precedence over the teaching of Maltese in the local educational system. Once again this 'compliance with colonial paternalism' must be viewed as a practical response to the dominant political situation which prevailed at the time. It was not an attempt to anglicize the people – as some of the local political establishment claimed – but a radical attack on the power structure of Maltese society. It was rather a Gramscian 'war of position', in which the workers aimed at 'mastering the tools of oppression' of both the colonizers and the local dominant classes, for their own liberation.

> We of the GWU measure the success or failure of our entire education services by the extent to which English (neither the quayside nor the grandiose type) manages to spread among the people. It is one of our strongest tenets. In practical terms, it equals that of our answering loyalty to the Church and the Empire ... May the worker's son be better equipped than his father to stand up for his rights, to exchange ideas with profit to himself and to the whole country ... We would like to see everyone in Malta capable at least of making himself understood, and consequently respected, by those who are masters, or equals according to one's knowledge of the only language they know.[13]

In a nation plagued by a high illiteracy rate – more than 48 per cent of the Maltese adult population claimed to be illiterate in the 1948 census – the GWU and Labour leaders also demanded compulsory schooling for the children of the working class. A resolution passed at the delegates' conference in 1947 also insisted that the University of Malta should fall under the control of the Maltese Minister of Education – rather than under the control of the British authorities – and that technical education should also be developed. The National Executive of the GWU urged its members to vote for the Labour Party in the 1947 general elections because 'the programme of the Party reflected the issues – including those about education – outlined in its resolution.' Eventually the Labour Party won these elections and implemented most of the recommendations made by the GWU in its 1947 resolution.

Although during this period the GWU never held its own educational programmes for illiterate workers, its leadership strongly supported the state-organized programmes for adult learners.[14]

Epoch III (1971–86): Economic Independence and the Welfare State

This period was dominated by three consecutive Labour governments and characterized by close collaboration between the GWU and the Labour government culminating in the official statutory 'fusion' of the GWU with the MLP. Throughout this period Dom Mintoff, the Prime Minister and charismatic leader of the MLP, and his ministers effectively led the fully cooperative union to support his governments' paternalistic, yet radical, Labour policies. Indeed, the union exposed itself to both internal and external criticism for abandoning its former militancy often leading to open confrontation with the previous government. Instead it now adopted a policy of dialogue and full support of government initiatives.

This collaboration effectively enabled the government to achieve its most important set objectives: those of ending the British military presence on the Island by 1979, the achievement of 'full economic and political independence', nationalization of the key sectors of the local economy and a reform of public institutions to enable government to establish a generous welfare state in which health, education and pensions were provided to all citizens in addition to financial benefits and housing for the needy. Simultaneously, efforts were made to raise working class status and living standards by narrowing income differentials. These reforms were implemented while the basic democratic institutions were retained.

TUE Initiatives

During the first 10 years of the 'workers' government', from 1971 to 1980, TUE was not high on the list of the union's priorities. Very few systematic initiatives were undertaken, apart from some occasional, short-lived ventures by a small group of volunteers within the Labour Party aimed at promoting educational courses in political economy. One such venture was the setting up of the Maltese Institute for Education, Politics and Economy, though it did not last long and was largely ineffectual. Systematic TUE remained sidelined and the GWU's education section continued to provide a motley collection of peripheral courses, which included subjects like flower arrangement, intended mainly for women.

Ironically, it was during this period that the concept of workers' participation became one of the policy options of the Maltese Labour Movement. The MLP-GWU tandem became heavily committed and involved in the introduction of different forms of workers' participation in industry particularly throughout the public sector. Experimentation was rife and the concept was introduced in different quarters with a high degree of flexibility. However, there was also a lot of confusion in people's minds about the meaning, goals, and practice of workers' participation and about the strategy to be adopted (Kester, 1980; Zammit, 1984). This vacuum clearly demanded a heavy investment in TUE.

The Labour government had tackled, with initial success, the Malta drydocks' problem through the introduction of a form of workers' participation modelled on the German codetermination system. This paved the way for self-management modelled on the former Yugoslav system, which was introduced in 1975. The drydocks workers were thus given the responsibility of running this major enterprise – which in the early 1970s employed around 5,000 workers – with hardly any previous training for it. Nevertheless, this experience gave a new lease of life to the industry and provided a psychological boost to workers and their trade union to pursue the goal of democratic workers' participation in other areas of the public sector.

Between 1975 and 1979, various workers' participation schemes were established in parastatal and state-owned enterprises. However, this policy was not pursued further by government or union in the private sector where employers were generally sceptical and even hostile to the idea. The strategy was to make the dockyard and parastatal enterprises models of successful firms run on a form of management different from the traditional one. Their viability under this system would eventually serve as an example for others, including the private sector, to follow suit (Kester, 1980).

Despite the initial euphoria, however, during the second phase of the Labour government (from 1980 to 1987), the workers' participation structures failed to meet expectations and the process was overshadowed by the political and economic problems of the country at the time and gradually discontinued.

In its heyday, the GWU leadership actually spared no efforts in encouraging workers, through the union papers and public speeches, to promote the system of workers' participation. The GWU also organized numerous TUE activities including seminars, workshops and short courses on workers' participation usually earmarked for its groups of shop stewards and other activists. These efforts however had limited impact. They were organized sporadically and there was rarely any follow-up on the conclusions which emerged. The suggestions were usually shelved until they resurfaced again in some subsequent seminar. Thus there was little improvement in the participative systems, and this proved to be a major flaw in their operation (Zammit, 1996).

There were, of course, also some practical reasons for the state of affairs, as almost all the available personnel and resources of the Labour movement went into the management of government institutions and programmes. The Party and union structures and their staffs were effectively depleted up to a point where they became mere appendages.

In the meantime, TUE – on an informal level – continued, as in previous years, by means of the GWU newspapers and publications. So did the 'stereotyped' TUE activities of the GWU's education section, including an annual seminar for the shop stewards of each section and participation in local and international seminars and meetings. Otherwise, systematic and sustained TUE for the union officials, activists and shop-floor workers was practically non-existent. At a time when democratic 'workers' participation' was the buzzword of the Maltese Labour Movement, TUE was conspicuous more by its absence.

However, the situation changed between 1981 and 1984. At this time, three new, significant initiatives were started from within the ranks of the Labour movement. These were: the establishment of the MLP's Department of Information; the Guze Ellul Mercer Foundation (GEM) as a joint venture between the MLP and the GWU; and the Workers' Participation Development Centre (WPDC) as an autonomous institute of the University of Malta, with the involvement of the whole trade union movement.[15]

The Information Department of the MLP, set up in 1981, was instrumental in organizing both formal and informal worker education projects including political courses for party cadres. This department also established its own publishing house – Sensiela Kotba Socjalisti – that produced popular, political and literary editions. The GEM Foundation[16] was set up as a joint venture between the MLP and GWU in 1984. This was a voluntary non-profit making organization, with its primary objective to provide 'educational opportunities to raise the consciousness and empower the workers and their families, in order to enable them to participate actively and fully in the political, economic, social and cultural transformation of society' (Caruana 1997, p. 360). To achieve this objective the GEM Foundation became involved in the organization of workers' education, community development, functional literacy, environmental and youth development and programmes promoting awareness of gender issues. It also organized art exhibitions and cinefora. The dominant role played by the MLP in GEM is indicated by the fact that its first chairman was the then president and later leader of the MLP and chairman of the MLP's information department.

Perhaps the most significant development in TUE was the setting up in 1981 of the WPDC at the University of Malta. In this case, both the GWU and CMTU played a prominent part in its creation. The WPDC was born as the outcome of a doctoral research project on the development of workers' participation in Malta carried out by a Dutch sociologist with a lifetime of commitment to worker participation and trade union development. The WPDC was conceived as a permanent structure to support, monitor and promote the processes of democratic workers' participation in a number of sites on the island, such as the Malta drydocks. The Centre aimed at providing worker and trade union education, carrying out scientific research and offering consultancy services on the development of worker participation and on the empowerment of people to become active agents of participation. In an evaluation of the role played by the WPDC, Mayo (1997) considered the efforts of the Centre 'as a breath of fresh air' in Maltese workers' education. He commented:

> The kind of worker education the Centre promotes is definitely not of the Human Capital Theory type. One may argue that this organization is concerned, in Freirian-Hegelian terms, with protecting the image of worker as subject rather than object of the production process, even though its initial and primary concern has been industrial democracy. Even its traditional links with the trade unions and the Malta Drydocks, where a self-management process had been in operation since 1975, this organization seeks to generate a culture of participatory democracy in its wider sense. In principle at least, this would render it open to the ideas and demands of other groups seeking greater democratic spaces within the wider community (Mayo, 1997, p. 311).

The subsequent epoch (1987–present day) is characterized mainly by the presence of the Nationalist Party in government, and its pursuit of moderate, liberal economic and social policies. The most important developments taking place are the result of government's determination to have Malta accepted as member of the European Union. With this aim, most legislation and many institutions are being harmonized with the requirements of the *acquis communautaire*. This includes a dynamic implementation of social dialogue and partnership as a central part of the EU's social and industrial relations policy, the establishment of European works councils and the recently adopted European Company Statute (see chapters 2 and 3 of this book).

In the meantime, one important boost has been given to trade union education in Malta since 1990, following the opening of a Mediterranean area office of the German Friedrich Ebert Foundation, with its own representative officer and secretary and a modest budget. The aim was to promote and assist workers' educational activities with a social democratic inspiration in collaboration with established local institutions working in this field. The Foundation has since funded many educational research publications and related activities organized by the GWU, WPDC and GEM, amongst others. All of these organizations were thus able to expand and diversify their activities and cater for a wider clientele. For its part, the Foundation has left each organization totally free to design and implement its own programmes and has monitored each programme only to ensure its effectiveness and the correct use of its limited financial resources. It can be safely stated that, were it not for this support, many of the union educational activities that flourished during the 1990s would not have materialized.

Conclusions

This chapter has traced the TUE activities organized by Malta's GWU since its foundation and juxtaposed them against the main experiences and developments undergone by the union at the different stages of its history. The main question posed is to what extent and under what conditions the various TUE strategies pursued over the years – both formal and informal – were 'transformative' or merely 'reproductive'. Given that the union, at least during certain stages, was promoting the establishment of systems of democratic workers' participation, the chapter has also sought to establish whether TUE was organized around this 'transformative' vision. If so, this would provide an empirical test case for one of the main propositions presented in the introduction to this book. This specific case study of Malta may thus be viewed from a wider comparative perspective, and its conclusions acquire a more general significance.

It was found that throughout the different epochs, TUE tended to be 'reproductive' particularly when reflecting the culturally patterned responses of Maltese society and when it aimed at propagating uncritically the Labour leadership's views on the national developments taking place from time to time.

Simultaneously, TUE pursued a 'transformative' role when it promoted the emergence and development of a working class subculture. This involved confronting and reshaping the established culture when mobilizing the union membership behind the leadership, when promoting popular access to education, when establishing the leadership, when establishing the welfare state and, to some extent, when promoting the concept of workers' participation. In reality, however, workers' participation was not promoted in a specific, systematic, structured and integrated manner. There was much emphasis on rhetoric and little on substance. Just as the inspiration for the initiatives and experimentation on workers' participation came mostly 'from above', the theory of teaching utilized followed mostly the traditional, hierarchical pattern. Therefore, for these reasons, it can be said that TUE was only 'partially transformative'.

Despite the significant contribution made to TUE by the university's WPDC, and by the other institutions in this field, their impact has been mainly that of providing training and development for the benefit of individual union officials and members rather than on the development of the union's policy-making organs.

This lack of a coherent, systematic and cumulative TUE programme by the union may be due to the fact that its message and ideology is diffused through its own daily newspaper which is widely read by the working class. There the public exhortations of the leadership as well as union activities and directives are given wide coverage. The TUE provided through the union newspaper effectively constitutes the main strategy to nourish and renew the commitment of union members and the union ideology. This powerful medium is also used to address the roots of social and industrial conflict and to mount a serious challenge to prevailing, culturally patterned social relations. Nonetheless it must be stated that although TUE may have bordered on the subversive, it ultimately conformed to a rationalized and reformist consensus which kept extremism at bay. Its educational role was ultimately grounded as much on traditional culture as on Fabian gradualism, that is, on the assumption that a society can by reformed from within, by consent.

Likewise, the present TUE strategy in the area of democratic workers' participation continues to support and reflect the union's official policy at a particular time, rather than to be inspired by a proactive, futuristic vision. This applies equally to the union's current policy on social partnership as to the direct forms of workers' participation at shopfloor level. If the union were to engage seriously in dialogue and commit itself to forms of direct workers' participation, it may find it feasible to integrate these into the traditional role of collective bargaining. TUE may play a vital role for such a development.

Like many other learners, trade unionists prefer TUE to be practical and directly related to the reality they have to cope with. In their speeches and actions, they exhibit a certain pride in their ability to engage in practical problems. They consider this to be their greatest asset because it makes them effective in dealing with bread and butter issues at the workplace. At a time when their role as social partners also requires them to discuss these issues at the national and transnational levels, they need to acquire new skills and knowledge. This form of democratic workers' participation, which is currently promoted as an integral part of the European Employment Strategy – with social partnership reflected in all its pillars – again requires a further investment into TUE, if it is to operate effectively.

Finally, the traditional culturally patterned forms of behaviour and the characteristic values of the working class subculture promoted through TUE are summarized in Table 13.2. These are subdivided along four key dimensions, namely: power relations, interactions, identification and future vision. In each case, the role of TUE has been to undermine culturally-patterned behaviour in favour of the working-class subculture.

Table 13.2 Impact of trade union education on forms of culture

Key dimensions	Culturally patterned behaviour	Working class sub-culture
1 Power relations	Compliance with paternalism	Us/them perceptions
2 Interactions	Patron-client relations (individual)	Working class solidarity (collective)
3 Identification	Local (village/parish) focus of loyalty and prestige	Loyalty to the Labour movement
4 Future vision	Progressive rise in living standards for all (social classes/strata are seen as superseded)	Political and social goals are defined by leadership Social justice and welfare state Workers' participation is seen as ultimate goal

Notes

1   The research for this chapter was sponsored by the Friedrich Ebert Foundation (Malta Office). The authors are also grateful to Ms Nerissa Sultana for her assistance.
2   The concept of 'workers' participation' refers to the active involvement of employees in decision making within enterprises, as distinct from 'labour participation', which normally refers to the passive contribution of workers and is the concern of labour economics and human resources management.
3   The empirical data for this survey was gathered through the systematic analysis of documents and other material reported in the newspapers published by the General Workers' Union, particularly *The Torch*. This was the first newspaper published by the union soon after its foundation in 1943.
4   For a fuller explanation of these adaptive responses, see Zammit, 1984, pp. 31–4.
5   As translated from Maltese, *The Torch*, 25 July 1944.
6   As translated from Maltese, *The Torch*, 15 July 1944.
7   As translated from Maltese, *The Torch*, 12 August 1944.
8   As translated from Maltese, *The Torch*, 11 November 1944.
9   Ibid.
10 Ibid.
11 Ibid.
12 As translated from Maltese, *The Torch*, 4 November 1944.
13 Ibid.
14 Particularly the literacy campaign organized by Captain Paul Bugeja (Vancell, 1997). Indeed the leaders of the GWU, including Reggie Miller and Vincent Dye, participated in Rediffusion discussions by Bugeja.

15 Both GWU and CMTU officials were represented on the WPDC Board from the beginning. This was a rare case of inter-union cooperation.
16 The Foundation was named after the late, prominent novelist, journalist and past Labour Cabinet Minister, Guze Ellul Mercer.

References

Boissevain, J. (1969), 'Why do the Maltese Ask so Few Questions?' *Ferment*, January, Royal University of Malta.
Caruana, D. (1997), 'The Labour Movement and Adult Education', in Baldacchino, G. and Mayo, P. (eds), *Beyond Schooling: Adult Education in Malta*, Mireva Publications, Msida, pp. 345–70.
Commission of the EC (1997), *Partnership for a New Organization of Work*, Green Paper, April, Brussels.
Freire, P. (1972), *Pedagogy of the Oppressed*, Continuum, New York.
Heaney, T.W. and Horton, A.I. (1990), 'Reflective Engagement for Social Change', in Mezirow, J. et al. (eds), *Fostering Critical Reflection in Adulthood – A Guide to Transformative and Emancipatory Learning*, Jossey Bass, Beverley Hills, pp. 47–73.
Holford, J. (1994), *Union Education in Britain*, University of Nottingham, Nottingham.
Hyman, R. (1994), 'An Emerging Agenda for Trade Unions', discussion paper on home page of the International Institute for Labour Studies (IILS), info@ilo.org.
Hyman, R. and Ferner, A. (eds) (1992), *Industrial Relations in the New Europe*, Blackwell, Oxford.
Kester, G. (1980), *Transition to Workers' Self-management: Its Dynamics in the Decolonizing Economy of Malta*, Institute of Social Studies, The Hague.
Kester, G. and Pinaud, H. (eds) (1996), *Trade Unions and Democratic Participation in Europe: A Scenario for the 21st Century*, Avebury, Aldershot.
Kester, G. and Sidibe, O. (eds) (1998), *Trade Unions and Sustainable Democracy in Africa*, Ashgate, Aldershot.
Mayo, P. (1997), 'Worker Education and Democracy: A Case Study', in Baldacchino, G. and Mayo, P. (eds), *Beyond Schooling: Adult Education in Malta*, Mireva Publications, Msida, pp. 309–32.
Mayo, P. (1999), *Gramsci, Freire and Adult Education*, Zed Books, London and New York.
Spencer, B. (1998), *The Purposes of Adult Education: A Guide to Students*, Thompson Educational Publishing, Toronto.
Vancell, J. (1997), 'Night School and Basic English – Adult Literacy Education in Malta (1946–73)', in Baldacchino, G. and Mayo, P. (eds), *Beyond Schooling: Adult Education in Malta*, Mireva Publications, Msida, pp. 55–65.
Welton, M. (1997), 'In Defence of Civil Society: Canadian Adult Education in Neo-Conservative Times', in Walters, S. (ed.) *Globalization, Adult Education and Training: Impacts and Issues*, Zed Books. London.
Zammit, E.L. (1984), *Colonial Inheritance: Maltese Perceptions of Work, Power and Class Structure with Reference to the Labour Movement*, Malta University Press, Msida.
Zammit, E.L. (1996), 'The Workers' Participation Development Centre', in Kester, G. and Pinaud, H. (eds.), *Trade Unions and Democratic Participation in Europe: A Scenario for the 21st Century*, Avebury, Aldershot, pp. 221–3.

Index

For Product Safety Concerns and Information please contact our EU representative GPSR@taylorandfrancis.com Taylor & Francis Verlag GmbH, Kaufingerstraße 24, 80331 München, Germany

T - #0089 - 270225 - C0 - 216/151/19 - PB - 9781138710016 - Gloss Lamination